Boats with an Open Mind

Boats with an Open Mind

75 Unconventional Designs and Concepts

Philip C. Bolger

International Marine
Camden, Maine

International Marine/
Ragged Mountain Press

A Division of The McGraw-Hill Companies

4567890 TGX/TGX 09876543210

Copyright © 1994 International Marine, a division of The McGraw-Hill Companies.

All rights reserved. The publisher takes no responsibility for the use of any of the materials or methods described in this book, nor for the products thereof. The name "International Marine" and the International Marine logo are trademarks of The McGraw-Hill Companies. Printed in the United States of America.

Library of Congress Cataloging-in-Publication Data

Bolger, Philip C.
    Boats with an open mind: 75 unconventional designs and concepts /
  Philip C. Bolger.
      p. cm.
    Includes bibliographical references (p. 408) and index.
    ISBN 0-07-006376-1
    1. Boats and boating—Design and construction.
    2. Boatbuilding.   I. Title.
  VM321.B677   1994
  623.8'—dc20   94-19978
                                       CIP

Questions regarding the content of this book should be addressed to:

International Marine
P.O. Box 220
Camden, ME 04843

Questions regarding the ordering of this book should be addressed to:

The McGraw-Hill Companies
Customer Service Department
P.O. Box 547
Blacklick, OH 43004
Retail customers: 1-800-822-8158
Bookstores: 1-800-722-4726

Boats with an Open Mind is printed on recycled, acid-free paper containing a minimum of 50% total recycled fiber with 10% postconsumer de-inked fiber. ♻

Printed by R. R. Donnelley, Crawfordsville, IN
Typesetting by Publishers Design & Production Services, Inc.
Design by Patrice M. Rossi
Production by Janet Robbins
Edited by Jonathan Eaton, Jane Crosen, Tom McCarthy

Dedication

I'm not at much risk of conceit as a designer, writer, or philosopher, on account of frequent salutary embarrassments. I am intensely proud of—awed by—the quality of my friends. I must have done something right for these people to come to me. This book is dedicated to them all.
I single out four for examples, and because they charmed or bullied me out of the contented inertia which is my natural state.

Susanne Altenburger

Holbrook Robinson

Dan Segal

Stanley Woodward

Contents

Note on Periodical Publication

About three-quarters of the chapters in this book are lightly edited articles published in various periodicals. For upwards of 10 years I had a regular feature in the bimonthly *Small Boat Journal*, in which I produced design concepts suggested by readers' wish lists. The letters are included here. These weren't supposed to be completed designs, but several of them were later carried on to working drawings; in those cases, the working drawings are used in this book in place of the original cartoons. When *SBJ* changed its identity (on account of steady unprofitability), I moved over to Bob Hicks's *Messing About In Boats*, which comes out every other week. The fictional scenarios (Chapters 36, 44, 46, 63, and 67) were published in *WoodenBoat* magazine.

The designs in Chapters 3, 5, 7, 10, 15, 18, 21, 25, and 45 are handled by H. H. Payson & Co. (see Sources). Most of these were designed in collaboration with "Dynamite" Payson, who built and tested the prototypes. His own books on boatbuilding and modelmaking include designs of mine not published elsewhere. The designs in Chapters 1, 2, 17, 19, 20, 29, 44, 46, 47, 48, 54, 57, 60, 62, 64, 68, 69, 70, 73, and 74 are handled by Bernard Wolfard's Common Sense Designs (see Sources). Some of these were worked out in collaboration with Bernie and some with his predecessor, the late Elrow LaRowe, starting about 13 years ago. The association with Dynamite goes back into the misty past, perhaps 30 years by now, when he and I were younger and more diffident.

Introduction

The Norfolk wherry was developed to carry bulk cargo on the twisting rivers of southeastern England. Fifty or sixty feet long, a wherry was sailed by two men. It set a boomless gaff sail, which might be 1,200 square feet, on an unstayed mast about 14 inches in diameter. The mast was counterweighted (lead-block weights averaged a ton and a half), and the whole rig could be lowered and raised so quickly that it was the practice to sail straight at a low bridge, lower sail, lower mast, shoot through on momentum, and get the rig back up and drawing on the far side without losing steerageway.

These vessels had no freeboard loaded, and full decklines at each end, but underwater the lapstrake hulls were fine-lined and graceful. They had long, shallow keels that could be dropped off and reattached with the wherry afloat. As related in *Black-Sailed Traders* by Roy Clark, the sail was black, "brushed over with a mixture of seal oil and tar, and finally with a coat of herring oil. Very often to get rid of some of the stickiness, black lead powder is added."

All this is fact: These craft were carrying cargo in living memory, and a few of them still amuse vacationers, though with less handling élan. I've seen no account of how often they hit bridges, or how much time they spent tied up because conditions weren't right. The patience of seamen of times past, and their tolerance of high accident rates, needs to be steadily in mind as we admire the feats they routinely accomplished.

The seal-oil-and-graphite treatment has so far not stimulated a profitable thought, except that it's better to live now than then, but that keel has been worth study, as have the arrangements for lowering that massive mast on the run. The underwater lines are an aesthetic experience.

History is a deep mine of such unexpected options in boat design, one beauty of which is that the requirement is hardly ever so sharply defined that the designer has to master a critical optimum. Even in the obvious matters of speed and weatherliness, an inferior option isn't usually bad enough to preclude use of an out-of-the-way idea offering some convenience, or simply amusement. The category of Entertainer includes boat designers along with classical musicians and strippers.

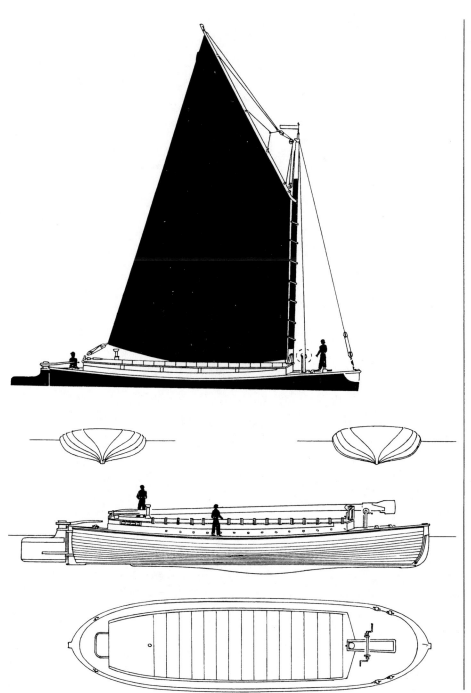

The Norfolk wherry. (Drawings based on Roy Clark's **Black-Sailed Traders.)**

Part One

Very Small Boats

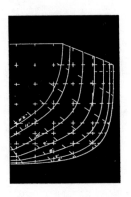

1 _Breakdown Punt_

5'6" × 3'6"

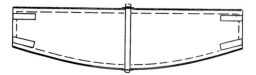

Dear Phil:

I'm in the process of building a 33-foot cutter for bluewater cruising and would like to carry a rigid tender on the cabintop. Space there is limited, so I've been looking for a two-piece, bolt-together dinghy that would allow one half to nest inside the other when not in use. None of the commercial nesting dinghies I've seen impress me greatly. Do you think you could design one? I'd appreciate it if you tried.

Jon Baxter, Hyannis, Massachusetts

This was one of several requests for a breakdown dinghy. I've seen quite a few, but never one that struck me as inspired, or that developed much popularity. The idea works better for a big dinghy than for a small one. If you take an 8-foot punt and add extensions, the result is a long, powerful skiff that stows in the place of the punt.

I tackled the small breakdown dinghy in the usual way first, with a 'midship section for the oarsman and bow and stern sections added on. I wasn't happy with anything I came up with. The rowing midsection had to be at least 45 inches long, and the ends either had poor proportions, made the passenger seat cramped, or had the bulkheads too low to be safe. My premise was that the two or three sections had to be independently watertight. Not only is a watertight joint hard to make and apt to be unreliable, but given the lack of deck space it seems that it ought to be possible to assemble the dinghy in the water. Moreover, I've had at least as much stowage grief over the breadth of dinghies as over their length.

I played with some over-crafty schemes for dinghies to be assembled out of a lot of

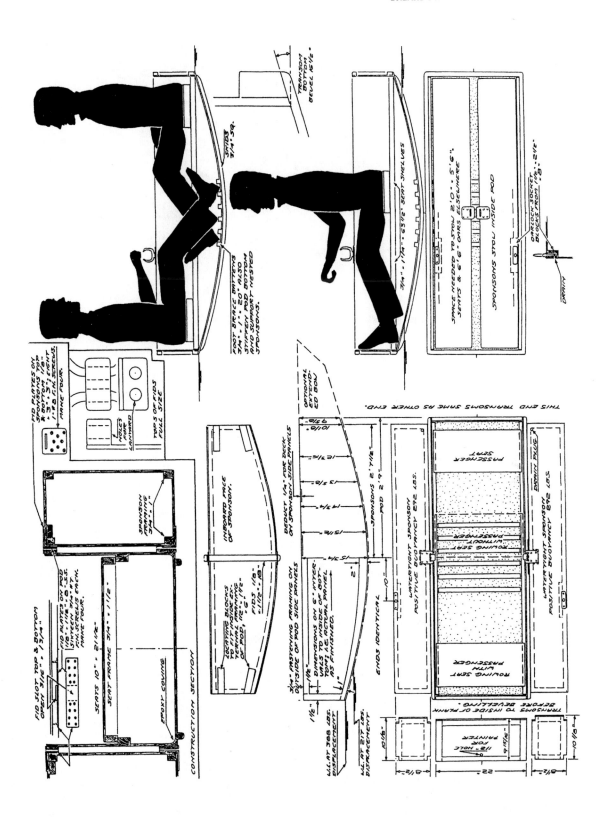

Breakdown Punt

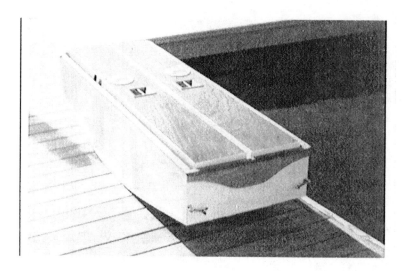

pieces, with joints running fore-and-aft as well as athwartships. If you carry this line of reasoning further, you end up with something like the primitive boats made up of bundles of bamboo or papyrus lashed into a boat shape.

The design shown will take $2 \times 5\frac{1}{2}$ feet of deck space, and will sit about 18 inches high. It could stow on edge or on end. For instance, I used one of my Tortoise Punts (6 feet 6 inches by 3 feet 2 inches) as a companionway shelter for a while, one end braced up 45 degrees. The dimensions here came from diagramming seat positions, with the boat trimmed and the oarlocks in the same position with one person alone or with a passenger. The center pod is wide enough to sit in and stable enough to crouch in afloat, to ship the sponsons.

The sponsons added on the sides give $3\frac{1}{2}$ feet of breadth to space the oarlocks and produce workable displacement. Completely watertight, they produce a lifeboat capability comparable with that of an inflatable raft. The boat can be launched (when assembled) by sliding it overboard on its side. The open center pod won't ship any water, and if it did, the sponsons would float it high enough for bailing even in rough water. Each sponson has almost 300 pounds of positive buoyancy. It would be worth considering installing some deck plates in the sponsons so emergency water and supplies could be stowed in them.

This boat would be more vulnerable to impacts than an inflatable, but would be less likely to deteriorate invisibly in storage and more useful between emergencies.

Assembled, the marked waterlines show that it would float lightly with one man and could be rowed quite respectably with a short, quick stroke. With two men or, better, a man and a woman, the transoms will come down to the water's edge. The punt will row sluggishly and spit if the water is more than rippled, but it won't be unstable or close to swamping. From there it will go down about another inch for each hundred pounds added. It could carry four men, two sitting as shown and two more sidewise on the sponsons, but there would be a tangle of knees in the way of the oars and very slow progress. Probably it would be faster to make three trips.

The plumb ends give the most capacity for the least overall length. If the stowing space allowed, the ends could be extended as much as you liked. But, vertical ends have one other advantage: In steep waves such as motorboat wakes, plumb transoms are less likely to ship water than raked ones. The bottom corner of a vertical transom will immerse and start lifting while the top edge is farther from the crest than that of a raked transom. The way to take a wave in this boat, however, is to lay her broadside to it. She'll react faster in roll than in pitch, and any slop will run off the decked sponson. It would take a real effort or a heavy breaker to capsize her. If she did get bottom-up, she'd be even more stable than rightside-up and would have to be parbuckled to right her. (A very small boat can be parbuckled by catching the painter in an oarlock and thence across the boat to give leverage to right her.)

The two movable seats serve three positions, as diagrammed. One instantly thinks of adding rollers to the seats, but it would be unrewarding since she starts to bog down in her own waves at $2\frac{1}{2}$ knots. The seats have to be movable in any case, for the nesting; I realized after finishing the tracing that they will stow on edge between the nested sponsons. The oars have to be stowed elsewhere.

I spent as much time figuring out a way to attach the sponsons to the pod as on all the rest of the design, but this kind of thing is not my forté. Probably the first 10 mechanics who look at the design will come up with better schemes. As designed, the sponson-locating blocks engage the outside fastening frame of the pod to line everything up, and the metal fid bar is dropped down through slots to hold it together. It all has to be loose-fitting or it will jam when the wood swells. I'm afraid there will be coarse language used while trying to get the end of the fid through the lower slot. The best alternative might be a hook on the bottom on which a sponson could be swung in and latched at the top—something on the order of a pelican hook. The dimensions allow some leeway for projections in the nesting process, and the sponsons could be slimmed an inch if necessary.

The worst drawback of the design is its weight. There's over 50 pounds in the plywood alone if $\frac{1}{4}$-inch fir is used. With the framing, I'd be surprised if the total weight were less than 80 pounds. Separated, the heaviest component is less than 40 pounds, which is handy at times, and the weight does make her less flighty, but I'd be discontented with a boat of this type that weighed that much. My Shoebox Punt is this design with the sponsons integrated with the center pod. It's 20 pounds lighter than, and half the price of, the Breakdown version, and a lot faster to get into action.

While I was trying one unsatisfactory idea after another, I indulged my frustration by recalling the times when big boats carried their tenders on outboard davits, and small boats towed their tenders. Towed tenders can be made seaworthy by watertight compartments and self-bailing devices. When I was towing the prototype Light Dory around, I noticed with pleased amusement that the wild dory roll threw any bilgewater high and far out of the boat. But, the self-bailers used in racing dinghies would be as effective and allow for a more practical sectional shape—one that doesn't make stepping on the exact centerline as crucial as it is in the Light Dory.

As for the davits, I see a lot of over-the-stern types, but a new look at side davits is overdue. They used to look very shipshape. The small boat could usually be carried swung out, leaving the deck clear. In a high-sided boat, you might get away with leaving the tender swung out over a marina float. I take it that berthing in marinas is the reason so few people tow tenders now. If so, some inquiry into parking the tender elsewhere around the marina might be in order, because the point of a towed tender is that it can be, and should be, a really good boat and a work of art. That's better than the most ingenious box.

2 *Brick*

8'0" × 4'0"

Brick started as an exercise in how much boat could be built out of three 4 × 8-foot sheets of plywood. It's a simple pleasure to come out even with no scrap left over. I try not to let this game become an obsession; there's an 8 × 32-inch rectangle here for which I didn't strain to find a place.

She's practically a scaled-up Tortoise Punt (6 feet 6 inches by 3 feet 2 inches, said with a little malice to be my best design). The sides are too high to row comfortably, but she'll carry four men and a big, frightened dog, with plenty of buoyancy left, still able to sail though with lots of noisy waves.

Built of ¼-inch plywood as specified, she is flimsy. I had a half-joking letter from a builder describing the distortions in her shape and her eventual disintegration as he and his crew hiked out to drive her. I retorted (with a bad conscience, as I'd totaled a Tortoise the same way) that since driving her wouldn't make her go faster, on account of bogging down in her own waves, there was no excuse for breaking her up. Brick would behave perfectly built of ½-inch plywood and slathered with epoxy fillets. That would make her rugged, but a lot more expensive and twice as heavy to carry around, whereas the disposable version will last a long time with humane handling.

It's disconcerting that these box boats do everything better than elaborately modeled boats of the same overall dimensions, if they both have to carry the same load. Rounding or tapering takes away volume; the boat settles deeper in the water and makes deeper, steeper waves. It's possible that running the bottom straight back to a perfectly rectangular stern would increase capacity more than resistance. The deeper transom would fit on the stipulated plywood if the rudder were made shallower (which it could stand), and the quarter knees displaced by the unrockered after sides would just use up that leftover rectangle. . . .

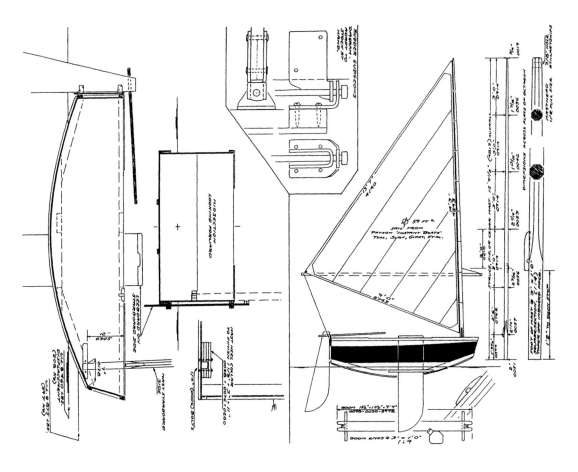

**Bernie
Wolfard's
tandem Brick**

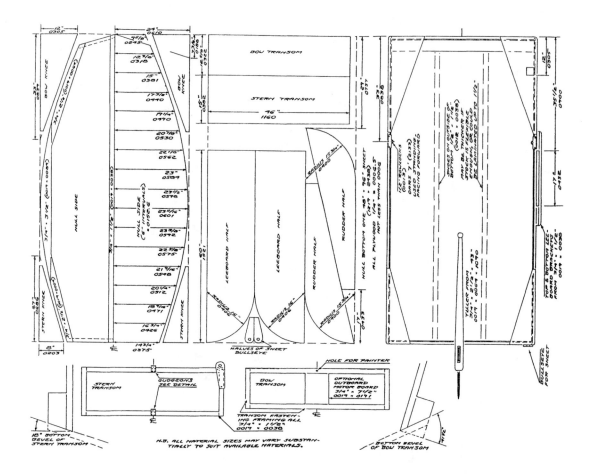

A good reason for the rockered stern is that she's designed to drive stern-first under power. The motor is mounted on the raked bow transom where it doesn't interfere with the rudder or foul the mainsheet. The side-stepped mast leaves the centerline motor mount clear. With rudder shipped or tiller lashed, and the sail rolled up, she goes backward as fast as forward; that is, not very fast.

The photo shows Bernie Wolfard's two Bricks pinned in tandem on a central spacer to make an 18-foot schooner, vastly roomy. The amalgam is clumsy to handle, but for a family outing it conjured up some pleasant scenarios. The central unit, *Grout*, was decked watertight to stow picnicking supplies, and the two dinghies could be freed in a few minutes to sail separately. The aggregate is much faster and more stable than the separated components.

3 *Payson Pirogue*

13'0" × 2'4"

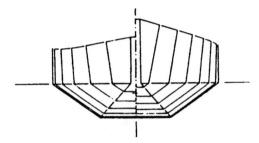

Dynamite Payson, who built the prototype, calls this a canoe. I call it a pirogue, "a canoe-like boat." It's an exercise in weight-saving without resorting to exotic materials.

A boat's weight is primarily due to its length, breadth, and depth. Reducing the longest dimension has the most effect since compact shapes have less surface for their bulk, and are less exposed to stresses. In the case of the Payson pirogue, this is the only option, since it's as narrow and low as is practical in an undecked boat. Thirteen feet is the least that allows clean lines to be drawn around enough volume to float two men.

Leaving off the deck eliminates a great weight and allows disembarking from the boat over the ends, as in an end-on beaching. It wouldn't be practical to build a deck strong enough to step on, and putting weight that high would capsize her. The bow is high enough to support a man's weight on the forward end of the bottom, without capsizing her if he is very careful. She could be given spray hoods forward and aft of stretched fabric or plastic. Perhaps a resilient material could be used, one that would yield until it reached the bottom of the boat, but any kind of cover will add a pound or two to the all-up weight.

Some of the weight saved by leaving off the deck had to be put back in the form of gunwale clamps and struts, to stiffen the sides. These are spruce and are sized and placed to serve as handholds. She can be carried on edge with a shoulder under the high side, or by two people, one on each side, to launch her with dry feet.

The taped-seam, double-chined shape is stiff enough to need no framing except for the two thwart struts, which are strong enough to lift the boat. With cushions on the bottom, the shape gives secure seating, or kneeling to use single paddles. The stiff ridge of the lower chine obviates applied stringers, which would be heavier, catch dirt if inside,

9

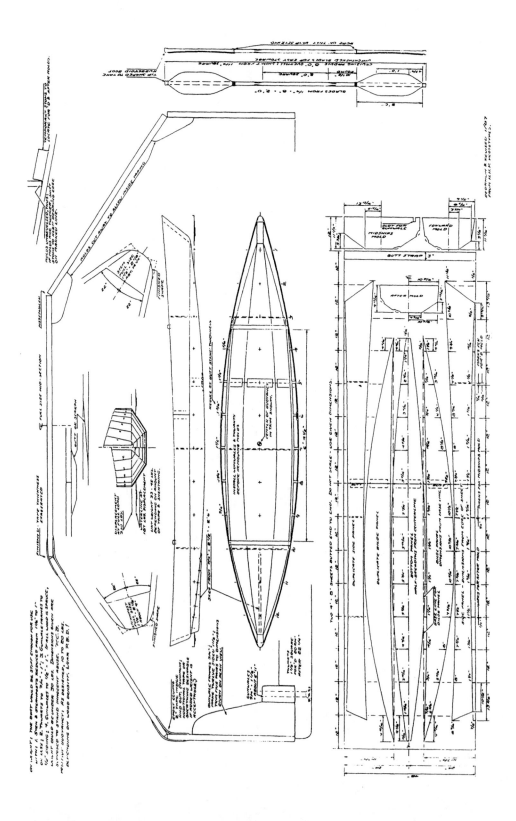

Jim Michalak's Payson Pirogue on an Illinois pond

or slow down the boat if outside. The only unnecessary weight in the structure is in the end posts, which were designed fat to get a good fastening surface for novice carpenters.

The prototype weighed 34 pounds, using 6mm lauan plywood, spruce or dry Eastern cedar for the natural wood parts, and a single strip of tape inside and out at each joint. Another boat built to the design, using heavier plywood, more tape, hard pine for the other parts, and with some decking, weighed nearly 60 pounds. The added weight doesn't make much difference when it's afloat, but since the point of a boat like this is easy carrying, I would call anything over 40 pounds a failure.

The heavy boat was fitted with a backrest, a hazard because safety in these slim boats depends on a paddler's sitting upright but keeping her torso loose, letting the boat roll under her. If the upper body is allowed to roll with the boat, its high center of gravity goes out to the low side and pulls the boat over. A backrest is not necessary if the paddler remembers to keep her back straight up, shoulders back, and butt out; backaches come of slumping, with a convex curve of the spine in the small of the back.

The shape of the boat, with all the panels prefabricated and assembled with gentle bends and no twist, has low drag and good handling as long as the chine is clear of the waterline. Loaded too deep, or meeting waves, the harsh forefoot makes turbulence, water eddying from the sides under the bottom. The deep rocker of the bottom mitigates the effect a little, but this is a boat for small ponds and slow streams.

Any kind of positive buoyancy would weigh too much (short of buoyancy bags inflated with helium). The wood structure won't sink; people depend on buoyant vests, without which I don't get into any such craft myself. Sobriety is prudent if the water is anything but tropical.

The boat is too high and wide at the gunwales for comfortable use of a double paddle. It's workable with practice, though noticeably harder on the arms than in a lower and narrower decked boat. The paddle design sacrifices a little power and wind resistance in favor of handy stowage. A feathering paddle is an awkward object to lay down, which I suppose is why the Inuit never used them. They do use something like the poling tips, indicated on the plan, but the use of household furniture boots is my own idea. A point in favor of the non-feathering paddle is that in strong wind it doesn't have the capsizing effect of the forward-going blade of a feathering paddle.

4 *Iceboat*

Dear Phil:

I have a winterized place in the Catskills, and I dream of an iceboat. Not a Scooter or a DN, though. What I contemplate is a daysailer. I'm not after speed or racing. I want something to cruise in on the mile-long lake. It should hold two of us and be both roomy and comfortable, with a simple sail plan. I was thinking of a stern-steerer.

I'd like it to be easy to build, but light enough that my wife and I can carry it the 100 feet down to the lake. None of the components should be longer than 15 feet so that I can store everything in the garage.

Gerald Molnar, Brooklyn, New York

Dear Mr. Molnar:

When it comes to iceboats, I have the advantage of having had no first-hand experience at all. A machine designed to generate wind-chill factors down toward absolute zero is not my idea of a vehicle for enjoying winter.

I do have a collection of designs for iceboats, ranging from a Swedish one designed sometime before 1775, through 1890s lateeners and gaff sloops, to a couple of supposedly futuristic types. Only two of them have enclosed cockpits, both single-seaters.

I don't see any reason why an enclosed, side-by-side two-seater can't be built. It wouldn't be hard to heat it, but I don't think there's much point. You'll be wearing outdoor clothes, and the enclosed volume is small. It could be that on a sunny day ventilation would need more care than heat.

My first thought was to follow your suggestion for a stern-steerer, and to use a bipod lateen rig, but it didn't work out. The main problem is the stipulation that all components be under 15 feet long. The lateen-rigged designs and the stern-steering gaff sloops all had long backbones projecting far ahead of the transverse beam, for the forward staying of their rigs. It wouldn't be hard to put some kind of joint in the backbone, but it would have to be a much neater connection than is needed for the springboard of a bow-steerer.

The special advantage in making this particular boat a bow-steerer is that the transverse beam supports the side-by-side seats well enough to keep them from twisting the backbone. Bow-steerers have prevailed primarily because they have more stability. The weight of the crew works on a long lever arm from the lee skate if the weather skate starts to lift, whereas crew weight in a stern-steerer is carried mostly by the centerline steering skate and does little to hold the boat down. The steering skates of bow-steerers keep being moved farther ahead to take still more of the weight off them and keep the weight on the spread-out stern skates, where it works to keep the boat from hiking.

The steering, with long tiller lines connecting two yokes, will be sloppy, but that may help damp out jerks from rough ice and patches of snow. Inside, the transverse tiller lends itself to dual controls. Each arm would hinge up vertically to get the drivers' legs under it, or pull out of a socket to stow out of the way. One crewman has both hands free to sheet the sail.

The enclosure is thin plastic wrapped around wooden frames top and bottom. The door hinge location allows getting in from a step on the transverse beam while the boat is moving, since I suppose that in light airs a push will be needed to start. If the boat should capsize, the upper door can be opened even if the mast breaks; for that matter, the flimsy enclosure could be kicked apart if the doors jammed. Seats would be foam cushions; in an upscale version they could be contoured for lateral support in turns, like those in sports cars.

I haven't indicated it on the cartoon, but I suppose an inside brake would be useful. This would be a lever on the backbone, looking like an automobile parking brake, with a simple ratchet to hold it. The brake itself would be an extension of the lever, ending in an edge to jam down into the ice.

All the usual iceboat types bear the stigma of the racer. None have enclosed cockpits because the weight and wind resistance would slow them down. Not only are they designed for speed, but the characteristic sail shape is typical of an arbitrarily limited sail area. I've beaten this subject to death, but one more time: Drive per square foot of sail area is not the best measure of efficiency. Drive relative to handling convenience, long and short-term cost, stress developed, storage space required, or any other functional considerations anybody can think of, are truer measures.

In any case, this particular requirement calls for a sail that is not efficient in the usual sense. On a lake only a mile long, a boat traveling at the speeds iceboats are known for will run out of ice in next to no time. In an iceboat that would keep to the speed of a waterborne sailing boat, say 5 m.p.h., you could cruise around the shores admiring the snow scenes without having to concentrate on looking where you're going.

With this cruising speed in mind, I would have no battens in the sail. Battens serve to increase sail area on a given spar length, improve the shape of the sail by eliminating the ineffective narrow triangle at the top, and keep the sail from fluttering and being blown aback in high relative wind speeds. The sail shown is set on three slender 15-foot spars to make an easily stored bundle. The mast and yard would be assembled lying flat and erected as if the boat were a jibheader, to save bothering with a halyard. A sprit boom is used to allow the draft of the sail to be adjusted for different wind strengths, and to allow luffing the sail in puffs without heavy slatting at the top. It might be worthwhile to lead the snotter back to the cockpit, perhaps to a reel winch, so it could be adjusted without going outdoors. This would give a better chance of moving the boat off from a standstill without having to get out and give it a push.

There are two sheets to control the angle of the boom without pulling it down hard. The sail can be backed with these sheets. In a fair breeze the boat could be stopped head-to-wind, then backed around to fill on either tack. If the lake has coves or inlets in its shore, or obstructions such as ice-fishing shelters, some neat-looking maneuvers would be possible. The sheets would not need shifting every tack; they could be made fast in such a way that each sheet was the right length when it was on the weather side. In tacking, control of the sail would be passed from one sheet to the other without shifting either. Contrast this arrangement with the usual iceboat sheet with its multiple-block purchase to flatten the sail. It reminds me of the parable of the barbarians who, needing to extract a screw, invented elaborate devices for gripping and pulling, in ignorance of how much could be accomplished by rotation.

The sprit boom could be a wishbone if you are offended by the girt (ridge) in the sail when the straight boom is on the lee side. I wouldn't bother with it myself, but if used it should be the Sidney Herreshoff–type with two straight arms joined by a straight strut ahead of the mast, forming a triangle around the mast and sail. The usual curved-arm wishbone is an awkward object at all times when the sail is not set.

I have no special ideas about rigging or skates and would just imitate some design on file. I wouldn't take on responsibility for working drawings of an iceboat on account of ignorance. I seized on your suggestion to make a favorite point—that it's often rewarding to question the way racing people do things. In this case, it looks to me as though a comfortable iceboat might be possible.

5 *Auray Punt*

9'9" × 4'2"

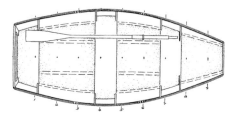

In the year 1912, Claud Worth was cruising on the south coast of Brittany in his yawl *Tern II*. Worth was a rare individual who never did anything or saw anything without giving it meticulous attention. Having thought, he would write—English prose at its unaffected best. In this passage from *Yacht Cruising*, I can hear the clear English voice speaking:

> At about 2 P.M. we left Le Palais (on Belle Isle), bound for La Trinité in the Crac'h River. The smooth sea was darkened in patches by a soft, warm wind, which made us think of Captain Marryatt's story of the gentle and beautiful damsel who was the wind, "sou'west, and by west three-quarter west." Six or seven miles away was the long chain of islands and vast numbers of detached rocks, which extends from the end of the Quiberon Peninsula to the Grand Cardinals. The main channel through this archipelago into the Bay of Quiberon is the Teignouse Passage, but there is another little passage, which we chose as being the more interesting. It lies between the Beniguet group of rocks and the large detached rocks which fringe the northeast end of Houet Island. It is marked by three little towers on the rocks, and, though very deep, is only about one cable wide. After sailing across the Bay of Quiberon we entered the Crac'h River, and moored off the village of La Trinité. Distance, 18 miles.

If I had been writing that, I doubt I would have refrained from trying to conjure up the scene there on November 20, 1759, when 21 French sailing battleships fought 25 British ships, in a gale of wind, on a lee shore, among those rocks.

As *Tern* lay off La Trinité, Worth noted the price of a meal for three at the Hotel Bretagne, and the characteristics of the fishing vessels from the various small ports in the neighborhood, each of which had its own distinctive style. The boats from Auray, a

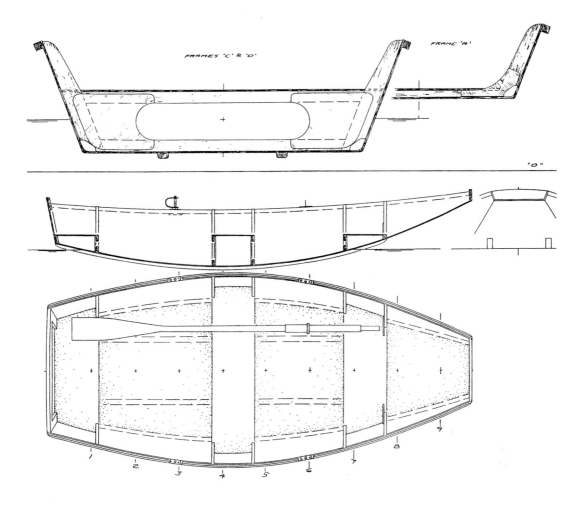

village at the head of a twisting creek a few miles away, had tenders that he thought interesting enough to rate a scale drawing as well as his usual description:

The Auray fishermen's dinghies are of practical interest to owners of small yachts. For steadiness, carrying capacity, landing on a beach, or dragging over mud they would be difficult to improve upon. Any amateur carpenter could build one. I made very careful drawings and measurements of one of them. At sea they are either carried in the lugger or are towed. The next day we saw one of these punts being towed in a fresh breeze; it seemed to be skimming along the top of the water like a hydroplane. The long bow is said to improve their towing qualities and to keep them dry in rowing to windward. Where space is limited there would be no harm in taking 9 inches off it. This dinghy might then be made to fit very nicely, bottom upwards, over the skylights of a small yacht. The working dinghies are heavily built. For yachts' use they might be planked with ¼-inch pine with fillets inside, or with three pieces of waterproof plywood.

Worth taught himself to be a first-class yacht draftsman, but at this time he was not one and I doubt that his drawing is accurate as to the detailed shape of the boat. It shows

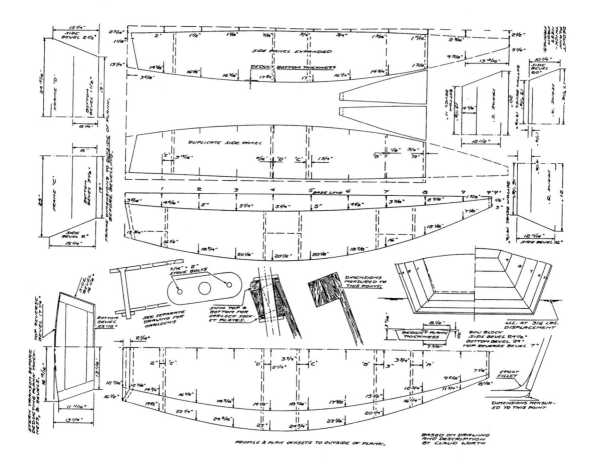

curves in the sides that would be hard to produce, especially with thick planking. I have smoothed out these curves, and also faired up the profile curve of the bottom (which was no doubt cross-planked) to take plywood without torture. Dynamite Payson tested my drawing with one of his pretty models.

There's a drawback to a snout like this, apart from the space it takes up: There's no buoyancy under it; stepping in it without another person to hold the stern down would put it underwater and swamp the boat. But it has the qualities Worth mentions, and gives style to a simple boat.

6 *Dart Dinghy*

11'6" × 4'6"

Most of the development work on shallow-draft boats has gone to centerboards. In their simplest and most efficient form, centerboards cut the accommodations and the structure down the middle. A lot of ingenuity has been devoted to mitigating this. Some of the results have been reasonably good, but often the board is made too small or has a tricky shape that works well only in good conditions with a skilled helmsman paying close attention, or uses a complex hoist prone to jams. Many designers opt for fixed-fin keels to house the centerboard rather than spoil the cabin. I've had fairly good results with long, shallow keels. I've tried bilgeboards and off-center centerboards and dagger-boards. All these can work well, but all create worse structural problems than center-boards, and all still take up a lot of space.

I've used leeboards a lot and will be using them more. They work well inshore and offshore, but they're even worse than bilgeboards for limiting hull shape, they're hard to design and build, and they're noisy and ugly and prone to collecting floating sculch.

Two distinct boat types hint that a different approach might work. One is a dugout used in some of the Caribbean islands, which has a striking ram cutwater sticking out forward and down from the forefoot. Peter Tangvald mentioned in a letter that he had sailed one of these and that it went to windward very well. Here was a boat with no lateral plane at all except out ahead of her bow! Eventually it dawned on me that the canoe had a big paddle at the other end for steering, and that the paddle might be doing more than steering.

The other type is the English Yorkshire coble. These are sailing surfboats whose keels slope from a flat stern at the waterline to a deep and sharp forefoot, deepest right at the foot of the stem. Again, the apparent effective lateral plane is all at the bow. The coble has a deep, narrow rudder hung on the raking transom, about 4 feet deep in a

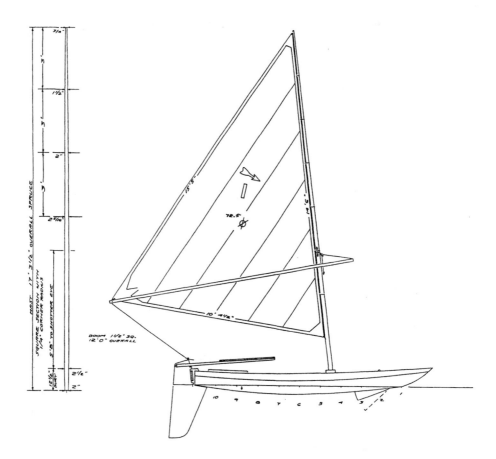

25-foot boat. I guess the rake is mostly intended to make the rudder bounce off its gudgeons when it hits bottom, instead of breaking, but it also delays stalling of the high-aspect–ratio foil.

I decided that the coble's rudder was doing most of the work of holding her against leeway. The narrow rudder with all its area close to the pivot axis supports the hypothesis. Most of her lateral resistance is converted into weather helm, but the shape of the rudder minimizes the force delivered to the end of the tiller.

A pleasant vision of a little cruising sailboat began to take shape. She would have a small centerboard close to her stem, a big, deep rudder on the stern, and wide open spaces for cabin and cockpit in between. With centerboard and rudder swung up, she would draw next to no water.

Dart was the cheapest boat I could work out that would give this idea a fair test. She was built of precalculated plywood panels, tack-and-tape fashion in the method described in Dynamite Payson's book *Build the New Instant Boats*. Brad Story of the Story boatyard in Essex, Massachusetts, built her quickly and easily.

Dart proved a good sailer on all points. She's wet in a chop like all boardboats, but more forgiving than most in stability and weight tolerance. She'll give two men a good sail, and only capsized once in several months of trials (actually, she capsized five or six

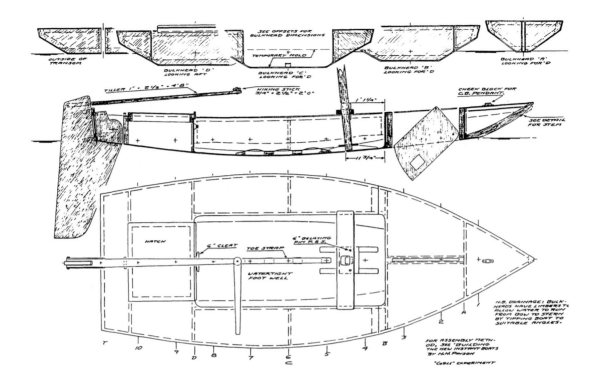

times, but all in one hour when a man used to keelboats took her out in a strong, puffy breeze). The compartment in the stern is a real amenity, and the whole hull can be bailed from there if the limber drains along the outboard sides of the footwell aren't forgotten.

The unusual mounting of the rudder was due to wanting a large balance area to mitigate the weather helm inherent in the concept. On a balanced rudder pivoted to swing up, the balance area can form a hook when the rudder is raised that will catch pot warp and marsh grass. I avoided the nuisance by hanging the rudder on a fin and pivoting the fin. It worked perfectly except that I located the pivot too low and too far forward, preventing the blade from swinging as far as it should. When it comes against the stop, the rudder is above the lowest point of the hull, but the boat can't be lifted at the bow without the weight of the stern coming on the rudder. The pivot pin should have been close to the top of the transom, using the same trunk in the hull.

The bow centerboard is barely big enough. I expected to carry it in the shallower position shown on the sail plan, but she doesn't handle well unless it's all the way down. I think she would be faster close-hauled if the board were bigger, or could drop farther.

Dart is easier to hang up in stays than a boat of this type should be. She pivots around the bow board instead of some point amidships as conventional boats do. The rudder has to slide the midbody of the hull sidewise through the water as she turns. I'd think twice about using this configuration in a boat with more resistance to slithering. An odd but not unpleasant characteristic of sailing Dart is that in turning, the stern goes out around the bow in such a way that the boat ends up considerably to windward of

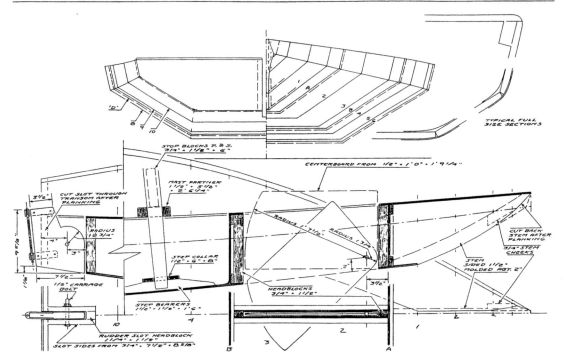

	11	10	9	8	7	6	5	4	3	2	1	0			T	D	C	B	A	
DECK	1.3.2	1.2.6	1.2.4	1.2.2	1.2.1+	1.2.3	1.2.4	1.3.0	1.3.4	1.4.2	1.5.0	1.5.3+	1.5.7	HEIGHTS FROM BASE LINE	1.3.2	1.2.2+	1.2.3	1.3.2	1.4.6	DECK
CHINE	1.0.3	0.11.6	0.11.0+	0.10.5	0.10.3+	0.10.3+	0.10.6	0.11.2	1.0.0	1.1.0	1.2.1+	1.2.7+	1.3.5		1.0.6	0.10.7	0.10.5	0.11.6	1.1.6+	CHINE
BOTTOM	0.7.4	0.5.6	0.4.2	0.3.1	0.2.3+	0.2.3+	0.3.0	0.3.7	0.5.0	0.6.2+	0.7.4	0.10.0	1.1.1		0.7.5	0.3.7	0.2.5+	0.4.5	0.7.2	BOTTOM
DECK	1.9.0	1.11.0	2.0.6	2.2.0	2.2.6	2.2.6	2.1.7	1.11.6+	1.8.4	1.4.0	0.11.2	0.7.0+	0.3.6	HALF-BREADTHS	1.9.0	2.1.1+	2.2.4	1.11.0	1.0.2	DECK
CHINE	1.8.3+	1.10.2+	1.11.7+	2.1.1+	2.1.7	2.1.6+	2.0.7	1.10.7	1.7.5	1.3.1+	0.9.4	0.6.3+	0.3.1+		1.8.3+	2.0.3+	2.1.4	1.9.1	0.11.4	CHINE
BOTTOM	0.11.3+	0.11.6	1.0.0	1.0.0+	1.0.1	1.0.1	0.11.6	2.10.3+	0.8.2	2.0.6	0.0.3	0.0.3	0.0.3+		0.11.3+	0.11.7+	1.0.0	0.8.2	0.7.1	BOTTOM

OFFSETS IN FEET, INCHES, & EIGHTHS TO OUTSIDE OF PLANK.
PLUS SIGNS (+) INDICATE BIAS, NOT NECESSARILY SIXTEENTHS.

BULKHEAD DIMENSIONS
TO INSIDE OF PLANK
BEFORE BEVELLING

where my programming expects her to be. I had to learn not to tack her too close to a weather shore.

The rudder itself seems to be all right. The boat has a normal-feeling weather helm and goes where she looks. Off the wind she's unusually steady; you can let go the tiller for minutes on end without her yawing much. I'm unclear why this is, though I note that it doesn't work if the bow centerboard is raised. Sharp angles of heel don't affect control much.

Dart demonstrates that a boat can be designed with practically all her lateral plane in her rudder, but I think that putting the fin right forward is not the best way to do it. I haven't done anything yet about the small cruiser, but my thinking is that she should be less extreme, with the small pivoting fin nearer amidships, to make bow and stern swing around the midbody in normal fashion. I had a similar experience while experimenting with bow-steering boats, which is discussed in Chapter 23.

The rig would continue to hang out over the stern in the cruiser. Since the sprit boom can be run inboard to furl the sail, this is no problem. Dart should have had a boomkin to sheet to; the bullseye shown had a propensity to hoist the rudder out of water at the wrong times. We put a span (not a traveler) across the stern over the tiller

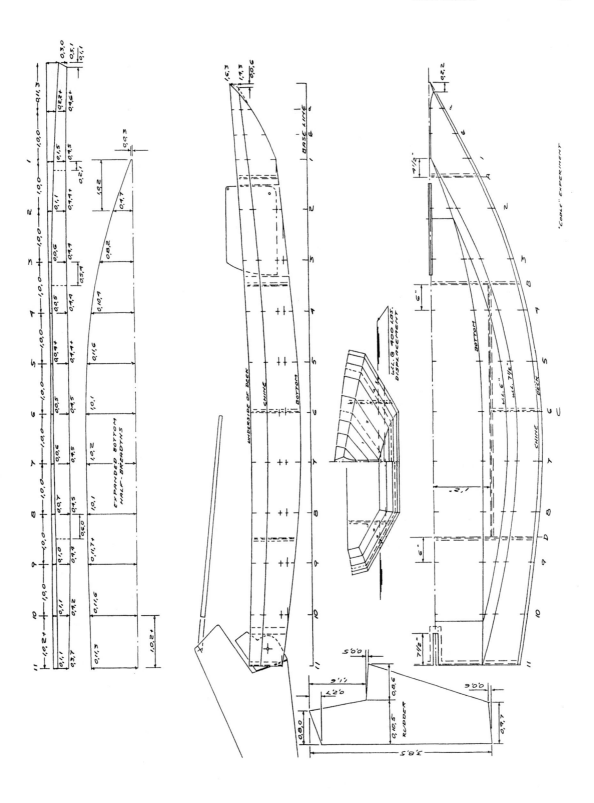

Dart Dinghy

for the sheet block, but the sheet comes in at such an acute angle that flattening the boom close-hauled takes an uncomfortable amount of force.

The rudder has to be quite deep to sail this way. The idea has the same drawback as many centerboards, that the boat can't sail well in very shallow water.

I think a very fast boat can be built with the Dart configuration because she can be balanced to carry her main lateral plane, the rudder, at an angle of incidence that will cancel all leeway while still being smaller than a keel or centerboard.

For cruisers, the lesson is that by using a powerful rudder for more or less of a boat's lateral plane, the rig can be balanced with much more freedom than has been assumed. I had a glimmering of this years ago when I found that the notorious Folding Schooner could be sailed to windward with her mainsail alone. The implications about centerboard location and rig proportions took some time to germinate.

7 *Cartopper*

11'6" × 4'0"

Dynamite Payson and I talked about this design off and on for years. We had in mind a small and light boat that could be built on the "New Instant Boat" system in which prefabricated sides and bottom are sprung around frames to form the intended shape without depending on a plumbed jig. This technique calls for a double-chined shape with a narrow bottom. If the bow is pointed, it has to be rounded back to fit the natural lay of the bilge panels. On 11½ by 4 feet, the bottom is less than 10 feet long and 2 feet wide. The waterline is 3 feet wide with a light load, or up to 3½ feet with more weight.

Such a boat will row badly and sail worse if crew weight is not concentrated amidships, where a normal centerboard is intolerably in the way. The shape of the boat makes leeboards an even clumsier option than usual. The Dart experiment (Chapter 6) showed the way and gave a good line on what we could get away with. The 'midship platform encourages the crew to sit where they belong, keeps their pants out of the bilgewater, and widens the seating base. This last is just as well, because sitting on the gunwale of a boat this light and tender is tense as well as uncomfortable.

A movable rowing seat allows the platform to be cleared for sailing. The long tiller needed to swing the big, unbalanced rudder brings the tiller end up to the platform. Besides mechanical advantage, long tillers discourage jerky steering by absentminded, or novice, helmsmen.

There's still no way to trim the boat properly with two people, one of whom is rowing. All that can be done is to have the passenger sit as close to the rower as possible. The strong sheer is partly to keep a heavy passenger from putting the stern underwater, partly to allow disembarking from her over the bow without swamping her from that end (and without capsizing her if great care is taken). The sheer and flare produce an

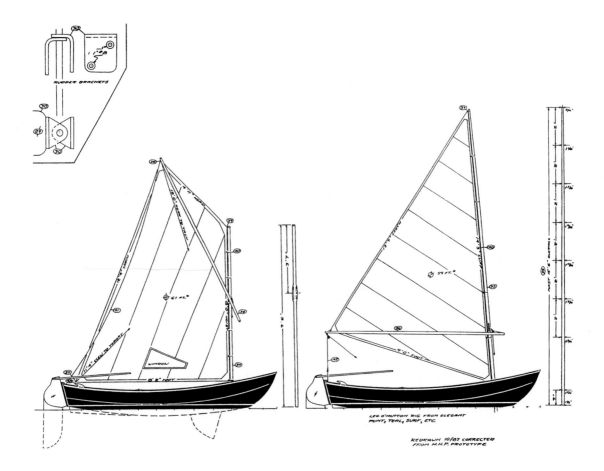

exceptionally dry boat in choppy water; she can carry three sober adults over a fair-sized powerboat wake. Absence of a stern seat helps keep the weight low, with a waterproof cushion for luxury.

These boats handle quite normally, without the idiosyncrasies of the more extreme *Dart*. They're decently spirited even with two adults. The boomless spritsail's only merit is its short mast; the peak vang shown helps somewhat to tame the nasty downwind habits of this rig. Close-hauled in a fair breeze, it's probably as good as the leg-o'-mutton. These two rigs show the distinction between a spritsail and a leg-o'-mutton sail with a sprit boom.

Cartoppers row well as long as they're trimmed with one person or three, and as long as they're not rowed hard. The short waterline makes waves rather than speed, with effort, even with a light load. For the same reason, only very small outboard motors make sense—say, 2 h.p. maximum. But a motor does allow decent trim with two people, if an extension tiller is added to the motor.

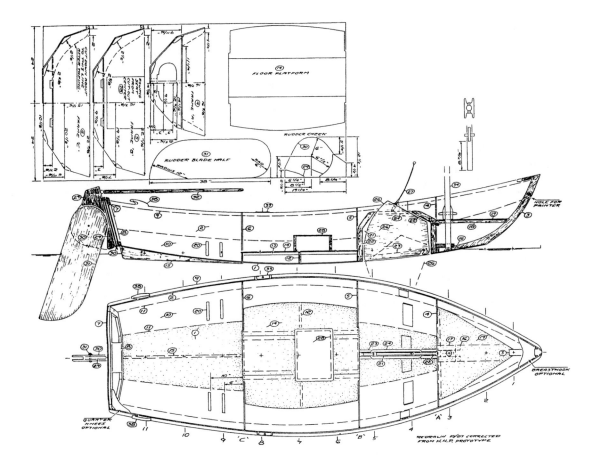

They tow lightly, straight, and dry even in rough water, and make good yacht tenders (see Chapter 63), except for the care needed to get in and out of a boat wide at the gunwales and narrow at the waterline. The taped-seam construction is easy to keep clean. Everybody likes their looks, which if anything benefit from the concessions to fast one-off assembly.

The open interior allows an adult to lie down at full length. I've suggested (in Chapter 63) that a cruising boat could tow one of these, fitted with an overall tent, as a guest stateroom. Two or more, towed in tandem, would accommodate still more and could be raced around the anchored mother ship. Arthur Ransome's *Coot Club* is about a cruise in this fashion. It could be an improvement on family cruising in a crowded boat.

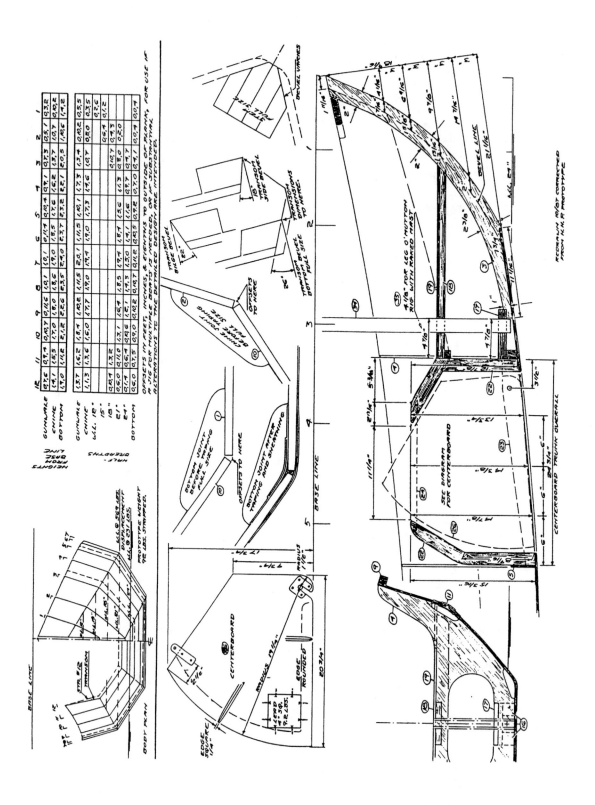

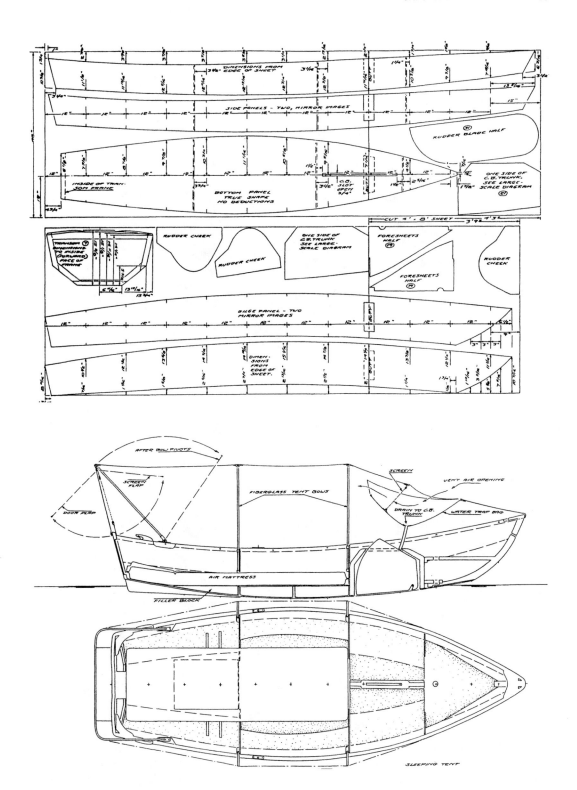

**Dynamite
Payson's
Cartopper**

8 *Three-Meter Multihull*

10'0" × 3'10"/ 7'10"

The fad for toy 12-Meters came and went, killed by cost, weight, slow sailing, and because the decadent *America*'s Cup class itself finally died. The International Three-Meter Multihull class is an attempt to keep the features that made the miniature 12-Meters intriguing, while eliminating some of their impracticality. John Marples got up the rule and built an attractive demonstrator.

The class is not supposed to be one-design. The rules call for overall length of 3 meters (10 feet), maximum breadth of 2.44 meters (8 feet), and 5.7 square meters (60 square feet) of sail. I understand that there's an official one-design rig that all boats can be required to use. I don't have accurate dimensions of it, but the rig shown is close enough to substitute one for the other.

Any number of hulls can be used, but the nature of the rule practically assures that trimarans will be dominant. It's possible that a monohull could be designed that would be competitive; in the heyday of the "bluewater bushmen" some Australian racing dinghies were as wide as they were long. If so, it would be an ugly little brute and not really in keeping with the spirit of the rule.

The shrewdness of the rule is in a requirement that the sailor stay in a fixed seat, and another that specifies a weight, including crew, of at least 350 pounds. The strength, endurance, and agility needed for hiking are factored out, and crew weights are equalized. Among other advantages, an afternoon of racing ought not to wear anybody out. The best sport would be produced by racing over very short courses, with several races in quick succession. One bad mistake wouldn't ruin a whole day.

In these light boats I'd also revert to the old rule that there has to be contact before a foul can be called. This was changed to "risk of collision" because the likes of Captain Charles Barr and Charles Francis Adams were playing chicken with 90-footers, but

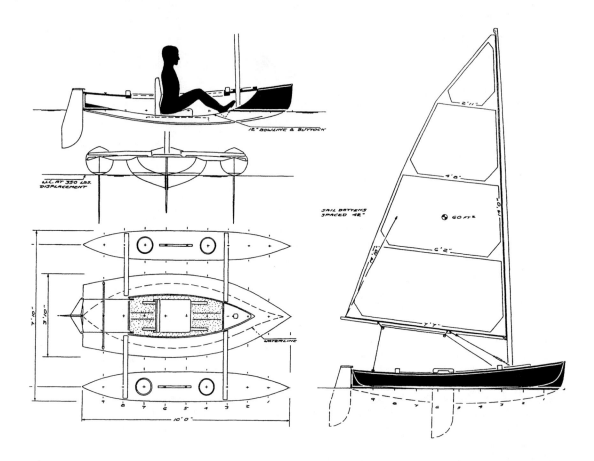

"risk of collision" was abused when I was racing intercollegiate dinghies. The trick was to tack before a port-tack boat had a chance to give way, then protest him for not giving way.

If the class grows to be hotly raced, it's a certainty that any sheet-plywood shape will be outclassed. A boat this short for her weight will be a better sailer if she's a complex shape. The form shown would be most readily built with edge-nailed strips of softwood sheathed with epoxy to slow down water absorption. I've put something like 5,000 miles on a strip-built cedar canoe that Dynamite Payson built for me 25 years ago, with resorcinol glue and no surface protection except paint, so the epoxy encapsulation is not critical. My boat has always been kept out of water when it wasn't in use, but it lives in the open, with no shelter or shade.

Since all the boat's power to carry sail comes from the buoyancy of the lee-side float, the floats are designed to bury to the deck without prohibitive drag: slim-lined, round-bilged, with sharp canoe sterns. (Appreciation is due to the memory of Arthur Piver, who first perceived that a trimaran's floats should be as long as the main hull since they would move at the same speed. For an embarrassingly long time, people who should have known better kept imitating flying boat wingtip floats.) These floats will support 270 pounds to the deck amidships, with a lot of sheer above that for reserve.

Apart from driving through squalls, it's handy to be able to step on a float to get into or out of the boat.

Daggerboards in the floats have not had the best results in trimarans, partly because they're too far off the boat's axis of rotation in turning, but mostly (I think) due to being too small and the wrong shape. Human anatomy precludes a centerboard in the main hull, but in these tiny boats a fixed keel might not be an intolerable nuisance.

An overall length limit naturally suggests upright ends to get as long a waterline as possible, but I've come to doubt that a sharp angled forefoot pays. It has to be either bulbous, which is likely to start eddies, or else so thin that it's all surface and no useful displacement. Also, all multihulls need to be quick-turning because they lack momentum to carry them through a wide turn, and rounding back the forefoot shortens the turning circle.

The main hull looks very wide by usual trimaran standards. Its weight of 350 pounds is a lot for a 10-footer to carry. If she is not wide she will float deep, and if she floats deep she can't go fast. I think the proportions shown are conservative; if the class goes on evolving, later hulls may be wider still. The speed of a wave 10 feet long is $4\frac{1}{4}$ knots. That would be the top speed of a deep hull that long, at which her ends would bog down in the crests of the deep wave she would generate. A wider, shallower hull will generate a shallower wave and have a better chance of getting ahead of some of the length of a longer, faster wave (one definition, not the only one, of "planing"). The reason I think an 8-foot-wide monohull might work is that it could carry the specified weight on a negligible draft, to sail with little or no wave drag. But, unless it was very craftily shaped, it would have a large wetted surface and lose out in drifting weather.

There's a common tendency to assume that a multihull will be light, whereas except for the lack of ballast they're inherently heavier than monohulls for any given volume, on account of the large surface area and high structural stresses. The result is that it's rare to see a cruising multihull that doesn't look overloaded. I'm still not convinced that wider, shallower hulls wouldn't pay, even in the racing catamarans that do float as they're supposed to. I have not designed many multihulls because the economy of the monohull's compact shape has usually had a higher priority than the multihull's ability to carry a bigger, higher sail plan.

The wide hull is also more adaptable. I guess one reason for the demise of the toy 12-Meters was that they were limited to solo sailing. This design, with seat removed and a tiller shipped, would be a respectable daysailer for two, or even three, sitting on deck with feet in the well. Another 350 pounds, doubling the displacement, will put her down in the water less than 3 inches.

The fixed-seat stipulation is well thought of, but for daysailing, even solo, I'd often prefer to sit on deck, as it's so much more convenient to look all around. I once had a sailing canoe of the ancient fashion, to be sailed from a reclining position. It was practically impossible to see aft from this position; irritating and unseamanlike. The bolt-upright attitude of the figure on the drawing is due to that experience; sitting up straight, it's possible to twist around above the waist to look through a large arc without resorting to mirrors. It's also possible to get your feet under you quickly if it should suddenly be desirable to get up or out.

Steering from the seat is with a foot bar, to leave hands free for the sheet and for the spinnaker the rule allows. I haven't detailed this, and I'm in two minds as to whether the bar should be the type that is worked with the toes and balls of the feet, with heels in fixed rests, or the type that has stirrups to be worked by knee action. The latter would be apt to lead to oversteering, with small leg movements producing large rudder angles—not a good way to sail fast. The former, we all learn to do delicately on the foot throttles of our automobiles, but the force available might be marginal for a rudder this size. The travel open to a foot fixed at the heel doesn't allow much mechanical advantage. However, I think I would probably go that way, with some balance area on the rudder if necessary.

The high and buoyant bow is an antidote for the pitchpoling propensities of short, heavy boats with tall rigs. Bows like this are tricky to fair, but good-looking if well done. This design has a more boatlike shape than most multihulls, and I think she would be quite attractive from most angles. I have not made any construction plan or detailing beyond what is shown here, and the lines and offsets. It would be in keeping with the general idea of the class if many contestants designed their own boats. Aside from the satisfaction of doing it, it's much harder to make a name as a boat designer now than it was when I was breaking in. Something like this gives an opening to ambition with minimal disaster potential.

9 *Supermouse*

11'6" × 6'6" × 1'3"

Lorry Sedgewick built a Fieldmouse dinghy from my plans. This is a clinker-built pram, 7 feet 6 inches by 4 feet 0 inches, very high-sided and bulky, with both transoms vertical. It carries a huge rig for its size in a fully battened cat rig. Lorry and his wife liked the boat and asked me to work on a bigger version that could have a cuddy cabin.

Since they liked the plumb ends of the small boat, these were carried into the bigger one without argument. Raked transoms make a faster boat less badly stopped by waves if they're raked out from the given bottom length, but in that case the boat would be better still if the waterline were carried out to plumb transoms at the new overall length. . . .

Even in much bigger boats, dividing the space into "below" and "on deck" means that both suffer. I look for a way to combine the functions, to use the whole boat day and night. The Birdwatcher layout (see Chapter 46) with the transparent raised deck is my favorite solution so far. It gives shelter and shade, is easy to close up entirely with fabric covers, and its high and wide buoyancy makes a boat uncapsizable in the context of small-lake sailing. High freeboard is an efficient substitute for low ballast. In this case, the sides open out; the assumption is that they would be closed before the squall strikes—a fair bet, though I'm more comfortable with fixed windows, which don't usually make the enclosed cockpit hot because there's an eddying flow of wind from the open centerline standing room.

The standing room allows walking with hands in pockets, standing up to look around, and an end-to-end tent at standing height. Stepping forward to the mast is an improvement over leading the halyards aft, whence somebody has to clamber to the mast to clear the jam at the turning blocks.

The watertight wells take care of oily objects aft and muddy ones forward. The

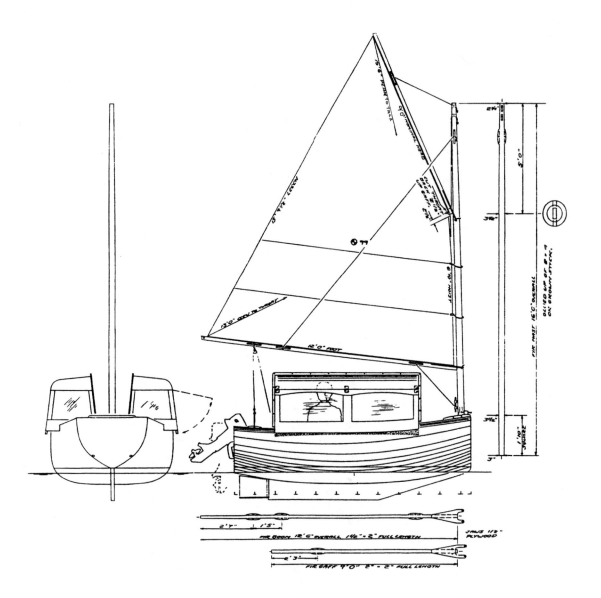

living room should never be worse than damp. A curtain can separate off the toilet for civility.

The Fieldmouse had big leeboards. These don't marry well with the glass house. A calf-deep keel seemed a minimal nuisance either in launching and hauling, or in shallow water; it makes the inboard rudder practical and, in turn, the most convenient and efficient motor mounting. This keel is not ballasted, but being thin, hollow, and free-flooding, it doesn't have much effect on the stability of this stiff hull. In a knockdown it would come out of the water and help right her before it could drain. It is stronger than it looks in the sectional view because the rocker of the boat's bottom offsets the ends of the keel from the middle for a good lever arm to resist a side stress. Keels like this hold on to windward quite well unless the wind has blown hard enough and long enough, over a

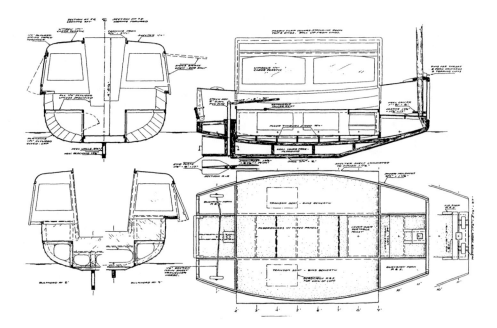

big enough stretch of water, to start the surface water drifting. In other words, they work on lakes and bays, and in gentle weather.

The high boom makes the nominal sail area less than that of more normal rigs of equal driving power and heeling effect. The gaff rig allows a shorter mast and is easier to lower and furl than the batwing sail of the smaller boat. It has the same advantage over a triangular sail—that the center of sail area doesn't shift so far ahead as the sail is reefed. (See the accompanying essay on catboat design.)

The inspiration for the superstructure was the bamboo-and-thatch shelter seen on liveaboard sampans all over the Far East. On them it's quaintly attractive.

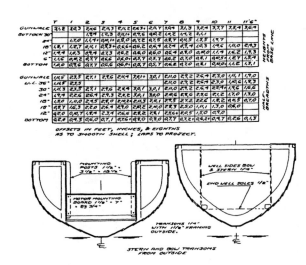

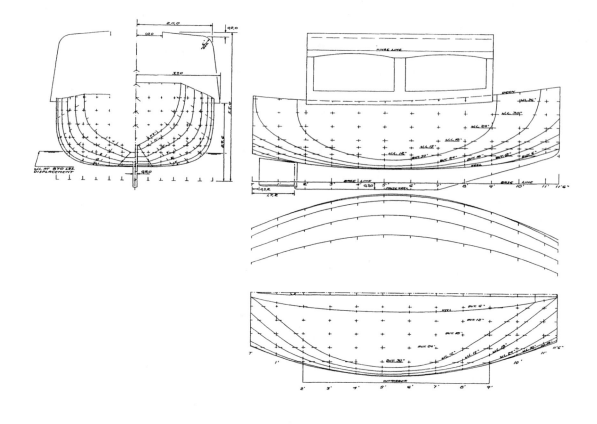

On Catboat Design

If you identify the midsection on the left on page 39 as a narrow boat, and the one on the right as a wide boat, you're right. The left-hand section is that of an English cutter six times as long as she is wide. The right-hand section is a Cape Cod catboat two beams long. But, how could you tell how long they are?

Apart from recognizing them for what they are, and noting that depth-to-beam ratio has as much to do with what makes a boat wide or narrow as length-to-beam, there's a good reason why the cutter midsection represents a narrow boat. If you built a two-beam boat on that section, it would be a very bad boat, slow, wet, and wild-steering. If you built a six-beam boat on the cat mid-section, that would be a good boat. The point is that you don't have to. A good short boat can be built on that section.

In the 1890s, when racing boats were measured for handicap by waterline length, several cats were built with long overhanging bows and sterns faired out from beamy catboat bottoms. The best of these long-decked cats was the Herreshoff-built *Wanda*. In the photo she is skimming along, seeming barely to touch the water, and you can take it that in the light air shown, or in more wind with a more modest sail and boom, she was a sweet-handling craft. Her beam was about what would be expected in a cat of her waterline length—her lines were stretched rather than enlarged. Besides allowing sleeker lines, the extra length added to her stability; she could carry more sail than a shorter boat.

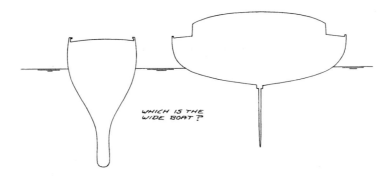

WHICH IS THE
WIDE BOAT ?

She's also potentially a better seaboat because out ahead of her massive mast she has buoyancy, to pick her up and let her drive when the short-bowed cat would plunge and root. To be a good seaboat she would need more freeboard, especially forward. The same concern applies to a short cat. Modern designs are higher than their ancestors, but most would be better in heavy weather if they were higher still. Their designers are wary of making a drastic departure from the traditional proportions of working cats built for lobstermen and longline fishermen, all of whom liked low-sided boats for obvious reasons.

Racing cats were kept as low as possible because a low boat has more initial stability and can carry a bigger sail without adding to the height of its rig above the waterline. Racing sailors can be expected to stay alert for the sudden loss of stability when the rail buries.

Notwithstanding the virtues of long boats, the usual reason for choosing a cat is that she can be made compact without being slow or clumsy. But, there's more to designing a good short cat than choosing a good midsection. Short and shallow boats naturally tend to have a quick turn from the stem into the keel—a "strong chin." Fairing the body of the boat into this profile shape is tricky on paper. The old-time cat builders designed with half-models, and they would stretch a string around the model to show up the fore-and-aft flow that no plane section can truly represent in a hull of that type. I guess that most of them were concerned with making sure that a cedar plank

would take the twist without splitting. Intended or not, the effect was to avoid the "club forefoot," a bulbous shape produced by making the chin too thick; this makes for an ugly bow wave and bad steering when the boat is driven hard. A well-designed boat with a strong-chinned profile always shows hollow in her forward waterlines.

A temptation that should usually be resisted is the raking midsection—that is, making the forebody deep and sharp, and the afterbody wide and shallow. As long as it's upright, this shape can be driven fast without making a lot of fuss. The sharp bow opens the water smoothly, and the shallow stern leaves it without pulling up a steep wave. But when such a boat heels, the big stern floats up and pushes the heavy bow down. She digs in at the bow, lifts her rudder, and tries to tear through the water cornerwise. A boat that shape has to be sailed upright. She needs an active crew to hike out and hold her up.

No cruising boat should be designed to be sailed that way. Even if the crew is heavy enough, they will get tired. Cruisers should have light afterquarters (see the elegant shape of *Wanda*'s stern), buoyant cheeks in the the upper parts of their bows, and hull depth carried well aft. All this allows a boat to be ballasted to bring her center of gravity back close to the middle of her topside buoyancy, which she will lean on as she heels. Her top speed will be less, but she'll be less demanding of endurance and vigilance.

Lastly, any catboat, and especially one that misbehaves if she heels too much, should be designed

The Herreshoff-built **Wanda,** *circa 1900*

to stand deep reefs without going out of balance. A great forward slope in the leech of her sail is a bad sign because the center of such a sail moves forward when a strip is taken off its foot. In that respect, a long gaff with a low peak is best; the triangular leg-o'-mutton is worst. Shortening the boom helps but reduces the sail's driving area; the boat won't stand up to adding the same sail area higher up. A cat with a tall, short-boomed rig will not sail as well as one with a bigger, lower sail.

The proportions favored in the 1890s still seem to be right, though now that engines do the ghosting, the sail can be smaller, with mast set farther back from the stem and less boom out over the stern, suiting a fair sailing breeze without reefing.

Part Two

Rowing
Boats

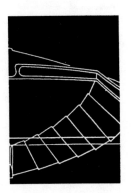

10 *Sweet Pea*

15'0" × 4'4"

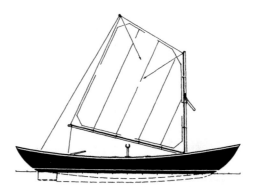

Market research is guessing whether something would be sold if it were offered. As good a way as any to make the guess is to build something that one of the parties to the enterprise wants, on the theory that what one person wants, others will want. Dynamite Payson wanted to row off to some islands in his neighborhood in the morning calm, and sail back when the breeze filled in. In summer weather the prevailing wind would usually make his return a broad reach. Being a State-of-Mainer and an ex-lobsterman, he likes to row standing up and facing forward, to see the rock before hitting it.

He had in mind a light, fast-to-build peapod, which is by way of a contradiction in terms since peapods are heavy and complex by nature. He settled for what I would call a surf dory, resembling a peapod in having a sharp stern and curved stem overhang. Surf dories had rounded lapstrake sides, for which the second chine in the new boat formed a fair substitute; it makes a more stable boat than a light dory with straight-flaring sides, in which you stand up at your peril. The new boat carries a load higher in the water as well.

We played with the wish list for some time. Dynamite turned down several schemes that I put to him (one was two Cartopper bows built end-to-end), until I came up with one he liked. Aside from getting the proportions just so, the hard problem was to give the boat lateral plane and a rudder without totally spoiling it for rowing, as usually happens if you yield to the pervasive impulse to rig a nice rowing boat to sail (fitting a good sailboat with oars is more profitable).

I thought of the slipping keels of the Norfolk wherries (see Introduction). With such a keel, almost all the parts that interfere with rowing could be removed when they weren't wanted. It made it possible to bring Sweet Pea's rudder inboard where a tiller of reasonable length could be reached by a solitary sailor sitting in the best place to trim the light boat. I made the keel shallow, since the boat wasn't called on to sail well to

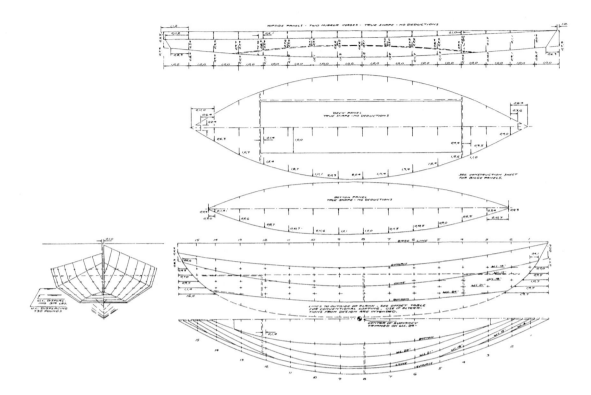

windward. A keel and rudder twice as deep would make a much more weatherly boat, but one dispiriting to row on account of all the surface friction. The drag of the 3-inch keel is noticeable; the difference with and without it is comparable to taking on a heavy passenger. If the passenger is present in any case, the keel's drag makes less difference. Dynamite was particularly tickled by the tiller lock notch in the sternpost.

The full-length deck carries movable rowing seats to trim the boat with one, two, or three people, and she could be rowed by two people without a passenger, which isn't practical with fixed seats. The seats could easily be made to slide, but the hull isn't capable of enough speed to justify the complication. Each seat is made up of five pieces of plywood stuck together with epoxy. The joints are supposed to be reinforced on each side with strips of 'glass tape, but I spent most of a summer trying without success to prove that they're not strong enough without the tape.

The deck also supplies secure seating on the weather side of the boat in a breeze of wind, a place to put down a sandwich neither in the bilge nor in danger of sliding overboard, and it covers enough foam buoyancy to allow rowing the boat completely swamped. The deck adds about 30 pounds to the stripped weight of the boat, which ended up at 125 pounds without the keel.

Dave Montgomery of Montgomery Boat Yard in Gloucester built a Sweet Pea, which he kept on my float-stages. She could be shoved into the water and be on her way 10 seconds after the impulse. He built the wells for the slipping keel, but we never did

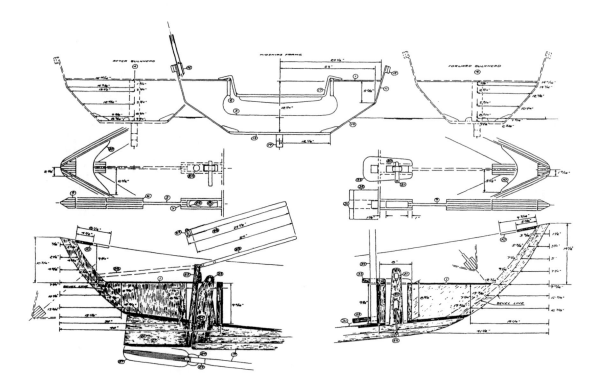

feel the need to sail her. Susanne Altenburger and another woman covered 20 miles in her one day, taking turns rowing (at one point, they had her bottom-up on a beach for shelter as a thunderstorm passed over). Dave and I found her best for quick spins of an hour or less, to unwind from work. With her short waterline she couldn't be rowed fast; 4 knots showed a rolling wake and needed hard pulling, but she made 3½ very easily and felt lively.

In rough water, usually motorboat wakes, she was perfectly dry. I never saw any spray come aboard. Her only vice was that in steep waves she would stamp and stop, on account of the flat bottom and full bow.

		15	14	13	12	11	10	9	8	7	6	5	4	3	2	1
HEIGHTS FROM BASE LINE	GUNWALE	9.6.0	9.7.3	9.8.7	9.10.0	9.10.7	0.11.4	0.11.6	0.11.5	0.11.2	0.10.4	0.9.3	0.8.0	0.6.1	0.4.1	0.2.4
	CHINE	0.10.5	1.0.6	1.3.3	1.5.3	1.6.7	1.7.7	1.8.3	1.8.4	1.8.0	1.7.1	1.5.7	1.4.1	1.2.1	0.11.7	0.9.7
	BOTTOM		1.11.0	2.0.3	2.1.5	2.2.6	2.3.4	2.3.7	2.4.0	2.3.6	2.3.2	2.2.3	2.1.3	2.0.1	(1.10.7)	
	KEEL LINE	1.5.0	(2.0.0)	(2.3.3)	(2.8.4)	(2.10.1)	(2.10.7)	(2.11.1)	(2.11.1)	(2.10.7)	(2.8.2)	(2.5.0)	(2.7.0)	(2.3.4)	1.9.6	1.2.2
		15	14	13	12	11	10	9	8	7	6	5	4	3	2	1
HALF-BREADTHS	GUNWALE	0.5.2	0.9.7	1.3.1	1.7.3	1.10.4	2.0.5	2.1.6	2.1.7	2.1.0	1.11.1	1.8.4	1.5.1	1.1.1	0.8.4	0.4.4
	CHINE	0.3.7	0.8.1	1.1.1	1.3.0	1.8.0	1.10.1	1.11.1	1.11.2	1.10.3	1.8.5	1.6.0	1.2.5	0.10.6	0.6.2	0.2.3
	W.L. 12"	0.3.2												0.5.7	0.1.4	
	15"	0.1.6	0.7.0											0.10.1	0.4.4	
	18"		0.9.0	0.11.1	1.4.4							1.5.7	1.1.2	0.8.1	0.2.6	
	21"		0.9.0	0.8.6	1.1.5	1.5.4	1.8.5	1.10.1	1.10.2	1.9.0	1.6.3	1.2.6	0.10.4	0.5.7	0.1.0	
	24"			0.6.1	0.10.5	1.2.0	1.4.4	1.5.5	1.5.6	1.4.6	1.2.5	0.11.4	0.7.6	0.3.4		
	BOTTOM		0.4.2	0.5.5	0.8.6	0.10.5	0.11.4	0.11.6	0.11.6	0.11.3	0.10.4	0.8.6	0.6.4	0.3.3		
		15	14	13	12	11	10	9	8	7	6	5	4	3	2	1

OFFSETS IN FEET, INCHES, & EIGHTHS
TO OUTSIDE OF PLANK. FOR CONVENTION-
AL LOFTWORK; STATIONS DON'T CORRES-
POND TO INSIDE-OF-PLANK EXPAN-
SIONS.

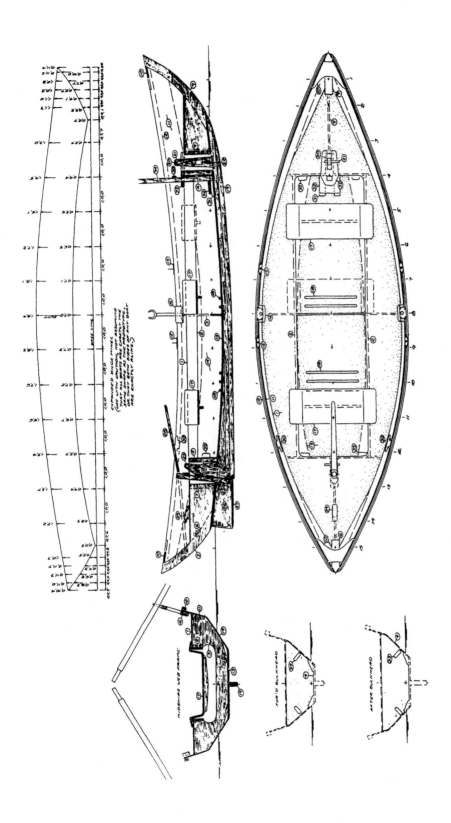

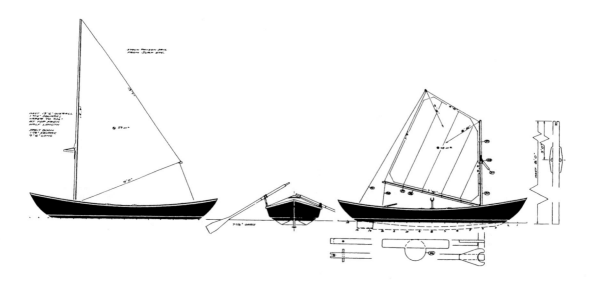

Susanne and Sweet Pea

11

Spur II

15'4" × 4'6"

Spur is named for a Whitehall type I had built in 1963, much admired but a failure in use due to its great weight, and because I designed the blades of her oars much too small and did not realize for a long time what was wrong.

The 1993 boat was built by David Montgomery for his and my use and as a standard model for his shop. *Spur II* weighs just under 100 pounds. Built in 85 hours complete, she looks very yachty, though Dave's usual policy is not to fret over minute imperfections. Successive boats will go faster, with patterns on hand for frames and planking.

The 6mm okoume glued-lapstrake planking is handsome and not a long job to build, at least for a professional. It works well for series building, since the laps allow some tolerance in prefabricated strakes. This is why clinker planking used to be considered an economical construction.

Spur II is as dry as Sweet Pea (see Chapter 10), cuts wakes more smoothly, and she's faster when the rower is working hard on account of her longer waterline on less weight. She disturbs the water noticeably less than some narrower boats with outriggers. With comparable weight, the narrow hull floats deeper and has to move the water she's encountering a greater vertical distance, generating comparatively deep waves.

Dave made the oarlocks detailed on the plans in about 20 minutes each. They're very pleasant to use, as the fixed vertical pin has no tendency to walk the oar as conventional locks do. Dave also made some spoon-blade oars from his own design, and showed me what a dramatic difference counterweights on the looms of the oars make in use. They allow a longer proportion of an oar outboard of the lock than I had thought was workable.

(text continued on page 51)

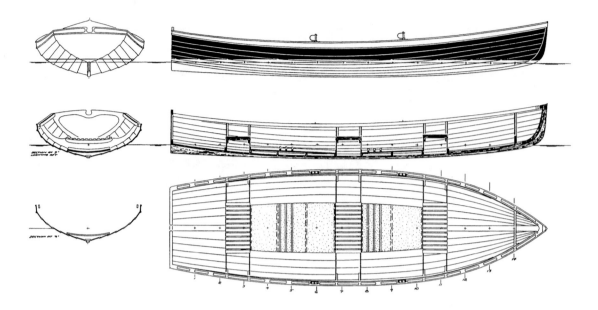

Spur II

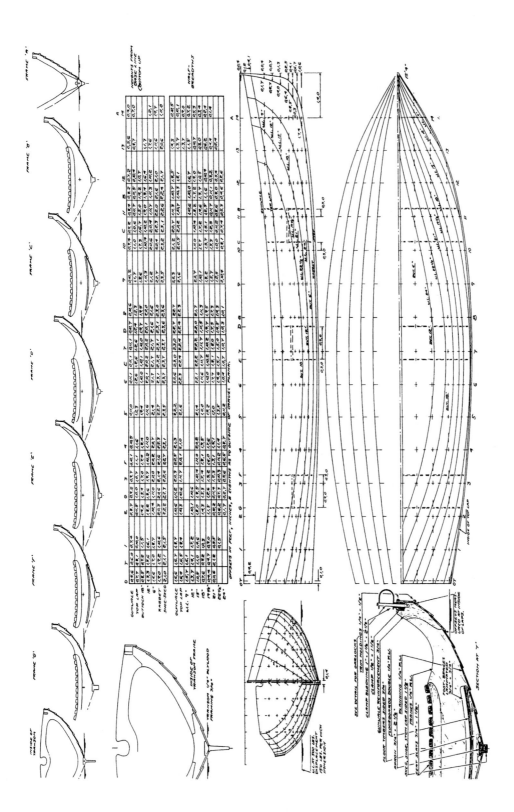

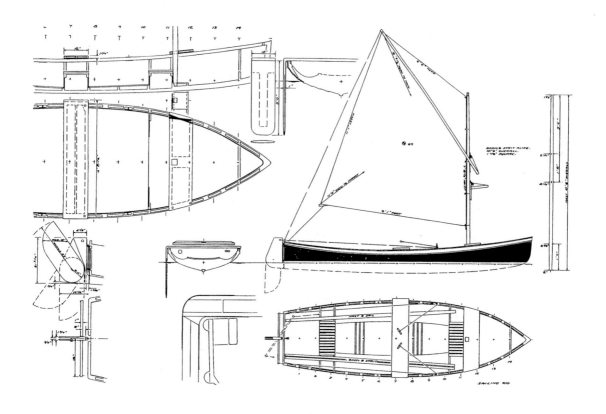

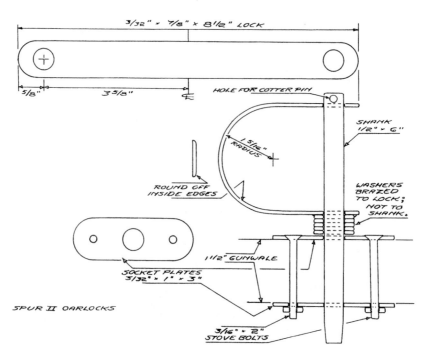

SPUR II OARLOCKS

The sail plan was made in response to the usual chorus of, "What a nice rowboat! Let's sail it!" It will add close to a thousand dollars to the cost of the boat, and clutter enough to spoil her for rowing. I made a genuine attempt to design a rig that will do the least harm to the rowing qualities. All the spars stow out to the sides. The leeboard is an awkward object, but it's quickly removable, as are all the components of the conversion.

This leeboard is supposed to combine the functions of leeboard and a sailing seat to allow a sailor to get his weight to the weather side without sitting on the thin gunwale. It's lashed to the gunwale at its forward corners to pivot up along the after edge when the leeboard hits something. The sectional shape of the boat precludes use of conventional leeboards, and there is not depth enough under the seats for a centerboard.

With this rig, *Spur* would sail respectably, though she would be tricky in puffy weather. The low and flaring sides would easily ship water. She wouldn't be fast compared with a real sailboat because of her soft stern quarters, which reduce her stability and would pull up a steep following wave if the boat were driven hard.

It's apparently a basic human instinct, when presented with something that does one thing very well, to instantly want to use it for something else. . . .

12 *Ceremonial Barge*

23'3" × 4'6"

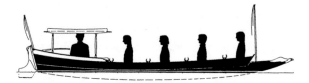

Dear Phil:

One of the pleasures of Mystic Seaport's Small Craft Workshop is the chance to row in one of the museum's multi-oared boats—from the seine boats to the four-oared race-boat *General Lafayette*. Inspired by this and other similar experiences, I have been day-dreaming about a four-person gig for day trips in sheltered waters.

She should be capable of being moved around on shore by a couple, so 200 pounds is a maximum weight, and I would hope for a good deal less. She should also be capable of being rowed by a couple, with or without one or two passengers, as well as by three people with a fourth as coxswain tending a rudder. A fourth rowing position would be nice if you could get it without too much length, complication, and bad trim. She should be stable enough that the crew can change places underway. Guide-model canoe stability is adequate. Finally, she should be good-looking inside and out.

I have no overriding preference as to model, although stretched adaptions of your Gypsy or Defender designs each appeal in their own way. Given the appropriate hull, a dipping lugsail would be appropriate to a toy gig like this, although it might not be used unless conditions were perfect.

If it all came together right, you could have a lot of satisfaction from such a boat: strenuous and spirited rowing, lazy paddling, and, by no means least in importance, the satisfaction of contemplating a pretty hull drawn up on shore.

Steven M. Weld, Milton, Massachusetts

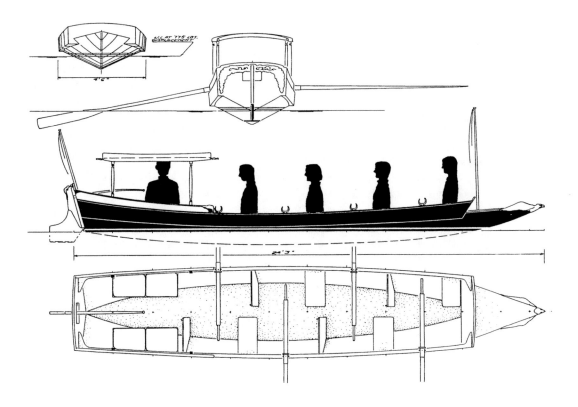

Dear Mr. Weld:

My first thought was the bateau I designed for high school students in manual training shops, like the one built for the Philadelphia Special Olympics, with six short oars to give many people some action. These craft are the most austere variety of Instant Boat, with sides prefabricated of straight, parallel-edged panels and flat bottoms with taped chines. They're built of ½-inch plywood to stand abuse, and with a big volume of positive buoyancy at each end. They weigh just under 350 pounds dry. Using ¼-inch plywood and other weight-saving materials, it would be possible to build a boat this shape and size (25 feet 6 inches by 4 feet 10 inches) not much over 150 pounds. I designed a 31-footer like this that weighed 182 pounds and lasted for years. This would be the way to get afloat with a minimum of delay and expense.

Next I thought about a complex-shaped, ultralight boat about this size, built glued-lapstrake as described in Tom Hill's book *Ultralight Boatbuilding* (Internatinal Marine, 1989). That would be as light, faster, and otherwise more pleasant to row, and an order of magnitude handsomer. In John D. Alden's *The American Steel Navy* (page 351) there's a hypnotic photo of a six-oared captain's gig of stunning whaleboat shape. I salivate at the thought of designing something looking like that. I did get a chance to design a half-size copy of it, which Dave Montgomery built for a Marblehead man a couple of years ago.

Larry Dahlmer designed and built a multichined, plywood-planked version of a Scilly Islands pilot gig for the Gloucester Sirens racing crew last year. It's bigger and heavier than you need but illustrates another possibility. A look through Howard Chapelle's or Edgar March's small-boat books will further stimulate the imagination.

The drawing here illustrates a less obvious thought. A couple of people who saw it on the drawing board instantly thought of the episode about Lord Nelson's funeral in C. S. Forester's *Hornblower and the Atropos*, but ceremonial barges came in handier sizes than those in that story. Chapman's *Architectura Navalis Mercatoria* of 1775 has pages of them, ranging from practical boats this size to an amazing royal galley 124 feet long with 32 two-man oars—about the ultimate in conspicuous consumption.

This boat I'm proposing couldn't be built as lightly as you suggest, but it seems to me that it doesn't really need to be. Even if it weighed 350 pounds, it would still be easy enough for two people to deal with on a light trailer. For two people to use in places where the boat couldn't be handled that way, it would make more sense to have another boat, much smaller, rather than constrict the design of the six-person boat.

She would go along well with two of the four 12½-foot oars. With four oars she would go fast, easily 6 knots. With some additional crutch positions she could pull with one to four pairs of sculls, allowing an odd number of rowers and incidentally less than the 22 feet of clear water needed by the long oars. She could also pull eight short oars using a side-by-side arrangement.

The shape is meant to be built of sheet plywood with taped seams. It's a scaled-up version of the Thomaston Galley, which I designed many years ago for Dynamite Payson. I used one myself for some years, enjoying her smooth and silent action. The wide sponsonlike sides will allow the proposed bigger boat to take as many people as you're likely to want without bogging down, and will keep her dry in a small chop. She's not fit for really rough water; the limit would be a steep enough sea to hit the forward ends of the sponsons. In spite of the sharp rake there, she would be badly stopped and throw up clouds of soaking spray.

The point of the sponsons is to allow the fourth rowing position without an outrigger or a much longer boat, and to make room for the pavilion over the stern above a fine afterbody. This boat would be tender for her size and weight. Though she would stagger if somebody stepped on the gunwale, the sponson would stop the heel quickly. She wouldn't go over or ship water, but her tenderness might be disconcerting to inexperienced people. I'd be open to an argument that she'd be better with a flat bottom about 18 inches wide, with more sharply rising bilges. Among other things, her draft would be reduced. However, the deep vee would have a smoother action and save one joint on each side. I think I could clean up the design of the bottom-to-sponson connection if I went around one more time in preliminary form. The shape of the spray rail now strikes me as unnecessarily complex and it might do more harm than good.

The low ram bow doesn't blow off as much as the usual profile, and with the awning aft she would have a strong tendency to weathercock into the wind. That's desirable in a squall, but it adds to the work of rowing broadside across a strong wind. I've often argued that the windage of hulls and superstructures is negligible, but that's only true by comparison with the tremendous drag of sailboat rigging. In a pulling boat, small resistances are exaggerated by the small power available. The four big oars here may develop as much as 2 h.p. total when the oarsmen are pulling hard. There would be times when it would be much appreciated if the awning could be taken down.

This boat could easily be made to sail quite well. A single spritsail, with all its spars short enough to stow well out of the way, would drive her respectably on all points. The sponson shape suits a clip-on leeboard of the simplest type. But, who needs it? The rig is expensive, adds weight, and makes a clutter that spoils the visual effect. I used the rig in my Thomaston Galley to get some rest on a long solo row, but the four-oared boat with six people can relieve one or two oars at a time so that everybody gets some rest in the shade without stopping the boat. If you row for an hour, then lounge at your ease steering and watching the others, you can keep at it for many hours. For that matter, in smooth water she could keep going well with two oars, still with six people, allowing stints of a half-hour at the oar with one-hour breaks.

Decorating something like this is a great artistic opportunity. I've roughly indicated a figurehead with squiggles representing carvings. Chapman's drawings are more elaborate, and Bjorn Landstrom's book *The Ship* has exhilarating paintings of the great age of shipcarving, including a baroque treatment of this kind of stern awning. Ship decoration is in a sad state of decadence, but it might be revived.

The best work I've ever seen was designed by Stanley Woodward, when he had his own yacht yard in Mallorca, and a sculptor able to execute his wonderful drawings. The only decorations I've ever done myself were forced on me when Stanley sailed off to Sicily leaving instructions—but no drawings—that the monkey rails of a ketch we were building should finish in lion's paws. The sculptor was good, but he'd never seen a lion, and what he came up with looked more like camel's feet. In desperation I looked up a copy of *Born Free*, with a photo of Elsa the lioness lying on top of a Land Rover with her paws draped over the edge at just the right angle. From that I made a full-sized drawing which the sculptor executed beautifully. I never had any calling to do more such work.

There must be some sculptors around with the requisite skill, but it's been a long time since I've seen any designs with both character and taste. Except for a rare natural talent like that of Stanley Woodward, it takes a lot of study and practice. I know two people trained in sculpture and painting who did admirable work at one time, but they both took to boatbuilding, had no time to keep their hands in on the fine art, and they've lost the dexterity. (Apparently the art schools are teaching that the design of applied ornament is degrading, an insult to the memory of Louis Sullivan, to go no farther back in history.)

Failing somebody with the skill and willingness to study what suits a particular boat, I'd finish the bow of this galley with a simple pyramidal spike and confine the rest of the ornamentation to painted scrollwork of the kind you see nicely done on panel vans.

Whether she has carving or not, this boat should blaze with color and gilding. A lapstrake whaleboat can be plain white and look exquisitely beautiful just from the shadows of the laps and the curves of her framing, but this boat was meant to be flamboyant, not subtle.

13 *Cruising Rowboat*

21'0" × 5'0"

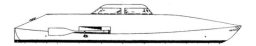

This boat was designed for cruising around Lake Michigan from the neighborhood of Chicago as far as Mackinac Island. Dr. Nenad Belic specified that she be able to carry half a ton of supplies and keep the sea in any weather, in case a dream cruise across the North Pacific came to pass.

At the power a single oarsman can keep up, a boat more than 15 feet long doesn't go fast enough for wavemaking to be significant. All her hydrodynamic drag is from wetted-surface friction. The most effective way to reduce wetted surface is to make the boat compact. The one-short-ton full-load displacement aimed at could be carried by a hemisphere 5 feet in diameter; the boat would be a complete sphere, half immersed. That would have the minimum of wetted surface, but at about 2 m.p.h. high drag from wavemaking and turbulent flow would set in, and she would not go straight without a big skeg which would put back a good deal of the saving in surface area. Some tank tests on a proposed hemispherical floating fort showed that at a very low speed, aimless eddies enveloped the rudder and made it uncontrollable. Besides, the 5-foot sphere has no place to lie down.

I've rowed a 19-foot-waterline boat a good many miles without much stress. In a dead calm and a smooth sea, that is probably more than the optimum length, but considering downwind rowing and wave encounter, it seemed a likely choice for Dr. Belic's boat. The bow was made sharp enough to split small waves, the stern full-lined but with a large skeg to control eddy-making. A deeper, shorter fin could have less area but would pick up floating weed. The vertical trailing edge will take a rudder the owner intends to try; it may pay when rowing before the wind. We discussed fitting a leeboard
(text continued on page 59)

Key to Construction Plans

1. Hull shell scant $1/2$" cedar strips, maximum width about $1\frac{1}{2}$", edge-nailed with 2" 14 galvanized Anchorfast nails on about 6" spacing, staggered 8". Epoxy-glued and sealed throughout, Dynel-sheathed on the exterior. Inside, in way of the rowing well, sheathe with 10-oz. glass cloth turned up the inside faces of the well.

2. Deck similar to hull but with center flat between the hatches $1/2$" plywood.

3. Stem and sternpost laminated, sided $2\frac{1}{2}$", molded $1\frac{1}{2}$".

4. Sheer clamp from $3/4$" × $1\frac{1}{2}$".

5. Deck transom $1/2$" plywood with $3/4$" fastening frame.

6. Web frames $1/2$" plywood; no fastening frames; cove out against hull and deck planking with epoxy fillets about $1/2$" radius.

7. Stem cap sided $1\frac{1}{2}$", molded as dimensioned on the lines drawing.

8. Skeg sided $1\frac{1}{2}$", built up as shown or as convenient (could be plywood), faired as shown to $3/4$" face along the bottom and $1/4$" face up the after edge. Seal with epoxy.

9. Sister keelsons of $1/2$" plywood form inboard faces of water tanks and bins, and walls of the rowing-sleeping well. Cove out with epoxy fillets to the bottom on both sides.

10. Transverse walls of fresh water cells $1/2$" plywood, all filleted watertight. (These water cells are supposed to be filled with seawater as they're emptied of fresh water, to maintain a self-righting ballast ratio.) At least two of them should always be full.)

11. Breasthooks from $1\frac{1}{2}$" × $3\frac{1}{2}$".

12. Bin flats $1/2$" plywood from end to end; $3/4$" × 1" cleats on hull side need not be continuous. Cove up against hull side. Take special care with fastenings and glue in way of the water cells,

as with the boat bottom-up the weight of water on each could be as much as 250 pounds.

13. Ventilators with baffles and flush ramps built up of $1/4$" plywood assembled with epoxy fillets. Don't alter the geometry of these vents without checking with me as they are designed to be immune to flooding through 360 degrees of roll. Hinged-plate dampers inside with screw adjusters as diagrammed.

14. Drains of ventilators about 1" square open straight through both sides of hull.

15. Stringers over oarports $3/4$" × $1\frac{1}{2}$".

16. Faces of oarport ramps $1/4$" plywood.

17. Sills of ramps $3/4$".

18. Drain channels of flush hatches 1" wide, 2" deep, with overboard drains at the corners adjacent to the web frames. The channels extend from Frame 3'4$\frac{1}{2}$" to Frame 18' to form deck girders. They're covered flush with the deck between the hatches.

19. Hatches $1/2$" plywood with $3/4$" square perimeter flanges to fit into the drain channels, with soft rubberoid sealing around the outside edges to minimize the amount of water the channels drains must handle. Each hatch is to have two lanyards which may be at the ends or sides, permanently fast to the hatch and made fast to an adjacent cleat under the deck, each side or end.

20. Struts to support partly-open hatches. They jam into the drain channels, with notches at the upper ends to fit the hatch flanges. One 9" (shown), three 6", and three $1\frac{1}{2}$" wedges, all with no-lose lanyards. Any edge of each hatch can be propped up to the selected opening and lashed down hard on its strut with the hatch lanyards. The hatches can also be removed entirely and stowed inside.

21. Oars: two pairs 8', one pair 9'; consult owner for design, leathering, etc. All stow under the deck as shown with shock-cord-and-toggle slings to web frames. $1/2$" shank offset oarlocks with two spare pairs; "Ashbreeze" type recommended if available. The oars are supposed to have fabric sleeves inside the ports, permanently fast around the port flanges with enough slack to allow a full stroke, and with large enough openings to allow the blades of the oars to be drawn in through them. The slack fabric at the withdrawal openings taken up semi-watertight with elastic lashings around the looms of the oars. It is supposed to be possible to lay the oars in to the position shown on the outboard arrangement drawings without disturbing the sleeves, and to unship the oars forward into the boat, with the port geometry shown.

22. Brackets to support outboard ends of laid-in oars.

23. Socket and bracket for seven-foot staff of radio antenna and radar reflector. The staff can be an aluminum tube. Mount VHF etc. in consultation with the owner, perhaps port side forward of and above the oarport.

24. Removable lids of stowage bins; provide hold-down latches.

25. Covers for bins at each end of rowing well $1/2$" plywood. All bin covers have holes for lifting and ventilation more or less as shown.

26. Plastic screw plates for water cells at least 6" diameter.

27. Spherical bulkhead-mounted 4" magnetic compass.

28. Ledges of canopy from $3/4$" × 1".

29. Side pillars $3/4$" × 6", rabbetted to take windows.

30. End pillars $3/4$" × 4", rabbetted and shaped to plan-view ellipse shape of canopy.

31. Windows $1/8$" Lexan bent to plan-view curves of the canopy.

32. Perimeter of canopy top carved from a laminated block to finish not more than $3/4$" thick, rabbetted to take windows.

33. Flat center of canopy top $1/4$" plywood.

34. Track for rolling seat about 33" long.

35. Rolling seat 12" × 23", slightly shaped as shown and fitted with a 3" foam cushion; consult owner about material of cushion cover. Four wheels about 2" diameter.

36. Rack for foot braces with detents on about 2" centers.

37. Foot braces pivoted on a full-breadth transverse bar. Seat and foot braces have to be removable to clear the rowing well for sleeping.

38. Four-footed 8" bronze cleats port and starboard, bolted through transom reinforcement. One 6" cleat forward in the vent ramp as shown.

39. Stem fitting made up from $1/16$" × $1\ 1/2$" stainless steel straps to form a $1/4$" thick eye for a $1/2$" shackle. Splice a four-foot $1/4$" 1 × 19 strand wire pendant to the shackle, with a T fitting on the outer end made up of about $3/4$" outside diameter pipe with 6" leg and 4" crossbar. Anchor warp, $1/2$" diameter by 200 feet, is made fast to the T and paid out until the pendant takes up the strain with the tail of the warp slack. This arrangement is supposed to eliminate chafe. The anchor can be a 14-pound Delta pattern and will also serve as a drogue with or without some added drag.

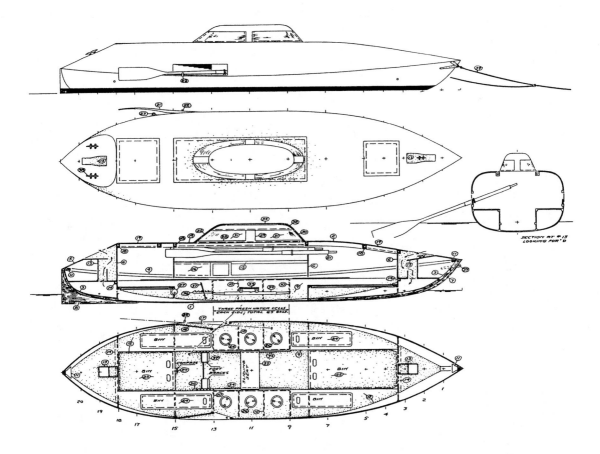

to keep her from crabbing in side winds, but my guess is that the shallow, rounded hull will make less drag by crabbing than the drag of a leeboard big enough to stop the crabbing. The leeboard might be a godsend if she had to work along a lee shore in an overpowering wind. It can easily be fitted to drop through brackets forward of the oarports.

If you could count on calms, this would be a fine singlehander, able to cover as much as 40 miles a day and get into places open to no other enclosed boat. I've been comfortable for a month in worse cabins. This one could be rearranged to accommodate a couple, with increased range by taking turns rowing.

A strong wind forward of the beam will break the heart of any oarsman. All that can be done is to wait it out, beached, anchored, or, offshore, riding to a parachute drogue. The pendant shackled to the eye in the stem takes the warp of anchor or drogue clear of chafe. With an air mattress in the footwell on the axes of pitch and roll, and with a radar reflector displayed, the oarsman waits out the bad chance in patient relaxation. The boat can be closed in tight, with ventilation from the baffled openings at the ends. These vents are ducted to preclude flooding even with the boat bottom-up, and she is instantly self-righting from bottom up. In better weather, ventilation is controlled by opening the three hatches at various angles, retaining shade.

I did everything I could think of to cut wind resistance, to enable her to keep going

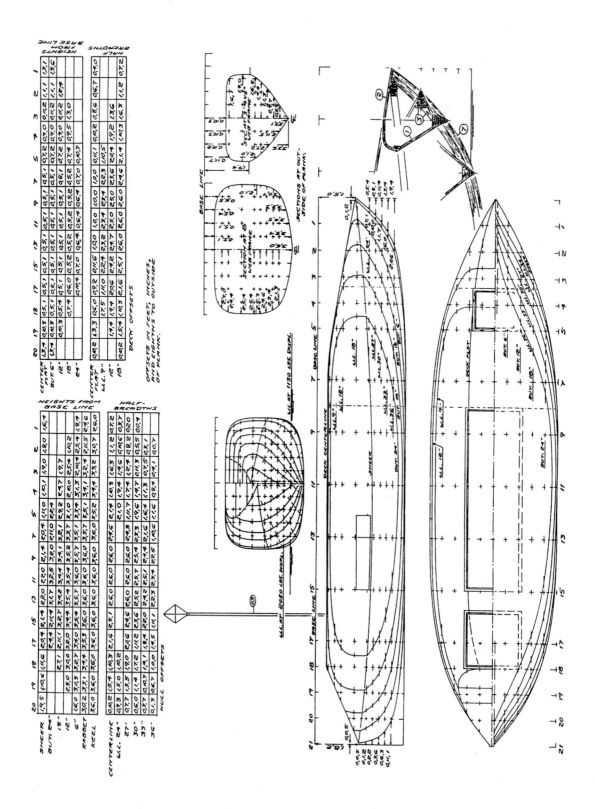

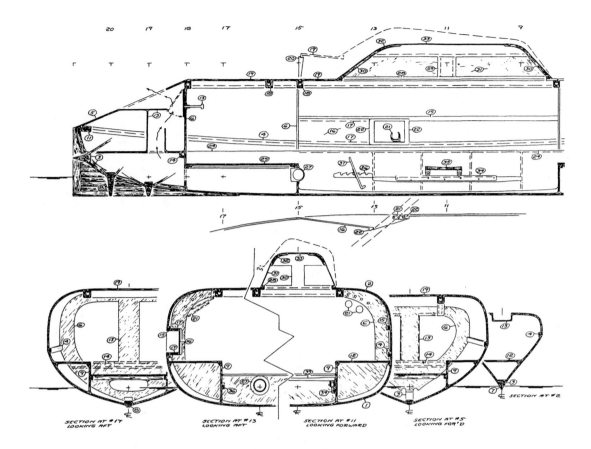

against and across some wind. The rounded-off raised deck with flush hatches and recessed ventilators, and the rounded hood for the oarsman's head, were designed for the least possible wind drag in all directions. Dr. Belic thinks that this is less important than I do. With his high-technology builder, Steve Najjar of Palo Alto, California, he devised an angular aluminum-framed hood with hinged windows, and fitted her with metal-framed hatches that protrude a couple of inches above deck. A lot of annoying drips may be prevented and ventilation improved. Wind resistance is doubled. The argument is that even the lesser drag is prohibitive, but I'm unconvinced that there aren't borderline situations that would justify the original design.

The oarports accommodate 9-foot oars with counterweighted looms, with two pairs of 8-foot oars slung up under the deck in reserve. The oars can be laid in almost parallel, and passed inboard from the laid-in position. The ports are valved with loose sleeves inside, slack enough to allow a full swing of the oars without binding. The wrists of the sleeves open wide enough to pass the blades of the oars through but are gathered around the looms, near the grips, with elastic lashings.

The boat was designed before Dr. Belic chose a builder, so I showed sheathed strip planking as the least demanding way to execute the complex shape. Steve Najjar is expert at cold-molding, which saved a couple of hundred pounds of weight with no loss of strength. An intermediate possibility would have been a foam-cored or balsa-cored fiberglass-sandwich shell.

**Cruising
Rowboat**

Part Three

Motor Trailer Boats

14 *Motor Canoe*

15'9" × 3'0"

Big-sterned canoes like this one appeared almost as soon as outboard motors to drive them. After a while, it was found that wide ones went as well as narrow ones—often better, because they floated higher in the water. By the 1930s they had evolved into the elegant outboard runabouts of that era, averaging about 5 feet in breadth. I now have an outboard utility about the same length as this design (see Chapter 16) but 7 feet wide. It's about as much like this Motor Canoe as a bird is like a dinosaur, but the heredity is not hard to see if you just look at the transverse sections and not at the plan view.

The 7-foot-breadth boat is much better than the 3-foot-breadth canoe in a good many ways. For instance, you can play a striped bass standing up and backing around, which would get you wet if you tried it in the canoe. Light 3-foot-breadth boats want light loads, low centers of gravity, and sobriety in their users. One reason canoes of this design are no longer built for sale is that they look like dangerous outboard utilities rather than comparatively forgiving canoes, canoes being widely exempted from the rules that are supposed to make utilities foolproof.

The 7-foot-breadth boat is thought small because it's less than 16 feet long, but it is not small. It's a short big boat, well onto half a ton, and it's not practical for cartop carrying, which the 3-foot-breadth canoe is. But, if anybody wants an outboard utility fit for a car top, it will have to be built one-off by a one-man boatshop without enough assets to interest a lawyer, on account of nightmares about liability.

So, I drew the plan for one-off wood-epoxy construction, like a stripper canoe. The best book I know of on this construction is *Canoecraft*, by Ted Moores and Merilyn Mohr (Camden House, 1983). Besides offering a lucid account of the method, the book has several extremely nice canoe designs as built by Bear Mountain Boat Shop of Bancroft, Ontario.

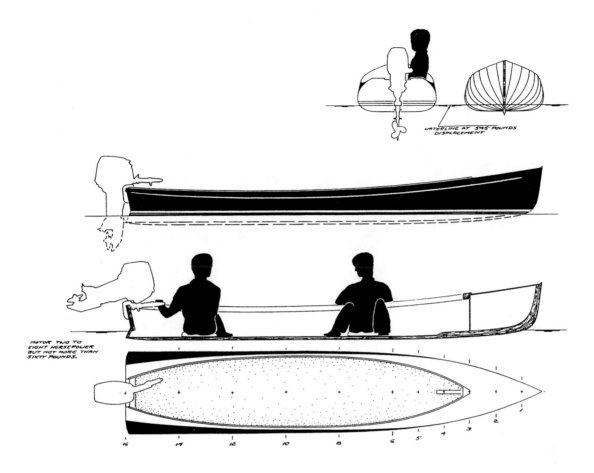

WATERLINE AT 545 POUNDS DISPLACEMENT

MOTOR TWO TO EIGHT HORSEPOWER BUT NOT MORE THAN SIXTY POUNDS.

The 3-foot-wide square-sterned canoe is a little less tricky to use than a sharp-sterned paddling canoe. The added bearing in the after quarters gives it stability equal to that of a sharp-sterned canoe 4 or 5 feet longer. The high power head of the motor is compensated for by sitting on the bottom of the hull instead of sitting or kneeling high in the boat with both hands preempted by the paddle.

The topsides tumble home for the same reason they do in a paddling canoe: to give a better angle of dip with a single-blade paddle. A square-sterned canoe is less degraded for paddling than might be expected, as long as it isn't heavily loaded. The tumblehome sides also give some of the reserve buoyancy of a half-decked boat; it takes a bigger angle of heel to ship water. A decked boat with vertical or flaring sides has more reserve stability, but the tumblehome sides don't allow an ignorant passenger to step or sit as far off the centerline, so the hazard ends up about even. The tumblehome sides make a lighter boat, decisive in a cartopper.

The quarters of the stern are tumbled in at the top still more (partly for style) and supplemented with some deck, because the commonest cause of swamping in all small outboards is shipping water over the corner of the transom while working on the motor.

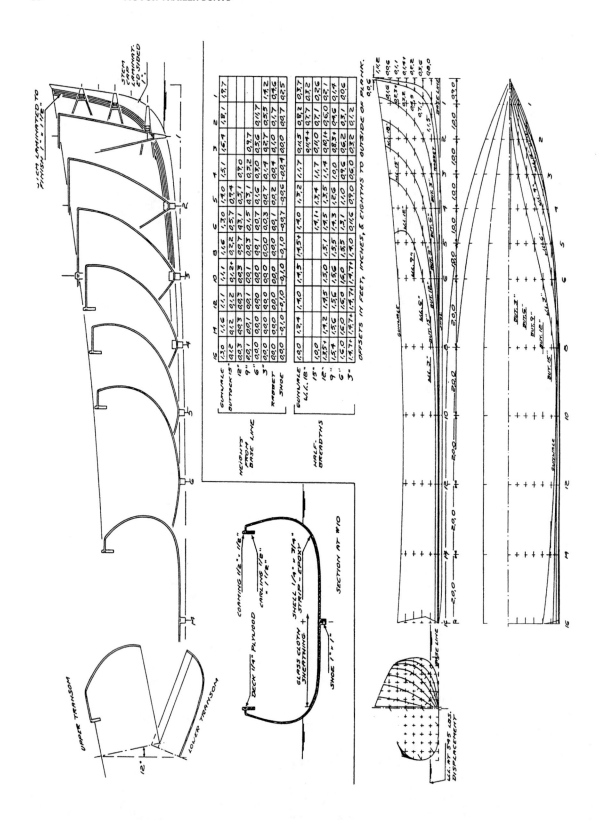

This can happen in more modern boats with double-bottom buoyancy, and often does because people tend to be complacent in these "certified safe" boats.

The shape of the stern—and the decking there, plus the deck forward—braces the gunwales well enough to dispense with thwarts across the open waist. There's room to spare to lay down an air mattress, which might be an incentive to prefer something like this to a jet-ski. The types are comparable in portability. The jet can go in shallower water and is faster because the canoe couldn't stand the weight of a powerful motor. The jet is foolproof for its riders but sometimes dangerous to bystanders.

I'm still waiting to see a young woman drive a jet-ski with her date behind her, though I've seen this once or twice on motorcycles. The motor canoe seems to have some advantages for dating purposes, for which canoes were once famous. It might be rewarding to see if a hybrid type could be developed. It might have the shape of this drawing with all the machinery aft and side-by-side seating low amidships. A production version could be molded with a flange along the widest part of the sections, sweeping up to the stemhead, so that the lower hull, and the upper sides and hull liner, could each be released from a one-piece mold.

The flange would make a good spray rail. I thought of showing applied rails on this design, and also tried it with a more flaring bow, but either option would add some weight and isn't really necessary in a hull as fine-lined as this. Even in a chop or steep wakes, a bow like this does not make much spray, or throw what it does make high enough to be blown across the boat. A little spray coming over could be a useful alert.

The narrow-sterned motor canoe, which amounts to a paddling canoe with the top of its stern shaped into a motor bracket, has persisted while the big-sterned canoe has evolved out of existence. I suppose this is partly due to being unmistakably a canoe, with less temptation to scant precautions. Narrow-sterns are significantly more efficient than the big-sterned type when they're heavily loaded. A heavy load to be carried a long distance is the best reason to put a motor on a canoe, and it often makes sense to retain a good paddling shape for light loads, short distances, and shallow waters. The narrow-sterned canoe can't be driven even moderately fast; at 15 knots such a canoe will stand on its stern, porpoise, yaw, and roll out of control. The big-sterned canoe will go that fast with a light 8-h.p. motor, with a clean, elegant action.

15 *Clam Skiff*

18'0" × 5'3"

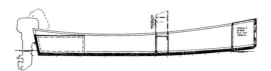

Clammers and fishermen are the last of the hunter-gatherers. Most people gave that up 4,000 years ago. It's almost over; the Deep Range that Arthur Clarke wrote science fiction about 40 years ago is in sight. Sea people are turning from hunting to farming. But, for now, civilization stops at high-water mark, and the people who go hunting and gathering are used to having no one to call to for help, and to doing all their own thinking. Some fine art and scholarship has been planned in commercial fishing boats, but most of the thinking is straightforward.

Dynamite Payson was a lobsterman before he began to write and teach. His orders for this design were for a solid skiff that could stand generous power, carry a big load, and have flat footing right out to the side. Nothing about it should be hard to explain.

Flat-bottomed boats with pointed bows get into trouble if their bows cut solid water. The sides push the water out harder than the bottom pushes it down. The water rushes from the high pressure at the sides toward the lower pressure underneath, and breaks into powerful eddies as it goes around the chine corner. The turbulence is unstable. The rush of water lets the bow drop, making the erratic flow still stronger, and the boat will yaw and broach. A garvey bow, like a toboggan, is much better in this way, but it has to have a long, sloping overhang at the bow to carry it over wave crests. If the slope of the wave is steep enough, a garvey can put the top of its bow into the crest before it starts to lift. The garvey is also noisier when it's working at a standstill.

The stern of this skiff is run straight back, to take all the bearing at the stern that her breadth allows. This floats the weight of the motor, and that of somebody working on the motor, as high in the water as possible. The sheer is cocked up aft to clear the water at the sides when the weight is off-center. When a skiff like this swamps, the water always comes over one corner of the stern.

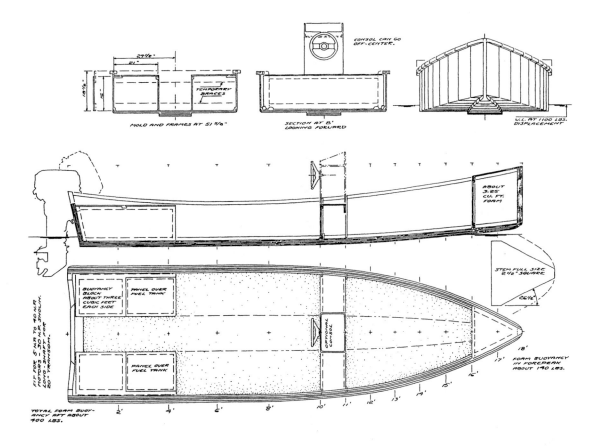

The bottom rockers up forward to keep as much of the sides out of water as possible, and to generate some pressure underneath to help hold the bow up. A rockered forward bottom pounds harder, but is faster and won't broach as often or as wildly as one with a straighter profile.

The big solid shoe is derived from the cutwater experiments I've discussed elsewhere (see Chapter 17 and Chapter 54). Cutwaters are too radical for people who can't afford to make a mistake when they choose a boat, and they make a less stable working platform, but this boat had to have a shoe to keep her from skidding her turns. I once designed a boat something like this but with a perfectly clean bottom. If you put her motor over sharply, the bow would swing, but the boat would keep straight on, sidewise, until she tripped herself. A very small shoe fixed her. This fat shoe has some effect toward picking the bow up when it tries to dive, it squeezes the air out to the sides before it reaches the propeller, and it adds solidity to the bottom. Running onto a pebble beach or an ice floe, or over a log, it's a comfort to have 2½ inches of solid wood piled up where it's likely to take most of the grind. The rest of the bottom is a full inch thick; fiberglass sheathed, of course. The positive buoyancy of that much wood is worth having, and it's in an ancient tradition of putting in enough timber to stand up after most of it is rotten.

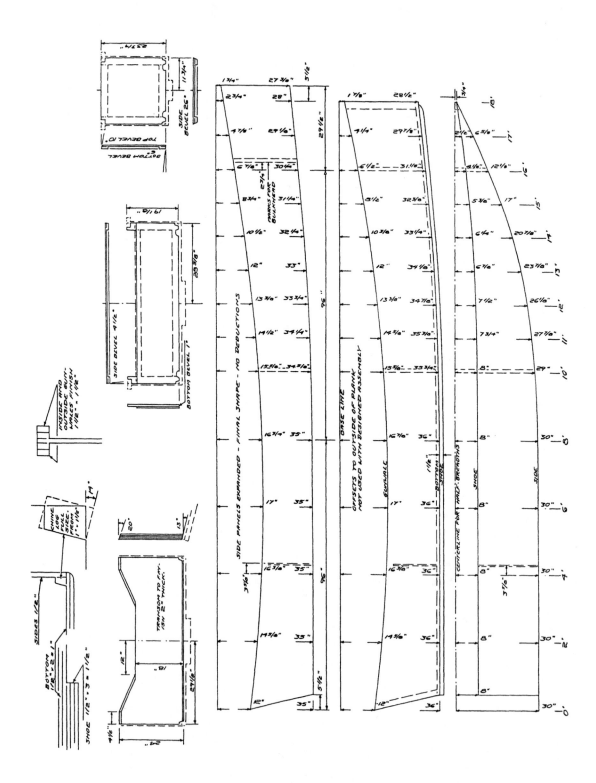

16 *Fisherman's Launch*

21'4" × 7'0"

Dear Phil:

I have an idea for a fisherman's launch. The boat would be similar to the launch on plates 52 and 53 of Howard Chapelle's *Boatbuilding*. This is a straightforward, honest boat that anybody could get out on the water with. I'd like it with a few modern ideas added, such as an outboard instead of an inboard with rudder, and plywood frames.

I'm not interested in a yachty boat, just one that's strong and durable. Maybe a boat that's overbuilt and low on maintenance, but one that could be put together at modest cost by any carpenter.

Any ideas you could share would be appreciated.

Matt Harman, Foster, Rhode Island

Dear Matt:

The design in the Chapelle book is a 21-foot 4-inch Hampton boat, a Casco Bay (Maine) workboat. They were originally sailing boats with spritsail cat-ketch rigs, but they stood the evolution into motorboats very well. Dick Pulsifer builds nice ones now in Brunswick, Maine. Traditionally they were strip-built, but at one time some were plank-on-frame like the Chapelle design. Probably Chap thought that method was more forgiving of inexperience.

I think so myself and have drawn the plan here for plank-on-frame. The small fresh-cut-oak frames can be snapped in at a great rate with no beveling or plumbing up. Irregular spacing creates no problems because the frames are spaced so as to back the

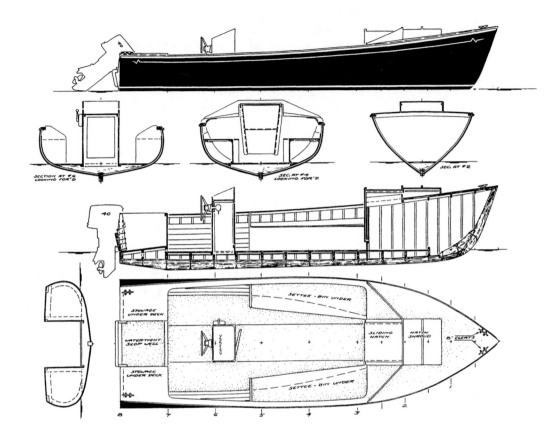

number of plank fastenings wanted, not because the planking has to be supported at such close intervals. Planking the boat from the garboard up will produce a fair hull, as the resilient frames will pull into alignment. (I've known a builder brought up on sawn frames to lock in unfair curves by planking up and down to a shutter plank at the bilge.)

Carvel planking on bent frames is as good a way as any to build a one-off boat, and the quickest way to build a complex shape. But a boat built this way has to be kept wet. If she dries out, the boat will not only leak, but may loosen up if she's used hard before the planking has a chance to swell tight. For a trailer boat, strip-building canoe-style with epoxy would be suitable, using ¾-inch strips plus a fiberglass sheathing. Cold-molding with four courses of ⅛-inch veneer laid up in epoxy would need no framing besides the bulkheads and settees. It would make a light and stiff boat, but an expensive one.

Eliminating the hollow garboards of Chapelle's boat produces a shape with smooth and simple curves ideal for cold-molding. It's a good shape for any construction that doesn't involve flat sheets—for instance, the lapstrake plywood used in the nice Lyman and Chris-Craft sea skiffs built in the 1940s and 1950s. A lapstrake lobsterboat would have to have the laps in way of the hauler davit filled and sheathed, but the construction makes an efficient boat, and a beautiful one if the strakes are lined off artistically. Plywood is better than natural wood for this because it won't split along the lap fastenings and needs little framing.

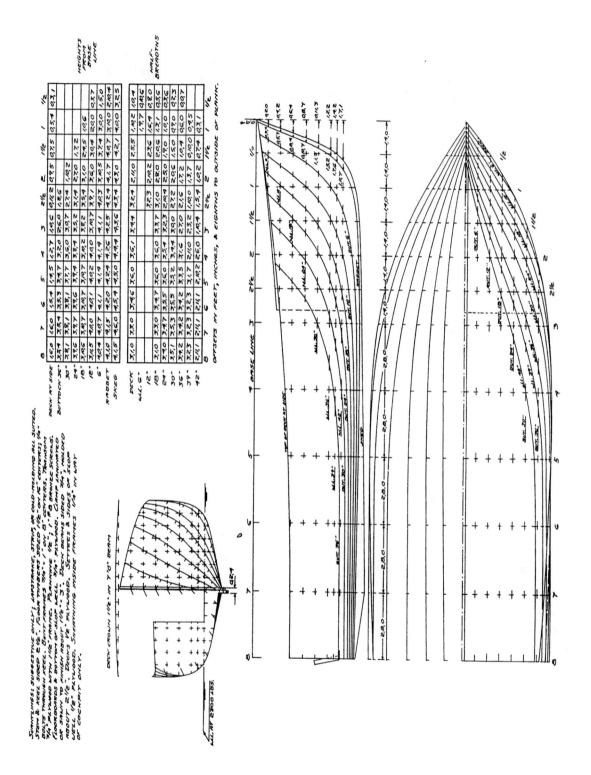

I have a nice outboard utility, only 16 feet long but 7 feet wide and high-sided. She's roughly built, with no finish to speak of, as a quick trial of a planking method in which wide-open seams are filled with adhesive seam compound. This construction method was not a success. Either the seams had to be very large or the planks very narrow; either way took too much of the expensive seam compound. The boat wasn't as quick to put together as I'd hoped. The idea might work better with a more stable wood such as mahogany in place of the Eastern cedar we used, but I doubt I'll do any more about it myself.

The 16-footer has been much admired. I've done several of these very wide boats and finally got the shape just right. This boat has no spray strakes, or even a molding at the sheer, but her bow has such a nice blend of sharpness and buoyancy that she's perfectly dry at all speeds, even in a chop with three people sitting forward. With two men, she made 29.8 statute miles per hour powered by an old Johnson 50-h.p. outboard; she planed level with her keel and took sharp turns smoothly. With the same load, she made 15 m.p.h. powered by the 25-h.p. Evinrude that's on her now, still planing cleanly with all of what little spray she made left behind her. You're welcome to infer that she would make 60 m.p.h. with 100 h.p., and I bet she would do close to 12 m.p.h. with 15 h.p. I mean to try the 15-h.p. one of these days. I like the way she can run slowly without dragging half the bay behind her with the light 25 as opposed to the heavy 50. The way she flew with the 50 was exhilarating, but I get enough of this very soon; you have to pay closer attention to where you're going than I find enjoyable for long.

I redrew the lines of this good boat with more space between the mold stations— 2 feet 8 inches instead of 2 feet even—to produce your 21-footer. The fore-and-aft stem dimensions were lengthened in the same proportion, making the bow rake out more. The heights and breadths were not changed at all. Nominal displacement goes up in the same proportion, from 1,750 to 2,300 pounds on the marked waterline. That's supposed to be with an average load. I suppose the 21-footer will weigh about 1,100 pounds empty.

"Stretching" a boat like this used to be routine. Boatshops would have a stack of molds left over from building a bent-frame boat; they'd set them up on a different spacing, just as I did on paper. They had to fair the new stem by eye, as they usually didn't keep a pattern for that. Stock boat manufacturers of the 1930s, such as Dawn and Matthews, used the same molds for boats of different lengths. Matthews at one time had standard models of 38, 46, and 50 feet all built on the same section molds. Many of the stock boats of that era were produced with practically nothing on paper.

The longer boats ran better than the shorter ones if they weren't overloaded out of proportion. This 21-footer will go faster than the 16-footer with the 25-h.p. motor in spite of her greater weight. With the 50-h.p. I'd expect them to run about even or with a little advantage to the shorter boat in smooth water. So much of the 16-footer is in the air at that speed that it doesn't matter so much what shape it is, while the weight and surface friction of the longer boat still count. But in choppy water, the long boat will win again by slicing through the crests more smoothly.

The stretched boat will be easier to build by any method because her fore-and-aft curves are gentler. The 16-footer's sections are soft curves to begin with—good especially for cold-molding—but her upper forward planks do have a hard bend that would be eased out as much as anybody could ask in the longer boat. In fact, the 21-footer looks a shade bland to my taste for extremes.

A cold-molded version of the Fisherman's Launch, built by Paul Billings in England, leaps a Cote d' Azure swell

If the 16-footer were scaled up all over instead of being just stretched, the 21-foot version would be 9 feet 4 inches breadth and the equivalent displacement would be 4,100 pounds. It would take 120 h.p. to drive her 30 m.p.h. In fact, she'd be likely to be heavier and need still more power, because nobody could resist filling a boat that roomy with heavy furniture.

The layout shown works very well. I meant to use a smooth-rimmed wheel 28 inches in diameter so I could reach either side of the boat without letting go of the wheel. But when I priced the big wheel, I flinched. I took advantage of the extra length to work in a cuddy for locked stowage and perhaps a portable toilet. The arrangement of the hatch, sliding into a fixed shroud, is to encourage the use of a spray hood—not for spray but for rain. In a hard rainstorm, an open boat this size will catch a phenomenal amount of water. I have an Edson diaphragm pump that throws a gallon of water with each stroke of its waist-high lever, and won't choke on dead rats and old overalls. But, with more usual equipment, the aftermath of a rainstorm is sore arms or run-down batteries.

I'm with you on fisherman-finish. I'm a nautical slob myself. I'm not proud of it, and I love to look at the boats of people willing to take more trouble. If I had my way, they would get a tax break for the improvement to the public view. I did make the outboard profile drawing suggestive of a yacht finish, with dark sides representing brightwork, and a gold covestripe marked. The effect would be spoiled by the registration numbers. It troubles me that I seem to be the only citizen who thinks it's demeaning to be made to wear a number on my boat and my car. Everybody is so docile about these insulting impositions that I foresee a law mandating the wearing of social security numbers in 50mm numerals across the back of every outer garment.

17 *Hawkeye*

18'6" × 7'9"

Hawkeye was designed around a weathertight deck, as a light boatyard workboat and general utility. David Montgomery built her as a joint venture with me; we use her as a tender for his boatyard. We hoped to sell some as pleasure boats and others as small-town patrol boats. She was completely prefabricated with all parts cut out from pre-planned diagrams and assembled bottom-up, using the flat deck as a base. Thirteen sheets each of ¼-inch and ½-inch 4 × 8-foot plywood were used, with a very small scrap pile left over. Her dry weight is less than half a short ton.

She accelerates without any planing hump, leaves little wake at any speed, and an old derated 25-h.p. outboard motor drives her just over 15 statute miles per hour with three people on board; she slows down with more of a load. The ideal motor would be a little more powerful—say, 35 h.p—to cruise at her present top speed without wearing out the motor. She could stand much more power, up to the point at which there would start to be a risk of taking off and flipping backward in a headwind—something on the order of a 60-m.p.h. relative wind, such as 40 m.p.h. against a 20-m.p.h. wind. But the weight of a motor to drive her that fast, and fuel enough for such a motor, would increase the wake at lower speeds. She would have to have her structure strengthened to stand the stresses, with still more weight. Her average speed wouldn't increase in proportion, on account of slowing down in traffic. The first cost of a lot more burst speed would be high, but the real objection would be the degradation of her behavior at more practical speed. The light boat, with a moderate top speed, often can run faster than a boat that is potentially much faster because her tolerable-wake speed is higher. *Hawkeye* drags less wake when overloaded than conventional craft because much of her weight is carried by the slim keel box, and the rest by her wide sponsons, on such a shallow

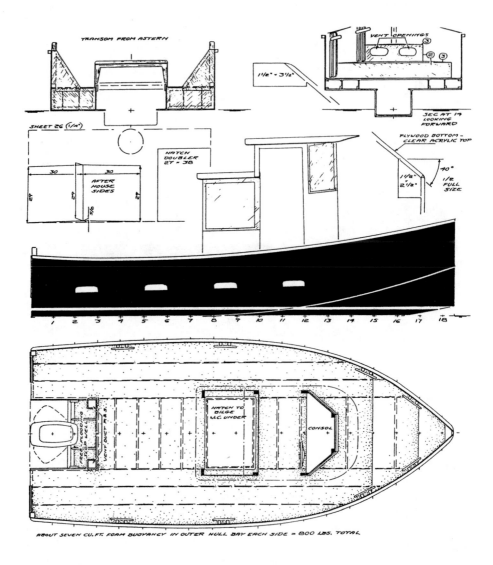

ABOUT SEVEN CU. FT. FOAM BUOYANCY IN OUTER HULL BAY EACH SIDE = 800 LBS. TOTAL

immersion that she can't generate a deep wave. But even with her shape, the more weight, the more wake.

In choppy water she is noisy and rough-riding; this is exacerbated by vibration in the flimsy superstructure. There are no other vices, unless you count blowing away while maneuvering at low speed on account of the windage of the high house. She tracks hands-off at all speeds and regardless of waves, and turns short at all speeds. She doesn't bank her turns, but doesn't skid or trip. The hammering in choppy water is less at high speed than when slowed down because she planes on the central ski with lighter impacts taken by the drumlike sponsons. She never brings any spray aboard for obvious reasons.

Accepting that she is not a good press-on-regardless heavy-weather boat (though she is very good in following and cross seas), she is spectacularly better than such boats

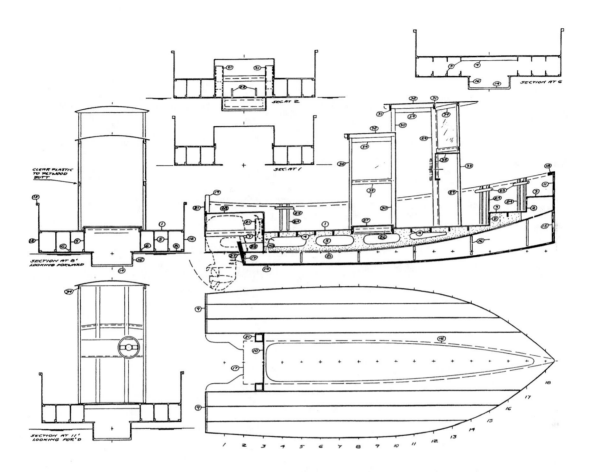

in protected waters, rivers, canals, and small lakes. The expanse of flat deck accommodates lawn chairs, sunbathing mattresses, toys. She runs her bow out dry on any beach, and sits upright when the tide leaves her. She needs 9 inches of water to float a good load. The inch-thick, 'glass-sheathed keel bottom can stand grounding on rocks.

The annex behind the wheelhouse encloses a portable toilet with standing headroom in the keel box. The view from the sheltered wheel is perfect. It's often suggested that she should have a more roomy house, and she certainly could carry one. It would look very bulky; the 6-foot-6-inch-headroom house looks well only because it is so narrow. Anything built on her has to be on top of the flush deck, because the space under the deck is full of web girders needed to make her stiff on such a light weight. Bottom and deck form a deep honeycomb sandwich. The ½-inch deck feels as solid as a concrete slab. The Microtrawler design (Chapter 54) shows what can be done by utilizing the depth of the keel box and by planning for cabin rather than deck from the first concept, but the freedom to walk all around *Hawkeye* is pleasant, useful, and unusual. We're thinking of pitching a tent over her, to have it both ways.

18 *Sneakeasy*

26'6" × 4'3"

Dear Phil:

I've just spent the afternoon reading and dreaming of a George Crouch–designed 1924 Gold Cup winner named *Baby Bootlegger*.

Could you please provide me with more fuel for my dreams by developing a cartoon for a boat that would capture the spirit and romance of *Bootlegger*? Please keep in mind: (1) I have built only two boats, both plywood. (2) Automotive engines, white oak, and Eastern white cedar are all readily available. (3) A quick construction method, preferably of plywood, would be nice. (4) Since I have four children, the boat should hold six and have a convertible top. (5) Funding will be tight.

I realize that none of the above conditions were considered in *Bootlegger*. I'm hoping for something more in the spirit and romance of that boat than in her actual performance. Please take any liberties you see fit in the design.

Richard Tremaine, Selby, Ontario

Dear Mr. Tremaine:

Baby Bootlegger (WoodenBoat No. 60, page 84) was the career masterpiece of a very talented man. George Crouch was active in his profession for 20-odd years after that boat came out. He designed some notable craft, including an experimental U.S. Navy torpedo boat, with blended sides and deck like *Bootlegger*, but he never had another artistic success in her class. John Hacker, a greater artist than Crouch, tried the type several times. He got one, *Locpat*, that was even more striking than *Bootlegger*

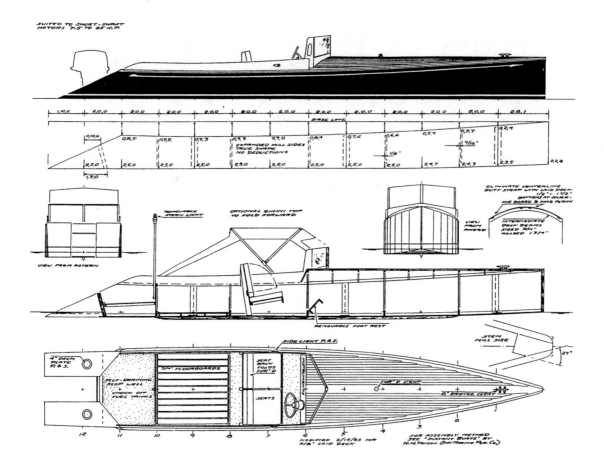

(partly because she was bigger), but the others did not quite come off. Most boats styled that way end up as ungainly affectations. The chances that I could produce something approaching the aesthetic equivalent of *Bootlegger* aren't good, even disregarding the handicaps of cost and function. Masterpieces are not produced on demand.

I did design, a few years ago, a boat that combines some "period" elegance with construction adapted to home building. She's nothing like *Baby Bootlegger*, but she could be an improvement on a degraded imitation of the great racer.

Sneakeasy was built by a high-class professional, Dan Shea of Sister Bay, Wisconsin, for Jim Shultz, who was not much concerned about cost. Jim wanted a fast launch to use in the canals of a Florida coastal development and nearby bays and bayous. Aside from some style and character, he wanted a boat that wouldn't have much wake to disturb a neighborhood in which everybody keeps a boat tied up at the back fence. When he got her, he liked her so much that he started to talk about putting her into production, though in fact the interest she arouses tends to be abstract.

The boat's long, perfectly flat bottom and plumb sides are optimum for keeping the wake flat. Almost all the water she displaces is moved vertically downward, and she floats so lightly even at rest that the water is moved 3 inches at most. So little pressure

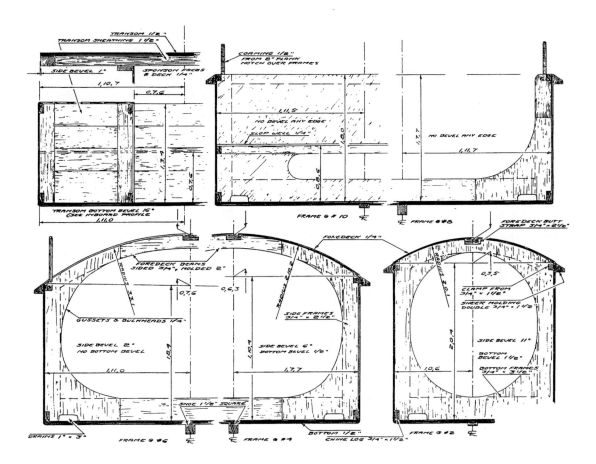

is needed to move it that far that practically no water moves sidewise in the form of waves. The wake is a flat carpet of foam from surface friction. To get this effect, the boat has to be light in proportion to the size of her bottom. Flare anywhere along her length would make the deck bigger—that is, heavier—or the bottom smaller and hence more heavily loaded. Either way, there would be more wake and, at moderate speed, more drag. Deadrise in the bottom would make whatever pressure is developed expend itself more to the sides, near the water surface where it would show up in waves. A small forefoot, as in *Baby Bootlegger*, wouldn't do much harm and would improve her steering in a small chop, which is its object in the Crouch design. Fortunately for the home builder, we decided to keep the flat bottom for its advantage in beaching.

She runs through her whole speed range with no change of trim. A Johnson 25 drives her as fast as the owner wants to go. No real speed trials were done, but a sister boat made 32 m.p.h. with 35 h.p., so I guess *Sneakeasy* can make about 25 wide open. I suppose she would make 12 m.p.h. with the 7.5 motor noted on the plans, not bogged down at all. The light motor and minimum fuel demand are elements of the light weight that's basic to no-wake running.

She showed no vices, banking her turns nicely at top speed, as did the more powerful boat. But, nobody should trust a hull like this when it's going really fast. Banking in

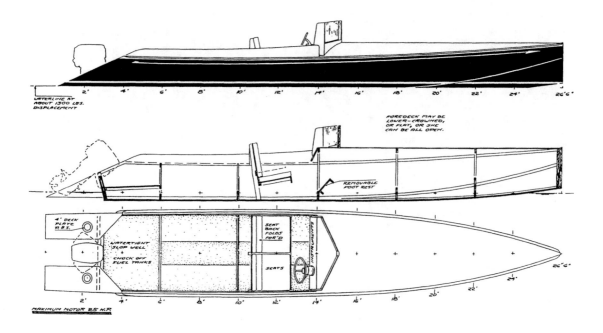

too sharp a turn, going too fast, it will break loose without warning, trip, and roll on its side if not all the way over. The long shoe down the middle of *Sneakeasy*'s bottom is intended to stop her from skidding, but at a high enough speed it will lose effectiveness. She's quite capable of making 50 or 60 m.p.h., and it wouldn't take *Bootlegger*'s Hispano-Suiza V-8 to make her do it, but nobody should take children for a ride in a high-powered boat like this.

For somebody who doesn't have more money than they know what to do with, it's nice that this bayou launch not only doesn't need a big engine, but for safety's sake ought not to have one. With 20 h.p. she'd be fast enough for any enclosed water, safe to turn heedlessly, and all the better to cope with any rough water she might encounter getting home. Despite her 4-foot beam, she's a stiff boat because her bottom extends out under any place you can step. A flaring side amounts to an outrigger, allowing crew weight to be winged out where it will heel the boat. The plumb side keeps people where they belong, near the centerline. I once designed a boat to ferry teams of sled dogs alongshore in the Bering Sea, and adopted this shape for that reason.

She could be made to pound hard, maybe hard enough to break her up, but no harder than any shallow-bodied powerboat. The only cure is a very deep vee, and even that is only effective up to a point; good deep-vee offshore racers experience 10- and 12-gravity accelerations. I'm not sure that perfectly flat is not better than—or I should say not as bad as—a shallow vee or other complex shape, because the flat bottom sometimes seems to benefit by an air-cushion effect. In any of them, a lot can be done by adjusting speed—and course, if possible—to the length of the waves. Pounding happens when a boat runs off a crest at such an angle that she starts to drop before her bow arrives at the next crest. It's often possible to make her follow the wave contours to some extent.

The cockpit has room for six people if most of them are small. It could be lengthened

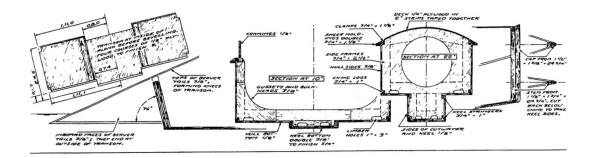

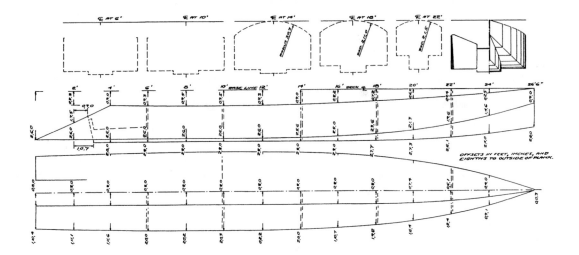

toward the bow, or a small cockpit could be cut in the deck ahead of frame #4. The latter would be better for our purposes since the long deck is one element of her style, like the long hood of a 1920s touring car. The long deck will shed rain and spray.

The top shown is a sunshade. I have a vivid recollection of taking my face off in a crackling, dark-red mask after a long day on Biscayne Bay straight from winter in New England. I take it that a nautical awning-maker will know how to add flaps to close it against rain and spray.

Granting her limitations for rough water and high power, this shape can't be improved on for fast and simple building. The hull can be cut out and nailed together like a time-lapse film, but would-be builders should practice on a smaller boat first, among other reasons because these plans were made for a professional who knew how to do it without instructions on the plans.

Whether it makes sense to build the ultra-simple hull, and then spend long hours on finicky styling features like the turtleback, is a matter of philosophy. Cold reason tells me that the bottom of a boat ought to be the last place to economize, not the first, but I admit to sympathy with the no-doubt perverse impulse to get the hull fast and then go leisurely about making a silk purse out of the sow's ear. I must say, this craft looks quite silky.

Sneakeasy

Afterword

Five years after I wrote the above, Don Caron commissioned a revision intended for the sometimes-rough water of Galveston Bay. He was concerned about control; flat-bottomed, sharp-bowed boats will run wild on their helms if they put their bows into solid water. Long ones like Sneakeasy aren't as bad as shorter ones because they develop less pressure against the sides of their bows, and because the long sterns help to keep them straight no matter what is going on under the bow; but even a six-to-one boat will misbehave in certain lengths of following sea. Don had me draw a modified bottom with the box cutwater I'd been trying out in *Hawkeye* and others. The rockered bottom of the cutwater equalizes the pressure between sides and bottom, with no water forced around the chine to make turbulence. This one won't have any tracking problems, but the simplicity is lost. Don was willing to loft her, and didn't want to pay for the time it would have taken me to project the panels for prefabrication, so I just got out a table of offsets defining the shape. He'll set her up the old way, with frames and molds plumbed on a ladder frame—more work for the builder, and more wasteful of materials, but the method does catch mistakes of mine and misreadings of the builder before they cascade through the work.

19 *Slicer*

29'0" × 5'2"

Dear Phil:

I have studied each of your books (devoured might be a better word) and followed your cartoon series in *SBJ* as well. There isn't one of your boats I haven't owned for a while, savoring the pros and cons as I turn the pages. But what I am most intrigued with today are the long, narrow powerboats. You mention somewhere L. F. Herreshoff's sweeping by at 12 knots with no wake. That's my kind of sweeping, but maybe a little slower and smaller.

I boat in lower Narragansett Bay, which is windy and choppy, I have a 14-foot aluminum skiff with a 25-h.p. motor, but I don't use it much—just too damn bouncy around here. I yearn for a day boat that will cleave the chop elegantly.

Outboard power of 7 to 10 h.p. would be best. I can leave the boat on my mooring, but leaving an outboard is a sure steal around here, and I don't mind carrying it home. I am willing to put up with small propellers and high r.p.m. in order to avoid all the gear and complications of an inboard installation.

I have built small boats of plywood and of cold-molded cedar, and prefer to use plywood. I don't mind springing for epoxy, but no more brain-cell-melting polyester for me.

I am fond of chines; the more the merrier. Construction à la tack-and-tape would be fun. Overall length of about 30 feet is about the most I can get home easily. Or, if it would stand infrequent ice, I could winter it in the water.

This might be an instance where putting the outboard in a well would make sense; I would put up with a lot not to bother with remote controls. The simpler this boat is to use, the better. Like a skiff: clamp on the motor, throw in the life jackets and lunch, and go. But, unlike a skiff: get a smooth and dry ride.

A cuddy cabin is unnecessary and undesirable. Fore and after decks, and side decks, too, are fine. Capacity for four adults, gear, driftwood, and lunch is needed.

Bruce Bender, Jamestown, Rhode Island

Dear Bruce,

I've been reading some early 1900s *Rudder* magazines that were published when small, fast motorboats were just starting to be built. "Autoboats," they were called then. These were boats to "cleave the chop elegantly," and they went fast with little power. There are, for instance, plans and pictures of Charles D. Mower's personal launch *Express*. She was 27 feet long with 4-foot beam, a clean shape with a sharp, deep bow faired through a round midsection to a flat stern just level with the waterline—what was called a double-wedge model.

With a motor rated 8 h.p. she made 12 knots, but the eight horses were a different breed from the ones that live in modern outboard motors. That motor had 185 cubic inches piston displacement, and developed its power at 800 r.p.m.—a high-speed motor when 300 or 400 r.p.m. was usual. It turned a 17-inch-diameter by 19-inch-pitch prop, with barely 5 percent slip (!).

By our standards she was a wet and tender boat. Designers then thought they had to put the weight of the engine far forward in fast boats, "to hold the bow down and prevent squatting." Several years later, Clinton Crane won three Harmsworth trophies because he discovered that fast boats were faster if they carried their weight well aft. The bow could then be made shallow as well as sharp, shaped to direct hull pressure downward toward the incompressible depths instead of laterally in surface waves. This is the basic principle of "planing," whether the boat lifts much or not.

I was tempted to suggest less length than you mention, but decided to take the 29 feet because it allowed combining the "slicer" proportions with the kind of middle and after body you're used to. You might think of this scheme as your stiff 25-h.p. 14-footer with a 15-foot fairing—literally, a cutwater—added onto her bow. There won't be any complaints about her stability, but she will slice cleanly through any chop short enough to allow her to bridge over two or three crests. Without the deep bow of the older boats, she will pound if she starts jumping through the air between longer crests, but I doubt this will come up with the kind of power you have in mind.

You haven't specified a speed, but any motorboat is unsatisfying if she can't buck a stiff breeze. I agree that 7 to 10 h.p. is about right for that, but motors in that class weigh 60 to 80 pounds. That's not my idea of something easy to unclamp and carry. The outboard profile shows a 10-h.p. motor. With a light load and a clean bottom, it might drive her 12 knots (13½ statute miles per hour); most of the time you could count on 10.

The inboard profile shows a 56-pound, 6-h.p. motor. Depending on the load, this would drive her 6 to 8 knots. A hull of this type suffers less from overloading than a stubbier boat, but the difference is still considerable. This boat would be happy with the 25-h.p. motor—slightly slower than the 14-footer in smooth water but able to maintain her speed in a chop.

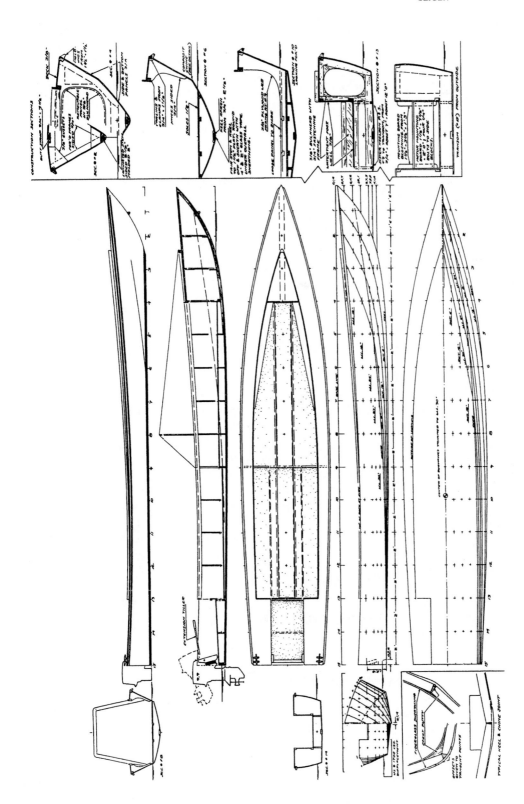

	15	14	13	12	11	10	9	8	7	6	5	4	3	2	1
DECK	0,11,5	1,0,7	1,1,6	1,2,3	1,2,5	1,2,3	1,2,2	1,1,6	1,0,7	0,11,7	1,0,4	0,8,6	0,7,0	0,5,0	0,3,2
CHINE	2,7,1	2,7,1	2,7,1	2,7,1	2,7,1	2,7,0	2,6,3	2,7,4	2,6,1	2,4,2	2,2,0	1,11,1	1,7,7	1,4,4	1,1,6
BUT. 18"	2,7,1	2,7,2	2,7,3	2,7,4	2,7,5	2,7,5	2,7,2	2,6,6	2,7,4	2,5,4	2,1,6	1,6,0	0,7,7		
12"	2,7,1	2,7,3	2,7,5	2,7,7	2,10,1	2,10,3	2,10,4	2,10,2	2,7,6	2,9,5	2,6,2	2,2,0	1,6,2	0,5,3	
6"	2,7,1	2,7,4	2,7,7	2,10,2	2,10,5	2,11,0	2,11,3	2,11,3	2,11,2	2,11,0	2,7,5	2,7,1	2,2,2	1,7,7	0,4,4
KEEL	2,7,1	2,9,5	2,10,1	2,10,6	2,11,1	2,11,5	3,0,0	3,0,3	3,0,1	3,0,4	3,0,0	2,10,7	2,8,1	2,1,7	1,7,4

NEIGHTS FROM BASE LINE

OFFSETS IN FEET, INCHES, & EIGHTHS
TO OUTSIDE OF PLANK.

	15	14	13	12	11	10	9	8	7	6	5	4	3	2	1
DECK	2,6,3	2,3,0	2,4,2	2,6,4	2,6,2	2,6,7	2,7,2	2,7,1	2,6,4	2,5,1	2,2,7	1,11,3	1,6,5	1,0,2	0,6,5
COAMING		1,11,0	1,11,4	1,11,6	1,11,7	2,0,0	1,11,4	1,10,3	1,8,2	1,7,7	1,0,0	0,5,4			
CHINE	1,10,3	1,11,6	1,11,0	1,11,2	1,11,3	1,11,2	1,11,0	1,10,4	1,7,4	1,8,0	1,6,0	1,2,7	0,11,0	0,6,1	0,1,7
WL.12"									2,5,0	2,2,0	1,9,4	1,3,5	0,8,4	0,2,6	
18"	2,1,5	2,2,6	2,3,6	2,4,5	2,5,2	2,5,4	2,5,3	2,5,0	2,3,6	2,1,6	1,10,4	1,5,7	1,0,1	0,5,4	
24"	2,9,6	2,1,4	2,2,2	2,2,6	2,3,0	2,3,0	2,2,6	2,2,1	2,0,6	1,10,4	1,7,0	1,2,0	0,8,0	0,2,0	
27"	2,0,1	2,0,6	2,1,2	2,1,5	2,1,6	2,1,5	2,1,4	2,0,6	1,11,2	1,8,6	1,4,4	0,11,0	0,5,4		
30"	1,11,2	1,11,7	2,0,1	2,0,3	2,0,4	2,0,4	2,0,1	1,11,2	1,7,7	1,5,1	1,0,3	0,7,5	0,3,0		

HALF-BREADTHS

If I meant to take the motor home, I'd think hard about using a 4-horse weighing 35 or 40 pounds. You might just get by, cruising at 5 or 6 knots; much better than rowing or sailing.

Devoting some ingenuity to dollies, davits, and other gadgets would make the 10-h.p. motor easier to move. Eighty pounds isn't so hard to handle if you can get it slung just so.

The hull is not a true developed shape, but it's close enough to plank easily with sheet plywood. It could be built with taped seams, but would have to be lofted and plumbed up on a building jig—partly to save drawing-board work in a design I doubt will be built in large numbers, but mostly because the shapes I'm able to project accurately for a prefabricated Instant Boat wouldn't be the best for a smooth ride in a chop. This ordinary V-bottom is a good compromise between graceful looks, low drag, smooth action, and quick building. In a boat this long for her weight, there's very little penalty in performance or looks over a full-molded shape. I see nothing to be gained by multiplying chines.

I'm not sure I'd bother with the bow centerboard shown. It would be handy at times maneuvering in a breeze, allowing her to drift, with motor tilted up, almost if not quite head-to-wind, and it makes a good beach anchor. It also has a steadying effect when running down a sea. But, it's a nuisance to build and maintain, and not at all necessary. In a 25-h.p. boat, the trunk would need a tight plug to keep it from hosing down the passengers.

The spray hood and awning are attempts to make the drawings more interesting. I would have the spray hood myself, and would try to work out a handy way to extend it back over the entire cockpit. It would keep rain out of her at her mooring, and once in a while would be a great comfort in a cold, cresting sea. The awning would be nice on a hot day, but I would build a couple of strong sockets for some big beach umbrellas. Even though an umbrella is one of the three things that should never be found on a yacht (the other two are stepladders and naval officers, the way I heard it), I once saw a fast

and shipshape sportfishing boat that had umbrellas permanently mounted. They were folded when she was running fast, open while she trolled. The idea never caught on, but I admired it.

I'm enthusiastically with you about eliminating remote controls. The nuisance and expense aside, there's always some slop in them.

I do *not* like inboard wells. I designed two boats for my own use that had them, the second in 1955, and since then have designed them only when my arm was twisted. I almost got asphyxiated once by exhaust fumes eddying out of an inboard well. If a well doesn't allow the motor to swing up, you lose one of the great advantages of using an outboard. But, if it's made long enough to swing the motor, it takes up more room than an inboard engine. Inboard wells almost always reduce a boat's reserve buoyancy, and fairing over the great hole in the bottom isn't easy.

The best-designed well I ever saw was the "concentric well" invented by Allan Vaitses. The motor was mounted on a separate box that fitted into the well, box and motor sliding up in such a way that the hole in the hull was both smaller and better-faired than usual. Incidentally, it was fitted into a beautiful example of a "slicer" hull, also designed by Vaitses.

In spite of Vaitses' ingenuity, I still think outboards should go on sterns, saving weight, space, and construction expense, and ensuring watertight integrity for the rest of the hull.

I left off the side decks when I made the drawing, thinking to save some weight, but on reflection I think she'd be better with them. The structure would be stiffer, and long objects like boathooks and oars would be easier to stow. No sole space would be lost, since the deck would just cover the flaring hull sides.

The cost of this boat would be comparable with a more normal 18-footer of similar construction. Except for higher berthing rents, she'd be much cheaper to run.

Part Four

Sailing Trailer Boats

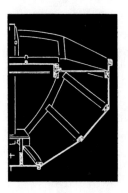

20 *Pirate Racer*

14'6" × 4'0"

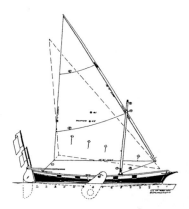

Dear Phil:

My next project involves, I hope, several small boats about the size of your Crab Skiff design. One day this summer, while trying to take 14 people for a sail in a 21-foot Venture, I began to suspect that we might all have more fun with several simple, small boats. What clinched it was watching three young lads having a wonderful time chasing each other around the harbor in Sabots. A young nephew of mine said that he would like something "piratical."

The enclosed Rules for Pirate Racing will give you a rough idea of what came of it all. I think it's a rather good idea that a pack of kids or uninhibited adults could have fun with.

Initially I would build a pair of boats. My daughter Emily, now eight [1990], and two of her cousins are interested. If I can sell two boats to the cousins' fathers, I will make two more, which would be enough to start playing the game I have in mind.

Rules for Pirate Racing

1. Races to be sailed around a course decided by the race committee.

2. Each boat to have a two-man crew.

3. The use of oars is permitted at any time.

4. Before racing begins, crews will be given sealed orders naming them Treasure Ships, Pirates, or Neutrals (numbers of each decided by the race committee).

5. Races start with boats in the water behind a chosen line. A horn will sound five minutes before starting time. Racing commences at the second horn or when a Treasure Ship decides to start.

6. Treasure Ships must display the yellow Treasure Flag as they cross the starting line. The Pirates fly the Jolly Roger and the Neutrals no flag of their own.

7. All others may start as soon as a Treasure Ship has started.

8. When an overlap occurs, the overtaken ship is required to surrender its flag. No boarding or physical contact between the crews is permitted. Flags are flown from staffs on the transom.

9. Pirate Ships are not obliged to show the Jolly Roger until making an attack on a Treasure Ship (i.e., trying to remove the Treasure Flag from another boat). The Jolly Roger, once shown, must be left in place.

10. Neutrals may not attack Treasure Ships—they must first become Pirates by capturing a Jolly Roger.

11. All captured flags must immediately be flown.

12. Boats may cut the course to make attacks, but will be disqualified if they do not subsequently complete the course.

13. Points will be awarded as follows: First Place, 3 points; Second Place, 2 points; Third Place, 1 point; Treasure Flag, 3 points; Jolly Roger, 2 points.

(These rules are subject to change.)

Tony Groves, Moreno Valley, California

Dear Tony:

How are you?

This is about as wide as I think it's well to go with a flat bottom: 39 inches bottom breadth, with 14 feet 6 inches length on deck. She'll be a stiff boat to move around in, though not very stiff under sail with her light weight and big rig. Wide, flat-bottomed boats need to be sailed upright, with agile crews, to get the best out of them. The narrow stern mitigates this; though it reduces her power to carry sail, she will lose less speed sailing heeled than a boat with a wide transom. This is partly because the corner of the transom isn't dragging in the water, and partly because the buoyancy of a wide stern would make her go down by the head as she heeled, an attitude that will kill the sailing of almost any boat. Reasoning aside, the narrow stern makes a more shipshape boat.

There's not much conflict between the best shape to use and the easiest shape to lay out and assemble. The straight lower edge of the side panels produces a likely bottom rocker with a moderate flare. I picked the flare and resulting rocker to give her 400 pounds displacement. I'd expect the hulls to average about 150 pounds, leaving 250 pounds for two children or an adult and a smaller child, trimmed with the forefoot clear of the water and the stern just at the waterline. She will go well enough loaded much deeper if the added weight is kept aft—another advantage of the narrow stern. This shape of bow should be kept well up out of water.

Taped seams, joints, and butts all work well and stand surprising tests. I think taped connections are less likely to result in defects from novice building than the constant-bevel fastening framing in the earlier Instant Boats. (If this idea catches on, I'd hope a good many Pirate Racers would be built by people without your experience.) The taped seams and joints are also lighter and probably cheaper, but what I like most is the clean and easily dried interior. *(text continued on page 98)*

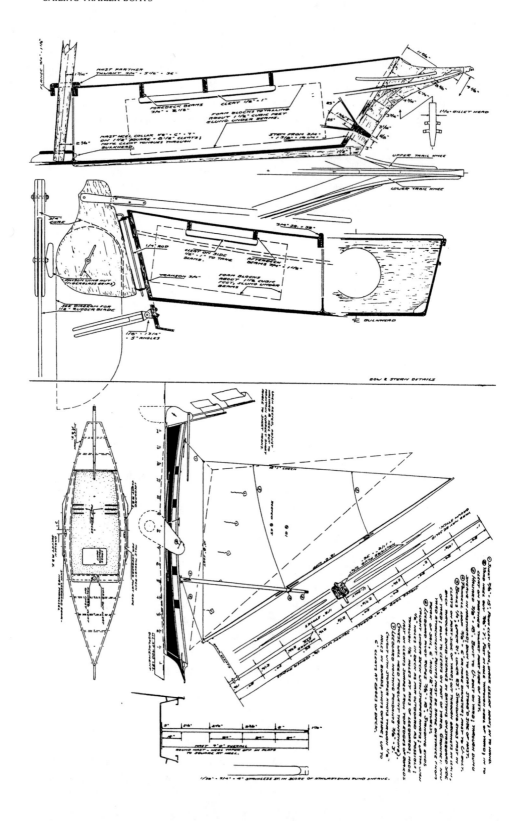

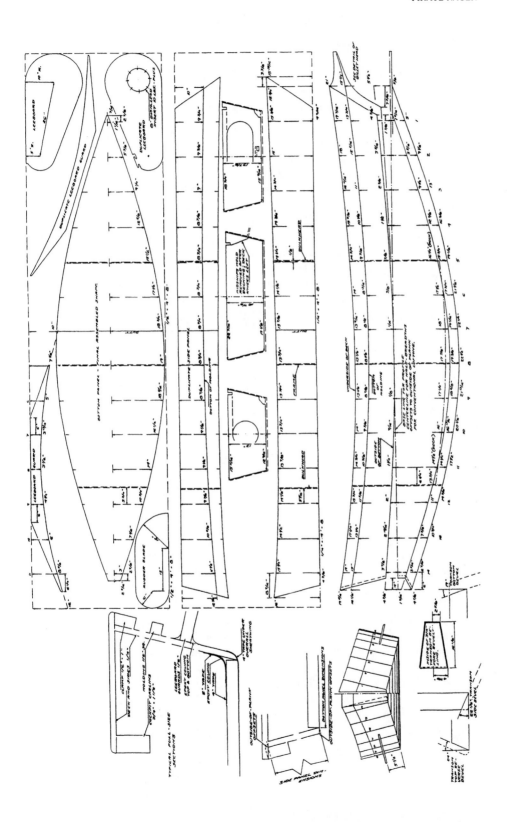

The narrow decks along the sides are mainly to give something flat to hike out over. I suppose there will have to be toe straps on the bottom if the racing gets hot. The decks give a little more margin of buoyancy in a knockdown, and they stiffen the gunwale enough to eliminate a 'midship frame. Wider side decks are nice in strong, puffy winds and choppy water; it would be quite possible to make them wide enough to float the boat on her side without shipping any water. But the wide cockpit is much better for all-around use. It is 6 feet 6 inches long, unobstructed, and could be tented in to make a respectable beach cruiser. Also, decking is heavy, which is why the completely decked board-boats and catamarans weigh so much.

The billethead is purely ornamental and could be left off without affecting performance. In fact, eliminating its weight would be all to the good. I think it has style, and if one or more of the youngsters has talent for designing figureheads, it would be fun to see what they produced. Dropping the beak below the sheer gives an effect of the Mediterranean fighting galleys. I suppose it's a vestige of a ram. Something like this would be an improvement on the clumsy catheads or "anchor platforms" on bigger boats.

The leeboards, hung entirely on rope, are hard to damage and easy to unship. They need a lot of ballast near the leading edge to work well; the 10 pounds specified is minimal. If they're not heavy enough, and before the wind in any case, they will kite out off their leeboard guards and skip along the surface. There's not much harm in this, though it will probably pay in racing to pick up the weather-side board; but if the boat then skids sideways, one board will come back in on its guard with a disconcerting jolt. I think this is worth putting up with for the simplicity, and because the leeboards need to be easily cleared out of the way of the oars.

The broad guards, necessary in a flared-side boat, look weak but in fact are pretty well braced by the curving interface with the sides. The "hinge line," where they would break, is about 6 inches out from the tips. I'm always in two minds whether to lay the boards parallel fore-and-aft, or to give them a trace of toe-in to try to cancel leeway; but I'm clear that there should be very little toe-in, if any, not much more than 1 degree to the centerline. After all, a good centerboarder ought not to make 2 degrees of leeway. Except close-hauled in light airs, I'd expect that it would pay to carry the boards raked aft more than the angle shown on the sail plan.

The lateen sail is handsome as an abstract shape and has romantic associations: Knights of St. John sailing from Rhodes and Malta; the war fleets of Venice sallying from the canals; Don John of Austria victorious at Lepanto. It will work quite well without a boom, eliminating tripping the boat in a knockdown and most of the hazards of jibing. The yard looks long, but it's actually shorter than a Laser mast and can be light because it's supported at one-third of its length and can be very slender at the peak. This last is the reason I think it might be worth the trouble to make the tapered spruce box spar instead of buying a stock aluminum extrusion, which would be heavier at the top where it counts. The taper adds a grace note as well.

The sail is a generous size and height for the weight of the boat. This is partly because you have so much light weather in California, but mainly because I don't think a children's boat ought to be too docile. Apart from not wanting to bore them, it's just as well if they have to deal with occasional emergencies, antidotes for complacency. Inducing complacency is too common, the most egregious example being the way children are taught to walk in front of automobiles on their way to school.

I like your racing scheme a lot. It may turn out that allowing oars to be used will

Pirate Racers in action

lead to the strongest oarsmen rowing over the whole course. I'd guess this will happen only in very light winds, in which case the rowing race would be more exciting and better exercise. The fact that the leeboards block the oars unless they're completely unshipped will complicate decisions about when to use the oars, which is as it should be. The fewer arbitrary rules based on preconceptions you can get away with, the better.

The International Rules of the Road will govern right of way, of course, but in these light boats I'd be tempted to revert to the old custom of calling fouls only for collisions. It saved a lot of argument and hard feelings about whether there really was "risk of collision." (The present custom does make sense in bigger boats. The tactics of the likes of Charlie Barr in 90-footers and Charles Francis Adams in J-boats put too high a premium on nerve.)

I'd suggest that the races be short and numerous. Some of the best racing I ever had was collegiate frostbiting, sailing six or eight short races in an afternoon, with that many starts and that many fresh chances for the losers.

Author's Note

Tony tentatively named the class for Roger de Lauria, knowing that the "Admiral of Aragon" is one of my historical heroes. De Lauria was Sicilian-born but was raised in Catalonia; he lived from about 1250 to 1304 A.D. He commanded fleets of war galleys in four major battles with 60 or 80 galleys on a side, and in innumerable small engagements and amphibious operations; he was never defeated. To me, he's a heroic example of imaginative thinking on all occasions, spectacular because in his time people were expected to follow their programming. His name is also appropriate for the class because he certainly was a pirate among other things, a reputable calling in his time.

21 *Bobcat*

12'3" × 6'0"

Dear *SBJ*:

Every issue, when I read Phil Bolger's cartoon offering, my dreamboat comes to mind. Each year, we vacation on the south shore of Cape Cod. We always take our trailerable sailboat with us (four different boats, so far), but I always find myself envying the Beetle Cat sailors.

The size, shape, style, and sailing characteristics of the little cat are great, but trailering a planked boat is almost an impossibility. To have such a boat in a freshwater lake in upstate New York, where we sail the rest of the year, invites rot as well as marina fees, and limits sailing venues. The new plastic cats from Nauset Marine are neat but far from cheap.

I propose a small catboat of light construction, perhaps a strip-planked, fiberglass-covered Beetle Cat built like some canoes of late. Or maybe a Cotuit Skiff–type boat built with the tack-and-tape method. A boat such as this would give some of us inland sea lovers a bit of salty style with a practical touch—shallow draft, and easy trailering, launching, and rigging.

I realize this is asking quite a bit, but I look forward to your ideas in this regard.

Tom Flynn, Syracuse, New York

Dear Mr. Flynn:

I've always thought the Beetle Cat would be more boat for the money if it were stretched out 3 feet on the same breadth and depth. I guess that the breadth and depth are right for you, and that you want it as short as it is, not to make it short but to make it

(text continued on page 103)

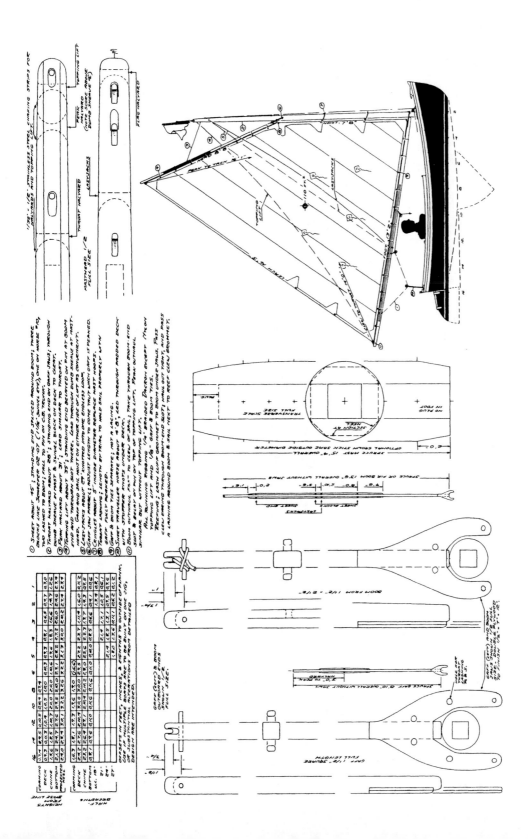

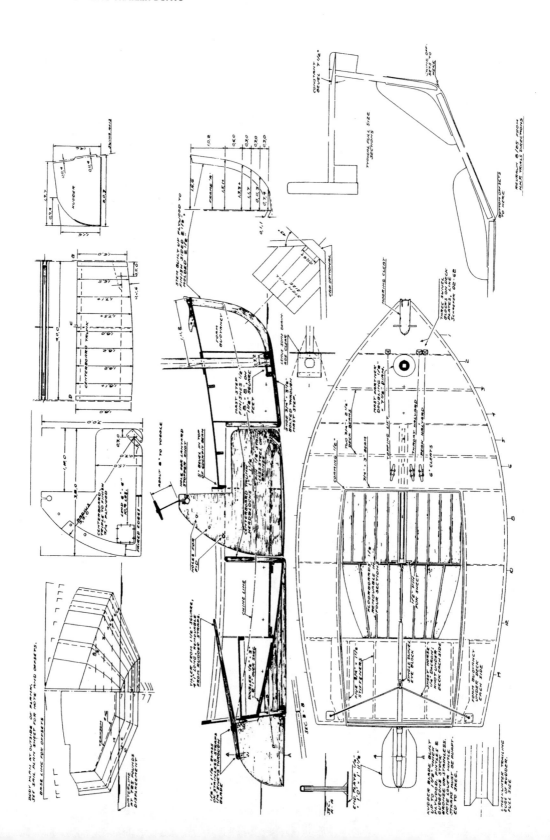

compact. More length would give you speed out of proportion to the added cost, but you don't need the speed.

Other things being equal, the short boat will be lighter than the long one. A boat in the lighter-than-air category would be flightier to move around in than you might like, but generally speaking, the lighter a trailer boat is, the less one hesitates to take it somewhere and launch it. (I've just finished a design for a trailer boat 40 feet long, weighing upwards of 7,000 pounds, but she's a custom job for a couple of professional cattle truckers, and even so I have some doubts about how good an idea it is.)

I agree that it's not fair to a Beetle Cat to dry-sail it. It should be kept wet, preferably with salt water, as you suggest. I suppose the reason salt water seems to inhibit rot somewhat is that the salt attracts moisture, so the cycles from wet to dry aren't as drastic as they are in fresh water.

The Beetle Cat is a living fossil. It was designed in 1920, but it was almost as reactionary then as it is now. In its proportions, shape, construction, and rig, it's a typical production boat of the early 1900s. They knew a lot about mass production in those days, but they depended on a pool of craftsmen who would work steadily at *demanding*, repetitive work. The threshold of boredom has been steadily dropping for 50 or 60 years, such that a team like the one at the Concordia Company, where the Beetles are now built, is phenomenal. I think it's much better to live in 1984 than in 1904, but a respectful bow is in order for the "do it right over and over, fast" craftsmanship that was once taken for granted.

As for fiberglass construction, once a craftsman has organized the operation, good boats can be built by people who haven't spent years learning how, don't plan to do it all their lives, and are thinking about something else while they work. But the production setup has to be so elaborate that unless you can spread the starting cost over more boats than the apparent demand for Beetle Cats, the price goes into orbit. Also, the most economical type of fiberglass construction produces very heavy boats.

I decided to pick up your suggestion for tack-and-tape construction, but I should mention that it's expensive to design on account of the tricky projections of the prefabricated panels, and it's not economical for a full-time professional to build because the job has to keep stopping while the resin cures. The first project of what became the Cape Dory Company was an experimental batch of light dories using this composite construction. The hulls they built for me were lighter and proved to stand up better than the conventional plywood dories I was ordering elsewhere at the time, but they weren't competitive in labor cost. The method is good for part-time builders who have to work in short stints with long gaps in between; similarly, it might work out for a moonlighting professional. The *only* way to get a one-off boat built cheaply is to find somebody who for some reason is willing to discount a lot of her time.

The nicely formed forefoot of the Beetle Cat can't be duplicated in sheet-plywood construction, but the difference in behavior is quite small. The Beetle would be better in a small chop if the two boats were the same weight, but the lighter weight of the plywood boat probably just about evens the score. The most noticeable sacrifice is looks. The snubbed, shallow bow of the plywood boat will stir up a shapeless heap of foam in place of the clear, curling bow wave of the Beetle. Some think the former is prettier; an advertising agency once retouched a photo of a powerboat I'd designed, to show more spray!

The plywood Bobcat's centerboard is well forward, as in the Beetle Cat and in 1900 practice generally. I used to think the rudder ought not to be made to carry any of the lateral-plane function, but I've changed my mind. Cats with shallow rudders have a bad name for weathercocking against a hard-over rudder when they're overpowered, but since I learned to put end plates across the bottoms of the rudders I haven't had any complaints about this. I started using end plates about 15 years ago, and I've reached the point where a rudder without one looks naked to me. It's astonishing how shallow a rudder can be and still steer the boat, if the water is kept from rushing off the bottom of the blade. I have an idea the principle could do wonders for shallow keels and bilge keels, though making the horizontal part strong enough is a problem there.

I haven't duplicated the curved cockpit coaming of the Beetle Cat. I like the looks of it, but it doesn't seem to suit the style of the plywood boat as well, and there's no functional advantage. It's an economy in a shop with a steam box going all the time and a steady supply of fresh-cut oak coming in, but not so in a plywood-and-glue operation.

The rig started out to be a standard Beetle rig, left over from a perished hull or bought new from Concordia. The boom, gaff, and sail shown are within the Beetle class limits. The mast is a little longer than that of the Beetle, partly because Bobcat has a higher bow and partly because I see Beetles sailing with less masthead above the gaff jaws than I like. I think a gaff sail sets and stands best with the peak halyard block well up—at a right angle off the middle of the gaff, if possible.

A gaff sail like this can be cut just as close-winded as a jibheaded sail. If the gaff "sags off," it's because the sail is not set or sheeted properly, and the sag can happen just as easily to the top of a triangular sail. It's true that this sail will twist up when it's slacked out to run before a stiff breeze, lose some power, and do that scary rolling-to-windward act. The modern dinghies don't have that vice. The reason is not their jibheaded sails but their elaborate vangs or "kicking straps" that control the boom. I'm sure you don't want to bother with one of those, and the foot of the sail would have to be cut a lot higher to take it. Another way to do it is to use a sprit boom with its heel up about where the lower mast hoop is shown here. I just came ashore from the first trials of a 450-square-foot gaff cat rigged that way. She's a good sailer with all-around good manners, and close-winded by any standard, but the rigging of the sprit boom is somewhat complex, and unfamiliar to most people. I settled here for a long traveler horse and the fall of the mainsheet taken to a lee side cleat to damp the gyrations of the boom somewhat.

A real advantage of the gaff rig in a cat is that the sail area doesn't move as far forward when you reef as it does in a cat with a triangular sail. The more a cat is expected to be reefed, the less her gaff should be peaked. It's even possible that a reef across the peak of the sail, tied up to the gaff and tying off a triangle from the throat out to some point on the leech, would be useful. They used to reef lateeners that way.

I can't fathom why the Beetles, and most cats this size, use purchases on peak halyards. All this does is slow down hoisting and clutter the boat with two or three times as much expensive rope as is needed. Gaff sails also usually have at least twice as many mast hoops as they need. If this boat were mine, I'd cleat the halyards at the foot of the mast instead of turning them through deck blocks, but a case can be made for keeping crew weight aft while hoisting and lowering. The rig shown works well if the deck blocks are big enough and have good bearings.

22 *Spartina*

15'4" × 7'0"

In 1921 Nicholas Montgomery built 85 hard-chined catboats from a trendy design he and Harry Friend, a talented amateur designer, had worked out. The boats cost $185 that year, but he had cut it too fine, even with his efficient production tooling; the next year the price went up to $225. Nick built several hundred more before sales slowed to a trickle in the Great Depression; the trickle continued through the 1930s and 1940s. Nick's son Herbert built one or two each year through the 1950s, 1960s, and 1970s, and grandson David built a few more in the 1980s and 1990s. Dave Montgomery made the first major change in the design, using a sheathed plywood-epoxy bottom in place of the nailed planking, so the boats could be dry-sailed. By that time they cost $6,000, which tells more about government than about value.

In 1992 there were no orders, which Dave thought might be due to prejudice against the hard chine. He and I worked out a new design for clinker plywood construction, doing our best to keep the spirited handling of the old boats, which had maneuvering elegance never equaled in all those years for precision and acceleration in crowded waters. While we were at it, we redesigned the rig with a Solent lugsail, to shorten the 25-foot mast and eliminate sail track and standing rigging. The shape of the sail was not changed, and the prototype retained the boom on the foot of the sail, but in later boats Dave intends to offer the sprit-boom rig as standard and the sloop rig to order. The length of the boat was kept the same. Breadth went up to 7 feet to keep the stability of the soft-bilged boat the same as that of the 6-foot 6-inch hard-chined boat.

The new boat is higher-sided to get some depth for seats (in the 1921 design, crew sat on the floorboards), and the bow is higher to stand harder driving before the wind. A tendency to plow when running off in strong winds is a failing of the older boats.

Dave named her *Spartina* after the boat in the novel of that name.

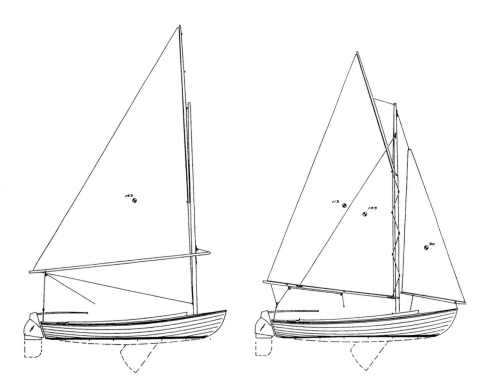

We retained the 1920s emphasis on thoroughbred handling qualities and ability to sail well without intense concentration and strenuous crew effort. The impression that a boat not designed for cutthroat competition must be clumsy and dead-sailing needs contesting. This design and its progenitor both demonstrate that a boat doesn't have to be either physically or mentally demanding to reward any level of skill.

Features biased to that end are a short waterline with the lateral plane concentrated in a short fin; a rounded keel profile with rounded underwater sections at each end; a powerful rudder carrying some of the lateral plane load (that is, the rudder shows weather helm when centered); buoyant fore quarters and high after quarters, to maintain fore-and-aft trim when heeled; and a powerful sail plan for the weight and wetted surface of the hull matched to breadth enough to carry the sail and freeboard enough to heel considerably without burying the deck edge. The added freeboard and increased deadrise at the stern in the new boat were improvements; she sails and steers well through a greater range of angles of heel than the old design. Most of the characteristics listed involve some sacrifice of potential top speed.

The smooth fairing of the new bow lines all the way up to the high deck eliminated the older boats' nose-diving habits. That and the plank laps much reduce spray-spitting on the wind in a chop.

Because the sailor is not distracted by complex gear, a boat with this kind of performance is faster through harbors, many of which resemble obstacle courses, than one designed for the cleared courses of formal racing. It may be faster over a long course because it doesn't exhaust its crew. Such a boat can deliver sport in small and crowded waters, because the pleasure of sailing it is less analogous to running than to dancing.

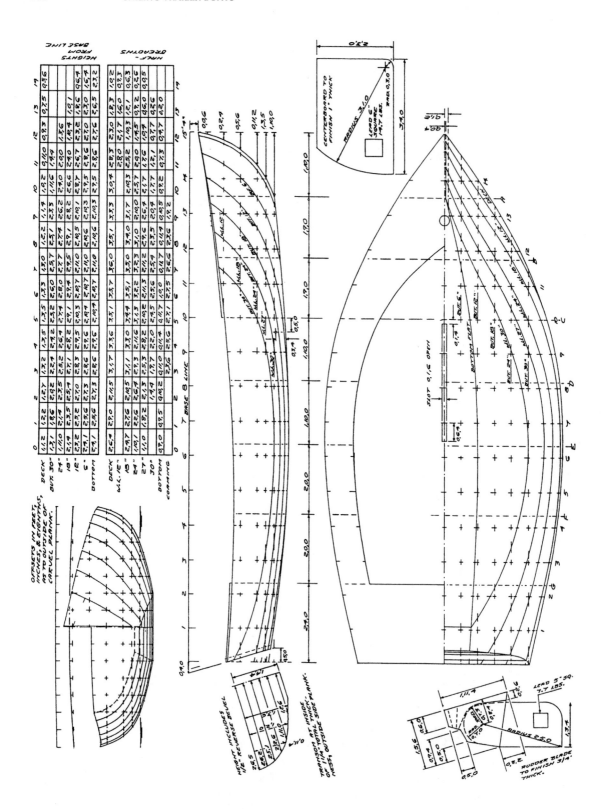

KEEL PANEL DOUBLE 1/2" PLYWOOD; BEVEL EDGES TO 1/2". STEM SIDED 3 1/2" (SEVEN COURSES OF 1/8"), MOLDED 2 1/2". CAP 1 1/4"
× 2 1/2". BULKHEAD-FRAMES & TRANSOM 1/2"; FRAMES FILLETTED, 3/4" FRAME ON TRANSOM. PLANKING, DECK, COAMINGS
1/2". CLAMP 3/4" - 1 1/2". CENTERBOARD TRUNK LOGS 1 1/2" - 3 1/2"; WALLS 1/2"; HEADBLOCKS & TOP FLANGES 1 1/2" SQUARE.

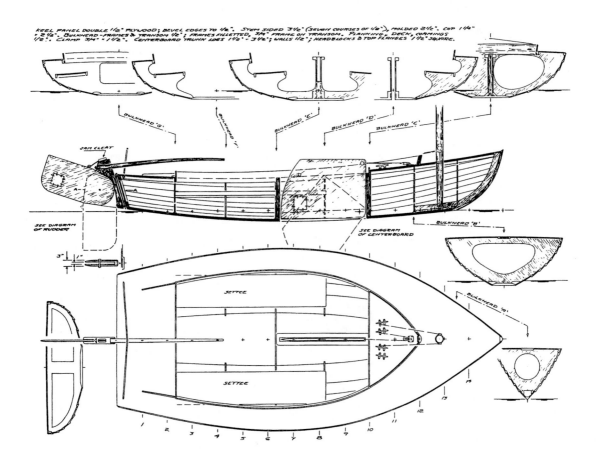

Spartina

23 *Canard*

20'0" × 4'6"

I had Brad Story build me *Canard* mainly to try to pin down the working of bow rudders. I used her for some other experiments, such as the variation on a square rig discussed in the next chapter. She also came in handy as a daysailer.

The hull is a sharpie skiff formed by wrapping straight-edged 16-inch-by-20-foot panels (two straight cuts through a 48-inch sheet) around bulkheads with sides flared enough to produce the sheer and rocker. Birdwatcher (see Chapter 46) is a bigger example of the type; the ubiquitous Teal skiff is a smaller one. It's not an especially good sailboat shape, as the sharp stern loses sail-carrying power, and the discrepancy between the plan-view curve of the sides and the profile curve of the bottom generates turbulence under the chines that makes them slow and unsteady-steering whenever they dig the forefoot into solid water. The trouble may be easier to grasp if you think of such a bow as an extreme case of a veed and rounded transom.

These craft can be made to sail tolerably well (as practically anything can, which is why boat designing is a relaxed profession), trimmed down by the stern. Their main virtue is that they're spectacularly quick and easy to design and build, without looking boxy.

I chose aluminum paint for the sides, having heard that this had the same reflectivity as pure white. People flinch when I suggest a metallic paint, but on the boat nobody noticed; it looked light gray and gave a seagull contrast with the white deck and bottom. The aluminum paint stood up well, taking care of itself for several years in the open, including some long bottom-up storage.

I designed the fins as shallow as I dared, hoping that setting the after one at a slight angle of incidence would compensate for its small size. The angle did help, though it was easy to crank in too much; 5 degrees slowed her appreciably. Eventually the

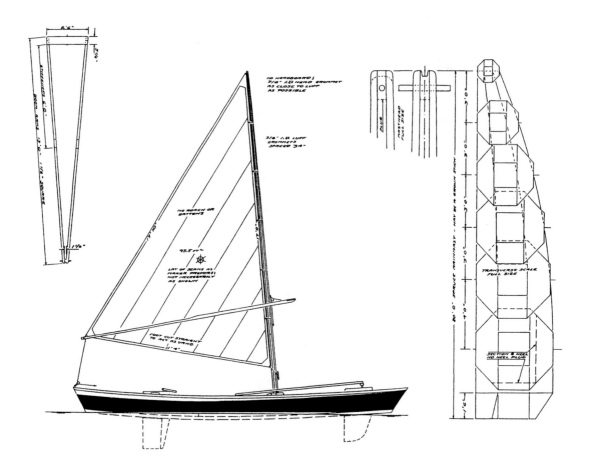

adjustable fin was replaced by a fixed one twice as deep, with an obvious improvement in windward performance.

Canard was never reliable in stays. With practice she could be tacked smoothly, but it didn't take much carelessness or bad luck to hang her up in irons. She then had to be backed around to fill on the new tack. The root of the trouble was that the after fin was abaft the axis of her turns, so the midbody dragged sidewise through the water as she pivoted on the fin. Contributing to this was the lack of momentum due to her light weight and modest speed. If I design another bow-steerer, I will arrange the two fins to be independently steerable for balance adjustment, but interconnected for sharp turns in such a way that the ends of the boat both swing around the center of gravity. An America's Cup boat with such a layout was astonishingly competitive, considering how radical the concept was. (I had nothing to do with her design except to admire its boldness.)

The stock of the bow rudder was set at right angles to the plane of the bottom to keep the gap over the top small, but it still caught weed. I thought the balance area ahead of the stock was needed to fair the blade to the round stock, but the sculch it collected must have slowed her down more than the bluntness would have. Such a rudder would be better under a bow with a low overhang, mounted clear ahead of the waterline, but it

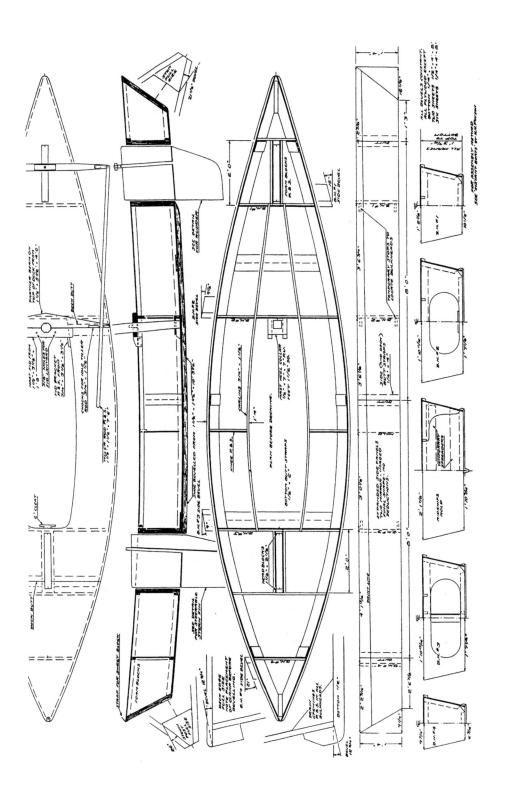

Canard *tries*
the proa sail

would still be a drift-catcher when the boat pitched. In *Canard*'s shallow hull the rudder
was "protected" by making it strong enough for the boat to lie on.

I've had trouble adapting to transverse tillers on stern rudders, but the action in
Canard felt perfectly natural, possibly because it was so visible. She was exceptionally
nice to steer running down a big sea, in spite of having a hull shape that is usually very
bad in such conditions.

The wide decks made her forgiving in gusty weather. She never capsized in the several years I had her. She did blow over in her berth a couple of times. Her sail was the
no-halyard type, which is furled by rolling it in from the clew, with the leech inside the
roll. This makes a neat furl if the leech is kept tight as it's rolled, but it is easy to leave
a flap at the top which a strong wind can get hold of, blowing out more of the head of
the sail. The cure was a light line made permanently fast at the masthead, which could
be pulled around the sail in a spiral after the sail was rolled up, to secure the roll. The rig
wouldn't do in a seagoing boat, but besides its simplicity it allows a very slender masthead, with no provision to hang a block or accept a sheave, and no downward stress
from a halyard fall. It is light in weight and aerodynamically good.

The luff of the sail was secured to the mast with separate ties of light twine. This
looked crude but made it possible to adjust the draft of the sail by varying the tightness
of the ties. Slacking the ties toward the middle of the luff threw more fullness into the
sail. It did not usually need adjustment for wind conditions because the flexible mast
would pull some of the draft out of the sail when it bent in strong winds, but the whip of

the mast was affected by the weight of the crew, so it sometimes paid to make some changes before setting out.

Canard was given a wishbone boom with curved, laminated arms. It looked well and no doubt was faster on what would have been the "bad tack" of a straight sprit boom, but it was often in the way and hard to stow, besides being expensive. I would tend to have the straight sprit boom in a day boat. In a real cruiser, like *Barn Owl* (see Chapter 74), a wishbone boom with secure goosenecks saves some chafing of the sail.

24 *Proa*

19'6" × 10'5"

Dear Phil:

After viewing a documentary on the South Seas, I couldn't forget the Polynesians and their proa canoes. These people are capable of traveling long distances at high speed with their low-tech, Stone-Age creations.

I sail on the south shore of Long Island. It is not unusual to sail across the Great South Bay to Fire Island on one tack and return on the other. Hence, a proa configuration could be optimal for average summer conditions.

Some thought-provoking problems are involved in designing a low-tech proa day-sailer that could carry a large crew but be handled by one or two persons. I'm thinking of a lateen proa with a symmetrical sail so that the sail's tack and the head are reversible. Two boards can function as rudders or centerboards as they rotate in or out of the case.

To be perfectly honest, the real point is to go showboating with a craft that is unusual, visually spectacular, and capable of outrageous speed.

Please run riot!

Peter Kaiteris, West Hempstead, New York

Dear Peter:

I've been thinking of building a proa myself, and your letter stimulated this study.

I was influenced by a sail I experimented with a few years ago and put aside to consider. Like a proa hull, it has dedicated weather and lee sides and interchangeable luff

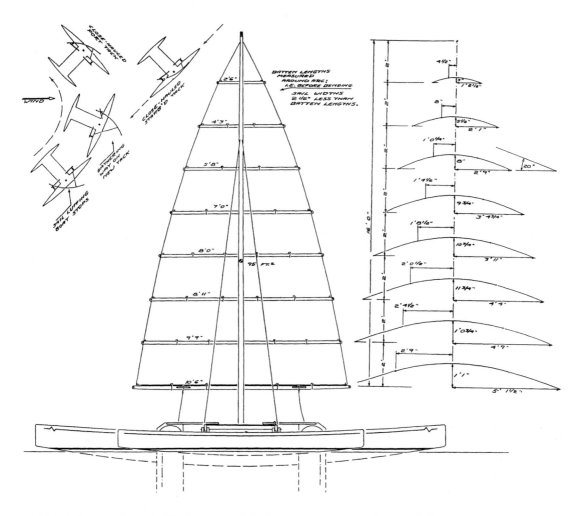

and leech (bow and stern). The battens and the boom are permanently curved. In a conventionally maneuvered boat like *Canard* (see Chapter 23), this sail is handled like a squaresail, tacked by backing it around the forward side of the mast. In the photo, which shows me sailing *Canard* singlehanded, she's moving well, but the picture doesn't convey the tangle I had just straightened out, or the one that happened a few minutes later. This is not a good singlehanded rig in constricted water! But you can see that the sail develops considerable power even when it's not sheeted as well as it might be.

For a proa, it's most appropriate to change ends, letting go the taut tack downhaul and hardening down the other. The one not acting as a tack downhaul serves as the sheet. The sail is pivoted around the axis from the tack downhaul up to the head. Four-fifths of its area is abaft this pivot axis so it will luff reliably (unlike a squaresail) when its sheet is started. It does not pivot on the mast and is attached to the mast only by the halyard. In the sail plan, the boat is supposed to be sailing from right to left, and if the sheet was let run, the sail would feather around a line about where the batten-length numbers are marked on the drawing. Reversing direction, the sail would be in the same

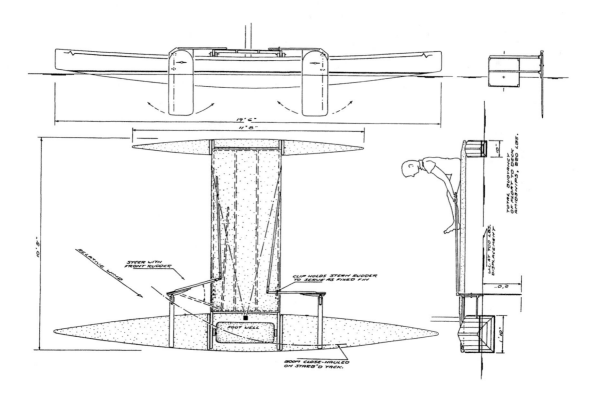

profile position, but the pivot axis would be shifted to the opposite one-fifth position, toward the new luff at the right-hand edge.

The system ought to be faster than swinging a lateen yard peak-for-tack, or than overhauling the sheet of a boomed sail with the tack on the mast. Jamie Richardson, a Massachusetts architect who designed and built a handsome Constant Camber proa with a leg-o'-mutton cat rig, tells me that he sometimes has a problem with the boat weathercocking before she can gather way on the new tack, which he thinks this more balanced sail might eliminate. He confirmed my idea that the usual diagram of a proa tacking is not the best way to do it. Such diagrams show the boat bearing away to a beam reach before changing ends. I show her holding a close-hauled course until the sail fills on the new tack, to gather steerageway with the wind as free as possible.

The existing sail is only 95 square feet, so a proa to suit it has to be small, which seems like a good idea in any case until we have a better idea of what we're doing. But in a very small multihull it's necessary to keep track of load-carrying ability. The flat bottom with deep rocker gives 700 pounds displacement as shown. A wedge hull would have to be twice as deep on the same waterline breadth and therefore much wider on deck. This flat hull has the same curve in its sides as it does in its bottom, so it will lose less to chine eddies than most sharpies. It will be noisy and bumpy in a chop, not a serious matter in this unserious boat.

By no coincidence, the hull looks like a close relative of Ray Hunt's International

110 (see Chapter 31). I follow Hunt's insight in sharpie design rather than Ralph Munroe's, because I believe that sharpies have to sail on their bottoms. The plumb sides and ends produce the most bottom for any given size of boat.

Russell Brown (son of trimaran designer Jim Brown and gifted with talent that must tear his father between pride and envy), whose elegant proas strike me as the best ones ever built, warned Jamie Richardson against flat-bottomed floats, which hike out and slam down when the boat is sailed hard. I've shown this one flat because it's the quickest shape to build that has the right buoyancy, and in this little boat the occasional crash won't be destructive of either boat or crew. I would think about making the float somewhat bigger. My first sketches showed it smaller, but when I figured the displacement I found that it would sink if somebody stood on it. In warm water and a minimum-clothing culture this may be convenient, but in many places, including Great South Bay, it's more useful to be able to get on and off the boat on the float side with dry legs.

Even in a cruising proa, I would follow Russell Brown in adopting the Pacific proa with the float on the weather side. In a small daysailer I can think of nothing to recommend the Atlantic proa with leeside float. A leeside float has to be as big as the main hull, running up weight and cost, and there's no efficient way to stay the mast. Any multihull with unstayed masts will be heavy and inefficient since the masts and outriggers don't support each other, and each must be stressed to stand the whole heeling force independently.

The steering and lateral plane arrangements in a proa become tricky as soon as you get away from the sweep steering of the Polynesians. I've designed several boats to be steered with paddles or sweeps and have yet to hear a good word about them from an owner, so I've tried to come up with something else. The two fins shown are balanced around pintle axes near the edge facing the nearer end of the boat. She is steered with the front one, on the left in the drawing as the boat sails from right to left. The after one is locked fore-and-aft to act as lateral plane. The proportions are about the same as those of the fins in *Canard* in the photo (see page 114), modified slightly from experience with her. A very small angle of incidence on the fixed stern fin improves its effectiveness close-hauled. Two degrees seems to be the most that ever pays, and if there's that much there should be alternate positions with less or none.

The blades are mounted to kick up if they hit something, as in beaching. They're supposed to be locked down by setting up one of Dynamite Payson's oversize fiberglass wingnuts, but I would have a big chunk of lead cast into each blade as well. The blades have to be free to swing up either way. The rudders are mounted on outriggers to keep the swinging blades clear of the hull while allowing them to be steered. The boat is supposed to carry lee helm to make the angle of the bow rudder set her to windward.

The mast is stepped on the weather side of the hull to leave some working space for gathering in the sail as it's lowered, with a deep footwell giving secure footing. In most weather I'd expect that some or all of the crew would sit on the inboard end of the outrigger with feet in the well, rather than in the uncomfortable position of the scale figure on the drawing. The outrigger should have cleats across it to keep people from sliding when the boat hikes. There should never be any more weight on the outrigger than is needed to keep the float just touching the water, or, better still, flying just clear of the water. This last is a balancing trick suitable for 10-square-meter canoe sailors and other acrobats.

Author's Note

This is a preliminary study, not a finished design. There's enough detail and dimensions for an experienced builder to work with in designing her own. The concept is too radical, and likely to be obsolete too soon, to broadcast a lot of formal plans. It would be embarrassing to have a few hundred of these under construction by the time somebody tried one and found that it needed to be drastically different. By the same token, if you found this book on an antique-store remainder shelf, it would be prudent to inquire what, if anything, became of the idea.

25 *His and Her Schooners*

19'6" × 4'2" × 3'0"

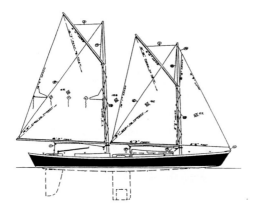

Dear Phil:

I would like my next boat to be small and traditional-looking, yet able enough to allow me to make small cruises from harbor to harbor along the Southern California coast and to make the 26-mile crossing from Long Beach to Catalina Island.

By "able" I mean that the boat should be self-righting and not liable to swamp. I am hoping that, if all the sheets could be led aft to a small cockpit abaft the mainmast, the area between the masts could be decked over with a hatch for access. I would like to have enough length under the deck to lie down, with space left over to stow camping gear. The hatch should be fairly watertight. It would be comforting to know not only that the boat would right itself after a knockdown, but that the sleeping bag, stores, and gear would stay dry.

The prevailing wind and current here on the Southern California coast are such that it is easy to sail south, but they often slow progress coming north again. Therefore, a small outboard would be a nice thing to have along.

I built one of your "Scooners" [23'6"] a couple of years ago and liked it very much. I am hoping that a smaller, one-man version could be designed to fit my requirements.

I live 75 miles inland and drive a small car. My building time and budget are both limited, so simple and cheap construction would be a big help.

I suggested to my wife that a pair of these, sailing along in company or rafted together at anchor, would be a pretty sight and a lot of fun besides. She was taken with the idea. So, I put it to you—could it be made to work?

Tony Groves, Los Angeles, California

Dear Tony and Mary:

I'm entranced with the idea of his-and-her schooners! Years ago Colin Mudie remarked how nice it would be to have two pretty boats alike, to sail one while admiring the other. You've perfected the idea.

My first thought was to make a race of it, but that would tend to separate the boats and might not be good for domestic harmony. What about reviving the ancient skill of station-keeping? When warships were sailed, every watch officer had to learn to match his ship's speed exactly to the rest of the fleet. The British, at least, are supposed to have been able to keep their ships closed up in tight formations and to tack and wear in ballet-like unison.

The rafting could also develop some intriguing ramifications. If the two main booms were lashed across four masts, the peak halyards could hold up the ridge of a tent that at night would look like a paper lantern.

The hull shape, formed by springing straight-edged panels around molds with carefully chosen flare and spacing, quickly turns a pile of plywood into a good-looking hull, and a good sailer if trimmed down by the stern as shown. I suppose the optimum is with the forefoot well clear of the water and the heel of the sternpost just touching still water, but the pointed stern doesn't drag badly if more weight is put in aft. Hulls like this will go very fast in smooth water and aren't badly stopped by a chop or motorboat bobble as long as there's a fair breeze to heel them. They're noisy at night, but a nice consequence of the layout you suggest is that with cockpit empty and somebody sleeping forward, the bow will go down into the water and not slap so much.

Any boat as light as this is happiest with live ballast hiked out, but I thought it would be best to lay her out to do as well as possible with her crew down on the bottom. Well chocked off with backs against the coaming and feet against the lee side, they could stand a long sail without weariness. The wide cockpit allows this. In a sharp knockdown, the weight carried low does more to get her back on her feet than it would high up on the rail. The drawback is that if she gets up on her beam ends, the cockpit will flood. As small as it looks, this cockpit on paper could hold close to 1,200 pounds of water; in practice, the buoyancy of the rest of the hull, beyond the watertight bulkheads, would float her so high that less than a quarter of that would get in.

The 100 pounds of lead in the daggerboard will right her quickly. It would take a big breaking sea to turn her bottom-up, and the odds are that the next sea would leave her upright again. If we're going to have nightmares, chain-reaction crashes on the freeway make a more likely scenario. The board is supposed to be more of a removable keel than a daggerboard in the usual sense, and it should be pinned in place at all times when she's afloat. The total weight of the board will be about 125 pounds so two people can lift it out and carry it to the car.

The forward cockpit is narrow enough to be clear of the water in all but the most extreme circumstances. I meant to give it a solid hatch cover, but after trying to find a place to stow it I decided that a fabric cover that could be rolled up could be made to shed water well enough for your purposes. The hold is 6½ feet long and about 20 inches deep from the top of the coaming. A tent supported by the furled and partly hoisted foresail can have as much headroom as you like.

Stripped, each of these hulls will weigh less than 150 pounds. The pair of them with all their gear won't overload the lightest trailer, which is just as well, as the picture of two cars and trailers going up the road in convoy is not as attractive as that of the two

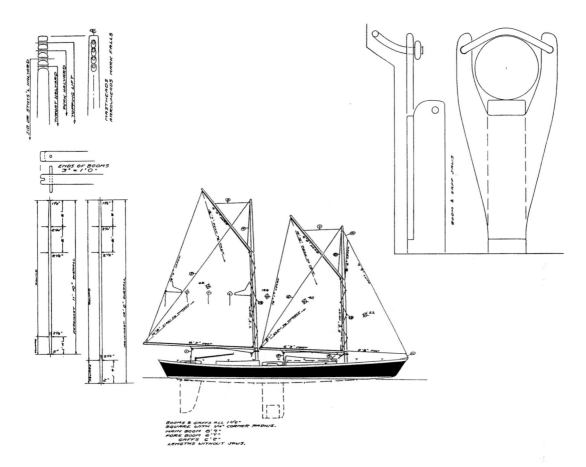

boats sailing in company. I've toyed with various schemes for racking the two hulls together: on edge deck-to-deck, bottom-to-bottom, or deck-to-bottom; or one on top of the other, both upright, both bottom-up, bottom one upright and top one inverted, or bottom one inverted and top one upright. Any of these would be possible if enough study went into racks to hold them and rollers to slide them into position. I'd guess that one on top of the other, both bottom-up, would be the best combination for good aerodynamics and minimal dust accumulation, and would be as easy as any to organize—especially if you can count on bystanders to lend a hand. All the spars can go on the car's roof rack.

The schooner rig looks like an affectation, and I admit that practicality wasn't a high priority on the first rig of this kind that I designed. I gradually noticed that it had some real virtues, starting with the traditional schooner quality of riding steadily to an anchor with the largest sail set. The next point is that a lot of sail can be set without going very high or using any very long spars. This boat has 126 square feet of sail, but the center of sail area is only 6 feet 3 inches above the waterline, compared with, for instance, almost 10 feet for a National One-Design. The schooner's mainmast is 14 feet long, and that includes a liberal head above the gaff jaws to make the gaff stand well without a heavy stress on the peak halyard. The foremast is 12 feet long. The main boom is 8 feet 9 inches long, just a bit over the ideal twice-the-beam rule. Both booms have topping lifts so the sails can be lowered with the booms broad off.

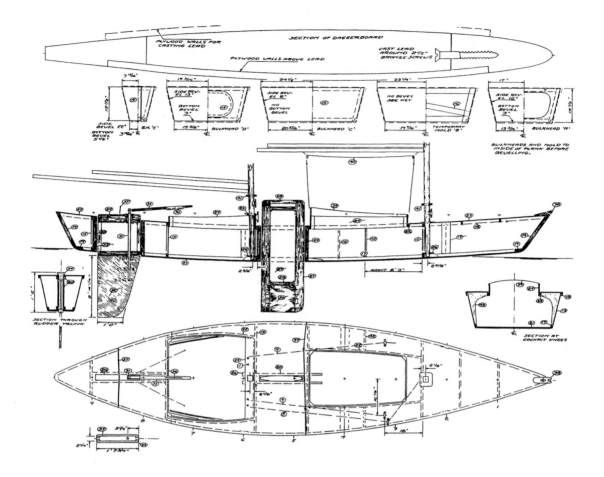

Schooners have always been most competitive on reaches. They're not close-winded because the mainsail works in the backwind of the foresail, but when the wind is abeam this turns into an advantage as the draft off the foresail increases the relative wind speed across the mainsail. Before the wind, they're better than might be thought at first glance. Trimming the mainsail a little will generate a flow across the sail that blows the foresail out wing-and-wing. Like all boats with conventional booms, their down-wind manners are improved a lot by vanging the booms down, to keep the tops of the sails from twisting forward. Bringing the sheets in to the masts produces some vang effect since it keeps the whole force of the sheets down to the ends of the traveler horses, but it will also be worthwhile, when there's a prospect of a long run, to rig a makeshift vang on the main boom—a clove hitch around the boom with the tail made fast near the heel of the mast.

When the jib is set, its halyard will be tightened to keep its luff taut. That ought to be adequate in moderate weather with a 22-square-foot jib. When the luff starts to sag in stronger wind, the jib should be taken in and the boat sailed like a cat-schooner. The over-size balanced rudder will take care of the resulting weather helm. A schooner like this can actually be sailed on all points including to windward with her mainsail alone, if the rud-

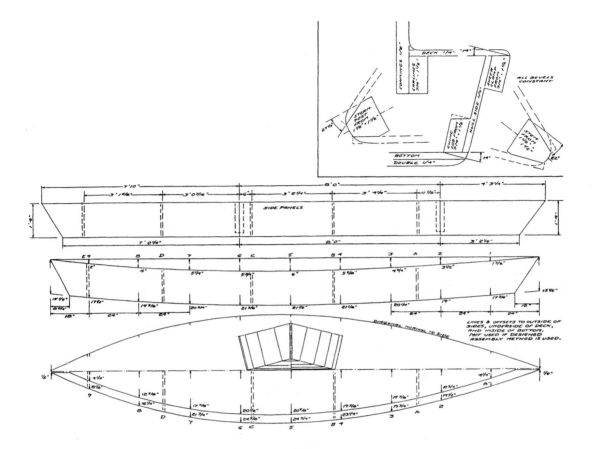

der is powerful enough; however, her real heavy-weather rig is full foresail and deep-reefed mainsail—a snug and handy cat-ketch with balance close to that with full sail.

I suggest the loose-footed jib, with two sheets, partly because it saves a spar, partly because the sail can be bigger, but mostly because it's handy and seamanlike to be able to back the jib from the cockpit. It's a pretty maneuver to back the boat through an anchorage with the tiller under your arm and a jibsheet in each hand, able to fall off and sail on either tack at any moment. It's now rare for any boat to be able to heave to with the jib aback and the mainsail flat, remaining almost stationary but under control. Schooners traditionally heave to under their foresails with the helm hard down, but they often fore-reach a lot. The famous schooner *Puritan* is said to have been lost because she moved much faster than her skipper expected, toward Sable Island, under her foresail.

I'm dwelling on these maneuvering niceties partly because I think they ought to be encouraged, but mostly by way of arguing that they're worth the trouble of tending a jib in tacking. I've spared you a main staysail.

As for the motor, I agree that it would be a lifesaver at times, but it's a mean thing to stow. I thought it might fit under the afterdeck, but it won't. It also doesn't mount very satisfactorily on the sharp-sterned hull. The best idea I've been able to come up with is a bracket fitted to clamp on the rail abreast of the after end of the cockpit. As for the stowing, I'd get a fuel-proof bag for it and try first putting it across the after end of

His Schooner leaps a Pacific swell

the cockpit. If that's intolerable, it will have to go in the hold, though the idea flits across my mind of shutting it into a streamlined watertight shell shaped something like a kayak, and towing it.

An engine as small as 2 h.p. is adequate power if each boat has one. If you could sell some other couples the idea, a fleet of these boats might support a towboat on call. Back when I used to day-race every summer weekend, I remember how pleasant it was, after drifting around in a flat calm, to see the launch coming with "race off" signal flying and a towline ready. To go farther back, I can just remember when there were two steam tugs in Gloucester, left over from the time when the fishing schooners often wanted a tow clear of the harbor.

26 *Japanese Beach Cruiser*

3.8 meters (12'6") × 1.8 meters (5'6")

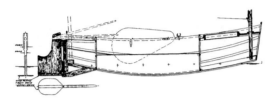

Dear Phil:

I wonder if you could design a leeboard cat-yawl, a craft that could have accompanied the *Swallow*, *Amazon*, and *Scarab* of Arthur Ransome's books, for my use on Japan's Inland Sea. A leeboard version of the loose-footed spritsail cat-yawl shown in your *100 Small Boat Rigs* would be about right.

Although I have made only your Tortoise and Teal, I want to build it myself. I feel that plywood lapstrake with minimal frames would be suitable for an amateur builder like myself.

This, I think, would make a unique boat.

Teruaki Imanaga, Nishinomiya, Japan

Dear Teruaki:

I've made this boat a little shorter and wider than those in the books; 3.8 by 1.67 meters, or 1.8 meters wide over the leeboard guards, as against about 4.1 by 1.35 meters. With the pram bow we can make her more compact, but I suggest the bow mainly because it suits the plywood lapstrake construction. The elm planking of the old British dinghies could be steamed to take the sharp curve in to their pointed bows, but steaming plywood is ineffective. Also, a leeboarder needs to carry her breadth farther forward than is usual in centerboarders to get bearings for the boards without a clumsy projection of the leeboard guards.

The stability of the pram shape is about the same as that of a well-faired, pointed-

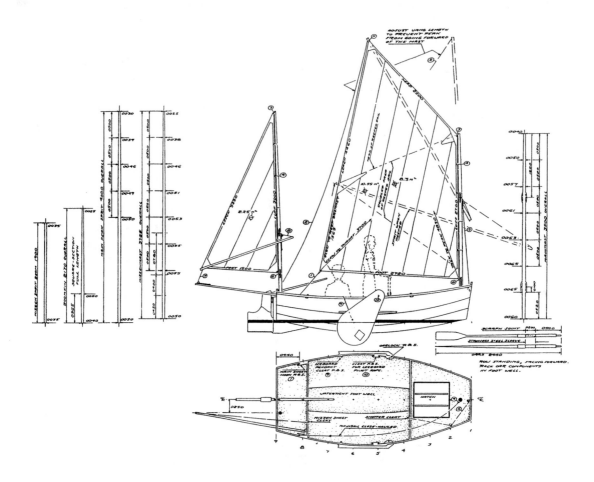

bow boat a meter longer. The longer boat could be driven harder in rough water but would be heavier and less agile.

For cruising, it seemed worthwhile to make your boat deeper inside than a conventional sailing dinghy so that adults can sit down inside, well braced, and able to sail her for many hours without growing dangerously tired and stiff. Added to the high sides is enough watertight volume to make her immune to swamping. These factors produce a boat that can face rough water and lose little time and distance to prudence.

The ends of the boat are shown bulkheaded watertight, and the chambers under the cockpit benches are also watertight. The boat can be sailed with all the water her cockpit can hold. Unless she went all the way over to bottom-up, she would recover from any knockdown. If a big breaking sea did put her upside down, she would float high and could be righted by wrapping a line around her parbuckle-fashion, to allow her crew to stand on the underside of the leeboard guard and hike out.

The last scenario depends on the security of the forward hatch, which should dog down on gaskets. The hatch opening gives access to the stowed camping gear, which should stay dry. The dry hold can make the difference between contentment and misery after a rough passage. The stern compartment and side chambers could have similar

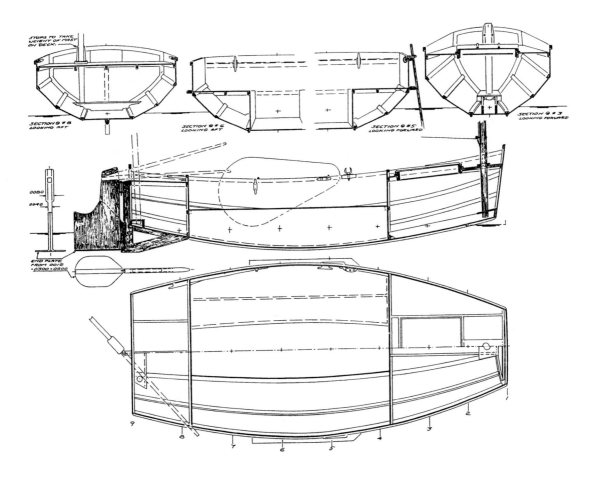

hatches, but the more openings there are, the more likely it is that one will be open at the wrong time. The drainage is arranged to get condensation water (or, perish the thought, leakage) to the accessible forepeak by canting the boat.

The sides and after compartments could be filled with foam to float her high if you should hit her against a rock. I would have some foam if she were mine, about a tenth of a cubic meter slung up under the bench seats, in case I wanted to put some ballast into her for singlehanding. That much foam would ensure that she wouldn't go out from under me if she had a hole punched in her, or if I lost the hatch cover. I wouldn't have much more because foam is heavier than most people realize; it would be easy to add enough weight to be a handicap on a steep beach.

The cockpit is 2 meters long with the benches and bottom clear for sleeping in the boat. It would be possible to use the mainsail for a tent by devoting some thought to grommets in the sail and padeyes on the hull located to compensate for the irregular shape of the sail. I haven't gone into that, as it's best done by mock-up on the boat.

An arched thatch shelter over the cockpit, as is or used to be common in your locality, is an attractive idea and suits the style of the boat. I'd use a Dacron cover on fiberglass bows in place of the thatch on bamboo, to make it easier to stow when it's not wanted.

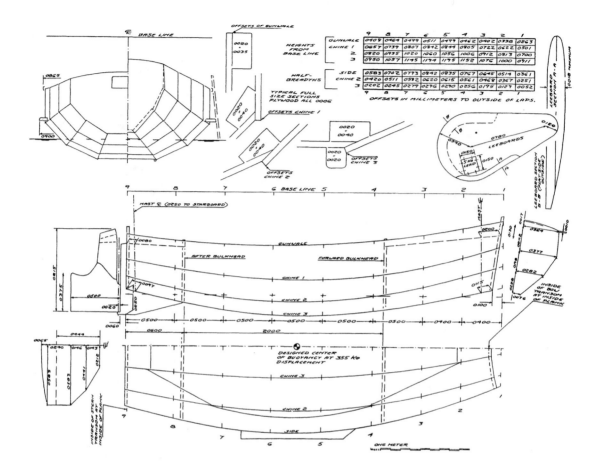

The leeboards are the simplest possible type. Broad, thin boards like these gain next to nothing by foil sections; they're flat except for enough edge fairing to avoid chattering. The pivots consist of 9mm rope caught with stopper knots through holes in the boards, taken over the gunwales and set up to cleats just inside.

Apart from being cheap and hard to damage, this arrangement makes it easy to take the boards off when the boat isn't under sail. They stow across the afterdeck. The pivot rope needs frequent tightening as it stretches—easy to do on the cleats. It doesn't hold the boards lined up fore-and-aft, and, if they're left down off the wind, they're apt to kite out off the guards and skitter along the surface. When the boat skids sideways, one board will swing back in with a bump and a jerk. I've known a boat with this arrangement to be capsized by the jolt in a hard jibe, but it's not hard to take precautions.

The boat is too high-sided to row comfortably from a sitting position, so I've marked the locks for rowing standing, facing forward. This isn't an efficient way to row far, but it's very good for seeing where the rocks are in a narrow entrance. It used to be the standard method in Maine, where the coast has a lot in common with the Inland Sea. The oars are shown with a joint, to be taken apart and stowed in the footwell, but I'd

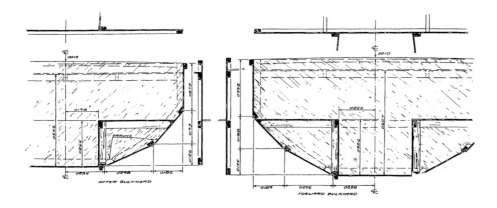

think about using one-piece oars and stowing them out along the boomkin over the stern.

For longer distances, a yuloh would be less tiring. One reason the rudder is mounted on a skeg is to allow plenty of fin area aft with the rudder pinned, to keep the tail from wagging the dog when sculling. The boat could be sculled with a cockpit shelter rigged, but I'd keep the rowing arrangement shown because it allows quicker and more certain maneuvering.

The cat-yawl rig allows the boat to heave to with her bow well up to the sea. The big spritsail is powerful for its heeling effect. With no boom to trip the boat, it's especially good in squally weather. The fall of the snotter is brought back to the cockpit so it can be freshened as it stretches, to keep the peak of the sail set up tight. The worst fault of a boomless spritsail shows up when you run free: The sheet doesn't control the peak of the sprit, which twists forward of the mast and rolls the boat to windward as well as losing drive.

The guy to the peak will keep the sprit from going forward of the beam. Its effectiveness is limited by the sail bellying out below the sprit, but the guy will help somewhat and not be much in the way. It will help to get hold of the peak when furling the sail.

The reef by folding the peak down to the tack has been tested. The reduced sail is not close-winded, but eases an overpowered boat dramatically. If you needed to sail in a really hard chance, a step and partner chock (not shown on the plans) would allow stepping the mizzen at the forward end of the cockpit with the mainsail furled or, better, with the mainmast unstepped. The tiny sail, 2.25 square meters, won't give enough thrust to drive the boat to windward, but she would go along under control reaching and running in a gale of wind.

This craft would make a good ship's boat with lifeboat capabilities. Compared with a liferaft, her ability to sail a shipwrecked crew to safety is something to set against her liability to damage in a heavy-weather launching. She would tow lightly behind a cruiser too small to take her on board, and it's to be noted that some 17th- and 18th-century explorers, Hudson for one, habitually towed sizable boats.

Swallows, Amazons, and Arthur Ransome

For those who don't know Arthur Ransome's books, they're about several families of children who go camping in sailing dinghies on a fictional lake resembling Windermere in the north of England. Later books place them on the Norfolk Broads, the Thames estuary, and elsewhere. There are 12 of the books.

The dinghies are between 13 and 14 feet long, lapstrake with full lines in the usual British fashion of the 1920s and before. They all have standing-lug cat rigs. *Amazon* and *Scarab* are centerboarders; *Swallow* has a shallow keel and is substantially ballasted—a dangerous boat by current standards, but they had a different attitude when these books were plotted. The father of "the Swallows," a Royal Navy officer on foreign service, wires his approval of the children's camping enterprise: "Better drowned than duffers. If not duffers, won't drown."

Ransome was a foreign correspondent for the *Manchester Guardian*, specializing in revolutionary Russia. He had no visible political preferences, but he became controversial by reporting that Churchill's counterrevolutionary policy was not working, and became suspect by close acquaintance with Lenin and other leading Bolsheviks. He also worked in Egypt, and in China during the warlord era. The character of "Captain Flint" in the books is a self-portrait. He wrote 50 or 60 books, mostly transient, but he knew that the children's books were his lasting monument.

Part Five

For Moorings and Private Landings

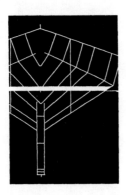

27 *Boy's Launch*

14'0" × 6'7"

Dear Phil:

Last spring I took my 10-year-old nephew along when I went to work on my Herreshoff Fish sloop. Young Blue hadn't been off exploring the yard long before he came to drag me off to the pier. "Uncle Dicky," he panted, "I've found the neatest boat!"

Nestled among the nondescript dinks was the yard's towboat, a cute little inboard launch, maybe 12 or 14 feet long, steered by a side tiller. She had a nice samson post aft and a big bow fender, both of which Blue eyed longingly.

One by one, he elaborated all the things he could do with the boat: tow his sister's Bluejay out to the starting line; fish the tidal rips off Sheffield Island; drag logs and things around the cove for his dad; take his mom and her friends out birdwatching.

Phil, could you sketch a boy's launch along the lines of a yawlboat of the type the coasting schooners use? The criteria would be straightforward: She should be pretty (since our yawlboat needn't live in davits, she could be stretched out a bit for either better looks or a smoother run); she should be able, so we need not worry about the fishing trips to the tidal rips; she needn't be particularly fast, 6 knots or so would do, but she should slip along smoothly. Accommodations can also be modest. She should be able to carry a bunch of people for short distances, but only four or so for any real outing. She should have a locker for flares and life jackets, and room under the floorboards for a pair of anchors. I favor plank-on-frame construction and diesel power plants; and I'm sure Blue would be disappointed without the samson post and bow fender.

Richard Trask

Dear Richard:

I empathize with this wish list. My first reaction was to point to the Molly's Cove Quahaug (15'11" × 7'6"), but I guess you found her a little too big and not pretty enough. I need frequent reminding that technical considerations shouldn't automatically override aesthetics. Quahaug was designed to be as able, fast, and floaty as a 10-h.p. diesel launch could be. I'm proud of the design, which runs and handles rough water better than any boat of that type I know of, but I have to agree that she doesn't have the endearing prettiness you're thinking of. The square transom with low and hard bilges is businesslike but not graceful.

I've drawn a shape with more curves for you, with the quarters of the stern elegantly lifted. The reflections and shadows around this stern ought to be very pleasant to see. The deeper, sculptured underbody is attractive when the boat is out of the water. The penalty is that she won't be able to leave her stern wave behind as Quahaug can. The 6 knots you mention seems a modest demand, but in fact a boat this shape, not much over 13 feet waterline, will have trouble making 6, regardless of power. When she gets near 5 knots she'll be pulling a steep, rolling wave behind her. Speeding up the propeller will make the waves deeper and steeper, without much increase in speed. *Unity speed*, the square root of the waterline length, is just under 3.7 knots. *Wave speed*, nominally as fast as a full-displacement hull this length can go, is 4.95 knots. If you towed her at, say, 10 knots, she'd be forced up out of the water with her bow cocked up 30 degrees and the stern wave right up to the rail. She has enough bearing in her quarters to go straight, but the effect would be undignified.

This boat's speed, 4 or 5 knots, is useful in plenty of places. Sailboat people get around contentedly at such speeds. Fast boats in crowded places are unpopular even with each other. The trouble with that argument is that a good fast boat can go slowly almost as well as a good slow boat. Nevertheless, the boat I've drawn for you would be handier and more economical at 4 knots than she would be if shaped to make 40.

Though I agree that cold reasoning doesn't have to prevail over romance, I'd still like a functional rationalization for the pretty, low-speed design. The suggested engine placement is one. A fast boat has to carry her engine well aft, where it's obtrusive in one way or another. In this low-speed boat there's little harm in putting the engine forward: partly because the engine is light compared with one in a fast boat; partly because buoyancy was taken out of the stern while I was making it prettier; also, the space the engine takes up in the bow wasn't very useful to begin with. The bow installation permits a tight bulkhead between engine and crew, and the tiller is as far from it as it can be. A couple of people sitting aft by the tiller ought to be able to talk without raising their voices.

What's more, the long shaft, mostly inside the boat, would lend itself to an effective soft mounting for the engine. You could put a thrust bearing just inboard of the stuffing box and universal joints ahead of that, and let the engine wobble around on soft springs that soak up all the vibration, as is done in automobiles. I suspect that tuning such an arrangement is not as easy as the auto engineers make it look, but it could be done if someone knowledgeable took the trouble. The reward would be a magic-carpet effect with the means of propulsion invisible and inaudible—something that can't be done yet (or at any rate is not done) in fast boats.

The off-center propeller isn't relevant to the forward engine placement, but it has possibilities. I developed this prop arrangement for auxiliary sailboats with shoal rudders, which don't work well if they have an eddy-making opening in front of them. The

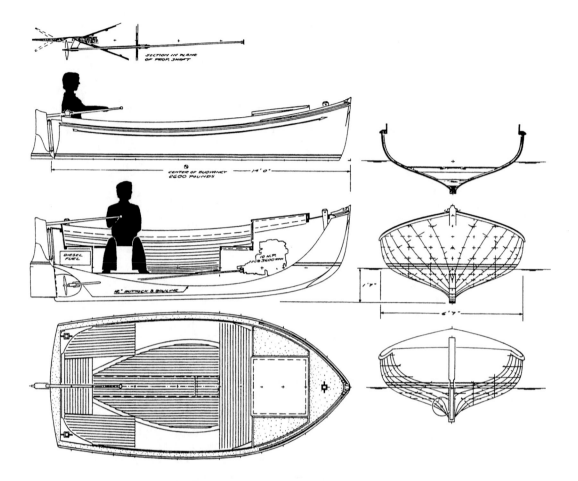

recess carved into, but not quite through, the skeg allows the prop to be mounted close to the centerline at a gentle angle. The critical point is to make the blade tips pass the deadwood abaft the deepest part of the recess so that water is supplied under pressure at the point where the propeller is accelerating the stream. I've designed about 20 of these installations, including several around here where the owners could rub my nose in any defects. None have. The boats steer well, under either sail or power; they show no imbalance going either ahead or astern; they turn equally well either way, including from a standstill; and they don't vibrate much, I suppose because the rudder isn't enveloped in turbulence from the propeller.

It first occurred to me that the idea could be useful in a straight motorboat when I was designing a lobsterboat for a local man. He wanted the prop in a cage, as most do, to keep out pot warp. I suggested that we build her with the prop alongside a solid deadwood on the side away from the hauler. The lobsterman wasn't willing to chance the experiment, since he had his heart's blood in the boat and I won't ever guarantee anything—not even that the boat will float the right way up. But, in fact, I think it would be a safe bet. Whether there'd be any noticeable improvement in speed or handling is doubtful, but it would be nice to have one side of the boat thoroughly protected from the meatchopper.

In traditional wood construction there are some advantages to the arrangement: the long bore through the shaft log is eliminated, as is the problem of getting the floor bolts past the shaft without using an inordinately thick deadwood or cutting the joining feathers. I suppose this kind of consideration is becoming esoteric, but there are still plenty of boatshops that build that way.

As long as there are carpenters working with it, carvel planking on bent frames will be an efficient way to build one or two boats. I share your liking for it. If you want the ultimate in style, it's the only way to go. There's no way to show off equivalent niceties in plastic or metal. In a small one-off, it's possible to get natural crooks for things like quarter knees, though I think laminations look just as pretty. I've indicated how the seats and sole could be made up in narrow strakes. Years ago I indulged myself in a rowboat with thwarts built this way, using some 40-year-old Burma teak, varnished. I'm not usually a varnish enthusiast, but there's nothing like dark old teak, well varnished, for a rich effect. The bleached teak stuck on fiberglass boats today just looks neglected; I'd rather have no wood.

Nicely lined-off carvel planking is elegant enough to be faked on fiberglass hulls, but the ones I've seen had been scribed by people who didn't understand the principle of planking. It helps if, as here, the shape of the boat has been developed with wood planking in mind—sheer, deck plan, and sectional shape matched up to allow the planks to spring around without undue spiling or edge-setting. The fair curve of the deck line as viewed from ahead is proof that the sheer won't show hard places from any angle. Many will think the stern would be prettier if the quarters were rolled in to form an elliptical transom and deck plan. I grant the point and would be willing to design a stern like that if you prefer it, but I have a mild preference for the shape that doesn't torment the wood so much.

I did try a fiberglass version of this boat with a round stern copied from John Lindsay's masterly treatments. Mine don't seem to come out as well as his, and it bothers me that a good many of his boats have spoilers built into the round sterns to stabilize them when they're towed. This design would be well suited to fiberglass as it is, if demand justified the tooling. It could also be built cold-molded, glued-strip, or lapstrake.

You're right about the tiller steering, but I'd skip the wheel forward. I once spent a couple of days with an Edson catalog, designing a hookup of my boat's outboard rudder to a console. Eventually I added up the components with a price list, and it occurred to me that if we bolted a long timber to the rudderhead, a push on the timber would turn the rudder. This insight saved $1,600 in 1978. The arrangement shown here is supposed to minimize the drawbacks of tillers. This one is stiff and fixed in the vertical plane, to hold up an extended arm and steady a standing helmsman. The height brings the end level with average buttocks, so it can be gripped there and free both hands for passing lines. For long runs, the forward-facing seat allows holding a course with one arm lying comfortably along the length of the tiller. With the engine forward, two people sitting together in the stern won't make the boat drag its tail.

This boat isn't well adapted to side-lever steering because of the sharp rise of her floors at the sides. I like the method in principle, but the usual hookup has too much slop for my taste.

The one thing I haven't done, that you laid stress on, is to show the bow fender. I think this ought to be removable, to show the nice sculpturing of her stemhead and bow chocks.

28 *Plywood 12¹/₂*

16'0" × 12'6" × 5'8" × 2'9"

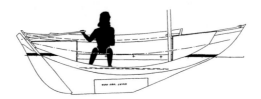

Dear Phil:

Your catboat design, Bobcat, was very pretty; I now hope that the building method can be applied to the Herreshoff 12½. If done in plywood, this classic design would then be available to amateur builders at a reasonable cost in materials and time.

The 12½ proposed would have to sail well for her size, but be reasonably simple to build, while similar in size and layout to the original. She must look classy in her own right. For safety, I'd vote for flotation in the ends of the hull and ballasting to closely approximate the behavior of the original in a seaway.

This is the definitive daysailer for those of us who prefer keelboats. I look forward to seeing what you can do with her.

Chuck Tringali, Millersville, Maryland

Dear Chuck:

It's hard to imagine anybody looking at a Herreshoff 12½ without smiling—except maybe Nathanael Herreshoff himself. Yet, while the record suggests that he was a cold-blooded calculating machine, consider the names he gave his personal boats: *Alerion, Swiftsure, Delight, Helianthus, Dilemma, Sabrina*. None of them are what I'd expect from a man said to never smile. Another anomaly is the 12½.

It's ironic that this modest design is Captain Nat's living monument. His engineering feats are as dead as so many triremes, yet the little sloop that looks as if a hundred other men might have designed it, but which in fact only Herreshoff could turn into a

masterpiece, sails on as Bill Harding's Doughdish. This fiberglass replica is a greater tribute to Herreshoff's memory than any museum piece. The first time I saw one, I remember thinking at once that Captain Nat would have nodded curt approval of the boat and the reasoning behind it.

There is, of course, no way to duplicate the intricate shape of the 12½ in sheet plywood, and I have not tried. One reason I've traced off the full body plan for each end of the boat is to emphasize that the shape has to be dramatically different to accommodate the way plywood behaves. The hollow flare to a full deckline in the bow has to go. To balance that, both to the eye and for the sake of the boat's action, the stern is narrower. Neither end will be as handsome as the original when seen in three dimensions with shadows and reflections.

To compensate, I made her lower-sided, increasing the angles of the raking ends. The sleeker profile is supposed to distract the eye from the coarse sectional shape. It will work from many angles but not all. This will be a very good-looking boat as long as there isn't a Doughdish alongside.

The reduced freeboard means that the plywood boat will get her rail down sooner than the Herreshoff. I made the cockpit coaming higher to get back some of the height. There is plenty of buoyancy in the end compartments to float the boat. Some of the original boats didn't have this. Waldo Howland's *A Life in Boats* has an anecdote about a 12½ that filled and sank while racing; the way he treats the incident suggests that it wasn't extraordinary. People used to be more casual about boats that could be dangerous when mishandled than we're expected to be now. They treated foundering potential about the same way we do the consequences of 40-knot speeds and meatchopper propellers.

The plywood boat is a little stiffer (has more initial stability) than the 12½, partly because she doesn't have the hollow garboards, buoyancy of which, down low, takes away some stability. A good part of the fin here would be hollow with plywood walls, free-flooding. This adds some ballast effect, but it's designed that way mostly to eliminate a mass of solid timber that would shrink and swell, and to make it quicker to build. It allows short keelbolts, saving the long bores that many amateur builders find difficult.

The ballast casting shown is 100 pounds lighter than Herreshoff's. My thought was to save that much cost, but I'm in two minds about it now. I know of many boats that were improved, sometimes dramatically, by giving them more ballast, and very few that were helped by reducing ballast. In a finished design I would think about putting back the 100 pounds, or more.

The square "garboard" of the plywood boat adds some wetted surface. In theory this should make the boat slower in light air, but I've grown skeptical about reductions in wetted surface. The resistance is real enough, but it's hard to reduce it without increasing some other drag. If you cut down a boat's effective lateral plane to reduce wetted surface, and as a consequence end up with a bigger leeway angle so that the boat goes through the water more crabwise, the tradeoff is often a bad one. The late Howard Chapelle tried to tell me this many years ago but didn't convince me at the time because I thought he was overly concerned with maximum, rather than average, speeds.

A sailboat keel is often thought of as analogous to an aircraft's wing, but there's a significant difference. All aircraft are powered (gliders are powered by gravity), whereas a sailboat has to operate efficiently with power input close to nil. It's possible that the flat keel forced on this design by the structural material is not bad for her performance.

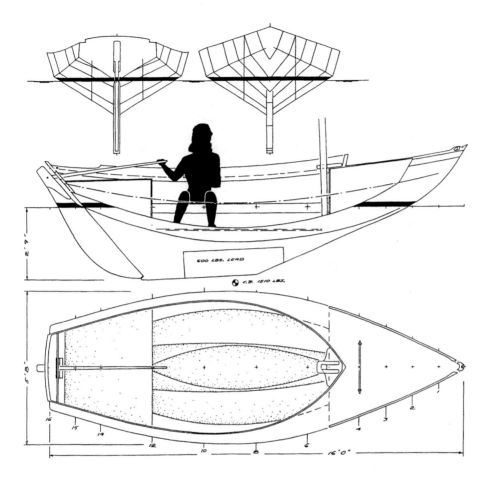

The original 12½ was gaff-rigged. It was meant, among other things, to be a school for bigger racing boats, all of which then had gaff rigs. Sometime in the 1920s the boat was offered with a jibheaded rig for the same reason. I understand that the jibheaded boats proved to sail exactly even with the gaff boats, with clubs like Beverly of Sippican, which had both, starting them all together as one class. Later still, the Herreshoff Manufacturing Company brought out another version with a wishbone boom, but this one didn't take. Wishbones are frustrating in boats that have their shrouds set up abaft the mast to act as backstays. Off the wind, the lee arm of the wishbone lands on the lee shroud long before the sail is squared out.

I adopted the jibheaded rig for this proposal because its rigging is a little simpler, and because most people now think a gaff is an affectation. I have no strong feelings one way or the other, aside from irritation at the falsity of most objections to the gaff. I do notice that it's getting difficult and expensive to buy sail track (a Herreshoff invention, by the way) for wooden masts, and would think that a point in favor of the gaff rig.

I haven't attempted here to make the rig coincide exactly with the 12½ rig, but it may be possible to buy complete off-the-shelf sets of Bullseye (the Bullseye is another fiberglass version of the 12½, more candidly adapted to its material than the

Doughdish) spars, sails, and rigging from Cape Cod Shipbuilding Co. of Wareham, Massachusetts. All these boats are about as simple to rig as is possible if you want a sloop.

The $12\frac{1}{2}$ was intended to be cheap to produce in the first place. The original batch of 19 boats, in 1914, cost $420 each, which was extortionate and upwards of double what they would have cost from highly respectable builders elsewhere. The Herreshoffs had worked into a position from which they could sell their boats to people who either didn't care what they cost, or actually valued a high price for its own sake as a status symbol. Nice work if you can get it, but the Herreshoffs had an expensive plant to maintain and tricky problems of production continuity. I think they took the chance offered by the order for the $12\frac{1}{2}$ fleet to develop a stock boat, something that would be economical to build on speculation, to smooth out the spurts and slacks of custom work. Hence the simple rig and, by Herreshoff standards, simple hull. It would have been business suicide for Herreshoff to put out a production boat that looked crude in any respect, but they had the tooling and the experienced craftsmen to build economically apparently expensive features like the hollow garboards and the characteristic molded sheerstrake. The inherent economies in the proportions and arrangement of the boat could be sold on a "less is more" argument.

I think the savings in this plywood imitation are less than you may expect, and that it makes sense only for a home builder. Lacking the tooling, it would take him forever to build an exact copy of the $12\frac{1}{2}$, no matter how skilled he was. The acceptance of the comparatively crude shape probably just about compensates for the costs of one-off construction. Any savings would lie in discounting labor time.

When I worked out the plywood imitation of the Beetle Cat (Bobcat, see Chapter 21), one of the main objects was to make a boat fit for trailer use. The $12\frac{1}{2}$ is too deep and heavy to be a good trailer boat in any case. The looks of the plywood boat don't match those of the Doughdish, or Bullseye, but the nice handling qualities and comfortable cockpit are preserved. Possibly something like this might serve a small boatshop in the same way that the $12\frac{1}{2}$ served Herreshoff, as a salable fill-in between major orders.

29 *Keel Daysailer*

18'10" × 5'6" × 2'6"

Dear *SBJ*:

Daysailing has always been my prime boating interest. This interest hasn't changed at all in my recent retirement, but the boat that will suit me has.

When I was in the Monday-through-Friday work force, sailing was a weekend activity. There were always friends along to share the pleasure of sailing and the work of making her ready and buttoning her up afterward. Now, with much more time available for sailing, there will frequently be only one pair of hands to do what two or three pairs used to share.

As a consequence, I've been conjuring up a specification for the ideal singlehanded daysailer—a maxi-pleasure, mini-fuss boat.

The first pleasure element I wish to maximize is the length of the sailing season. The boat will be kept on the Yeocomico River, a tributary of the tidewater Potomac, which in its turn is an arm of the Chesapeake. A long sailing season is practicable in the Bay, though winds are brisk and chilly in spring and fall. The boat must be suitable for cold-weather sailing—that is, too stiff for capsize to be a reasonable fear, and dry for all hands. This requirement calls for a ballasted keelboat with fairly good freeboard. Although the boat must be easy to sail alone, it will also have to accommodate four or five people on occasion. Length in the 15-to-18-foot range seems about right, though it could go to 20 feet in the extreme, depending on the hull form.

The first fuss-free requirement is a self-bailing cockpit. Bailing rainwater or striking and rigging a boom tent are a drag on sailing.

The next fuss to eliminate is the jib. Handling jibsheets and tiller simultaneously is more work than one pair of hands needs. Even a self-tending jib is still one more sail to hank and unhank, fold and stow. I'd like a cat-rigged boat, if you please.

Even without a jib, there will be times when the helmsman has to leave the tiller, to adjust the outhaul or open a can of beer, for instance. Such activities are made almost impossible if the tiller swings 90 degrees the instant it's released. A reasonably placid helm is a must. The rudder can be attached to the keel or to a fair-sized skeg, but balanced spades are out. To kill the tiller problem for sure, I'd like a tiller comb.

Although simplicity of gear and ease of handling are the main target, these virtues are not to be gained at the expense of good performance. I don't want a racing machine, but the boat should be lively and fun to sail—sailing is the point, after all! I'd like the boat to be fairly close-winded, with a light and sensitive helm. It should also move on a light evening breeze, while being capable of sailing reefed in 25 knots of wind and handling a foot and a half of Chesapeake chop without ingesting much of it. Reefing is to be quick and simple. Because of these performance requirements, oddball rigs are out. I believe that the jibheaded cat will give the best combination of simplicity and enjoyment.

I'd like the rig's aspect ratio to be medium to high. I welcome your recommendations as to whether full, partial, or no battens at all would be best. I am not sure how valuable a curved roach is when it's not free (unrated) sail area for racing, and battens can be a nuisance. A four-part mainsheet suits me fine, as I'm at the opposite end of the physical spectrum from the average gorilla, and although cam cleats seem fairly trustworthy for the mainsheet, I don't want them anywhere else.

I dislike boats that become hard-nosed when heeled, so beam should be kept moderate. I'd like to keep the boat at my pier, where the water is 3 feet deep. I could keep it at a mooring, but that is much less convenient. A mooring means a dinghy, and a dinghy means bailing, and—there we go again.

To assure minimum maintenance, the boat should be of foam-cored fiberglass. This seems to eliminate constraints on underwater shape, and I have no preferences in that regard. The required load capacity and draft will dictate shape to a large degree, I expect.

Aesthetics are important to me, and I have fairly strong preferences. Underwater, where function is everything, modern shapes are fine. But above the water I prefer a traditional look. I want a springy sheer, with stem and stern profiles that fit the rig. I have an aversion to the tumblehome stem of Cape Cod cats, and think that either a spoon or clipper bow looks incongruous on a cat. A slightly raked and slightly convex stem, with a bit of turn down near the waterline, would be just right. The transom would be well-raked and have a nicely curved shape. Either a transom or counter stern is fine with me, as long as it looks like it belongs with the bow. I'd like enough freeboard to assure comfortable seating in the self-bailing cockpit, with a bit of flare up forward to keep spray where it belongs.

Amenities should be kept simple, with vented and lockable stowage forward under a deck or cuddy. I am not going camp-cruising and only need to stow life jackets and other paraphernalia for daysailing. There should be some wood aboard to avoid a sterile look, but oiled teak coaming and hatch trim and a varnished tiller is about as much as I want to care for. I want no specific provision for an engine. However, if sculling is practicable, I'll need a lock and oar, and a place to stow them.

I can visualize this little boat at my pier on a summer evening, with an hour or two of daylight still left. There is enough breeze for a pleasant sail. We step aboard, snap off the sail cover, untie the stops, sway on the halyard, secure, cast off. Elapsed time: maybe three or four minutes, with the same time spent on our return.

Neil Wilson, Lottsburg, Virginia

Dear Mr. Wilson:

I'm heartily with you in everything you write about how to get the most pleasure out of a sailboat. It troubles me whenever I notice the time that goes into getting ready to have some sport. Not only sailing. A friend once had a two-seat high-performance sailplane. I flew with him sometimes, once on a long cross-country flight that I treasure in memory. I never argued with his claim that soaring was a greater thrill than sailing, but it appalled me to see how much trouble he had to invest for each hour of flight. Not for me—I even have my doubts about the overhead in sailing. Rowing boats and canoes have a still-better potential for reducing downtime. In my own case, I have trouble making time to exercise, so a boat that combines recreation with a controlled workout is very desirable. If I didn't have this obsession with paper and ink, I might feel differently about sails.

I started this study with a midsection, and soon concluded that $5\frac{1}{2}$ feet of breadth was about right. The cartoon figures show why. The live ballast is in an effective position without gymnastics.

It then seemed to me that a self-draining footwell of comfortable depth put the seat too high. The higher the seats, the less effective live ballast is when the boat is heeled— hence the way crews of Stars and other boats that race at sharp angles of heel are called on to climb out and wrap themselves down over the turn of the weather bilge.

The height of deck shown here looks like the best compromise between keeping the crew weight low and allowing enough freeboard for her to heel a lot without burying herself. The light crew does imply heeling, since a fixed-ballast keel functions, as ballast, only when the boat heels appreciably. The hull shown has about 10 inches of freeboard along the sides, a foot to the centerline of the crowned deck. The part above that is a bulwark for shelter, spray suppression, and security when moving around on deck. Incidentally, it produces the traditional sheer.

There will have to be scuppers in the bulwarks at the sides, stem, and transom to let rain run off. I'd have flaps or check valves, or plain plugs for these scuppers, except those in the transom, so they won't spit in a chop.

The open footwell or standing room is contrary to instructions. I show it for its comfortable depth and for the handy access to the space under the deck. I have trouble envisioning a hatch that would allow the 8-foot sculling sweep to be stowed below, for instance. I thought this well could have a solid cover that would be light and easy to put on and off to keep rain out. You could leave it on the wharf when you went sailing. A fabric cover with two or three stiffening battens might not be much of a nuisance if it had some shock cord worked into its edges to snap around a flange in the coaming like a kayak's spray skirt.

A compromise would be a watertight tub to fit down into the opening, with a flange to fit over the coaming. The tub would be hinged to tip up and dump accumulated water onto the deck. Without an overboard drain, it could be as deep as we liked.

Some Mediterranean beach boats have ingenious overlapping hatches that hinge outboard. The underside is built to form a shaped seat on the deck when they're swung open. They're neat if well done, but in this case I think it would be more satisfactory to have slatted seats loose on the deck to keep the crew out of the damp. In heavy weather when there's no use trying to keep dry, these can be kept racked where you won't stub your toe on them.

Having selected $5\frac{1}{2}$ feet of breadth, close to 19 feet of length is needed to carry a

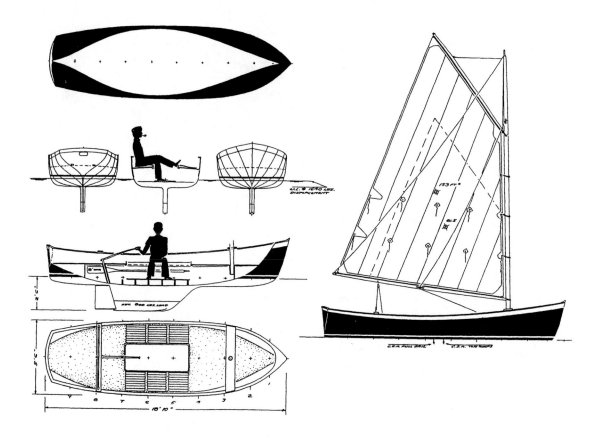

ballast keel that will give real power to carry sail without depending on crew weight, and to carry the five people mentioned, without feeling sluggish. The 800 pounds of lead shown ought to give her good momentum to carry her way through stays in a chop.

I agree pretty well with what you say about proportioning boats to behave well when heeled. This hull, with its sharp waterlines aft and lifted quarters, won't go by the head as it heels. I'm hoping that the wineglass shape of the transom and its plan-view curve will please you. If you would like it raked more, I'll oblige, but I like transoms nearly upright, to take all the waterline length I can get for a given overall length. I think this would be a graceful shape, as I've tried to convey with the full body plans and the view from below. The white area in the latter is the waterplane, not the boottop shown in the other views.

The flare of the bow is moderate, like everything else about this design. With her easy entrance lines and the high sweep of the sheer, I'd expect a lot of spray to drop back without reaching the rail. I'm in two minds about whether she'd be improved by flaring the bulwarks a little more through the midbody, keeping the deck breadth about the same. The sitting position when heeled would be more comfortable. She has power enough not to feel flighty when a guest steps on the rail, which is about the only drawback to flare in a boat of this type. She looks a trifle pinched amidships in the plan views. Perhaps 6 inches more breadth at the rail?

The bottom is dead flat over the keel, the most powerful shape to carry sail on any given displacement. The shallower the body, the less overall draft is needed to make the lateral plane effective. You can see at a glance that 2-foot 6-inch draft allows ample fin area. She'd hang on with as much as 6 inches less, though you'd notice the difference at times. It's been established in recent years that sharp deadrise is not a good idea if you don't need to stow inside ballast. The flat bottom also produces a good displacement distribution around the hull-fin interface without any Coke-bottle distortion.

It seems to me that rudders hung on the fin, as here, give smoother, more pleasant steering feel than when they're separated. In this case, the tiller comes just where it's wanted for good crew weight placement. Three or four types of tiller combs could be arranged. I have an ordinary pin rack in my boat, but some kind of clamp allows more delicate adjustment.

I like cat rigs, especially when they're stepped in long hulls with plenty of buoyancy and deck space ahead of the mast. They have a problem with lee helm when you pull down deep reefs. The cure is to carry the breadth of the sail well aloft. It can be done with a fully battened batwing sail, and full battens have the added advantage that the sail can be luffed without slatting hard. The battens are less of a nuisance with Dacron sails than they were in the days when they had to be taken out of the cotton sails before you could go home. On paper the battens can be laid out to allow the sail to be lowered and furled without detaching it from the mast. Some people swear by them, but my own experience is that the best-designed battens are more trouble than no battens.

I suggest that we go back to the gaff rig. The mast is 21 feet 4 inches overall, as opposed to 25 feet 9 inches for a jibheaded sail without battens of about the same area. The center of sail area is 9 inches lower with the gaff sail; 13 inches lower with two reefs in both. The center of sail area shifts 9 inches forward with two reefs in the gaff sail; with two reefs in the jibheader, 14 inches. There's not much doubt that in strong winds the gaffheader would be faster, more weatherly, and easier to control.

It's a great pity that racing rules have almost always been biased against the gaff sails. Aerodynamicists often point out that a triangular airfoil is not an efficient shape, even disregarding the fact that a gaff sail set with hoops and jaws streams from the mast better than a jibheaded sail on a track or in a slot. I would give quite a lot to know what gaff cats would be like if racing rules hadn't discouraged their development. Perhaps I wouldn't have liked the outcome any better than Francis Herreshoff liked what came of his inventions that allowed big jibs to be carried to windward!

However that may be, I'd say that the gaff sail meets the Little Fuss test. It will furl in an even cylinder, not all bunched up at the luff. Three or four gaskets will hold it neatly; one will do for a temporary furl. A shock-cord furling line along the boom would be even faster. The lowered sail hangs at a handy height by the topping lift at the end of the boom, with a single lazyjack on each side. The whole bundle can be allowed to swing outboard for hoisting with the wind abeam. Halyards are single-part; that is, short. (I once had the use of a cat with 600 square feet of sail and four-part halyards. The falls piled up about knee deep by the time the sail was set.) Hoist with the gaff horizontal, gripping both halyards at once. It doesn't matter which side of the topping lift the gaff picks, and the gaff is always between the lazyjacks. Belay the throat halyard when it comes up two blocks, and peak the gaff to taste.

To lower sail, reverse the process. Gaff sails aren't immune to jams, but they average fewer than tracked jibheaders, to say nothing of sails set in luff slots or with double luffs. You can count on getting the peak down in a hurry, which is something when you've underestimated the squall. In this proposed design, the halyards would belay on the mast thwart, giving the most direct possible lead and a secure position while your hands are busy.

I show the boom on the foot of the sail, as it makes for a quicker furl than a sprit boom or a wishbone. The long traveler horse for the sheet holds the boom down close-hauled off to a beam reach. The sheet is four-part; I'd have it double-ended with two single blocks on the same bail on the boom. I indicate a wire vang to hold the boom down when broad-reaching or running. Without this a conventional boom will lift at the clew and let the peak of the sail fall off, killing the power of the sail and tending to roll the boat. The trouble has nothing to do with the gaff. The top of a jibheaded sail will do the same. The problem is the boom in either case. This vang would have some kind of purchase on the end, four- or six-part, to hook onto the mast just above the deck. In light weather it can clip up to the boom jaws out of the way.

As for finish, I've assumed that the railcaps and the two thwarts, the tiller, and the spars would be bright wood, since you want her yachty. It would look nice, and make good footing, to lay teak veneer over the fiberglass deck with narrow planks nibbed into a covering board.

30 *Staysail Cat*

31'0" × 6'1" × 5'0" (original design)
(CorSair 24: 23'6" × 5'10" × 3'4"; see author's note, below)

Dear *SBJ*:

I have often read about boats that Bolger has designed to fill the requirements of sailors who are unable to fill their need from production builders. I presently own one of his Instant Boats—Teal. She is a delight, fun to row, fun to sail, easy to take care of, and great for my 100-pound daughter.

My needs, however, are different. I dream of the fastest, cheapest, stiffest, simplest daysailer ever built, a boat that will be close-winded and capable of great speed around a triangular course. She might be developed from Zephyr (a skim plywood 19-footer; plans from Dynamite Payson) or the Folding Schooner (an ultralight 31-foor schooner with a hinge in the middle; plans from Dynamite Payson). She might have an arc bottom if it doesn't cost too much. A metal keel with a bulb on the bottom might give enough stability, and a conventional masthead rig should help her weatherliness. But no jumper stays, no running backstays, and no mast bending.

The cockpit should be deep enough to make you feel as though you are sitting in the boat instead of on it—a Herreshoff-type cockpit. Flotation can be in the ends. No cabin required. No engine is required.

The ability to singlehand is important, but for racing I'll use a crew of three or four. Feel free to add winches if required, based on the size of the sail plan. I want to use the boat for afternoon races and casual sailing in moderate winds and smooth seas. A length of 35 to 40 feet should generate exciting sailing. She can be built of wood or 'glass, depending on how much money I'd spoil.

Bob Pearlman, Ridgewood, New Jersey

Dear Mr. Pearlman:

First, some history: There used to be a fleet of day racers hereabouts called I-boats or Class I. The proper name was Massachusetts Bay Yacht Racing Association 18 Foot Waterline Restricted Knockabouts, so they had to be called something for short. They were built to a measurement rule made up in the 1890s and were about the most competitive class in the country for eight or ten years. Charles Francis Adams, for instance, had several of them—a new, up-to-date design every year or so.

The boats gradually got kinkier, as happens when designers try to build the most boat inside a set of restrictions. By 1908 they were all about 31 feet long on deck, still with 18-foot waterlines. They were rigged as gaff sloops, with sail area limited to 450 square feet. They had big fin keels, about like the one shown here except that the roots of the fins were faired into the hulls with planked-down fillets. For a while most of them had separate rudders like today's racing boats, but toward the end they went back to rudders hung on the fins as shown here. I'll be interested to see if this happens again in the next few years.

They gradually went out of fashion as the top sailors went into other classes. The last of them were still racing at Sandy Bay Yacht Club in Rockport, Massachusetts, after the Second World War. I once saw one of them humiliate the North American Champion 5.5-Meter over a triangular course. They finally all perished of old age, but (the point of all this preamble) many people still remember their speed and power with nostalgia. Even the most extreme modern keel racers look like bulky cruisers alongside them.

This suggests that we can get the sensations you're envisioning without going longer than 31 feet, which happens to be a convenient length for plywood construction (three butts).

The I-boats were essentially flat-bottomed, though the bilges were rounded off and the sections had reverse curves over the keel. We don't have to respect the restriction to 18 feet waterline, so we can eliminate the rule-cheating hollows in the end profiles. The fairer sweep of the bottom will compensate for the square bilge. I don't think there's anything to be gained by an arc bottom. It would be structurally stiffer, but it's best to have a thick bottom anyway, and some stringers won't add much expense. It's my opinion that the vertical sides make the fastest boat as well as saving some time in assembly. In a boat as low-sided as this, with exaggerated tumblehome of the transom obscuring the rectangular stern sections, the boxy shape won't be very obtrusive. If you'd be happier with a little flare, I wouldn't give you much argument. I'd split the difference between the bottom and deck, making her slightly wider on deck and slightly narrower on the bottom.

Not all the old I-boats had trunks and cuddies, but all the late survivors did. I like the looks of it myself. It's handy for locked stowage, and I've slept a good many nights in such cuddies, dry and screened. Add a cockpit tent, and you'd have a weekender.

There's no doubt about the speed potential of keel sharpies. If you put an IOR-type sloop rig on this hull, you'd have a fast and weatherly boat. However, your stipulations about the rig touched a chord. I agree with you that bending masts in compression is undesirable, to put it mildly. But the fact is that a bendy-masted sloop will beat a stiff-masted sloop every time. We don't have to beat everything afloat, but you say you'd like all the speed you can get. This rig here, which I'd call a staysail cat, is what I think almost happened to masthead sloops at one time. Remember when the ocean racers

(text continued on page 153)

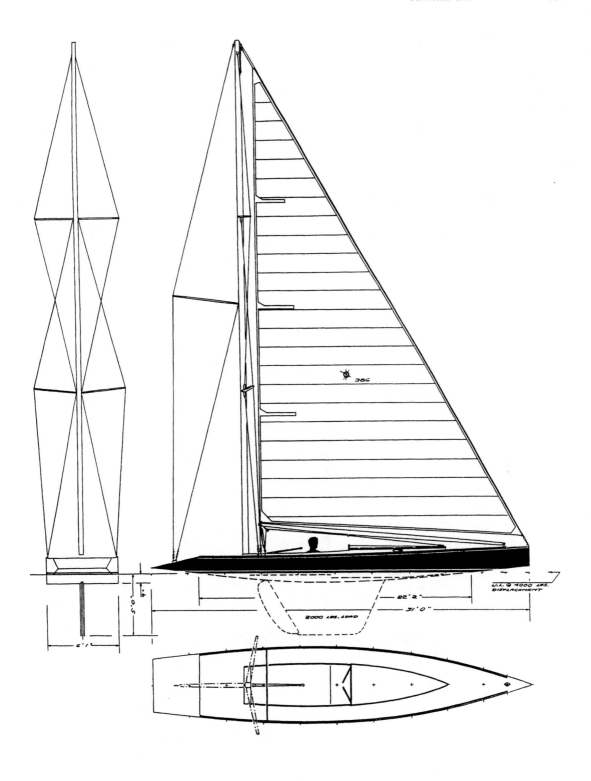

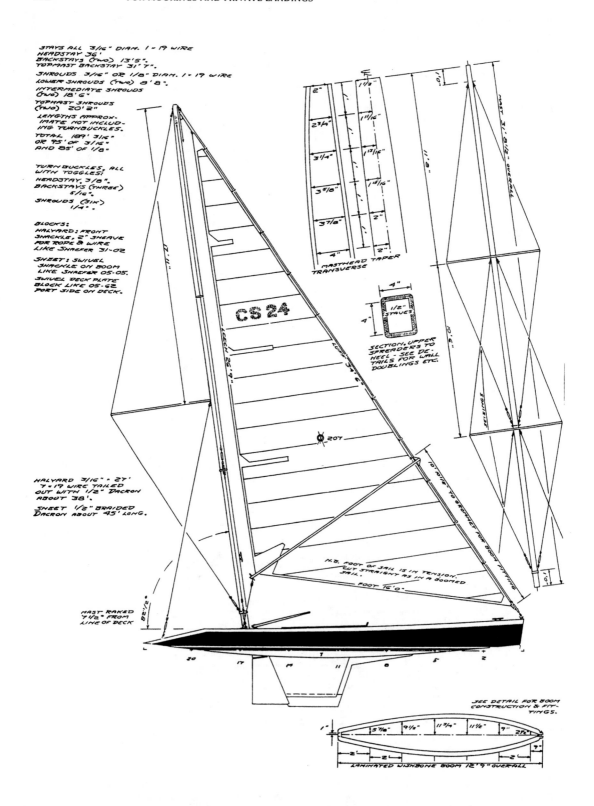

STAYS ALL 3/16" DIAM. 1-19 WIRE
HEADSTAY 36'
BACKSTAYS (TWO) 13'5".
TOPMAST BACKSTAY 31'7".

SHROUDS 3/16" OR 1/8" DIAM. 1-19 WIRE
LOWER SHROUDS (TWO) 8'8".
INTERMEDIATE SHROUDS
(TWO) 18'6".
TOPMAST SHROUDS
(TWO) 20'2".
LENGTHS APPROX-
IMATE NOT INCLUD-
ING TURNBUCKLES.
TOTAL 189' 3/16
OR 95' OF 3/16"
AND 85' OF 1/8"

TURNBUCKLES, ALL
WITH TOGGLES:
HEADSTAY, 3/8".
BACKSTAYS (THREE)
5/16".
SHROUDS (SIX)
1/4".

BLOCKS:
HALYARD: FRONT
SHACKLE, 2" SHEAVE
FOR ROPE & WIRE
LIKE SHAEFER 31-02

SHEET: SWIVEL
SHACKLE ON BOOM
LIKE SHAEFER 05-05.
SWIVEL DECK PLATE
BLOCK LIKE 05-62
PORT SIDE ON DECK.

HALYARD 3/16" × 27'
7×19 WIRE TAILED
OUT WITH 1/2" DACRON
ABOUT 38'.

SHEET 1/2" BRAIDED
DACRON ABOUT 45' LONG.

MAST RAKED
7 1/2" FROM
LINE OF DECK

CS24

207

MASTHEAD TAPER
TRANSVERSE

SECTION UPPER
SPREADERS TO
HEEL - SEE DE-
TAILS FOR WALL
DOUBLINGS ETC.

1/2" STAVES

N.B. FOOT OF SAIL IS IN TENSION.
CUT STRAIGHT AS IN A BOOMED
SAIL.
FOOT 16'0".

SEE DETAIL FOR BOOM
CONSTRUCTION & FIT-
TINGS.

LAMINATED WISHBONE BOOM 12'9" OVERALL

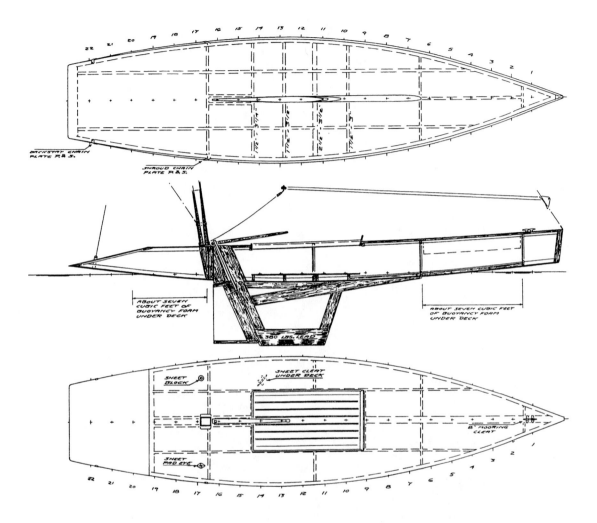

started to black-band their mainmasts farther and farther below the masthead? Finally, A. E. Luders had his *Storm* measured with no mainsail at all, and with that the rule-makers put a stop to the process, as they always do when somebody wins with anything they're not used to. It's quite possible that without the bugger factor in the CCA Rule, all the ocean racers would have had rigs something like this one, at least for a while. It's barely possible that the bendy-mast business would have been left to the dinghy racers.

However that may be, the idea of a staysail cat has intrigued some able designers. My own teacher, Nicholas Montgomery, built one about 1922, which he claimed was fast in light airs. Sherman Hoyt designed a Six-Meter called *Atrocia* with such a rig. She had a small sail set on her mast, making her what might be called a staysail cat-yawl. She wasn't a success, probably because in 1925 they couldn't get the long headstay tight enough. I've heard that Starling Burgess was interested in the rig, and just lately read that Ray Hunt was tinkering with an aft-mast International 110 in the last year of his life. Anything Hunt did was worth pondering. Incidentally, his work supports my opinion that sharpies are best without flaring sides.

CorSair 24

The main advantage of the rig is that the sail has a perfectly clear luff and perfect aerodynamics if you can make it hold its shape. That's why stiff-masted ocean racers had big jibs and small mainsails.

The secondary advantages are that the weight of the mast is aft, where it doesn't drug the boat's bow in a chop, and that the windage is aft, where it acts as a riding sail to steady the boat at anchor and keep her head up under bare poles.

This rig needs tremendous tension on the headstay, the luff of the sail, or both, as does any rig with a big staysail. Without such tension, say a couple of tons in this proposed boat (that's *initial* tension, what you screw in with the turnbuckles when you rig her), the luff will sag and the sail will bag in a good breeze.

Stepping the mast aft and setting no sail on it has great advantages in arranging for this tension. Since the staysail doesn't have to extend abaft the mast, the spreaders can be long, with the shrouds coming off the mast at large angles. A big shroud angle reduces the stresses on the mast and the hull produced by any given tension on the headstay, and makes the whole rig stiffer. With no sail on the mast, there's not much penalty attached to using a fat, box-sectioned spar. A four-stave wooden mast might be competitive with an aluminum extrusion. I wish it didn't take nine big turnbuckles and all that wire to set it up, but a masthead sloop needs them, too.

The plywood hull is designed as a stiff girder, with big glued-up chine logs and clamps, so the rigging tension won't break her back under the mast. The mast would be stepped on deck with a bulkhead under it to carry the thrust of the mast to the hull sides. The hull has to be stiff as well as strong, because bending the ends of the hull up will slack the luff of the sail. The box-section hull is very good for rigidity, better than more complex shapes.

I show the sail with a boom, partly so it will be self-trimming to tack without touching anything but the tiller, and to sheet without a winch, but mostly because the hull is not wide enough to sheet a boomless sail this long on the foot without using an awkward outrigger on each side.

This boat wouldn't be really cheap. You have to pay for a 2,000-pound lead casting and all that rigging hardware. But she would be substantially cheaper, something like 50 percent, than any self-righting singlehander with a comparable windward performance. She should be able to sail away from a Soling or J-24, and cost less even custom-built in a good shop.

Author's Note

This essay was written in 1984. C S Boat Works of Marco Island, Florida, had me design a scaled-down version of the proposed boat, 23 feet 6 inches long, 5 feet 10 inches breadth, 3 feet 4 inches draft, with a 380-pound ballast casting and about 200 square feet of sail, which they called CorSair 24. This boat, shown here in plans and photo, was said to be extremely nice to sail, with no bad habits and great speed, especially in strong winds.

David Montgomery and I repeated his grandfather's 1922 staysail cat experiment in a duplicate of the 1922 boat. This boat also was a good sailer with all-around good manners, but she was consistently outsailed by several boats of the same class with the original 1921 jibheaded cat rig. The staysail cat rig's geometry requires a smaller sail for any given mast height than a jibheader. This is supposed to be compensated by improved aerodynamics in the staysail, but it wasn't, as sailed by Dave and myself. The boat showed occasional flashes of close-winded speed in which she would sail right by and up across the bows of the standard boats, but neither of us could make her do it consistently. I conjecture that this is an expert's rig, which needs phenomenal skill and concentration to exploit its potentialities. The perfect airfoil of the staysail must be extremely prone to stalling and, sailed by a mediocre helmsman, will develop no more power than a sail stalled by mast interference.

31 *Tarantula*

keelboat version: 23'6" × 3'11" × 3'7";
trimaran option: 23'6" × 16'0"

Brad Story picked up a junk fin keel with the idea of building a daysailer in the style of the 24' International 110 class. He and I shared an enthusiasm for the admirable art of that Ray Hunt design. I had published an essay in *Nautical Quarterly* about art in boat design, in which I used these seminal boats as one illustration, as follows:

C. Raymond Hunt was not a Master. He never troubled himself to learn to draw finished plans. He did not take the profession, let alone the Art, seriously. But he was a genius. When his attention was engaged he could follow a chain of reasoning uninhibited by prior programming.

In 1938 the George Lawley Corporation drew his attention to their need for a stock boat to fill gaps in their custom yacht work, with the problem that anything they did would be expensive on account of high overhead. The Herreshoff Manufacturing Company had addressed the situation by offering small gems at prices supposed to entitle the buyers to boast about how much they had paid. This formula was to work later and elsewhere, but it wasn't working there and then. The Lawley managers thought they might do something with the new waterproof plywood. They assigned the ingenious Bror Tamm to take up the slack in Hunt's attention span, as William Harris had done earlier, and Fenwick Williams and John Deknatel were to do later. It was a privilege to sort the golden debris of Hunt's intuitions.

Hunt started with a plywood box. Out of his insight into the behavior of molecules he rockered the bottom and pointed the ends. Lawley craftsmen and tools could produce intricate rounded, routed and rabbeted moldings to grip and protect the edges of the plywood. A production jig threw an arc into the bottom panel, to stiffen the sheets and float the chines higher in the water. A distinctive fin keel exploited Lawley skills and equipment. A trendy sloop rig was stepped; Hunt had incendiary ideas about rigs, but this was no time to pursue them. Besides, the faddish rig was handsome.

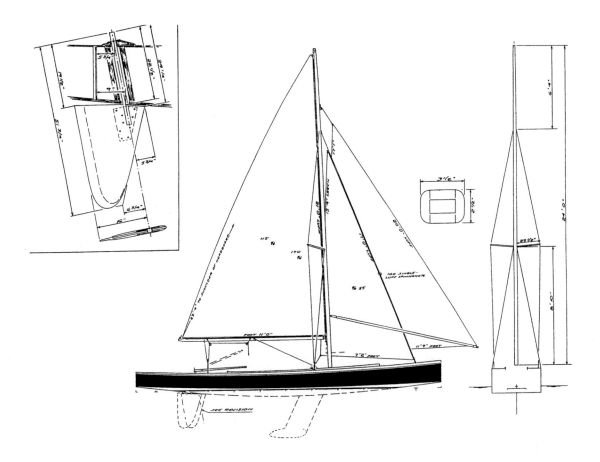

Hunt turned the aesthetic problem, the flat sheets of plywood, into a striking theme. He outlined the panels with sharp paint contrast. The profile sweep of the bottom was dictated by hydrodynamics, which he grasped as few people have, but the sheer and height of ends had lesser functional implications. He tapered and swept the side panels just enough to soften the basic rectangle, to compensate for the optical illusion that would have made a true rectangle look humped and down by the head, and to convey lift and lightness.

Hardly anybody appreciated the aesthetic purity of Hunt's design. It did not "look like a boat." It multiplied on its functional merits, but yachting writers sneered at the "cigars," and insensitive owners painted out the crucial outline contrasts. Hunt was not a zealot. Five years later he snubbed the ends of the bottom of his 29' 110 to wring out curved overhangs. The improvement was widely applauded.

Brad and I worked out *Tarantula* as a 110 clone, with simplified construction for one-off building, and a bigger sail plan and added bottom profile rocker to suit the keel in hand, which was heavier and deeper than that of the 110. Brad judged that the 110 paint scheme did not fit the sharp-edged panels. I thought she could be driven harder if the cockpit were narrower. (I was right; in strong wind, water has been halfway up the lee deck. With the wider cockpit of the 110 she would have had to be eased.)

The fin-keeled *Tarantula* had no vices, unless you count pounding at anchor, not a

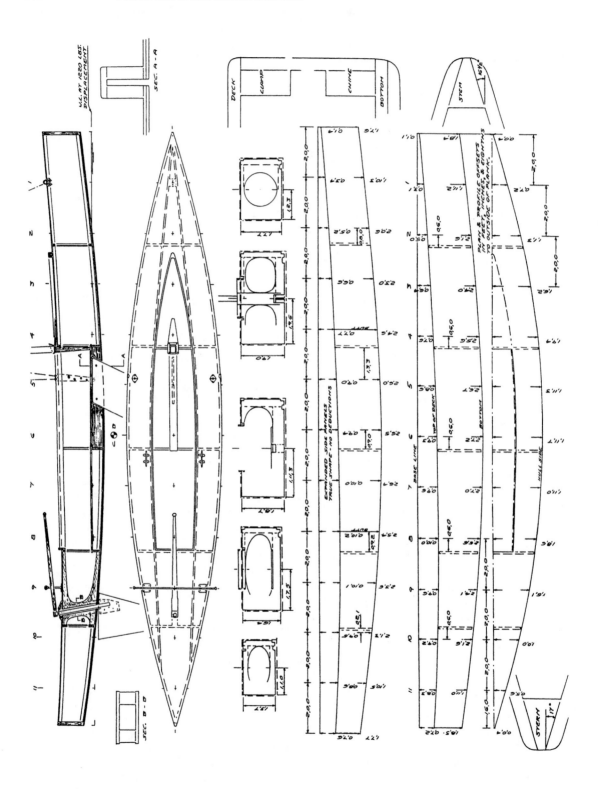

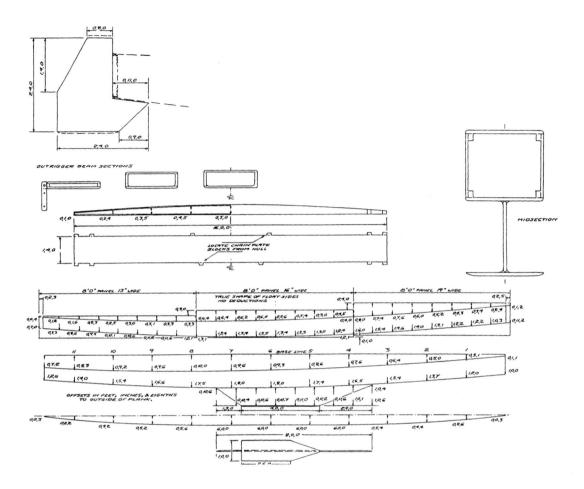

serious matter in a daysailer. She is a very fast boat; it takes something like an Etchells 22, among the keelboats, to get by her. But, one season of putting up with the constrictions imposed by her draft around the sandbars of Essex Bay was enough.

The obvious move was to sell her off to Marblehead and build something more practical, but Brad was reluctant to budget the time and asked me to look for some way to eliminate the keel—ironical, considering the hull's genesis.

We looked at a shallower keel. I thought one could be designed that would let her sail on as little as 16 inches draft, but with a drastic performance penalty and dubious reserve stability. The spindle hull doesn't have enough initial stability to stand up to a high sail plan, and it can't carry enough ballast to work without the long lever arm of deep draft.

Eventually we settled on the trimaran. It was supposed to use a single leeboard pivoted on the side of the hull, a centerboard being out of the question in the narrow cockpit. But with her existing rig, the board had to go well forward of the widest part of the hull. I thought her sailing would be killed by drag at the interface of board and hull side, due to the leading edge of the board standing off the hull more than the trailing edge. I

Tarantula *in her trimaran incarnation.*

proposed the shallow fins on the floats, arguing that the big end plates would let them hold on with the bottom of the float heeled down on the water surface. If so, she could sail to windward over a flat with a foot of water. The fins would be even quicker to build than the leeboard, and she could more easily be reconverted to the fin-keel mode. The risk was that she might become unreliable in stays. This last was a concern since we were increasing her wind resistance and decreasing her momentum. The two long fins far off the boat's axis of rotation would have to be twisted through the water as she was turned, and the drag might be more than the boat could tolerate.

However, trying the fins didn't preclude the leeboard option, so it seemed worth trying. We judged that the alternative was to cut a daggerboard slot alongside the cockpit. That would result in more efficient lateral plane and less hindrance to turns, but less freedom in shallow water.

If I designed a trimaran from scratch along these lines, indifferent to noise in choppy water, I'd be likely to draw a narrower main hull with more rocker, like the Auckland catamaran (see Chapter 33). The deeper midsection would allow deeper fins on the floats without extending them below the line of the main hull, and the shorter waterline would let her turn faster. The trimaran incarnation of *Tarantula* went quite well. My concern about trouble tacking did not materialize. She's not nearly as fast as a multihull ought to be, especially in strong winds when the stern, shaped to sail heeled, leaves a roaring following wave. She *feels* fast, and the freedom to roam the sand-choked bay is exhilarating. We're talking of building a more appropriate main hull and rig.

32 *Newfoundlander*

29'0" × 8'3" × 3'6"

Charlie Ballou spends his summers on the Bay of Exploits on the northern coast of Newfoundland. This is supposed to be the land the Vikings called Vineland the Good, but they saw it in a stretch of global warming, and they came to it from Greenland by way of Baffin Island. It looks harsh now, jutting rocks and dark forest facing the Labrador Sea. The bay is full of wooded islands and isolated coves, demanding a different order of vigilance from that of the crowds of Megalopolis.

Vokey Shipyard in Trinity, Newfoundland, built her in between commercial fishing boats. She was designed for the usual Newfoundland construction, nail-fastened carvel planking on sawn frames. Charlie shipped in the ballast casting, some of her timber, and most of her equipment. He already had the make-and-break Lunenburg-built engine shown on the drawing. It seemed very appropriate, but we couldn't work out a good enough way for a singlehander to deal with a direct-reversing engine so far from the helm. He swapped it for a Volvo diesel before she was finished.

He kept the coal range, also from Lunenburg. One like it has kept me warm and fed for most of nine years. I'm fond of it and proud of having learned to make it carry a fire for up to 20 hours without attention, but I guess the 19th-century technology is about finished. Anthracite coal isn't as easy to find as it was, and diesel stoves are much better than they used to be.

The raised-deck hull is for simplicity, and for ability to sail through a squall without burying herself. The long, deep keel, heavy outside ballast, and powerful hard-bilged shape are for ability to weather the evil lee shores. The forefoot is cut back to turn sharply among the islets of the bay, but the keel is carried back to a gently raked rudder to make sure she can be kept on course, running off in a bad chance.

(text continued on page 165)

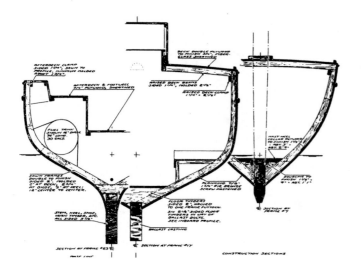

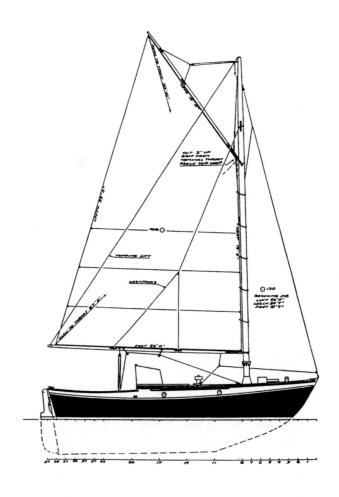

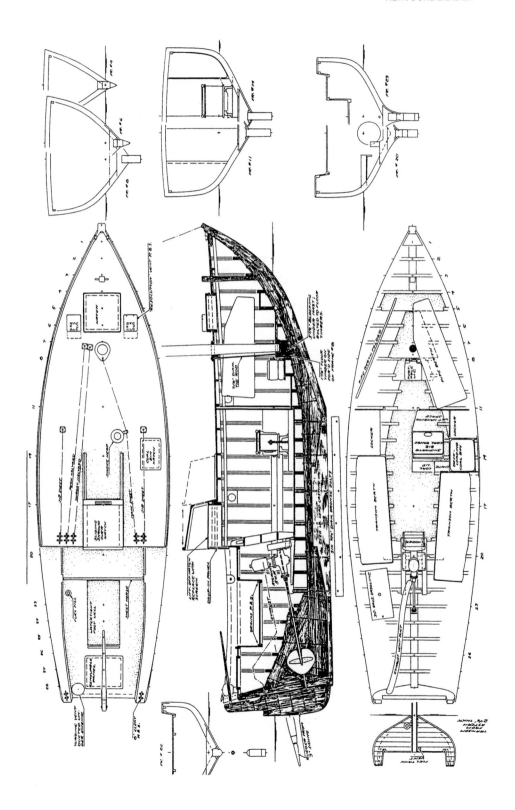

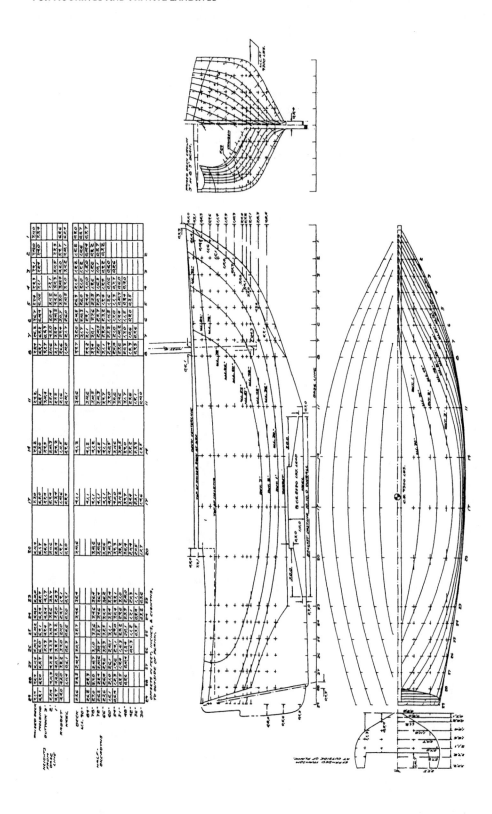

The tall gaff cat rig obviates standing rigging, with a tree for a mast, knots and all; one sheet for quick-reaction singlehanding. The vices of the cat rig don't appear in a boat long enough to build a long bow out ahead of the mast and to keep the boom inboard of the stern. One mast is much lighter than two. A jib would add driving power, but would demand wire standing rigging with high wind resistance and much more stress on the nail-fastened hull.

33 *Auckland Catamaran*

31'6" × 15'10"

Colin Frankham built a small catamaran to a design of mine that was a total failure. It is not easy to design a completely unusable boat since almost anything will work after a fashion, but it can be done. On the principle that the day after a crash is the safest time to fly, he came back for another one. (I had done a couple of other boats for him that weren't so bad.)

He had the rig of one of the Auckland 18-foot racing dinghies, fierce carnivores demanding large, strong, fearless crews. He was retired from that kind of sailing, but he thought it would be fun to put the rig into something he could sail singlehanded without a lot of strain, but still fast. He wanted to be able to assemble it quickly, without a big investment, and keep it on a mudflat off his landing. It did not have to be seaworthy, smooth-riding, or tolerant of an absent mind.

He didn't rule out any type, but the catamaran had the best mix of simplicity and speed if I could make it behave. The long, upswept bows are supposed to have enough lift to make cartwheeling over a dug-in lee bow rare. The short waterlines keep the wetted surface small and let her swing quickly, to get through stays against high wind resistance with little momentum. The centerboard is on the axis of her turns for the same reason, swinging down through a backbone reminiscent of a 1900 iceboat, and like the iceboats in its forward extension to take the jib. I did not expect the jib to be used much—only in light airs, with crew.

The strongly rockered bottom profile limits her speed by comparison with the D-cats she somewhat resembles. A straighter bottom, to plane more efficiently, would have to be a more complex shape to tack reliably and not pitchpole without provocation. She's fast enough—in a breeze, faster than the big monohull dinghies with the same rig but overloaded with live ballast.

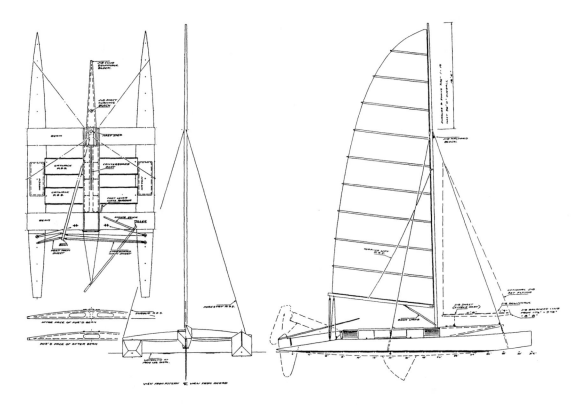

The rudder is large, deep, and set far aft on a hinged extension of the backbone, to take some of the lateral-plane function when the jib is not set. Hinging the backbone arm rather than the blade of the rudder avoids the problem of locking the rudder blade down while allowing it to kick up at need. In the lowered position the rudder axis has a slight rake that produces a downward force on the blade and increases steering effectiveness by reducing flow off the bottom of the blade.

Use of catwalks instead of a complete platform saves weight and increases the sensation of speed with the view of the water whipping past. The open spaces can be filled in with a tarp when there's too much spray. She doesn't make much spray in most conditions, but the flat bottoms are impressively noisy in ripples.

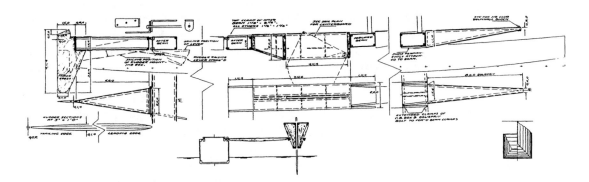

34 *Snow Leopard*

28'0" × 7'0"

"Consistency is the hobgoblin of little minds, adored by little statesmen, philosophers, and divines."

Ralph Waldo Emerson

Bradford Story and I started this project on speculation for his custom boat shop, to fill a hiatus in custom orders. The design was meant to be a conversation piece or mobile sculpture, to be looked at with pleasure or amusement. If abstract art is traveling at 40–60 m.p.h., and weighs two tons, whoever is directing it should see where it's going. If it can carry several people, showing it off can be doubled with some other recreation.

It's not true that round-bilged hulls are inefficient at high speeds. Hulls of this type ride so high at speed that what little spray they make doesn't reach the areas where the chine would be if there were one. I suspect that a chine, spray strakes, and steps increase drag by making eddies in the air that carry spray over more of the bottom than would be wet in a smooth hull. Streamlining the underbody of a boat that will often be in the air seems at least as reasonable as streamlining the upper works. In this case, the visual effect of doing it fits the theme.

The pointed stern is really an extreme case of a curved transom rather than a double-ender in the usual sense. The hull was designed to a flat, vertical transom, with the bottom lines running straight back as in any fast boat. The sides and deck were then rounded in and down, with no change in the lines of the bottom except that some of it was cut away where the corners of the transom had been. This was done for style, in imitation of some much-admired old boats. For a temperament like mine that has to ratio-

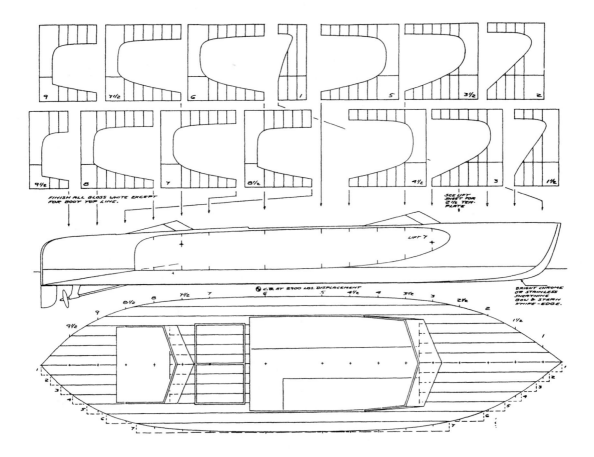

nalize everything, removing some buoyancy in the quarters allows finer bow lines on a given weight placement. The vulnerable corners of the stern are removed, as in lifeboats, and exhaust fumes aren't carried along with the boat.

Fast boats spend a lot of time running slowly, and the slow running is apt to be where they're most visible. Most of them look ungraceful when they're slowed down, dragging their sterns in undignified fashion. Snow Leopard was designed to clip along in purposeful fashion at displacement speeds. Her bow is razor sharp to make a neat feather, and the weight isn't centered so far back that the stern lacks buoyancy to support it. She's comparatively light; the single engine is a V8 of about 180 h.p. The 350 h.p. shown on the drawing might drive her 70 m.p.h., but the 180 (top speed around 40 m.p.h.) saves weight in itself, requires a smaller fuel load, and allows lighter construction. The chances of using more speed than that, in a boat that doesn't have three-axis, active, aerodynamic controls (that is, can't fly under control), are so rare that I don't think it's reasonable to put up with ugly running at low speeds to get the potential. She will not only look better, but in no-wake zones can run faster than the boats that can outrun her in open water.

We discussed using a light Porsche engine, but one of the qualities we were aiming

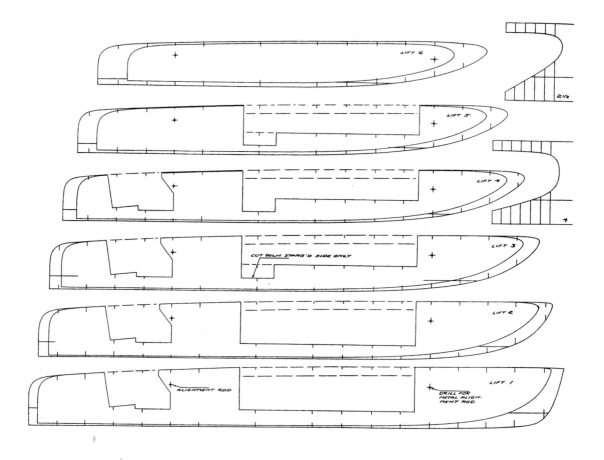

at was style with a minimum of demanding maintenance. It's also planned to use some of the empty space under the deck to arrange effective mufflers, as bulky as necessary. I would opt for complete silence, but I'd accept a contented purr at low speed and a deep growl when opened up.

These rounded-off decks are apt to look bulbous. I've never seen one with its stem-head rounded down in profile that struck me as handsome. With the angular stemhead the curves close in to a tight focus, complementing the upright stem that lengthens and sharpens the waterline. The fad for long bow overhangs is getting ridiculous. Some of the later boats come close to getting their decks in the water before they pick up any buoyancy from the forefoot, in a steep sea. Even if the effect is good in profile, snubbing the waterline makes an ugly line viewed from the forward quarter; even the magnificent J-boat *Endeavour* shows this bad angle, as I noticed while admiring her last year.

I tried curved windshields, which seem appropriate but in fact don't look well to my eye. The big forward cockpit is supposed to be self-draining, cushioned all over for sprawling, but with a hatch near the after end to allow two or three people to sit facing forward with their feet down. This cockpit could have a tent over it at anchor if some privacy were wanted.

The helmsman stands in the small after cockpit with a long line of sight over the heads of people in the forward cockpit. The big smooth-rimmed wheel can be worked from either side for a good maneuvering view. There's a jump seat for long runs. With the forward cockpit tented, the after one could double as an outhouse with a portable toilet. For a canal cruise in style, the good low-speed running would be appreciated. It could be that arriving in this boat might lead to exceptional hospitality along the way, whether camping on board, or, more likely, pulling up to a hotel at each port.

It's been customary to finish boats like this in bright varnish, but we thought we could get at least as dramatic an effect, and spend a lot less time polishing, with the all-gloss-white finish trimmed with mirror-silver for the stem and stern sheathing plates, hatch bindings, windshield frames, wheel, and so on. Cushions and padding around the cockpits would have white covers. Aside from the visual effect, the silver and white finish is cool in strong sun and not liable to cracking and discoloration from ultraviolet radiation. I'm in two minds whether to have the boottop stripes

Brad is as capable of as fancy varnishwork as anybody, but he shares with me a distaste for making boats (or anything) expensive and laborious if the effect sought can be had some easier way. In this case, the glittering but easily maintained white finish would be produced by encapsulating a strip-planked hull with epoxy sheathing. She would really be a fiberglass boat, but without the unsightly seams and flanges that led to the epithet "Clorox bottle."

So far, Brad hasn't run out of custom work, so the concept hasn't progressed beyond preliminary studies. The model shown in the photo was made by Dynamite Payson to illustrate one of his books on modelmaking (*Boat Modeling the Easy Way*, International Marine, 1993). The shape was unusually suitable for demonstrating the vertical-lift method of modelmaking, in which the block is assembled from layers following the bow lines and buttocks instead of the usual waterlines. I made plans for the book with patterns for each lift and templates for carving the sections. The photo was taken with the model resting on top of a clean, shiny, blue automobile with the St. George River for a background. The model is 21 inches long, at a scale of $\frac{1}{16}$, or $\frac{3}{4}$ inch to the foot.

Both the drawing and the model are oversimplified, exaggerating the clean effect. I've been toying in a desultory way with schemes for arranging ventilators, lights, cleats, exhausts, and tank fill caps without cluttering the style. It's possible to make stylistic accents with these things; John Hacker was the master of the technique. His designs, including some "torpedo runabouts" with this kind of shape, have all this business shaped and placed like jewelry on the dark mahogany hulls. He would have appreciated the Lamborghini Countarch car, a haunting example of a low-drag shape studded all over with aerodynamically dirty afterthoughts that actually contribute to the stunning effect.

I plan to try to keep the final design genuinely clean, except for the turbulence-inducing cockpits which I can't help. The ventilation outlets will be arranged around the cockpits to take some advantage of the turbulence. Intake vents will be flush NASA type with the recesses painted white to be as unobtrusive as possible. She may have under-

Dynamite Payson's model of Snow Leopard

water exhausts with pop covers over the above-water relief pipes. Most of the other excrescences can go into recesses with hinged or removable covers.

The windshields are a bad aerodynamic shape and almost useless for their ostensible function. The Emerson quotation is one of the most useful aphorisms I know. I found it in *Bartlett's Familiar Quotations* and have not looked up the context. . . .

Part Six

Period Pieces

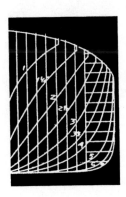

35 *Dugout*

11'9" × 3'0"

Dear SBJ:

Here's another one for Bolger: How about a modern dugout canoe, laminated, built up, and glued together? To dig a boat out of a log would be a big job, even if one were fortunate enough to obtain a suitable log. Spreading the sides to adequate beam would also be difficult. I've read that Indians of the Northwest would fill a dugout with water, then drop in hot stones to heat it; the hot water softened the sides enough to spread them.

Could common 2-inch lumberyard construction stock (1⅝ inch dressed) be laminated together with a suitable waterproof glue to build up a canoe hull in lifts? In modeling, we call it bread-and-butter construction.

With the high cost of even the cheapest lumber, perhaps wood could be saved by using vertical lifts. Some might remember that ship modeler Captain McCann worked out a Chinese sampan model with vertical lifts; *Popular Science* published an article on it in the 1930s.

For a full-sized canoe, the lifts may need to be thicker than 1⅝ inch. Chesapeake Bay log canoes were hewn from timbers drifted together. A dugout of glued-up lifts would undoubtedly be heavy, so it couldn't be very long. Fourteen or fifteen feet would do, and it could easily be slid into the box of a pickup.

Instead of playing the game of fitting the components of a boat into a minimum number of plywood sheets, the challenge here would be wasting as few board feet of 2 × 12 as possible. Could Bolgerizing a stack of planks into a boat bring a revival of the primitive dugout? I, for one, have always wanted to try one but need help. Could a canoe be carved from Styrofoam?

Marion McClure, Bloomington, Illinois

Dear Mr. McClure:

The only boat I know of that was built somewhat the way you have in mind was designed by L. Francis Herreshoff for his own use. It was a kayak (LFH insisted that they should be called "double-paddle canoes"; a kayak, he said, was stretched sealskin) with the deck forward of the cockpit bubbled up high enough to sleep under and all streamlined like an airplane. It's on display at Mystic Seaport, and there's a photo of it on page 38 of *The Common Sense of Yacht Design*, Volume 1 (in the chapter on cabin arrangements!). *WoodenBoat* magazine featured an article about this boat some time ago (*WoodenBoat* No. 14, page 54) that's worth looking up. As I remember, the plans were quite elaborate, but it was such a complex shape that it took the combined talents of LFH and Bror Tamm to get it fair. I've kicked myself often, recalling how many times I was within arm's reach of that boat without noticing anything remarkable about the construction. LFH had it smoothly painted and slung from the ceiling in his drafting room. Seeing it only from the outside, I thought it was cold-molded. I now realize that it was easier to carve all those curves than to bend them.

I take it that this is what's at the bottom of your suggestion—that carving softwood can be pleasant exercise even if it takes a long time, whereas bending wood and making it hold the curves can be frustrating and punctuated by crises. I assume from your letter that you're more interested in the building of the boat than in using it afterwards.

Still, it would be a pity to end up with nothing but abstract sculpture, so I cast around for some kind of boat that would benefit in use by the dugout construction. I naturally thought first of a canoe. This wasn't satisfying—partly because a slender boat like that is better adapted than most to using bent planks or strips, so the carved construction seemed wasteful, and partly because a paddling boat is hurt by weight more than any other type.

Next, I thought about a small pram, which would carry out the experiment with a minimum of materials. This seemed unenterprising, and weight reduces the usefulness of a type of boat that you'd often want to pick up and haul around.

I settled on this small outboard utility. With a motor, the heavy boat isn't at such a disadvantage. This one would go along nicely with anything from 2 to 5 h.p. It won't be hurt by the big stern as much as a paddling or rowing boat would. The breadth can be carried back in straight lines, adding to capacity and stability while economizing on timber. I took advantage of the carved construction to give it bow lines as nicely faired as I could imagine, with plenty of flare and a soft-nosed stem. This boat will slice sweetly through a small chop.

I made it as small as I thought would be fit to stand up in, in smooth water, without being an acrobat. The weight helps in this. If the boat weighs 180 pounds, give or take a lot—depending on how thin the sides end up, and on how wet the wood is, and on what kind of wood it was in the first place—it'll be less flighty underfoot than a 50-pound cold-molded shell.

The capacity is comparable to that of a 15-foot canoe; that is, two adults make a good load. Built of soft pine or cedar and pared down to ¾ inch at the sides, the dugout will float in 3 inches of water—when she's dry. Like a real dugout, she'll soak spectacularly if left in the water long; eventually she will absorb her weight.

Though she's primarily an outboard motorboat, I've shown a sculling notch on each side of the stern. You sit straddling the thwart, facing athwartships, with the sweep in the notch on the opposite side. Sculling seems to be making a mild comeback, and it's

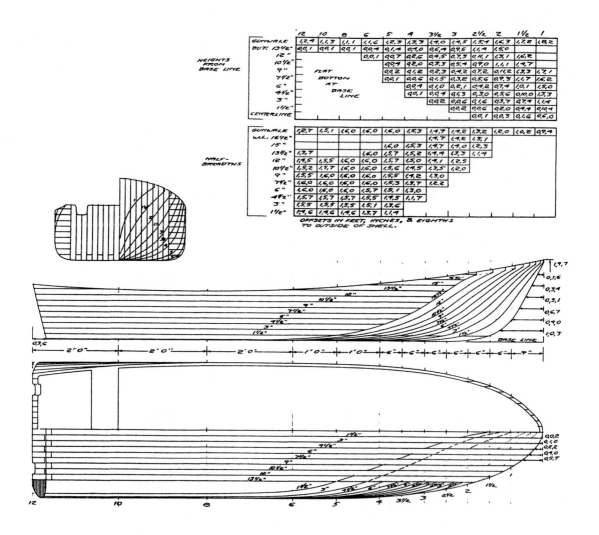

a good way to move a heavy boat a short distance. The continuous thrust of sculling works better than the intermittent strokes of oars or paddles in a boat that tends to stop between strokes, as this one would.

I thought of showing a rowing position forward, using a portable rowing seat, but she's not really wide enough to use oars without using outriggers, which would look ridiculous on a boat of this type. Scull or pole her a little way, or motor her for a longer haul.

One or more thwarts besides the one shown could be added, and would be useful to brace the sides. But a boat like this is safer and looks better if people sit on the bottom. Duckboards might encourage this.

The hull is intended to be built up from 1½-inch lifts. I don't trust that 1⅝-inch standard much, and the waste from running all the stock through a planer doesn't amount to that much. In any case, the lifts can be rearranged in lofting to suit what stock

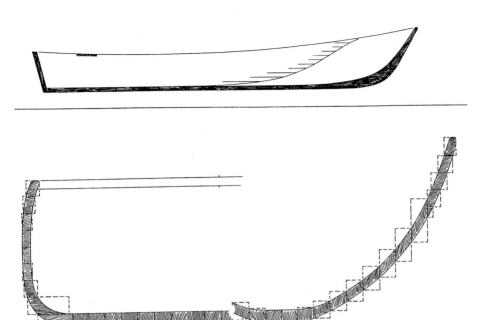

SECTION @ #10   SECTION @ #3

you can find. The boat ought to be lofted full length, as I lined it out rather hurriedly and the spot check showed the offsets to be less accurate than I usually expect to deliver. However, any shape something like this, that's fair, will do. I understand that owners of racing log canoes do a little carving after an unsuccessful season, which is one of the opportunities presented by the thick-walled construction. With epoxy, it's no longer true that "if you take off too much, you can't put it back."

The flat part of the bottom is 1½-inch-square strips. That ought to give confidence enough to beach the boat on rough shores. The transom is the same, with alternate strips caught between two bottom strips for a neat mortised joint.

Wider planks, still 1½ inches thick, are needed where the vertical seams of the bottom sweep up forward. There'll be staggered butts where the curved forward planks join the straight stripe of the after bottom. I think nothing wider than a 2 × 6 will be useful, and it could probably be done with 2 × 4s if enough joints were used.

The horizontal lifts along the sides avoid some acute feathering out at the seams, saving some timber and some cutting.

I faired this shape with diagonals and laid out the waterlines all the way to the stem when I drew the hull, but in the final tracing I've eliminated all the lines that don't represent seams, except in the body plan sections for templates. These lines give some idea of how the boat would look if the glue lines were dark and the finish clear varnish or oil.

Epoxy glue would be best because it doesn't need pressure to set up. Sawing out the inside edges of the lifts before assembly saves some timber and a lot of chipping, but it would make bracing the staggered lifts against clamp pressure a problem, as they'd tend to collapse like a canted stack of poker chips. Dynamite Payson's books on modelmaking would be useful reading before starting any dugout. See Sources for his address.

Some wood dust is as toxic as many more nasty-seeming chemical vapors. As far as I know, working with plane, drawknife, and chisel, or a broadaxe for that matter, is healthy exercise. Power sanders are not healthy without a state-of-the-art breathing mask.

I think I'd like a clear finish to show up the seams; it would be too bad to take this much trouble and end up with something that can't be distinguished from fiberglass. Clear epoxy will slow down soakage, but it needs some additive to protect it from the sun, or it will turn purple or milky, or crack, or get some other kind of skin cancer.

If the boat looks good enough to be worth the trouble when you get that far, some kind of railcap, with laminated knees at the stem and quarters, would be nice.

I'll be surprised if there's much of a revival of the dugout, unless somebody comes up with a better idea than this one. But this would be a neat-looking and useful boat in a modest way, and cheap in material cost, as boats go.

As for the Styrofoam: If you can lay hands on a copy of my out-of-print book *Different Boats* (try interlibrary loan), you'll find plans and a photo of a sailing dinghy carved out of foam (not Styrofoam!) in Chapter 28. You might find it rewarding to buy the catalog of Aircraft Spruce and Specialty Company, P.O. Box 424, Fullerton, CA 92632, to see what can be done with foam. Beautiful and light structures are being built this way. But it's not as easy as it sounds, it's not cheap, and the materials aren't as pleasant to work with as wood.

36 *Marina Cruiser*

21'3" × 7'10" × 2'4"

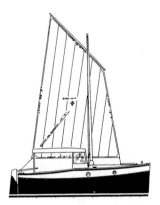

(A fictional scenario commissioned by WoodenBoat *magazine, one of several illustrating small boat cabins designed for, or adapted to, differing circumstances. A couple of the others are further along in the book. They were all loosely based on experiences of mine.)*

The Friends

Why a miniature power cruiser is steaming into Bucks Harbor, Maine, in the month of March, manned by three middle-aged men, is a long and irrelevant story. She was built as a "marina cruiser"—a substitute for the summer cottages that were cheap in their day but were built on land that only rich people can now own. This boat was meant to lie through summers at crowded float-stages. She'd be plugged into shore electricity, and her crew would have access to marina washrooms. Her original owners were a city couple whose children were grown and gone. On hot days they might motor to a nearby anchorage. There, or in their marina berth, they would sit in folding lounge chairs in the cockpit shade (the standing shelter had a white fabric top over an open frame that reflected the heat of the sun while transmitting a glow of light). They would eat ashore, or picnic-fashion.

The cruiser was designed as short as possible to reduce the marina bill. The rudder can be swung 90 degrees if there's a threat to include it in her length-for-charges. She steers with a tiller to save the cockpit space of a wheel and console; the tiller can be unshipped when she's not underway (the normal condition). She is carvel-built on bent frames, and her builder complained that the bow is so full that he had to steam all the

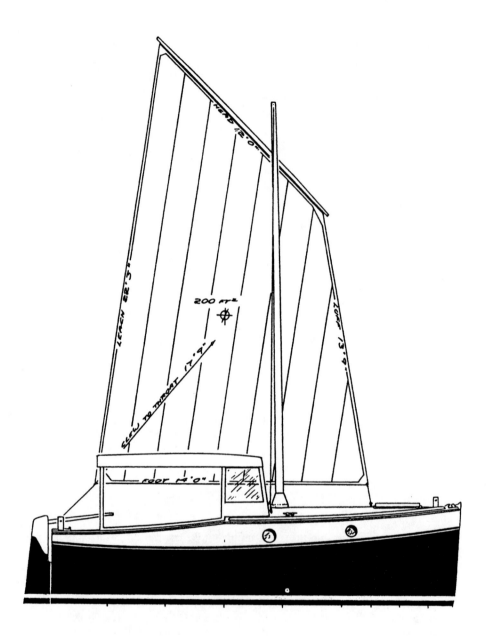

upper planks; otherwise, she was quite cheap to build in New England. The cedar sheathing inside the frames has a pleasant smell, and the gravity-powered air circulation behind it keeps her cuddy unusually dry—there is never any apparent condensation inside.

The original owners fondly imagined that she made 10 knots; they were under the impression that no motorboat ever went slower. In fact, the two-cylinder 13-h.p. diesel drives her 6½ knots. If she had a 3:1 reduction gear to swing the larger prop allowed by the aperture, she would make 6¾ knots. With twice the power (which would not fit in the designed compartment) she might make 7 knots—with 10 knots' worth of wake.

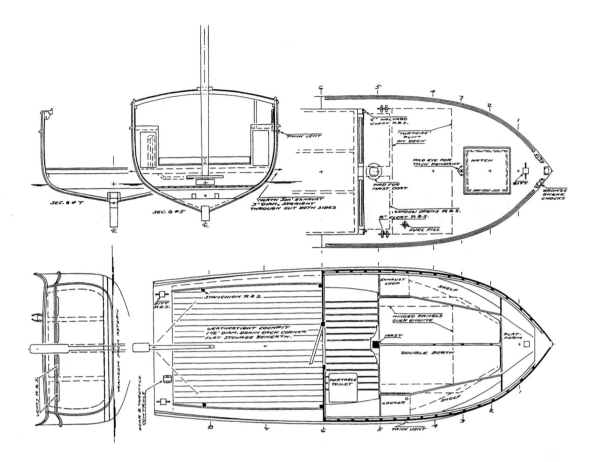

The engine has very low time, and the mast, yard, and sail usually were stored ashore to clear the cabin and reduce windage and bridge clearance. She never went anywhere where a tow wasn't available for the asking. But it was established, when she was new, that she could sail after a fashion, even a little to windward.

Below, the double berth was made up with tucked-in sheets and blankets. The forward hatch was used only for ventilation, since it was easier and cooler to anchor by the stern in the only conditions in which she ever anchored; if a shower threatened, she would go home. A plastic sheet was propped up over the hatch in warm, rainy weather so it could be open without dripping. Some craftily placed hooks on the topsides stretched the store-bought square sheet in place with the strutted peak facing in any direction. The effect was highly unseamanlike. A portable television set stood on the forward platform.

Other people in the marina did not understand this boat, but they were tolerant. A few of them knew that she was a loose imitation of a production cruiser of the 1920s, but even those who did not bother with history thought her quaint. She became a marina mascot. Children would shout, "Look! The *President Coolidge* is going out!"

The notable difference between this boat and her ancestors is that the engine has disappeared under the double berth. High-powered boats were once built with engines in this position, but they were long and slender, and, even so, were slow for their power

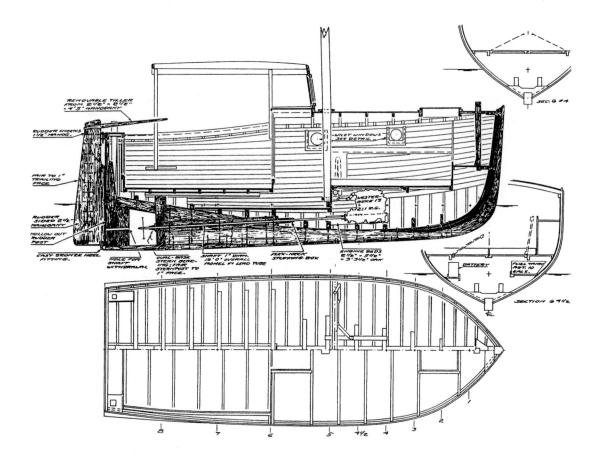

and wet and wild-steering in a seaway. The small modern engine in this boat is so light that it just about compensates for the weight of the helmsman at the tiller. The bow has a complex forefoot shape showing deep hollows in the waterlines. The lines of flow are sharper than most, and the bow wave is turned over in a clear roll indicative of a dry boat and a steady steerer.

The present skipper has done what he could to make her fit for a coastwise passage. He restepped her mast, and the dipping lugsail has brought her up Penobscot Bay on the brisk southwest wind as fast as the engine could have. Because her fuel capacity is very small, the auxiliary propulsion is welcome. The sail tames the exhausting bouncy roll that makes the buoyant little boat intolerable for any length of time in rough water.

Insect screens have been battened out over what is suspected to be plain plate glass in the windshield, the skipper having read Captain Alex Moffat's account of how a screen an inch from the glass saved the wheelhouse windows in Kaiser's War sub-chasers. The fabric shelter top has been replaced with plywood fitted with grabrails, and the open sides have been paneled-in almost to the stern.

A tarpaulin has been laid over the double berth, turned well up the sides. To handle the anchors, the current crew walk over the tarp-covered mattresses and stand chest-deep in the hatch. A bundling board runs down the berth centerline, since the skipper

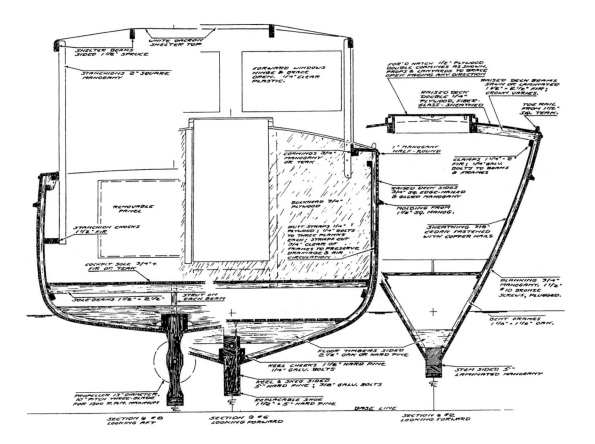

and his friends are neither homosexuals nor quiet sleepers. The third man sleeps on a folding cot in the cockpit. They all have good sleeping bags and wear overall oilskins with long johns inside. They plan to wash and shave in Bar Harbor.

An anthracite stove is bolted down where the control console should have been. It faces aft; they wish it faced forward in a boat that pitches as hard as this one does, but at any rate it does not face athwartships and has not yet spilled a substantial amount of hot coals. A stiff stanchion is bolted at the after inboard corner of the stove and has so far prevented any bad burns resulting from falls against the stove. Three 50-pound bags of coal were stowed under the cockpit, where the lounge chairs used to be put away; this much fuel will last a week if they run the stove full blast whenever they're awake. The stove will carry a fire 20 hours if it's knowledgeably banked, but at this time of year they bank it only to sleep. At anchor, with the cockpit tented in, the stove puts out so much heat that in 40-degree evenings a forward port is left open, giving air circulation through to the transom openings. One of the men smokes and has agreed to light up only abaft the after shelter stanchions. The cuddy door had to be removed, as the width of the stove blocked its swing, but they would have kept it open in any case.

They have another type of smoke problem. When the transverse "North Sea" exhaust rolls its lee outlet underwater, the diesel fumes belch out on the weather side and

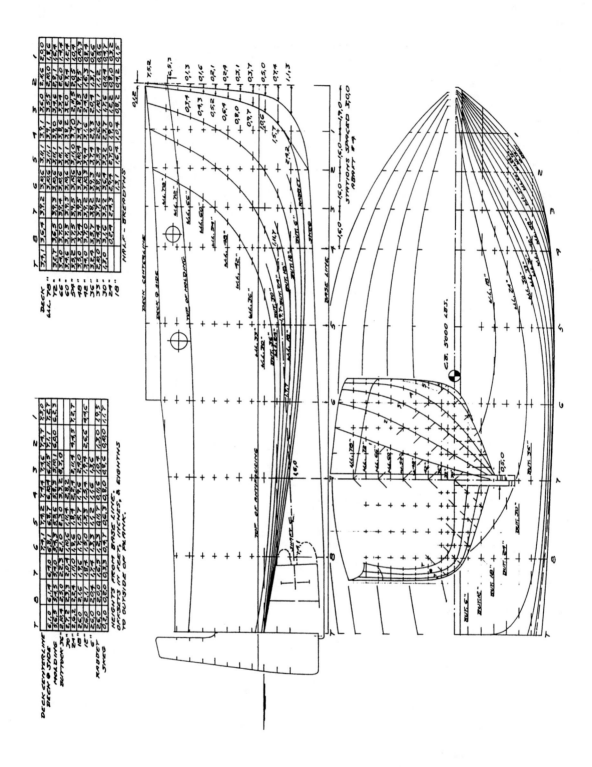

blow back over the boat. The crew all wish the boat had a dry exhaust—up the mast, ideally—even the man who once grabbed an unlagged dry-exhaust pipe with his bare hand.

Underway, the stove heat goes away fast through the cabin's open after end, but socks dry and water keeps hot. The men will boast later that it snowed on their cruise, but in fact it was just a flurry. They took care not to start in a northeaster and were ready to run in and wait it out if one had blown up on the way. They counted on, and got, offshore winds and plenty of calm. The high-sided boat will live in a very wicked sea, but she makes little progress in a head sea and quickly wears out her crew with her wild rolling and pitching. This "winter cruise" is an anomaly, and soon the boat will again become a summer cottage.

37 *Alice*

28'0" × 7'10" × 2'9"

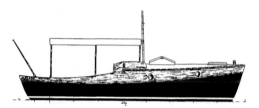

(The following appeared in WoodenBoat *magazine as a design commentary.)*

Recreation suffers from thinking too hard. By definition it ought to be spontaneous. The people motoring through rivers and harbors look as though they were doing it right, but the boats they've been sold don't. The designers have studied harder than is appropriate.

The boats are great performers, whatever you think of the looks of some of them (the stylists have been thinking too hard). They go faster, are stopped less in rough water, and have fewer handling vices than anything that ever floated. They have accommodations on deck and below like Arabian Nights fantasies. They carry huge loads without complaint.

But, none of them ever look tranquil, though their people often do. The boats look tense, affected, impatient. They're fast, but inelegant when they slow down; able, but out of place in smooth water; comfortable, but obtrusive.

In the years around 1910, motorboats were built without much knowledge or deep thought. There had not been time for a lot of study. They were just starting to emerge from the habits of rowing and sailing types. The engines were huge, dangerous machines, noisy (though the deep pitch of their exhausts had something to be said for it), with vibration hard on human nerves and mechanical hull fastenings.

The boats were wet and badly ventilated. They were staggering rollers and pounded their seams open in head seas. Those were the years of the powerboat races to Bermuda and Havana, every race an endurance test at 7 or 8 knots.

Even on lovely days in protected water they weren't pleasant, on account of the demanding machinery, but there they *looked* at home, seen from a distance or in a photo. They moved graciously, with clear, curling bow waves and gently rolling wakes. Ladies

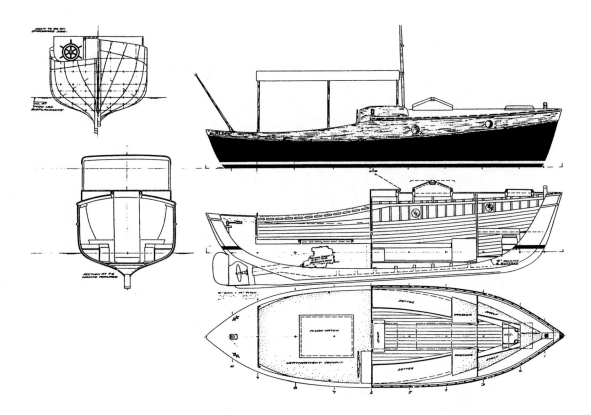

in long skirts and huge hats sat in wicker armchairs in the cockpits. Men with blazers over stiff-collared shirts, wearing square-crowned yachting caps, managed to look competent. All these people looked as though they were where they wanted to be, rather than impatient to be elsewhere.

Now, the people give the same impression (and look, and are, much healthier and better able to deal with unexpected developments), but the boats don't.

When I drew the design for *Alice* (as in Wonderland), I tried to recover some of the tranquility of the 1910 boats. Not the innocence; that "cometh not again," nor would many of us want it. But it might be possible to build something in keeping with a relaxed mood. Fast and able boats can go slowly in smooth water, but there's a sense of unrealized potential that doesn't contribute to the spirit. At 6 knots in a crowded waterway, with much to look at, a boat like this is where she belongs, doing what she does best. She looks it, and her well-being is infectious.

Resembling the 1910 boats, she can really do what they only seemed to do, thanks to the compact, quiet, reliable 1980s engine out of sight and almost out of mind under the cockpit. In 1910 it would have been three times the size and planted in the middle of the cabin, leaking gasoline and lube oil under the galley stove. (It's hard to understand why they didn't all blow up, but the Lord looks after the pure in spirit.) *Alice* is a magic carpet by comparison. The little Japanese diesel purrs at half its rated r.p.m. Vibration is negligible. The fuel tank is so small that it doesn't show on the plans. Enclosing walls damp mechanical noise. Air flowing smoothly around the pointed stern carries the diesel smell away.

The cockpit is deep, roomy, and clear. Perhaps some wicker armchairs can be found. The view is not as good as that from a flying bridge, but access to it is better, and the smooth water sliding by within arm's reach is more relaxing than a mass of foam seen from on high. The white fabric awning glows overheard. No glass or plastic dims the view. The ladies need not wear long skirts, nor the men stiff collars.

Below, the cabin is roomy and bright. It is arranged for day use; this is not a cruiser. Serious cooking is done ashore. The wonderful portable toilet, one of the greatest achievements of the age, has space, light, privacy, and no built-in plumbing. For the occasional after-dark homecoming there are 12-volt lights, but no other electrical equipment, no electronics, and no radio.

It's a safe assumption that this boat will be one of a kind, since her conception calls for thinking hard about how not to think hard (like the magic spell that would work if the magician could remember *not* to think about a hippopotamus). This has the advantage that *Alice* can be built of wood, since there are still enough good carpenters and boat lumber to produce a single boat. Such boats are not very expensive, especially this one with her single small engine, lack of extensive equipment, and minimal joinerwork. The hand-built wooden skylight with its handsome mortised corners is the most expensive luxury on board.

The wood is most striking below deck, where the unpainted cedar sheathing glinting with the heads of copper nails produces a steady airflow right around the boat in the bays between her steam-bent oak frames. Dark topsides force this flow by heating the air on the sunny side as the cooling seawater sucks it down the shady side. This cabin, or cuddy, is fresh and dry beyond the experience of people who know only plastic or metal, or even those who have wood sheathing in contact with a plastic hull.

The sides of the raised deck are bright-varnished. The cockpit is soled with laid teak, also varnished, which makes it ridiculously slippery but can't be matched for a rich appearance. The raised deck may also be laid teak or white pine, but is more likely planking sheathed with cotton duck lightly painted for its soft texture. The skylight and wheelbox are, of course, bright mahogany, as is the spoked wheel itself.

This outboard finish needs constant care to keep its rich brilliance. It really ought not to be left in the sun. In middle age the boat will fall into the hands of somebody who does not like thinking hard about polishing. He will roughly scrape the perished varnish and roll on latex house paint, and replace the perished cotton deck sheathing with fiberglass. Then she will need no maintenance for years on end. Later still, when she is 40 or 50 years old, she may have the luck to find an owner who will lovingly (without thinking too hard about why) restore her original glitter.

She has a small signal mast, a straight round stick with a decorative taper. She will show textbook-correct colors, and her owner will feel comfortably superior to the boats displaying pre–Second World War Polish naval ensigns or Scottish royal standards, even while he admires the beauty of the exotic banners.

This boat's inspiration was a modest craft for modest people, with no pretensions to style or status. She hovered on the outskirts of the occasions of the rich and famous, enjoying without much envy the spectacle of big-schooner racing, processions of steam yachts, and the vicissitudes of the primitive racing motorboats. She had been built by a boat carpenter of local reputation who was not modest and had a fund of stories about somebody's discontent with a Herreshoff or Lawley boat. Yachting reporters did not focus as their eyes passed over her, unless she engaged in an exploit such as the New

**Dynamite
Payson's
model of
Alice**

York-to-Marblehead powerboat race. (This was a real race, not a navigation contest, and since the Cape Cod Canal was not yet open it could be a real adventure in an easterly breeze.)

Some such boats were much better than others, no consensus having been reached at the time about their shape. *Alice* is harder-bilged and wider than most of them, with what passed at the time for moderate flare. Her displacement is spread out forward and aft as much as is compatible with a bow that will slice cleanly through the wake of a modern boat without either bringing water on deck or throwing it wide with a noisy splash. She is not a bad seaboat, though bouncy in her motion compared with a 1980s boat slowed down to her speed. The modern boat's motion is damped by her load of machinery and fuel, and by the heavy construction needed to stand the stresses of her speed.

The virtue of this boat is that she will bolster everybody's self-satisfaction. Her owner will congratulate herself on her good taste as she admires the wood grain and the unaffected style, her good sense in taking an afternoon on the water without a foolish excess of power and equipment, and her independence in choosing distinction without pretensions.

At the neighboring landings, the owners of the 70-knot catamaran on one side and the four-story seagoing condominium on the other will feel just as contented, knowing that their boats are faster, more seaworthy, more comfortable, and much more expensive.

38 *Keelboat*

38'9" × 8'0"

The commission called for an upper–Missouri River keelboat "representation," a much better word than the much-misused "replica." But in a sense this *is* a keelboat, though different in shape and construction from those that worked in Andrew Jackson's day. The promoters were interested in demonstrating the performance and handling of the boats rather than their construction.

These craft were the equivalent, on the High Plains river during the "winning of the West," of stagecoaches on land, as the canoe corresponded to the express rider and the flatboat to the ox-wagon. They carried passengers and premium cargo, and serviced the fur trade; the representation's name, *General William Ashley*, commemorates a field commander of the traders who handled the catch of the Mountain Men.

The Missouri River below Great Falls is not a fast stream. It is shallow except in flood. It runs in a deep gorge which channels the wind, hence the square sail to make best use of fair winds and to be easily struck down flat in headwinds. The stream is too strong to row against; the oars are for crossing deep places and for steerageway downstream. Battened walkways along the low sides allow poling her. It's possible to carry the pole forward, leaning in against the tumbled-in house side, as the men pushing lean out on their poles. A mile an hour was good progress. As these keelboats labored up the river, the unthinkable patience people once had to learn was nearly over. Elsewhere, railroad track was being laid and steamships were moving.

The single much-published drawing of one of these keelboats shows a big one. Several oars are impossibly placed, and a peculiar rudder is shown that I thought for some time must be the figment of another misunderstanding by the artist, until I came across a photo of a rudder much like it on a French river boat. I suggested the steering sweep, copied from a New Bedford whaleboat of the same period, arguing that being

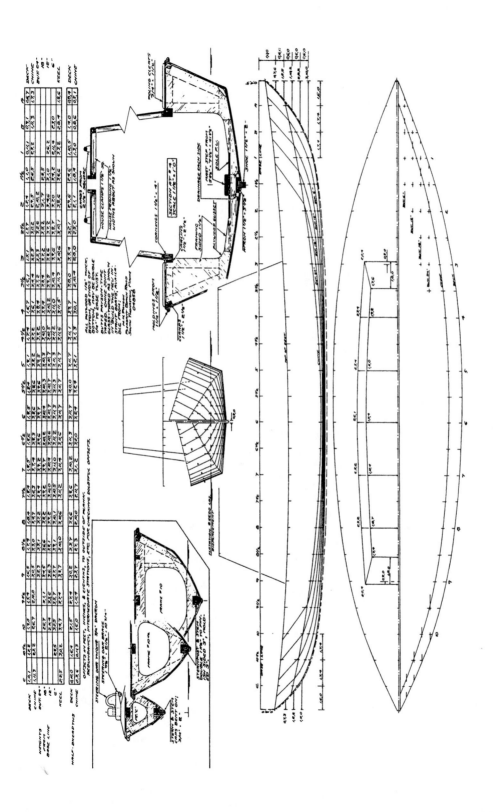

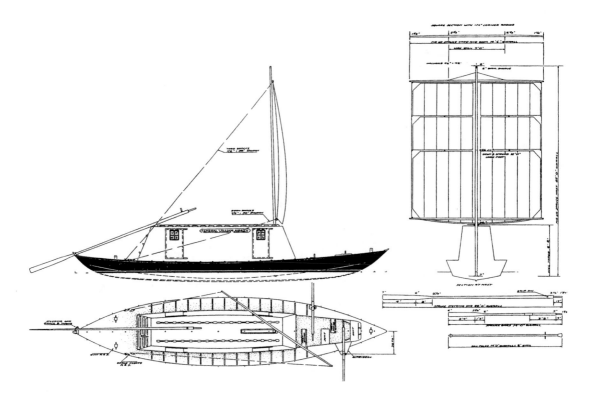

able to row the stern around with no way on the boat would be so convenient on the downstream run that the sweep must have been used. The helmsman can steer from on top of the house part of the time, to see for himself what he's about to meet. If the boat has way on, such a sweep is best worked by twisting rather than by sweeping; it can be treated as a rudder rather than an oar.

The two big oars have decent geometry. We discussed giving her auxiliary power, but my suggestion that it would be more satisfactory to hire a motorboat to stand by was accepted. I'd seen a photo of the big keelboat built for the film *The Big Sky* in action, with men straining at oars and poles, most realistically except for a very visible propeller race shooting back from her stern. . . .

We followed the deckhouse shown in the old drawing, which was probably not typical. The 55-footer that took Lewis and Clark up as far as Fort Mandan in 1804 was open amidships and pulled 22 oars. She drew 3 feet of water and didn't attempt to go on into Montana. I would have made the house a foot lower if I'd had my own way.

The V-bottomed hull shape was intended to be similar in behavior and handling to the round-bilged 19th-century boats, and to look something like them afloat and loaded. Plywood sheet construction was primarily to speed up building. It also allows her to be taken out of lengthy dry storage and used at once without having to go through a long swelling process. The plywood keelboat is much lighter than the old boats, but most of the total displacement would have been crew and cargo: moonshine and muskets upstream, beaver pelts downstream.

39 *Longship*

38'0 × 8'0" × 1'11"

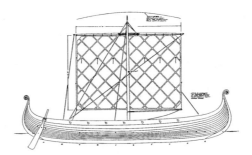

This small representation of a Viking ship was commissioned by The Society for Creative Anachronism of San Antonio, Texas. I suppose the motive was entertainment.

The people of whom these ships are the symbol were callous, rapacious, vindictive, and quarrelsome. The Vikings admired weapon-skill, good luck, and self-respect. Among them were craftsmen who produced some of the greatest art in history, and their vessels were the most highly perfected wooden structures ever created.

The perfection was not due to genius. It was the culmination of a thousand years or more of minute improvements. The Vikings were very patient: The Oseberg ship, from which much of this design is derived, was the yacht of a lady who in her youth had been kidnapped and raped, and her father and brothers killed, by a neighboring warlord. She lived with the killer for 16 years, until her son was old enough to inherit the chieftainship. *Then* that warlord was speared by her bodyguard. The son was Halfdan the Black, and his son was Harald Fairhair, first king of all Norway. The lady's name was Aasa, and when she died Halfdan buried her in her ship like a king. He killed her maids to keep her company. (All this is how it *may* have been. I'm a dilettante historian. But I would say it without a pause, they were like that, as the Icelandic Sagas tell.)

The seaworthiness of these vessels is defined by the Greenland expedition of Eric the Red. He set out from Iceland with 25 boats. Eleven were lost in the Denmark Strait. Fourteen made it and founded his colony. . . .

These boats were designed to reward hard driving under sail. The long, shallow keel has high drag if it's pinched close-hauled, but it's efficient sailed free with a good breeze. For a raiding beach-landing craft, it allows the vessel to be run onto a rough beach without hesitation, and launched again in a hurry if the enterprise ashore doesn't

(text continued on page 196)

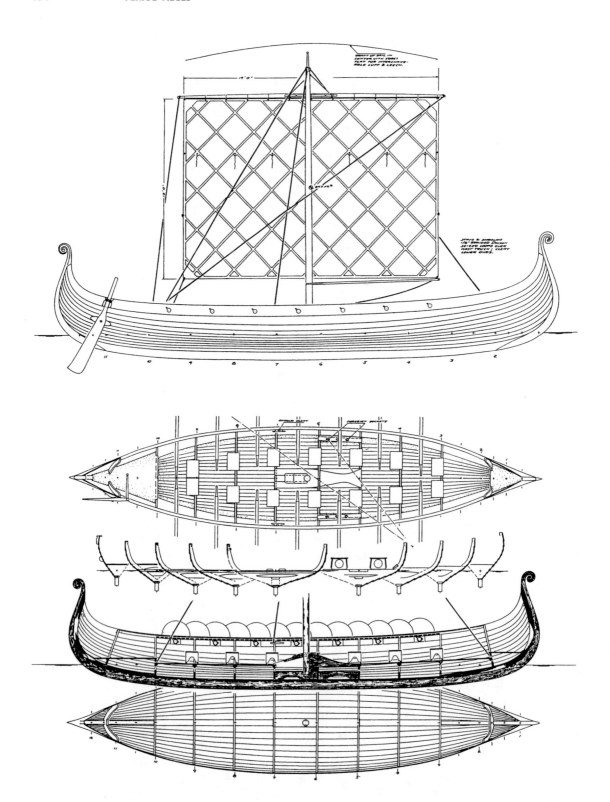

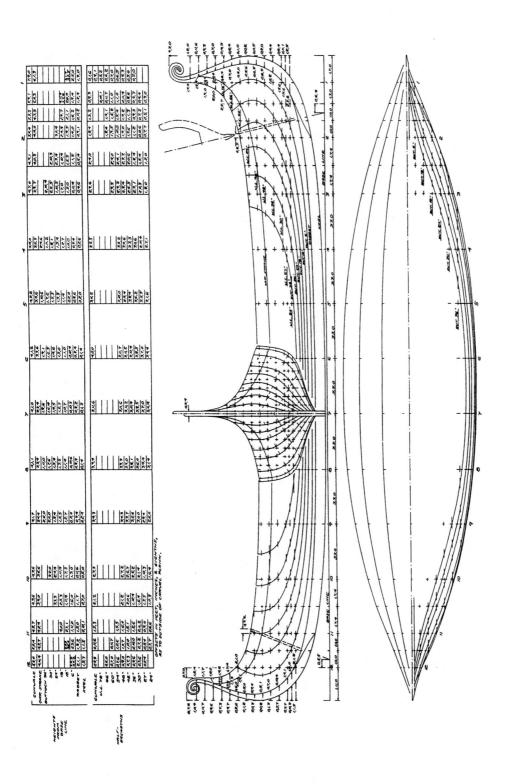

go well. The large surface area of the keel makes for hard rowing and shows that they meant to sail most of the time, but the oars have perfect geometry. The oarsmen usually sat on movable chests. With a strong headwind they could run the oars two or three feet inboard and stand up to them, for a shorter stroke with better mechanical advantage.

The construction is laid out to have no wood rigidly attached across the grain. Where the planking bears cross-grained against the frames, it is secured with resilient rawhide lashings. The natural-crook clinker planking is swept up to land on the stem and stern posts with grain almost tangent, all secured with iron rivets. This structure could shrink in the boathouse and swell in the sea without stressing itself. Every part is perfectly proportioned for the stress it has to bear in rough water and hard grounding.

This design uses plywood planking and laminated frames, and epoxy instead of iron and tar. It apes, as if without understanding, features due to other materials. It's possible that the shipwrights who built the great originals did not understand the design, but blindly followed a Master's formula. They produced great art, and I a tribute to their art.

40 *Schuyt Houseboat*

28'10"/ 26'0" × 10'5" × 2'0"

Dear Editor,

I have a retirement boat in mind, one which could comfortably and economically follow the seasons up and down the Eastern Seaboard via the Intracoastal Waterway, serving as both home and transport for a newly retired couple.

I've always thought along the lines of the old Dutch craft, but one that could be put together in the backyard by a home handyman. A couple of sailing scows have appeared in *National Fisherman* lately, and they seem to be the right idea; maybe 30 feet long or less, with accommodations for two. There would have to be a cozy cabin with kitchen, bathroom, living area, and sleeping arrangements. A wheelhouse or enclosed steering station to keep out the weather would be a fine addition.

Sails could be the primary power. I'm not sure what kind of rig would work—loose-footed mainsail and jib, junk, schooner? The masts would have to raise and lower for bridges and for painting. Leeboards would be simple to use. There should be an engine, maybe a small diesel or Saildrive.

There should be room aboard for a couple of bikes or mopeds to be used for running errands ashore, and space for tools, books, the painting easel, and the dog. Natural light through the roof would help with the painting and reading.

Of course, the old folks' income is going to be fixed and rationed, so economy both in construction and operation should be a major concern. Then again, the owners will have plenty of time to devote to the boat's upkeep. The wife might grow some vegetables in window boxes, and the old duffer might hook a cod or cunner for supper.

Speed would not be a concern. After all, the fun is getting where you're going, not in arriving. But, the boat should be able to take care of her occupants if accidentally caught on an open stretch.

Yes, I can picture such a craft—gaily painted like the canal boats of Europe, wandering the edges of Penobscot Bay in the Maine summer, and poking around the Florida Keys in winter. Would such a retirement boat be feasible? I'll bet a bunch of folks would like to know. Don't forget the ground tackle and the dinghy.

Richard Randall, Hampden, Maine

Dear Mr. Randall,

Schuyt (prounounced something like "scoot") is the generic name for the array of traditional Dutch types: Boeier, Hoogaars, Tjotter, etc., including the Botter mentioned below. This concept is eclectic.

Back when *Small Boat Journal* was new, there was some discussion about how big a boat was small. Strictly, a small boat is a boat carried on board a ship. But if the ship was a battleship, her small boats included a 50-foot steam launch. She might not have carried any boats under 30 feet long.

The ruling from the editor at the time was that a boat under 30 feet long would be considered small. By that definition the craft proposed here is a small boat, being 26 feet between perpendiculars, and less than 30 feet over the rudder and cutwater—which might be the dimension a marina proprietor would notice. It's close to 11 feet wide, not counting the leeboards, and it's designed to sail displacing 13,000 pounds. We'll agree to call it small.

Looked at as a permanent home, it's just workable. The beds are good-sized. The starboard berth could be a double, but I don't like doubles that can't be reached from both sides for making up. Bookshelves go above the foot of each berth on the faces of the chain boxes.

Closet space is barely adequate if you don't have too much that has to be hung up. With some ingenuity, and not keeping things around that you never wear, a year-round wardrobe could be disposed of.

Some will say that the bathroom is overdone. I've had my leg pulled now and then for devoting too much space to toilet functions. I thought the shower stall might be arranged as a tub of the seat-and-footwell type. It would take a lot of water, as the seat would have to be high enough to get out into the turn of the bilge, but it might be appreciated when you're tied up alongside a hose. A basin set far outboard as shown is a hazard to the absent-minded. I have one like this, and I ought to post a large notice above the door, "IS THE SEACOCK CLOSED?" One of the more advanced portable toilets is shown. I think there's just space for a holding tank, if necessary, mounted outboard and rather high. There is not space for a mulching toilet, much as I like the idea.

I first meant to have the dining settee L-shaped. That would give more bin space but take up available flat floor and cause people to brush against the painting easel set up where the guest chair is shown on the drawing. The couch pulls out into a double berth for guests, but you have to step on it to get into the bedroom.

The kitchen seems as good as could be asked. The sink is on centerline, so its seacock can be left open. The stove can be gimbaled, and the refrigerator is top-opening, in case you really do sail sometimes. The refrigerator is over 10 cubic feet inside 4 inches of insulation all around, one example of not having cheated on this cabin. There's good working and locker space, light, headroom, access to outdoors, and a fine view out. It would be possible to hook up controls, so the boat could be handled from this area under power, if you put up a periscope to see around.

The back porch is low-sided for stepping off onto the float but cocks up aft for a secure seat underway. An awning can be rigged over the boom in its permanent gallows, or over the lowered mast. It's possible to get at the motor from all sides.

The raised deck would have more lifelines and grabs than I've gotten around to showing. The punt is the type that can be slid over the side on end to spare launching gear. The mopeds needed hard thought, but eventually I saw that they should be slung in side davits like a ship's lifeboats, swung inboard during voyages, outboard for lowering to the float. The dog is your problem. I suggest that a good-sized python would be better adapted to life afloat and probably at least as effective in discouraging intruders.

The mast can be raised and lowered with the gypsy of the anchor windlass via a strut, not shown, socketed into the mast to give a direct lead through the whole arc. When down, the mast sticks far out over the stern, being close to 35 feet overall. A 6-ton boat is hardly oversparred at that.

I haven't tried to make the hull a simplified backyard project because: 1) The upper works, interior, and rig and engine are too big an investment to degrade by tying them to a cheap-looking bottom. 2) However simplified, the hull would be too big and heavy for most backyard builders. 3) A really simplified hull would be noisy at anchor and lack the floor space forward that this hull has. 4) It wouldn't stand up to groundings and heavy weather, or last as long, as this curvy shape. 5) I've never yet [see Chapter 68; 1993] been able to produce a scow with this much interior volume that works well as to deck arrangement. I've tried hard!

I think the elaborate character boat stands a chance of being a good investment; the simplified hull, probably not. The executor of your estate will think kinder thoughts in your memory if you pick this one.

Her remote ancestors are often mentioned as having been built of oak. For strength, you'd think. No doubt, but also because oak could be steamed to take all those quick curves and twists. Later, they built them of steel. A Dutchman used to wave his magic wand and make steel spring into sweet compound curves for riveting. Later still, they welded them and smoothed over the wrinkles with cement.

The shape would be perfect for ferrocement. I wonder if there's still anybody around who thinks that method is the home-builder's friend? I designed four ferrocement boats, and all I can say is that the last one wasn't as bad as the first.

The one-off fiberglass methods would be suitable. C-Flex, which tends to be heavy, would be the obvious choice. All fiberglass methods that don't involve a complete female mold produce a rough finish without an intolerable amount of finish work, but this type of boat doesn't have to glitter to look shipshape. It doesn't even have to be clean. The displacement allows for a massive layup of cheap mat an inch or more thick on the bottom. If you run her onto a coral reef, the hazard will be a lawsuit for damage to the coral.

The high sides and heavy bottom give her a seagoing range of stability. The shape can't be driven hard, but if she were caught in a blow offshore, I'd be surprised if the consequences were any worse than a mean bouncing around.

She'll cruise at 6 knots with around 10 h.p., but ought to have more power than that

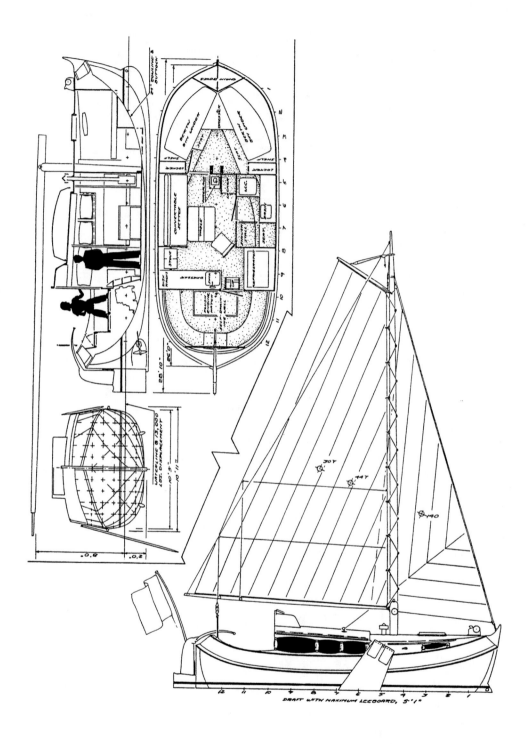

for control in bad conditions. Top speed would be 7 knots regardless. Since you'll be living wherever she is, there wouldn't be much hurry to be elsewhere.

For her sailing, read the voice of experience—Claud Worth. His facts were always accurate and his opinions always sensible. He described sailing a Schuyt in *Yacht Cruising*, written in 1910:

> During our Autumn cruise in Tern on the coasts of Germany and Holland in 1897, Bennet took a great fancy to the Dutch schuyts. With the tide under them, they turned to windward well in their own shallow waters. With the wind free, the splashing of water under their bluff bows made them appear to be sailing a great deal faster than they really were. They certainly looked very comfortable sitting upright on the sand when the tide left them.

Bennet bought one.

> We tried her during two weekends in the Thames estuary, but she was altogether too slow and heavy for the purpose. The sails were light to handle, and her powerful winch made the ground tackle easy to work, but she made a very poor show to windward, except with a good breeze and a favorable tide. In light airs she was quite helpless. . . .

They tried her offshore.

> . . . at first made good progress to windward. But when the sea began to get up, she soon showed us that she was not designed for this kind of work. She had to be sailed hard to keep her going at all. When she pitched into the trough of the sea, instead of rising gently over the next one, she would ram it hard with her square bows, completely stopping her way. There was as much wind as she wanted with a single-reefed mainsail. The sea was rather high, but easy and regular. Tern [a deep, narrow, English cutter] would have made no trouble of it. At 10 PM we were nearly up to the Royal Sovereign lightship. We turned to windward all night, standing far out to sea in hopes of making better weather, but we never managed to weather Beachy Head. Next morning, having had about enough of it, we brought up in Pevensey Bay at 8 AM. We had made good 26 miles in 25 hours, in a good sailing breeze!

To buy a working boat, or a boat of special type, and use her for a purpose for which she was never intended, usually leads to disappointment, and at best is only a makeshift. These schuyts are not the best boats for sailing, even in their own waters. They are specially designed to carry a maximum load on a shallow draft, and to stand a great deal of bumping on hard sand. The Thames barge model would fulfill the former conditions, but the square chine and flat bottom would not stand the bumping so well as the Dutch build.

41 *Scow Schooner*

28'0" × 9'10" × 1'3"

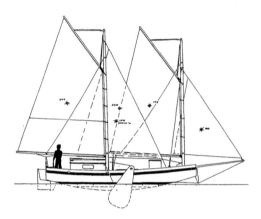

Dear *SBJ*:

Here in northern California there used to be a sort of working craft called a hay schooner. These were big scows with a bowsprit and a nice sheer that looked as pretty as any schooner in profile. The sides were flared, but they were scows with squared-off bows and dead-flat bottoms. They worked in shallow, narrow sloughs where they could navigate right up to the edge of a hayfield to pick up cargo.

I've often thought that something smaller along these lines would be a most useful craft here in my backyard, along the Sacramento and San Joaquín Rivers and their delta, which is a 1,000-mile maze of sloughs and channels. The wind howls across these, while the water remains flat in all but the most exposed channels.

My idea would be for something around 28 feet on deck, with a stockless rudder and small deckhouse aft just like the big boys had. I have a sort of junior cargo vessel in mind that would also serve well for daysailing with two or three couples. One or two crew ought to be able to make her go, and with all that deck space there ought to be plenty of room for non-working crew to lie about.

In the house, I'd need room for two people to sleep or four to six to sit—perhaps on the bunks with a foldaway table in between. Standing headroom would not be needed, but good ventilation would.

Forward of the house, I'd like a normally configured cargo hatch with boards and tarpaulin, just so I could haul stuff around or let kids crash below on air mattresses. I could keep bags of sand and a portable toilet there under some cruising conditions.

The rig could be sloop or schooner, gaff if possible, and the mast(s) should be in a tabernacle to allow passages beneath drawbridges that are no longer manned. It would be nice if a boat such as this could have a powerful engine to allow relatively painless upstream runs when the wind dies.

The old-timers had centerboards, but I'd go for leeboards if I heard a compelling argument. Plywood construction would suit me fine.

Walter Wiley, Sacramento, California

Dear Mr. Wiley:

This looks pot-bellied at first glance, but if you compare the profile of the bottom with the bow-buttock lines of a normal auxiliary, you'll find they're in the same class. The advantage of using plenty of rocker is that the boat can be deep in the middle without enormous displacement. Lots of rocker also makes for quick turning, useful in a boat that doesn't have much momentum relative to her resistance.

The advantage of being deep is that the point of maximum sail-carrying power, when the weather chine starts to fly, comes at a big enough angle of heel to go into a head sea with as little slamming as anybody has a right to expect in a flat-bottomed hull. The ballast can be placed low relative to the height of her sides. Unlike very shallow scows, which behave more like catamarans, sailing bolt-upright until they suddenly flip bottom-up, this boat has a range of stability similar to that of most monohulls. The deeper scow can be driven in a breeze without intense concentration because she'll warn you when she's over-pressed.

Her upright waterline is short, which cuts down wetted surface in light weather; but, as she heels, the waterline lengthens for fast sailing. She draws quite a bit more water heeled than she does upright—handy for the kind of sailing you describe. You can hold a board till she feels the bottom. Putting the helm down to tack will reduce the draft enough to go through stays clear of the mud.

I tried various angles of rake on the bow transom and decided to leave it plumb. She must sail on her bottom, and a vertical transom means the bottom can be longer and carried higher, so it takes a deeper pitch or a steeper wave to dig the transom in. A raked transom has less drag than a vertical one, but it's still prohibitive when immersed. Left to myself, I'd put it vertical, but I wouldn't be vehemently against more or less rake.

The cuddy cabin is built all the way out to the sides. Advantages: more room inside, and quite a bit more reserve stability and buoyancy in a knockdown. The drawback is climbing over it every time you go forward or aft. There's a good rectangular transom berth on each side, with the galley across the forward end between them. The toilet is in the outhouse up forward.

The hold is 8 feet long, about 8½ feet average breadth, and around 3 feet deep, give or take 6 inches depending on where you measure it. The hold hatches open wide for bulky objects, but for obvious reasons the outboard panels are supposed to be dogged down tight when sailing. A boom for lifting cargo could be rigged on the mainmast.

The stockless rudder works in neatly since we have to use wheel steering anyway. There's too little room for the length of tiller she'd need. These arrangements have built-in slop that irritates me, though stiff springs in the steering cables might take care of most of it. The main advantage is that the components are all easy to build, strong, and readily inspected.

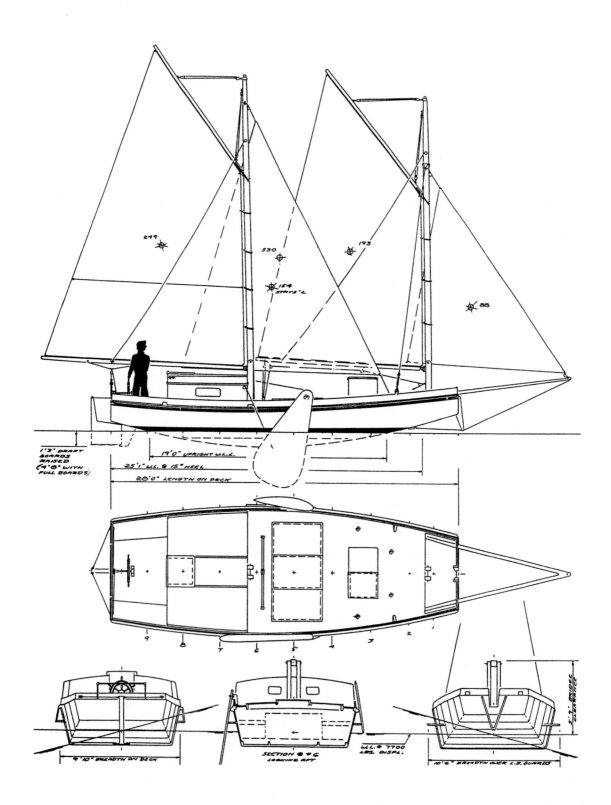

249

530

154
STAYS'L

193

88

1'3" DRAFT
BOARDS
RAISED
(4'0" WITH
FULL BOARDS)

19'0" UPRIGHT W.L.L.

25'1" W.L. @ 15° HEEL

28'0" LENGTH ON DECK

9'10" BREADTH ON DECK

SECTION @ #6
LOOKING AFT

W.L. @ 7700
LBS. DISPL.

10'6" BREADTH OVER L.B. GUARDS

S.T. BRIDGE
CLEARANCE

No auxiliary engine is shown. An inboard engine could be put either in the cuddy or in the hold, but it would spoil one or the other. An outboard could be carried on a bracket, but I'd opt for a yawlboat, a stiff tender with a big outboard and heavy padding to lash up to the stern or on either quarter. If the gear is imaginatively set up, this will drive the mother ship at least as well as a bracket motor and is less likely to be swamped or pitched out of water, because the small boat conforms to wave shapes. It also encourages keeping an able tender. A discount-store jonboat would be appropriate.

Besides your suggestion, I have a letter asking for pontification on leeboards. I used to mount them as close to parallel with the centerline as I could get them, but lately I've been trying a very small toe-in, about 1 degree. In theory, toe-in should be just enough to cancel leeway. In practice, it's terribly easy to overdo it, converting the leeboard into an effective brake. A very slight toe-in keeps the weather board from kiting out, though leeboards should be designed on the assumption that the weather board *will* be left down and *will* kite.

They should be mounted at an outward angle, rather than vertically, so that they'll lie quietly on their guards and not swing out and bang back. The exception is the type that has bearings both above and below the pivot, as in my Dovekie design among others, but the arrangement can have high drag unless the boards are matched just right to the shape of the hull.

Hulls with flaring sides need very wide guards, but these are hard to build strongly enough, are apt to pound in a seaway, and collect weed and other sculch. This is a bad habit of leeboards in general.

Each leeboard should be equal in area to whatever the boat would need in a centerboard or fin keel. But if the boards are braced well clear of the hull, as here, the area can be figured from the waterline so the boards' draft when lowered will be less. I wouldn't advise anybody to get crafty with high-aspect-ratio boards with sophisticated foil shapes. Among other problems, these have to work at high angles of incidence to be effective at low speeds. Without the slots and flaps of aircraft, they may stall and let the boat sag to leeward. Even if they don't stall, the drag of the boards and hull will be large as the boat is pushed along partly sideways. An aircraft designer doesn't usually care how high the drag is when his plane is flying low and slow, but a sailboat ought to aim for low resistance in light air. Leeboard area should be something upwards of twice what aeronautical-type calculations may suggest. (If someone is thinking of gliders, they are gravity-powered, and if you fly in one you'll find, especially when it comes in to land, that it doesn't fly slowly!)

There's always a problem making leeboards stiff enough to prevent them from warping under press of sail, because they're braced less comprehensively than centerboards. If they're built thick for stiffness, they have a lot of buoyancy and need so much ballast to sink that they're heavy to raise. I've tried making them hollow and allowing them to flood, but the flooding and draining is too slow when they're wanted up or down in a hurry. Best make them as thin as you dare, and, if they're as big as these here, arrange a three- or four-part purchase on the pendants. There's a lot to be said for a dedicated winch on each board.

In this proposal, the hull and rig are both proportioned to place the leeboards at the point where the flow of water around the hull is more or less parallel to the boards' section. Conversions of centerboarders to leeboards aren't usually satisfactory because the leeboards have to be too far forward, where the hull forebody is pushing the water across the leeboards. The guards have to be too broad, with a bad hull interface. Boats with bilge keels have the same problem, the reason so many of them are not very good sailers.

Leeboards can be mounted and pivoted in a wide variety of ways, much too big a subject to go into here. A test of whether the student grasps the subject is to examine the difference in the action of the boards in the Dutch geometry I usually use, and the alternate principle invented by Francis Herreshoff. Study where and at what angles the boards end up as they swing off the hull at various lowered positions. The Dutch boards stay parallel with the hull even if they swing out off the hull to horizontal. The Herreshoff boards cant their leading edges downward as they swing out, which forces them back to their intended position on their guards.

The rig is designed more for fun than economy. She'd be substantially cheaper to rig, and very likely faster some of the time, with a gaff cat rig. A cat-yawl would be more forgiving to handle, but not as fast as the straight cat. However, once you've paid for all the spars and sails, a schooner like this is great sport. With the big main staysail set, there's 684 square feet of sail, and she'll stand up to it because it's carried low. I haven't bothered to figure her ratio of sail area to wetted surface, but I can see at a glance that she would probably astonish anybody who thought he knew what fast boats look like. Her best point of sailing would be reaching in light to moderate winds; her worst, close-hauled in light air and a leftover slop or bobble of motorboat wakes.

In strong winds, with the jib and the staysail furled, a deep reef in the mainsail, and a full foresail, she would be weatherly and fast, coping with a head sea as well as most boats.

The masts pivot down aft for bridge clearance of less than 6 feet. They're short and stiff enough to lower without complicated gear. Their location and the general arrangement of the boat allows this to work without having to cut holes in the deck for the heels to swing through—a plus for the schooner rig.

Construction is intended to be all plywood, and could easily be laid out for prefabrication. I've designed sizable flat bottoms with regular cross-planking, with glued-strip cross-planking, and with multiple layers of plywood. One boat had a thin plywood bottom sheathed with natural timber laid fore-and-aft and tapered to make her bottom about 4 inches thick amidships but only ¾-inch thick at the ends. I've also done bottoms fore-and-aft planked on transverse frames, and with various framing systems in steel and aluminum. A metal boat of this model is practical, but needs deep longitudinal stringers to stiffen it.

The multiple plywood bottoms have seemed the best combination of economy and freedom from trouble. I'd have this bottom at least 1½ inches thick overall—say, three courses of ½-inch—with a couple of stringers and little or no framing in between the bulkheads. I'd sheathe it with fiberglass all over the outside to save finish work, or if copper prices stayed low I'd think about copper sheathing below the waterline; 16-ounce copper sheet is about the ultimate in low maintenance and pays for itself long before it wears out, if it ever does.

For a long time I've tried to design a boat of this type with her house carried the full length or nearly so to make a sailing houseboat. It isn't easy.

Author's Note

I did later design a 36-footer with a long house, but she hasn't been built as this book is written. See the Superbrick design, Chapter 68, for the nature of the problems.

42 *Racing Schooner*

39'9" × 29'0" × 8'11" × 4'6"

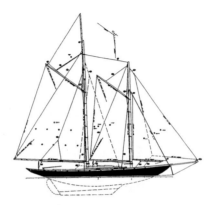

Leonard Crask's famous statue of The Helmsman has looked out over Gloucester Harbor for 70 years, a memorial to 10,000 lost fishermen and to the era of the sailing fishing schooner. When the statue was made, the fleets of sailing fishermen and coasters had dwindled. Memory was already selecting their splendor as works of mobile art over their significance as technology of an excellence that drew enterprising men from Newfoundland and the Azores and Sicily, but with deficiencies that killed those men by the hundred.

It's a fact that the sailing fishing schooners were killers, created and sailed by people who were callous by necessity, as, at the time I'm writing, people are callous of the killers and works of art on highways.

Brad Story and I pictured a fleet of small schooners, built by him and others, moored in a row under the eyes of The Helmsman, off the public beach and esplanade there, and raced in and out of the harbor to liven the scenery. Some would be privately owned, crewed by friends. Others would be business enterprises, skippered by a professional with paying passengers as crew. The size was chosen as fit to be raced by as few as three people, but to carry as many as eight without a speed handicap. My recurring thought is that such a fleet could be a lively gambling device, better than betting on dogs because a bettor could ride the boat of her choice. (I had a good time elaborating this theme in my novel *Schorpioen*; its working title was "The Sea Jockies," but the publisher said that that was "a wimp title.")

These boats would be small enough to be numerous, with some flavor of the harbor scene in the era of sail. The size allowed proportions reflecting those of the last sailing fishermen, with graceful style paramount. They needed no more below-decks accommodations than followed the style. Labor devoted to more elaborate cabins would be diverted to increasing the numbers of the fleet.

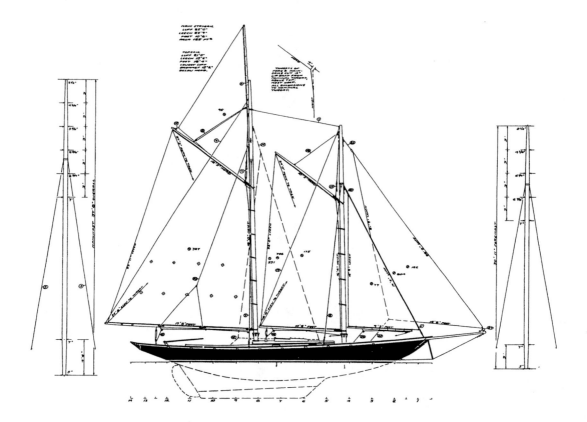

The shape is similar to many racing classes designed in the 1920s and earlier—thoroughbred boats as rewarding to sail as anything since, though not quite as fast or close-winded as can now be designed. Some were schooner-rigged, and it's possible to rationalize a functional case for the rig, as its sails can be set and furled in the handiest sequence while riding to a mooring—small forward sails quickly and easily, large after sail more at leisure. Such boats are more tolerant of mistakes in handling, and maneuver more gracefully, than the later designs that outperform them.

Dr. Joe Geary had me design a 44-foot schooner along these lines, which he and his family have much enjoyed; but, though she is noticed and admired, she has not been imitated.

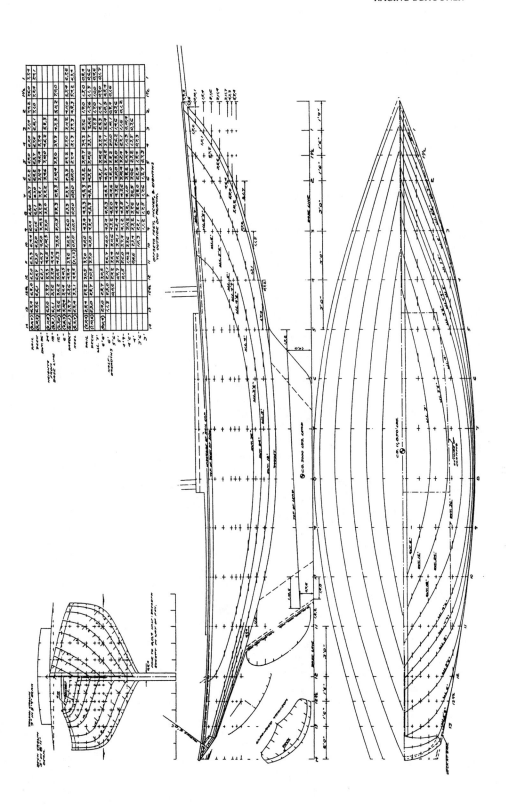

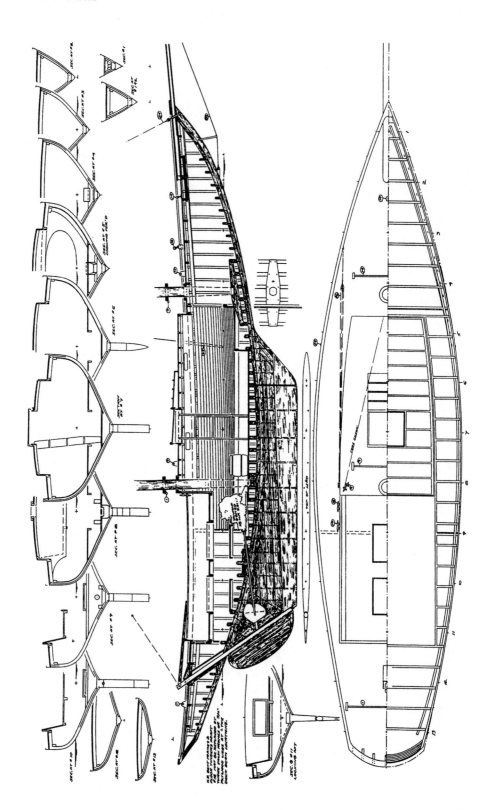

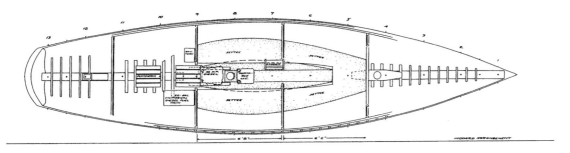

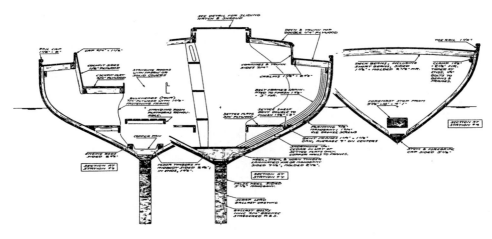

Dr. Joe Geary's schooner

43 *Brigantine*

32'0" × 9'0" × 3'0"

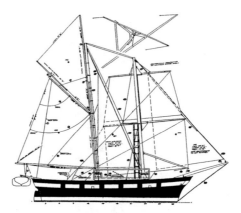

Charles Andrews specified the brigantine rig as an attraction for customers; she was intended to carry paying guests daysailing initially from Cleveland or thereabouts; later on the Chesapeake and points south. Her yards standing out on the waterfront set her off from the nondescript fleet. Once any kind of premise is adopted, it pays to take it seriously and see how good a seaboat and performer can be developed on the premise. All pleasure boats are toys, but there's a temptation to slack study on an unusually toylike one, which may be fair enough in dealing with a model, or a true replica, but which can miss good chances in a boat meant to be used as well as exhibited.

The first study was lower-sided, with the 'midships raised deck as low as would give a fair margin of reserve stability and buoyancy in a squall. The cabin was a cuddy, to wait out a shower at anchor. The owner suggested that it would be useful if a couple of berths could be arranged in the engine room, so he could rent the cuddy overnight occasionally, with the crew out of the way of the charterers. The intended low afterdeck left no room for berths. I made a rough drawing showing her with a foot more freeboard all along. I meant this drawing to demonstrate that the idea was impractical, but when I tacked it on the wall and stepped back, I liked it better than the lower hull; it had a pert and buoyant look. The flat sheer, adopted from the beginning to keep the height of the ends from getting out of hand, fitted the higher sides still better. This kind of style, including the painted ports and the lack of trailboards, was common in the first half of the 19th century. It appears in ship portraits by Antoine Roux. Some show the elaborate carved headwork of earlier times painted over in this fashion.

The added buoyancy made her fit for offshore work. Conor O'Brien's famous world cruiser *Saoirse* (pronounced something like "sheer-she," and damnation to whoever was responsible for the ridiculous way Gaelic is transliterated) was like this in many respects. O'Brien touted the rig as ideal. I do not; it has too much wind resistance and is much too complicated (there are 44 pieces of running rigging!), but it's workable with enough hands or enough time, and does have some advantages. Alan Villiers' book *The Way of a Ship* is the best primer on the workings of square-riggers.

Locating the center of effort in such a rig defies analysis. The long, straight keel with a lot of forefoot common to all square-riggers is intended to make the vessel insensitive to the effects of many combinations of sails. Lee helm is as bad for windward performance as in any rig, but it isn't dangerous as it is in a fore-and-after; in fact, a strong weather helm is more dangerous because it increases the chances of being caught aback, which could dismast or capsize many old-fashioned square-riggers, though not this one. With all plain sail, and certainly with the club topsail set, she should carry a mild weather helm.

The hull is flat-floored, hard-bilged, and full-ended to carry the weight of the rig and to sail upright. Her hard-driven speed is not fast (I'd be skeptical if told that she had done much over 7 knots), but she has plenty of sail and a respectable all-around performance, given hands enough to keep the rig trimmed. The long, flat-sided keel enables her to hold on well. It has high drag if she's pinched in light airs, but her rig geometry precludes doing that. The square-rigger's ability to turn at a standstill and to back down under control could lead to less use of her engine than those of many modern cruisers.

The hull is simpler than it looks. The stern is a straightforward transom, flat across and just notched in profile for effect. She is carvel-planked on bent frames, copper-sheathed underneath. Above the main sheer she is all plywood, fiberglass and epoxy sheathed, to be tight and trouble-free in the sun.

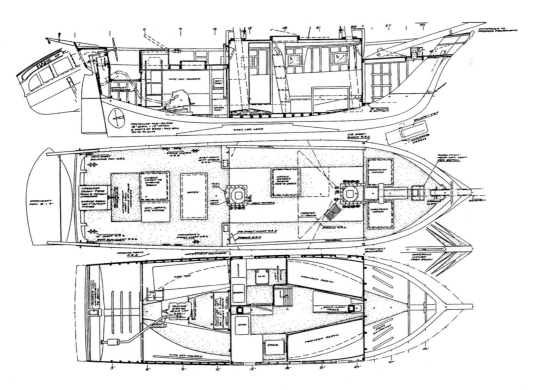

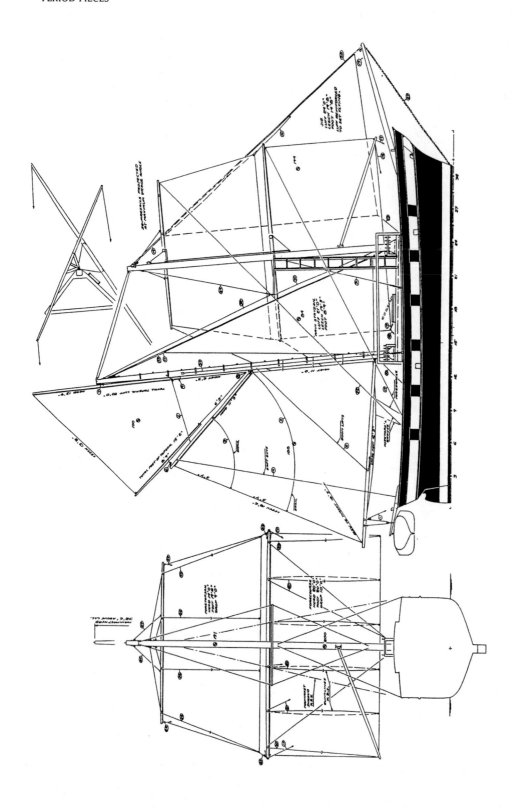

Rigging Details

Running Rigging

1. Main sheet $3/8$" × 70'. Standing end on a boom bail 2 feet inboard of clew end; through a block traveling on a $1/2$-inch removable horse between the stern davit arms; up through a swivel block on a boom bail; fall to leeside belaying pin in davit arm.

2. Main boom lifts (two) $3/8$" × 28' each. Standing ends on the mast just below gaff level; through cheek blocks on the sides of the boom 7 feet inboard of the clew end; fall in to cleats on the boom close to the gooseneck.

3. Mainsail brails (two) $1/4$" × 40' and 35'. Standing ends on the side of the gaff at the throat and 6 feet below the peak; out through leech grommets diagrammed; in to blocks on the gaff opposite the standing ends; upper brail taken in to a turning block near the throat; falls to pin rail.

4. Main gaff guys (two) $3/8$" × 30'. Fast to gaff sides 12 inches below the peak; falls direct to cleats marked on the deck plan. (The guys will usually be slack and may be tied off forward as convenient.)

5. Main peak halyard $1/8$" × 24' 7 × 19 wire tailed out with 7 feet of $1/2$-inch Dacron. Standing end 3 feet from peak of gaff; in to a block on a mast bail 7 feet below the masthead; fall to pin rail. (Normally used only to make small adjustments in peak angle.)

6. Main topsail sheet $1/4$" × 50'. Standing end at midpoint of topsail club (find best point by trial); through a block on the peak of the gaff; in to a block on the gaff close to the throat; fall to pinrail.

7. Main topsail halyard $3/8$" × 58'. Standing end 6'10" below the peak of the topsail yard; through a block under the masthead cap; fall to pinrail.

8. Main topsail tack downhaul $1/4$" × 15'. Straight from the tack grommet to the pinrail. (Take all the topsail gear to the leeside pins when setting the sail.)

9. Main topsail yard heel downhaul $1/4$" × 22'. Straight from the foot of the topsail yard to the pinrail. (This line may not be necessary.)

10. Main staysail sheets (two) $1/4$" × 15'. Straight from clew of sail to cleats marked on the deck plan. (Consider using one sheet brought over in tacking.)

11. Main staysail halyard $1/4$" × 55'. Standing end on the head grommet or headboard of the sail; through a block on a tang under the mainstay tang; fall to mainmast pinrail.

12. Main staysail tack downhaul $1/4$" × 3'. Straight from the tack grommet of the sail to a cleat lashed across the mainstay turnbuckle.

13. Jib sheets (two) $3/8$" × 30'. Standing ends on the clew grommet of the sail; to swivel blocks marked on the deck plan at forward end of raised deck; aft to cleats on the after face of the raised deck.

14. Jib halyard $3/8$" × 55'. Standing end on the head of the sail; through a block on a tang under the forestay tang; fall to pinrail.

15. Jib tack outhaul $3/8$" × 28'. Standing end on the tack of the sail; through a block just inboard of the forestay tang; fall to the mooring cleat or to a dedicated cleat after trial.

16. Jib luff downhaul $1/4$" × 39'. Standing end on a grommet 8 feet above the tack of the sail; through a grommet 8 feet below the head; through the head grommet; fall to the pinrail. (Used to control the sail when setting and taking in.)

17. Forecourse braces (two) $1/2$" × 31'. Straight from yardarms to cleats marked on the deck plan. (These may need a purchase but try single part first. The leeside brace will normally be slack.)

18. Forecourse sheets (two) $3/8$" × 28'. Standing ends on the clew grommets of the sail; lead aft through the scuppers at the after end of the raised deck, to cleats placed by trial on the inside of the bulwarks.

19. Forecourse tack lines (two) $\frac{1}{4}$" × 18'. Standing ends on the clew grommets of the sail. Lead through hawseholes to cleats on the inside of the bulwarks.

20. Forecourse clew garnets (two) $\frac{1}{4}$" × 36'. Standing ends on forward side of the yard 12 inches inboard of the yardarms; down through clew grommets; up, through a cringle on the after side of the sail, to cheek blocks on the after side of the yard 12" inboard of the yardarm; fall to pinrail.

21. Forecourse buntlines (four) $\frac{1}{4}$" × 34' each. Reeve like the clew garnets.

22. Foretopsail braces (two) $\frac{3}{8}$" × 35'. Reeve similar to forecourse braces.

23. Foretopsail sheets (two) $\frac{3}{8}$" × 12'. Standing ends on the clew grommets of the topsail; through blocks or bullseyes on course yardarms; lead in to cleats on the course yard within easy reach of the foretop.

24. Foretopsail halyards (two) $\frac{3}{8}$" × 36'. Standing ends on the topsail yard 4 feet 9 inches inboard of the yardarms; up through blocks on the sides of the mast 6 inches below the masthead; falls to pinrail.

25. Foretopsail clew garnets (two) $\frac{1}{4}$" × 37'. Standing ends on the forward side of the topsail yard 12 inches inboard of the yardarms; down through clew grommets of the topsail; up, through cringles on the after side of the sail, through cheek blocks or dumb sheaves on the after side of the topsail yard; through blocks on the mast 2 feet below the masthead; down to

cleats on the mast within easy reach of the fore-top.

26. Foretopsail buntlines (two) $\frac{1}{4}$" × 32'. Reeve the same as the clew garnets, through blocks 2 feet 6 inches below the masthead.

(All running rigging except the wire main peak halyard can be braided Dacron.)

Standing Rigging

All except the chain bobstay $\frac{1}{4}$-inch diameter 1 × 19 strand wire with swaged jaw terminals. Lengths approximate pin-to-pin including $\frac{3}{8}$" turnbuckles. Total wire 206 feet plus turnbuckles.

27. Bobstay $\frac{1}{4}$" × 12' galvanized chain. $\frac{3}{8}$" turnbuckle at the outboard end.

28. Forestay 28'9". Masthead to bowsprit end.

29. Foretopmast shroud upper legs (two) 12'11". From near masthead to corners of fore-top. Turnbuckles at the lower ends.

30. Foretopmast shroud lower legs (two) 10'0". From corners of foretop to mast near deck, see detail.

31. Foremast shrouds (two) 12'4". From after side of mast under top platform to hull chain plates.

32. Foretop guys (two) 18'0". From corners of foretop up to mainmasthead.

33. Maintopmast stay 28'0". From mainmasthead down to foremast near the deck.

34. Mainmast shrouds (two) 20'8". From tangs on sides of mast 8 feet below the masthead, to hull chain plates.

Part Seven

Bed and Breakfast, Sail

44 *Micro*

15'4" × 6'0" × 1'9"

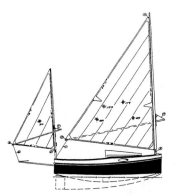

Micro was originally designed for the late Elrow LaRowe, a retired clergyman and founder of Common Sense Designs, to sail on Tampa Bay. The cuddy was for shelter from an afternoon thunderstorm. The design turned out to be one of my best efforts, and a fleet of the boats has been built from New Zealand to Finland. The following fiction, written for WoodenBoat magazine, is an amalgam of different people's experiences plus some of my own in the waters of the setting.

The Lovers

An April sun is rising over Italy, far out of sight over the lee quarter of the tiny cat-yawl making her way toward France. The little boat has been bobbing along at 4 knots, close-hauled in a gentle westerly breeze, all night and since dawn the day before. The mountains of Corsica went under the horizon about noon. The young woman at the tiller is sitting on the weather side, her weight reducing the angle of heel. If the wind were much lighter she would move to the lee side, since the flat bottom is noisy if the boat is sailed bolt-upright.

A very small inflatable boat is in tow. The tiller is held in a rack, and the boat is keeping a good course unsteered, with the mizzen sheet slightly freer than the mainsheet. The woman occasionally turns a flashlight on the box compass that is chocked off against the break of the deck. Near her feet, in the open hatch of the hold under the after-deck, are dry-cell navigation lights ready to show approaching ships. She used them once during her watch when a large power yacht crossed their course—bound for Genoa, she guessed.

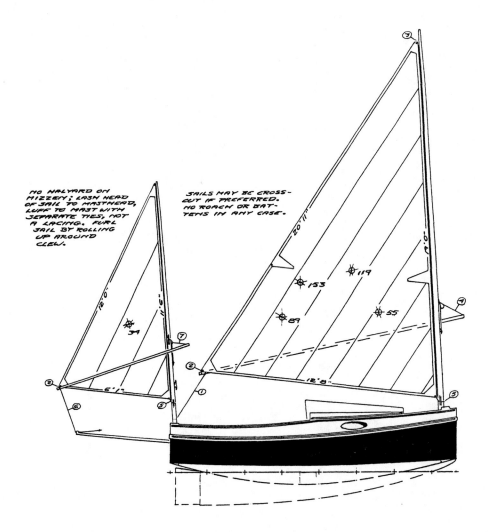

NO HALYARD ON
MIZZEN; LASH HEAD
OF SAIL TO MASTHEAD,
LUFF TO MAST WITH
SEPARATE TIES, NOT
A LACING. FURL
SAIL BY ROLLING
UP AROUND
CLEW.

SAILS MAY BE CROSS-
CUT IF PREFERRED.
NO ROACH OR BAT-
TENS IN ANY CASE.

Her husband is sleeping below, his feet under her left buttock, his head on the sloping forward end of the cuddy sole. A length of canvas laid under his mattress and stretched up 30cm above the inboard edge of the berth would hold him in place if the boat heeled much. He sleeps on the weather side, to be live ballast—not necessary in this weather, but a great help to the boat when there's more wind. His weight is centered well back from the bow, and his wife's weight, in the cockpit, is far from the stern, keeping the ends of the boat light as well as balanced. This is especially necessary because, while the boat is nominally all of 4⅔ meters long, each end is a free-flooding well, more of cutwater and stern platform than boat proper; the actual watertight envelope is barely 3 meters long. The arrangement makes certain that outboard motor fuel, stowed aft, and muddy anchors and warps, stowed forward, won't contaminate the cuddy. Some of their other supplies are also stowed in the end wells, including a 4-liter jug of red wine wrapped in life vests.

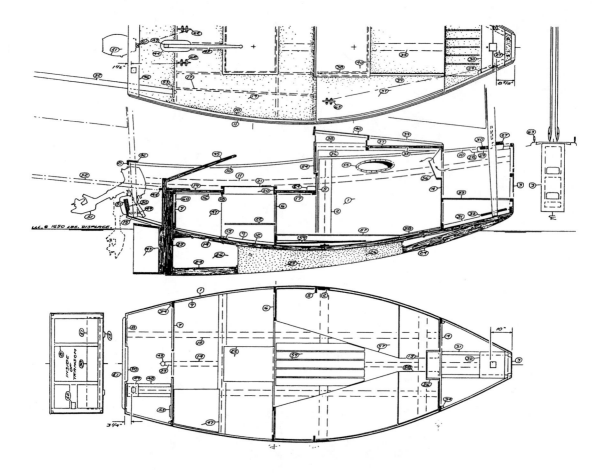

The cuddy is reasonably clean, but it's hardly dry. The berths have the same problem that quarter berths do in more reasonably sized cruisers: they're in the way of drips and splashes from the companionway. The forward ventilator has been known to spit when there's a strong headwind. The cockpit hatch is supposed to be kept shut underway, but the couple find it so comfortable to sit with their feet in it that they usually have it open. Through ventilation is good between the openings in the forward bulkhead and the one in front of the sternpost; the draft will work with either bow or stern to the wind, so the cuddy dries quickly whenever the air is dry. They scrub it out with fresh water when they can. On one glorious occasion they found themselves within reach of a large yacht's deck hose, with a group of amiable deckhands looking down at them. They stripped the cuddy and half-filled the boat with fresh water without making an appreciable inroad on the yacht's seawater conversion capacity. They had a memorable soaking bath in the flooded cuddy, and took no offense when a voice from above was heard to say, "I knew there had to be some reason for a boat that shape!"

They normally keep their few clothes, including some large bath towels, in waterproof bags. A portable toilet lives under the forward end of the cockpit, between the feet of the berths. It is slid forward under the companionway hatch for use. They dump it furtively over the side as far offshore as possible.

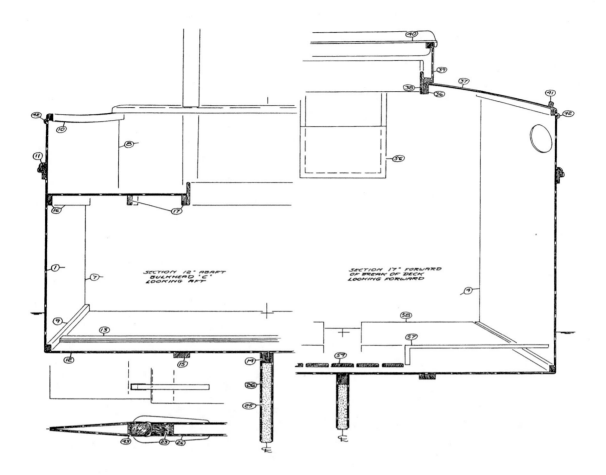

SECTION 12" ABAFT
BULKHEAD 'C'
LOOKING AFT

SECTION 17" FORWARD
OF BREAK OF DECK
LOOKING FORWARD

They have found that a boat with a keel drawing 53cm with the boat trimmed level (and less when she's down by the head) does not always have to lie in the crowded and quarrelsome ranks of Mediterranean yacht harbors. Nearly every port they've visited has a shallow place somewhere, that has allowed them to lie out of the way and have some privacy. They motor around in search of it, frequently pursued by a harbormaster trying to warn them away from the shoals. They have arranged supports for the cuddy floorboards at the slightly higher level of the berths, to convert the cuddy into a bed almost 185cm wide. A square awning shades the companionway and most of the cockpit; it hangs slightly cockeyed between the mainmast and the off-center mizzen. The long sprit boom forms a ridgepole; mizzen boom and boomkin serve as transverse spreaders.

A propane stove is used in the cockpit, when they're in port. Underway the couple lives on bread, cheese, fruit, and the red wine. They have two Walkman cassette players and a paperback copy of *El Conde de Monte Cristo*, the latter now almost perished. There's a dry-cell riding light which is more often used for cabin lighting. For reading after dark they use candles, four at a time in a socketed block of wood mounted between the heads of the berths. There have been some nights when the heat of the candles was welcome.

They were lucky in their weather, and they hopped from port to port around the

Dale Amundson and his Micro

Gulf of Genoa with increasing confidence, fulfilling a dream by reaching Montecristo. They considered pushing on to the Strait of Bonifacio but decided they did not have time. If they had passed the strait they would almost certainly have lost the boat. The Libeccio, a southwest dry gale, blew up out of a clear sky as they neared Cap Corse, and even under the lee of Corsica they got the scare of their lives and just made it into Bastia with deep-reefed mainsail and motor wide open. They came close to being blown over to the Italian coast. If they'd been on the west coast of Corsica, they would have piled up on the lee shore.

After the fright, they ventured the long jump to France with their hearts in their mouths, but they will boast later that none of their gear shifted or got wet. In truth, the shifts weren't disastrous and the wetting was limited. While waiting for the gale to blow itself out, they added some more hooks and eyes and bought some net material to improve restraint against beam-ends knockdowns.

The woman looks ahead and sees the mountains of Provence catch the first sunlight behind a gap that ought to be the Gulf of Saint-Tropez. Her cry, "Tierra!" brings her husband's tousled head out of the hatch. It's a good sign that he looks good to her after a month in that boat.

45 *Chebacco Boats*

19'8" × 7'5" × 1'0"/ 3'11" (sheet plywood)
19'8" × 7'5" × 1'6" (higher sides and shelter house)
19'6" × 7'9" × 1'0" (lapstrake)
25'4" × 7'11" × 1'4" (stretched lapstrake)

The Essex River north of Cape Ann on the Massachusetts coast is a long, twisting tidal creek. Its head of navigation used to be a world-class center of mass-production wooden ship building—fishermen, coasters, whalers, now and then a yacht. For 200 years the foreshore was lined with rising timbers. Looking at the creek now, it's not to be believed that 150-foot three-masted schooners were worked through it. It looks as though it couldn't be negotiated by the steam tug, let alone the vessel.

Nowadays, it really couldn't be done because the creek is solidly filled on both sides with boat slips. The slips are full, and the remaining marshy banks are out of bounds. Any more boats have to be hauled away from the water when they're not in use.

The Story Shipyard has built vessels for seven generations, father to son, since 1813. Now it builds fewer and smaller craft than it did in its famous years. The yard is no longer on the too-valuable foreshore, and its boats are not built on the assumption that they'll be wrecked in a few years (those massively timbered ships were as short-lived as automobiles). The lower tempo of production introduces a sequencing problem: building one or two boats a year, a single cancellation can create a cash-flow problem. There's a need for standard models for which there's a steady demand, to build on speculation when there's a gap in bespoken work.

The crowded slips point to a trailer boat, overproduction of utilities and cruisers to a daysailer. Bradford Story and I conceived the Chebacco boats to fit a niche market: a trailer boat/daysailer. (Essex was once called Chebacco Parish of Ipswich, and its first distinctive product was a cuddy-cabin fishing boat, so-called.)

The first batch were cold-molded, expensive for their capability. The second group were built from the sheet-plywood design here (see plans) with a huge saving in labor time. The motor centered on the stern replaced the makeshift (and ugly) off-center

The first sheet plywood Chebacco design, 19'8" × 7'5" × 1'0"

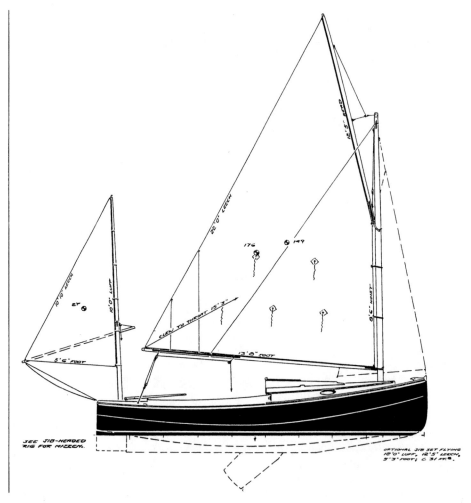

bracket of the first series to make them handier under power for running up the narrow channel between the rows of boat slips. The motor's position called for an inboard rudder, which also improved the tiller position in the cockpit. The mizzenmast could be centered and set inboard, allowing use of sheets to the quarters, eliminating a long boomkin. With two sheets thus, the weather-side sheet controls the sail. The lee sheet hangs slack. The sprit boom's downward thrust keeps the clew from lifting and slacking the leech. Neither sheet has to be touched in tacking; both can be set up tight to hold the boom on center, making the best use of the cat-yawl's ability to weathercock for reefing, or to lie steadily to an anchor.

The inboard rudder needed a skeg to protect it on the trailer, and by extending the skeg forward some of the centerboard could be buried under the hull, reducing the intrusion inside. We found that this shallow keel allowed the boats to sail to windward and maneuver reliably in 12 inches of water, opening up sand flats usually useful only to rowing boats and jet-skis. (They sail and maneuver much better with the centerboard down in deeper water.)

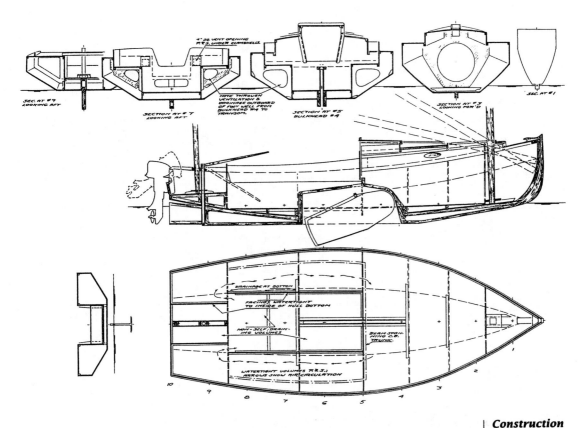

*Construction
drawings for
the first sheet
plywood
design*

Rudders as shallow as this used to be unreliable, but the addition of end plates on the bottoms of the blades made them very satisfactory. Pressure that used to be dissipated off the long lower edge is now maintained by the end plate, improving not only steering but lateral-plane effectiveness. The same effect is produced at the top of the rudder by keeping the gap between the rudder and the bottom of the hull as tight as possible. In some designs I put the rudder stock at right angles to the bottom to sweep the bottoms all through the steering arc, but a vertical axis reduces the gap as the helm angle increases, and avoids increasing the drag of the end plate at large helm angles. (With the rudder stock raked either way, an end plate is canted to the water flow when the rudder is put over.)

The Chebacco's flat bottom, or wide keel, allows the shallow draft. The high and wide chines give reserve stability and buoyancy. These boats have no ballast, but they can't be capsized by less-than-hurricane winds or any sea that is not breaking heavily. With their low freeboard and big cockpits, they're meant to be fair-weather boats, but they can deal with rough water given prudent handling.

The third version (see plans), with higher sides and shelter house, was designed for Doug and Kelly Wood to sail on San Francisco Bay, where wet and windy days are more usual than they are on Massachusetts Bay in summer. To make the cabin more inviting, the centerboard was eliminated, replaced by a ballasted keel and deeper rudder. This boat needs 18 inches of water, still tolerable for trailer hauling. Her range of stability is increased almost into the offshore category by the extra freeboard and the small

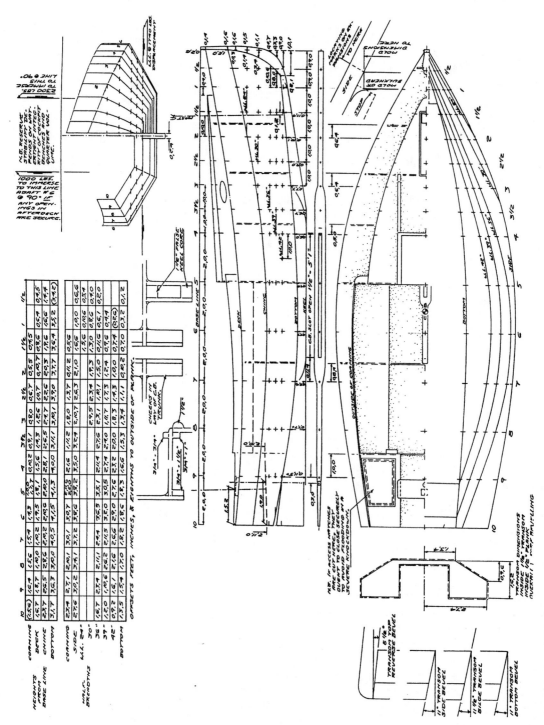

Lines and offsets for the plywood Chebacco, version #1

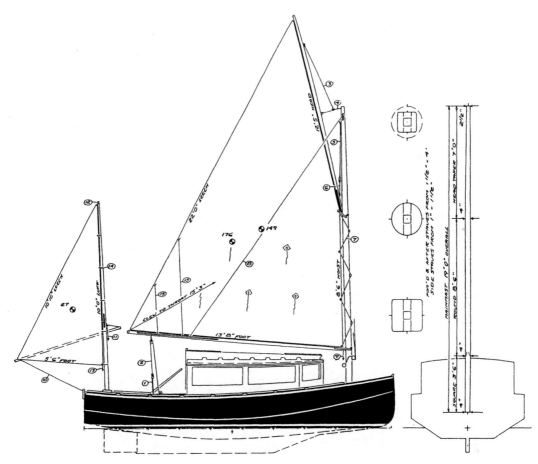

Sheet plywood Chebacco #2, with higher sides and shelter house, 19'8" × 7'5" × 1'6"

outside ballast casting. Very shallow keels are unweatherly in open water and sustained wind because they work in water so near the surface that it is blown to leeward by wind friction, carrying the boat with it. Given sea room, this is a virtue; the drift reduces the force of wind and the impact of waves on the boat. It has also been argued, by the famous Commodore Ralph Munroe among others, that there's merit in a boat which runs into knee-deep water if she's blown onto a lee shore. (The proponents of this theory all live on shelving coasts.)

I call this glass-house version a motorsailer, but it has practically the same sailing performance as the daysailer. What difference there is, is due to the sail area lost by the higher boom. Laying out the boat to be sailed from inside the house doubles the cabin space, since nothing has to be withheld for a cockpit. It puts crew weight just where it belongs in a light boat. The helmsman can stand up in the companionway, with the tiller lifted up to swing clear abaft the bulkhead, for close maneuvering.

A sheet-plywood boat with a prominent forefoot, like this, has a twist in the bilge panels forward, which makes the panels difficult to coax into place. The first boat had ½-inch-thick bilge panels. This was changed on the following boats to two courses of ¼-inch, which made the work easier but took longer. Brad suggested that a glued-

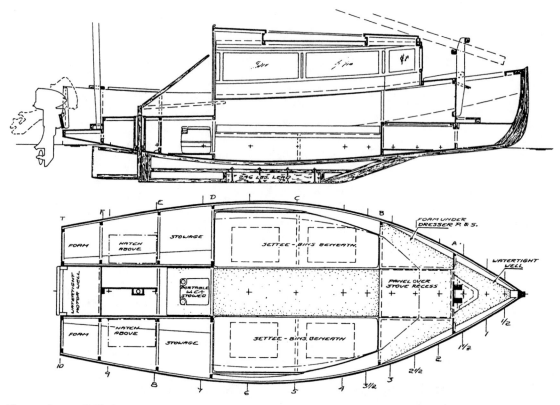

Sheet plywood Chebacco, version #2

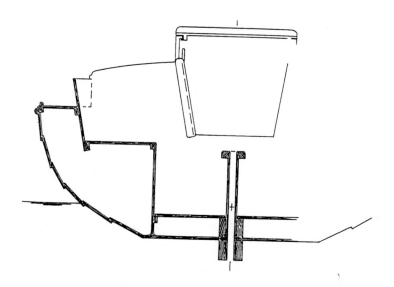

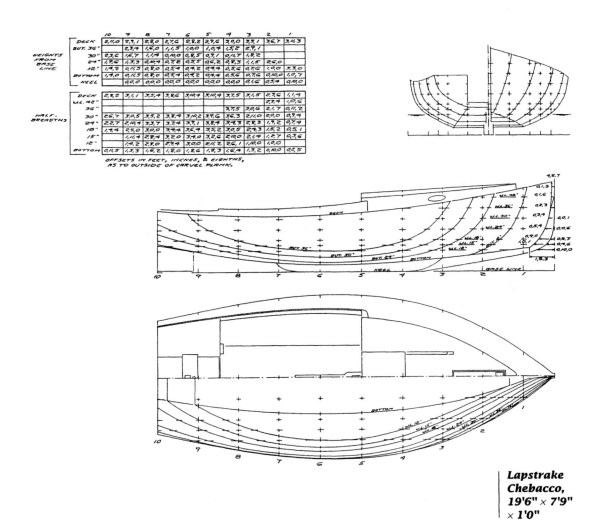

Lapstrake Chebacco, 19'6" × 7'9" × 1'0"

plywood clinker hull might be less work and look better (see lapstake plans) It actually took a few more hours to plank than the sheet-panel boats, and there's some difference of opinion about which has more character. The clinker boat heels less easily to small angles due to her wider waterline. As far as can be judged without a long series of races, performance is the same.

The 25-footer is a stretch of the clinker 20, to make a roomier cuddy. The raised deck increased useful space still more, besides adding buoyancy in a knockdown. Everything else is the same. The extra length adds several hundred pounds to the half-ton weight of the 20-footer. That, plus the increased wetted surface, means that with the same rig, the long boat is not as fast in light wind. However, the long length lets her go faster in a good breeze, or under power. She planes cleanly with a 15-h.p. motor at low cruising r.p.m.

The 25-footer could carry a lot more sail, but we kept the rig of the 20-footer practically unchanged because it had proved so handy to rig and unrig. It can be set up in a

(text continued on page 233)

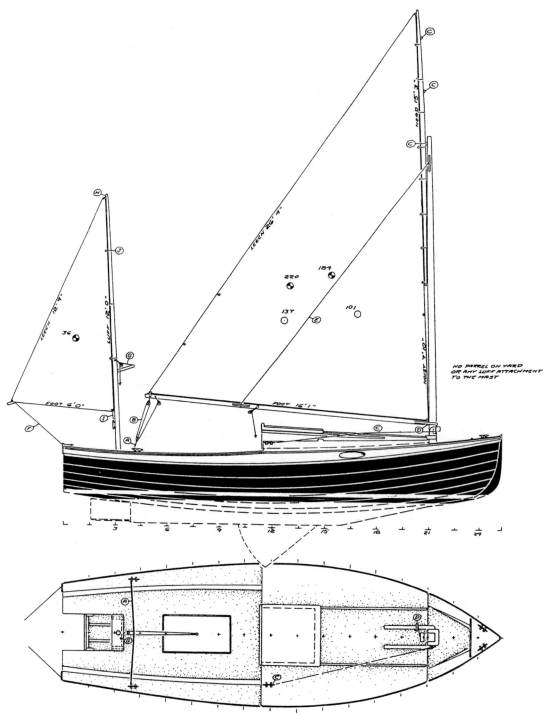

The 25-foot lapstrake Chebacco

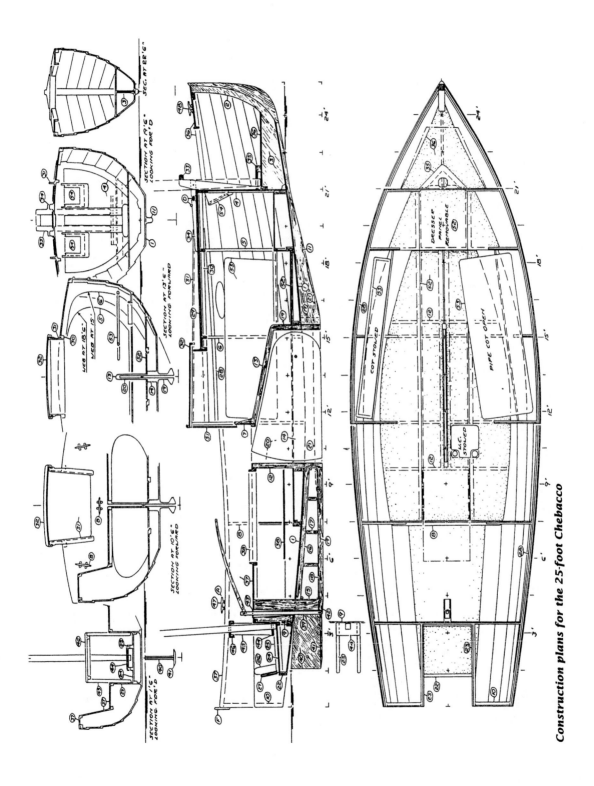

Construction plans for the 25-foot Chebacco

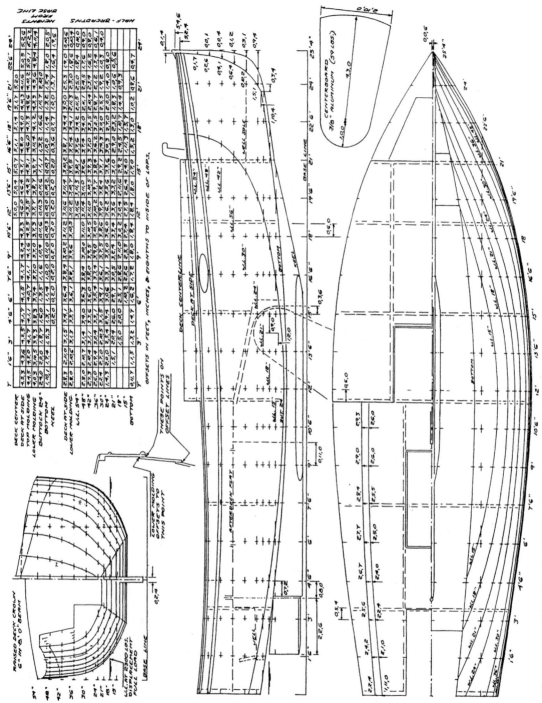

Lines and offsets for the 25-footer

19-foot lapstrake Chebacco

Ted Ratcliff's cold-molded Chebacco 20, built by David Montgomery

few minutes, afloat or on the ramp. The mast slot of the 20-footer (which is hard to keep tight in the rain) and the over-under partner of the 25-footer (all outside the watertight envelope) work well with masts as short as these. The mast is run in at a low angle, then walked upright. It doesn't have to be held vertical before stepping, as with regular partners, and is not fixed on centerline at some fixed height, as with a pivoting tabernacle.

46   *Birdwatcher*

23'6" × 5'7"

In 1975 I designed a camp-cruiser called Dovekie, which was intended to test the theory that a light boat with oar auxiliary instead of a motor was a practical sporting proposition. I used the prototype myself for a couple of seasons and liked her very much, as did Peter Duff of Edey & Duff, who built her for me. By very imaginative demonstration and advertising, his firm of Edey & Duff sold upwards of 150 Dovekies.

The publicity led to requests for plans for amateur builders, but the Airex-cored fiberglass boats built with elaborate tooling were as unsuited as possible to be built one-off by unskilled people. I had a couple of tries at adapting the general layout to a ply-wood boat, but the results weren't happy. Eventually I realized that it would be better to start from first principles, working toward the same objectives: the oar auxiliary, the rig so quick to strike down that there would be no temptation to try to row her with the rig standing, the general simplicity, and the combining of cabin and cockpit into one large space for living, sailing, and rowing. Looked at in that direction, a much better idea appeared, which I named Birdwatcher—after reading an article by Jack Dunn in which he used that word for "craft in which one might poke through a marsh or backwater in search of nothing more than a pleasant lunch and a tan."

I think the concept of an unballasted boat, deriving her power to carry sail from people sitting out at the side under a transparent raised deck buoyant enough to float the boat dry in a beam-ends knockdown, is genuinely novel; there has never before been a boat with Birdwatcher's capabilities. The class has been slow to catch on, partly because the principle is alien; using the boats to best advantage calls for learning a different technique of handling. A great many people are not willing to work with the limitations of oars. Some people are really confronted with situations for which oars are

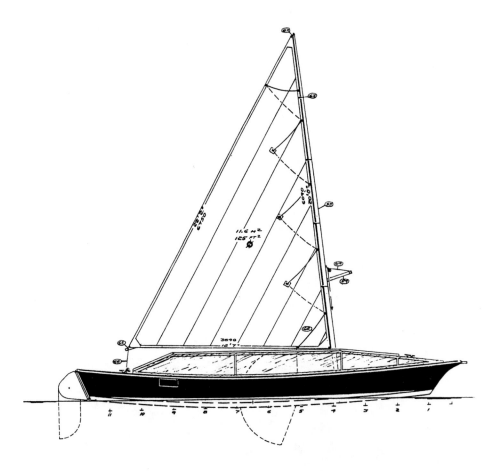

inadequate, others have learned to deal with the problems of motors and aren't interested in beginning a new course on oars.

The people who have Birdwatchers like them very much, almost the only complaint being that they're undercanvased for lively performance in many places. I made the second sail plan to meet this criticism. It's a little more complicated, but the mast is actually shorter than the original one, and I find it very good-looking.

The following fiction, another of the group I wrote for *WoodenBoat* magazine, is based partly on reports from Birdwatcher owners and partly on experiences of my own. It's close to reality.

The Family

Birdwatcher is entering Carquinez Narrows close-hauled in a rising chop and a stiff breeze. The standing room down her centerline is battened down with fabric flaps all the way back to the break of the deck over the tiller. The stiff flap that forms a door at the after end is in place but propped up as high as the swing of the boom allows. The family is on the weather side—parents aft, one child just forward of the mast, the other child

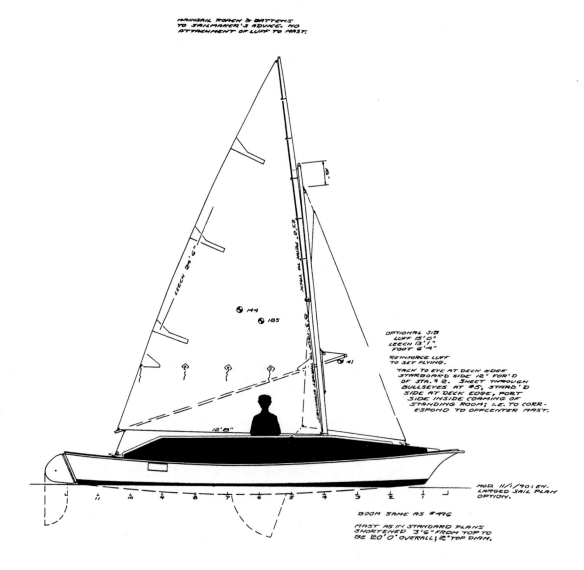

lying on the pile of sleeping bags and mattresses in the big bin outboard of the off-centerboard trunk. They all have a wide view through the all-around picture windows that form the sides of the raised deck.

The dark glass of the windows takes the curse off the glaring July sun but makes the sky look more threatening than it really is. The adults can look aloft through the transparent part of the deck to sail the boat full and by. The sheet comes into the enclosure from the stern, so nothing needs to be open, but the standing room cover is not absolutely tight and the off-centerboard trunk spits, so their gear is stowed on the assumption that there will be water flying and underfoot.

They have great confidence in the boat, having learned by trial that even if she's

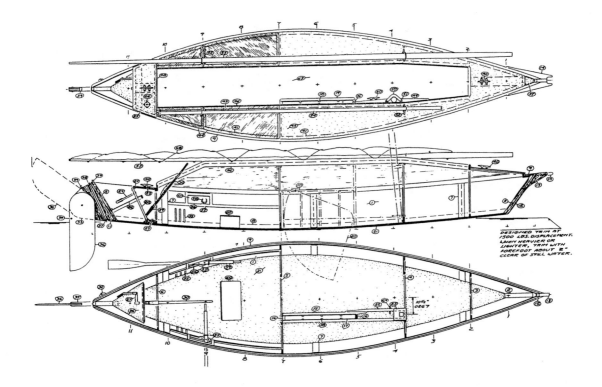

DESIGNED TRIM AT
1500 LBS. DISPLACEMENT.
WHEN HEAVIER OR
LIGHTER, TRIM WITH
FOREFOOT ABOUT 2"
CLEAR OF STILL WATER.

knocked down on her beam ends, she will float high on her side with the standing room
well clear of the water. The weight of the 1-inch-thick plywood bottom will right her
immediately. On the clear Colorado lakes where they normally sail, they sometimes
heave her down deliberately for the underwater view through the submerged windows.
Today they're avoiding knockdowns, the murky Sacramento Delta water offering nothing to look at. Also, they don't want to create alarm among other boats in sight, some of
which will rush to the rescue if they see a boat on its side. When they first had the boat,
they thought this was amusing, but later decided that the joke was in poor taste.

The fact that *Birdwatcher* is sailed with all hands under glass allowed them to start
sailing on the high lakes before all the ice was out. If it rains, the boat can be rowed with
everything battened down. The one-way effect of the tinted windows allows close
approach to wildlife. One of their most treasured memories dates from a trip down the
Missouri River from Fort Benton to the Fort Peck Reservoir. They rarely used the sail,
the wind being chaotic in the steep-sided gorge and the fair stream encouraging rowing
or simply drifting. In a backwater behind an island they suddenly found a dozen young
bighorn rams looking down at them from a steep bank a boat length away. They had
grown almost matter-of-fact about mule deer and golden eagles. They also saw several
rattlesnakes and were glad they slept in the boat instead of on shore as other campers
did. Their feeling of superiority was enhanced by a day of cold rain, which hardly
affected them.

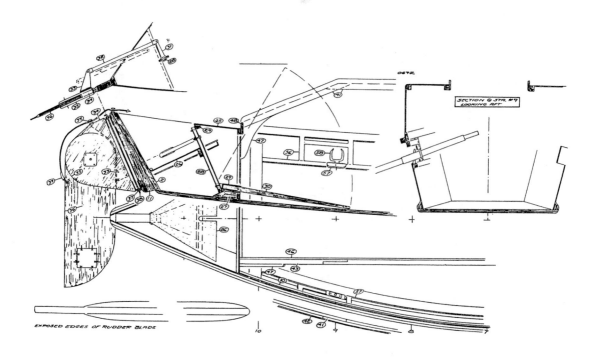

EXPOSED EDGES OF RUDDER BLADE

The adults sleep aft, the children amidships. The space to port of the off-centerboard trunk is not really wide enough to be a double berth, but they have not told the children. The inevitable portable toilet is forward and forms a seat for a child looking out with eyes just above deck. A curtain across the mast bulkhead allows the adults to relax. The children have not yet learned to worry about such matters.

In calm weather, if they're out for more than a few hours, a couple of the air mattresses are kept inflated to sit or nap on. The other mattresses, the rolled-up sleeping bags, and all their camping gear are piled in the huge bin outboard of the off-centerboard trunk. The bin is supposed to be filled in a standard order to minimize burrowing at random.

The 30-pound Bruce anchor is on the cathead at the stem, its warp stopped down, flaked across the foredeck. The kedge is a 15-pound Danforth hanging with its flukes hooked over the starboard gunwale at the stern. Neither anchor is ever brought into the living quarters. One of many reasons the boat uses oars instead of a motor is to exclude oil as well as mud from the inside of the boat. Other reasons are silence, economy, elimination of a theft apprehension, freedom from fouling in weeds and plastic bags, shallow draft (they can pass a 6-inch-deep shoal), and the satisfactions of moral superiority. Either of the adults, or the two children each with one oar, can cover three miles in an hour in smooth water and dead calm, as in the upper reaches of the Delta which they've just been exploring. With the mast struck down (which they can do in a minute) they can row a short distance against a strong wind. For rivers and tideways it has become second nature to make a downstream plan, as on the Missouri. The oar ports close seeping-tight under sail; at anchor they're usually open for ventilation.

The children, when not needed as oarsmen or as ballast, are free to run around

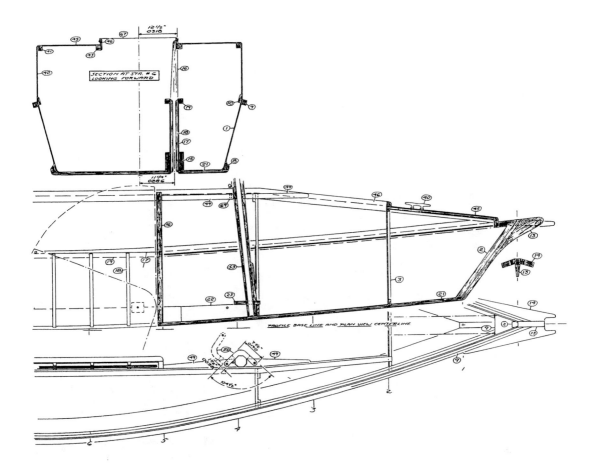

untethered and unencumbered. They can wrestle and skip rope, or spread a full-sized chart for piloting instruction. Their growth has been marked by the rising of their eyes above the coaming, from the time when they had to chin themselves on it. The adults stretch their legs by strolling the length of the standing room, waist-deep in the boat.

They had been concerned about heat buildup in the greenhouse shelter, but it turned out that a breeze usually eddied through the standing room. When there was no wind, they at least had shade. They have toyed with a plan for a cruise on the Texas lagoons, and have looked longingly at a chart of the Bahamas. At least while the project is remote, they see no great imprudence in a crossing of the Gulf Stream.

On the highway, with the standing-room cover in place and the spars inside, *Birdwatcher* is aerodynamically clean and stable. Cruising at 65 m.p.h., the fuel consumption of their subcompact sedan is hardly increased at all. *Birdwatcher* weighs less than 600 pounds empty. She has more than once been launched without a ramp with eagerly offered bystander help. The heavy external clamp stringers give a good grip for a dozen or more people to pick her up and walk her along. Such help is rewarded with conducted tours of the boat and a demonstration of the rowing arrangements. The invisibility of the rower always generates amusement, but the performance under oars never seems to make the impression it deserves.

Jim
Michalak's
Birdwatcher
on an Illinois
Lake

47 *Whalewatcher*

29'0" × 6'6" × 10½"

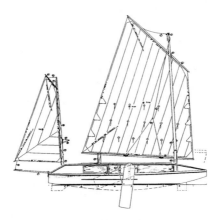

A long correspondence led to this design, but the gist of George Anger's wish list was thus:

1. The boat would be sailed mostly on Chesapeake Bay, including the shallow parts. The Bay can be rough and the boat should be able to cope, but much of the time the winds are gentle and the water smooth.

2. Berthing is scarce and expensive. The boat should be readily launched, hauled, and rigged, for dry-sailing and trailer-hauling back from the waterfront.

3. She should be a fast and weatherly sailer over a good range of conditions, with emphasis on handiness in crowded places and shifty winds. Auxiliary power should be generous and instantly available.

4. Cruising would be of the overnight-picnic variety, seldom more than two nights at a time and usually only one night. Necessary accommodations amount to mattresses for four people and a portable toilet. Flat surfaces for a camp stove and for making sandwiches, plus space for a cooler or two out of the sun, would be desirable. All equipment should be detachable and portable.

5. Construction should be as simple as possible. George was in two minds about whether to build her himself or to contract with a boatshop, but in either case he wanted realization to come quickly.

6. George is 6 feet 6 inches tall and has a son who is 6 feet 10 inches. They're both tired of boats proportioned for the middle 80 percent of humanity. Moreover, George has a back problem that calls for chair-height seats if he's to be comfortable for long.

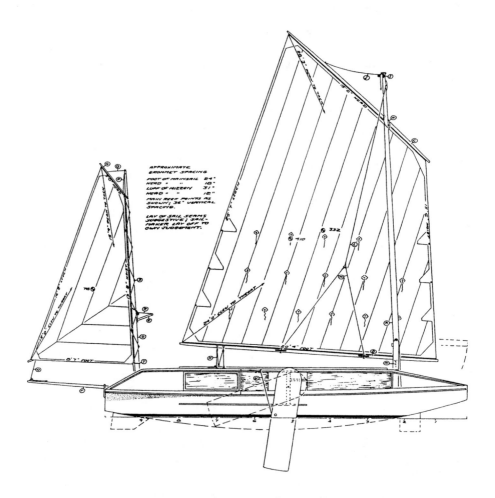

George had been thinking about modifying my Martha Jane design (see Chapter 48). These boats sail and handle respectably but they're high-sided already. I doubted that making one higher was a good idea.

I suggested pulling out the length to 29 feet and the breadth to 6 feet 6 inches. The length leaves the whole rig, including a compact 4 × 4 tow car, within the legal limit of most if not all states, and the breadth will just go between the wheels of a trailer, to ride low to the road and float on and off at a shallow angle.

It's possible to design a trailer from which this boat can be launched without wetting the wheel bearings. (Trailer design is out of my line, but I've seen it done.) The trailer can be quite short, with highway lights and plate clamped on the stern of the boat rather than on a long tail on the trailer. The boat's construction amounts to a giant box girder and does not need any support from the trailer.

Designed displacement in use is 4,700 pounds, but upwards of 1,000 is allowance for crew and camping gear and supplies. The water ballast totals 900 pounds. On the highway, the weight is supposed to be about one ton plus the weight of the trailer. The ballast tanks flood and drain automatically as the boat is launched and hauled. They won't flood without opening the inside vents, but they will drain, though slowly, with the

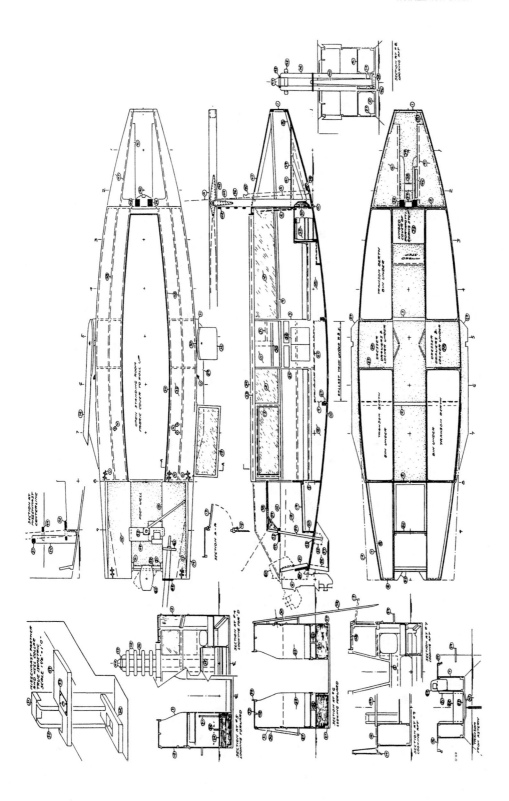

vents closed. As the boat is designed, somebody has to wade alongside to open and close the flooding plates, but it wouldn't call for a lot of ingenuity to fix up a remote control. George is toying with arrangements to pump the tanks while sailing, to float her up and improve light-air performance. I doubt that the advantage would amount to much, and sooner or later some embarrassment will come of being caught with the tanks empty.

Water ballast is effective only when there's enough buoyancy to lift some of it above the waterline as the boat heels. As long as the neutral-buoyancy water is submerged, the stability of the boat is whatever it would be if the volumes containing water were removed entirely. A couple of years ago, one of my water-ballasted designs met with an accident that completely flooded her. The wood structure had positive buoyancy, so she didn't sink, but she floated bottom-up, with the outside of the ballast tanks awash. Some foam high up in the hull would have righted her and saved some inconvenience, even danger in cold water.

I suggested dealing with the "big and tall" problem by using the Birdwatcher principle outlined in the previous chapter, with the transparent raised deck and open standing room down the centerline. The open part is well clear of the water, even in a knockdown past 90 degrees. The buoyancy of the high raised deck, working against the weight of the heavy bottom and more than half of the ballast water, will whip her back onto her feet. The crew sits under the raised deck, in the shade and sheltered from spray, on seats high enough to bend the knees normally. A 7-foot crew has height to sit straight, and can walk upright from helm to mast in the standing room. Shorter mortals have windows at eye level, and their heads clear the deck in the standing room. With a flush cover stretched over the opening, headroom averages 4 feet 8 inches. At anchor, a tent using the lowered mast as a ridgepole can be any height up to tepee proportions.

The interior is not hot because the downdraft off the mainsail ventilates it powerfully. One of the beauties of the arrangement is that people spread out all through the boat and don't crowd together at the stern where they're not only cramped but make the boat drag her tail. They can stroll with hands in pockets through most of the boat's length when she's driving hard in a head sea, or sprawl and watch the hypnotic race of water close below the lee-side picture windows.

In Birdwatcher, the helmsman sits inside with the others, but George wanted to be able to see over their heads without standing up. He was also particular about seat-back and foot-brace proportions, so we added the stern sponsons overhanging the sides where the bottom has to tuck in. (If the bottom were carried back as wide as the deck, the corner of the transom would drag when the boat heeled, and the boat would go down by the head.) The sponsons are a construction complication, but they're appropriate in that they're something like the "patent stern" of her Chesapeake ancestors, the bugeyes. There will be cushions shaped to the helmsman's bottom fitted to the deck each side.

George insisted on the big hinged windows in the sides of the raised deck. The attraction of being able to open her up there is clear, but I resisted at first, arguing that Murphy's Law ensured that she would sometime get a knockdown with the lee-side window open. Eventually, he talked me into showing them on the plans. I decided that she had so much reserve stability that she would recover before she swamped, and the worst case would be the boat back upright with a mess of loose water and wet clothes to dry out. If she were mine, I would make a fetish of keeping the windows closed whenever sail was set.

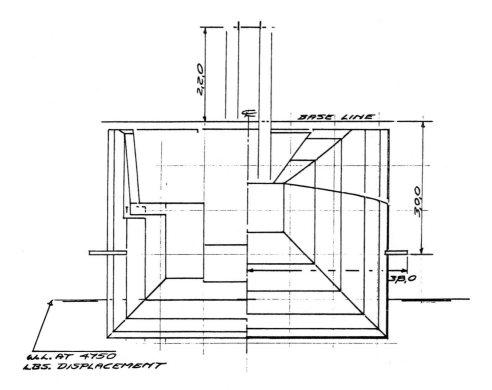

BASE LINE

2.2'0

30.0

38.0

W.L. AT 4750
LBS. DISPLACEMENT

The motor is so handily within reach of the helmsman that no remote controls are needed. It can be tipped down and started in a few seconds, and tilted clear of the water as quickly. It will probably be an 8- or 10-h.p. four-stroke and cruise her at 6 knots, well below peak r.p.m. An engaging characteristic of motors mounted in this way is that if they're loose on their pintles, the motor will follow the rudder of its own accord. The rudder is free to swing in a complete circle, and with rudder turned past 90 degrees and the motor hard over, the boat will chase her tail inside a circle of her own length—handy if they don't open the bridge.

The tiller can be swung up to a vertical position to allow the rudder to move at anchor without loosening the tiller bolt, or it can go over 180 degrees for steering in reverse, but in its normal position it has a bracket to support the weight of an out-stretched arm. The rudder is no deeper than the boat's bottom. It will give positive steering because the stock angle allows it to sweep close against the bottom of the boat, while the big end plate on the blade holds the flow of water there. There's no loss of steering force up or down off the rudder. A drawback of this geometry is that the rudder's trailing edge is deeper when it's swung over than when it's fore-and-aft, 7 inches deeper if it's reversed. However, if she grounds on the rudder, it is pressed against the bottom of the boat, and with luck the stock won't be bent.

The scow shape allows the swell of the forward sides to match the bottom profile exactly. The idea is that water pressure will be the same above and below the chine, with no flow around the chine to make the eddies that slow down sharp-bowed, flat-bottomed boats in a chop and make them steer erratically in a following sea. The penalty, aside from the looks, is booming pounding if waves are met upright.

This boat is supposed to be sailed heeled. The ideal angle is 10 or 12 degrees, with the weather-side chine close to the waterline. At that angle, the waterline length, nominally 20 feet when upright, lengthens out 6 feet or more as the lee overhangs immerse. Exhilarating bursts of speed with started sheets will be frequent. She'll also be a good drifter since the short upright waterline keeps the wetted surface small.

Leeboards are unpleasant devices—ugly, noisy traps for floating debris. But all the alternatives are unacceptable; they would ruin either the trailer handiness or the spacious interior. The long and narrow boards with low pivots are necessary to clear the windows. Their trouble is that when they're swung up to sail in shallow water, their lift moves aft and the boat develops lee helm that kills her windward sailing. This problem is one reason I've kept tinkering with bow rudders; I thought of using one here, but the control linkage would be complicated and so would any way I can see of keeping the beaching capability. I settled for the daggerboard in the bow. I doubt that it will be used much, but it doesn't take up much space and can be dropped in quickly to help her get to windward over a shallow flat, say 16 or 18 inches deep. The trunk will need a close-fitting plug in a head sea!

I settled on the balanced lug rig because it has considerable area set on masts short enough to be lowered without a lot of preparation. A spritsail main might be faster if it were well cut and set, but a big peak sprit is strenuous to set up compared with the light yard of the lugsail. Balanced lugs are handy and light to sheet, and will drive a boat respectably. They'll drive better if there are ever enough of them to give the sailmakers some experience with the shape that works best. It's arguable that sailmakers have more responsibility than designers for boat performance.

I realize that this design looks peculiar to most people, but it's the latest step in a 35-year evolution. Whalewatcher is a close relative—the construction is almost identical—of Pointer, which I sailed through the 1960s, and every feature of the design has been tried in practice. As I said to George Anger, the question is whether he wants what she offers enough to put up with the derision of the bystanders.

Author's Note

This boat was nearly ready to launch when George Anger, "the gentle giant," died suddenly. I hope the boat fell into good hands, able to let "the derision of the bystanders" roll off. Bernie Wolfard of Common Sense Designs has been trying to find somebody else to test the design. He called the design Whalewatcher, intending her as a big sister of Birdwatcher.

48 *Martha Jane*

23'6" × 6'0" × 7"

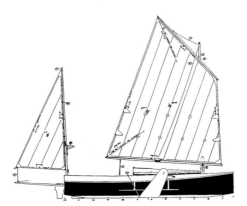

The 25½-foot leeboard sharpie Mike O'Brien named Black Skimmer is one of the three or four most popular designs I've produced. They've been built and cruised far and wide, and work so well that I'm afraid to tamper with the 25-year-old plans.

They're tantalizingly close to being good trailer boats. The 34½-foot mainmast is the most obvious problem. I did finally work out a way to shorten it enough to fit it with a tabernacle, but the boats are still too heavy. Massive trailers, powerful tow cars, and steep launching ramps are more satisfying in imagination than in reality. The amount of use a trailer boat yields is in inverse proportion to the capital tied up, and the overambitious boat nags at her owners when they're tired of the mental and physical effort her use demands.

The late Elrow LaRowe (of Common Sense Designs) asked me to try to design a viable trailer boat comparable to Black Skimmer, with dry sleeping space for four people if two of them are small, or for two people with supplies and camping equipment for a month's cruise; able enough to go into open water on a fair-weather prospect; spirited enough under sail to be usually satisfying and occasionally exhilarating; fast enough under power to go up rivers; and simple enough in construction to be within reach of many amateur builders (or quick work by professionals without a production investment).

The length is two plywood butts. In Martha Jane we save 2 feet from Black Skimmer's length by clipping the point of the bow and the rake of the transom, keeping the bottom length—on which a sharpie has to sail.

She is wider on the bottom than Black Skimmer, to float her weight on a shallower draft and on the short upright waterline that allows the light boat to turn easily, to get

(text continued on page 250)

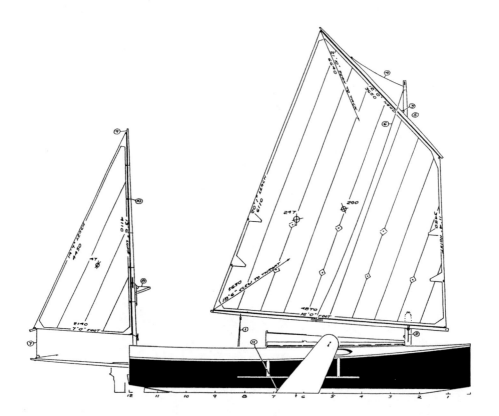

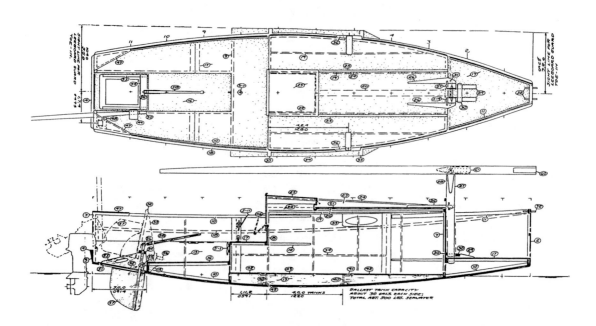

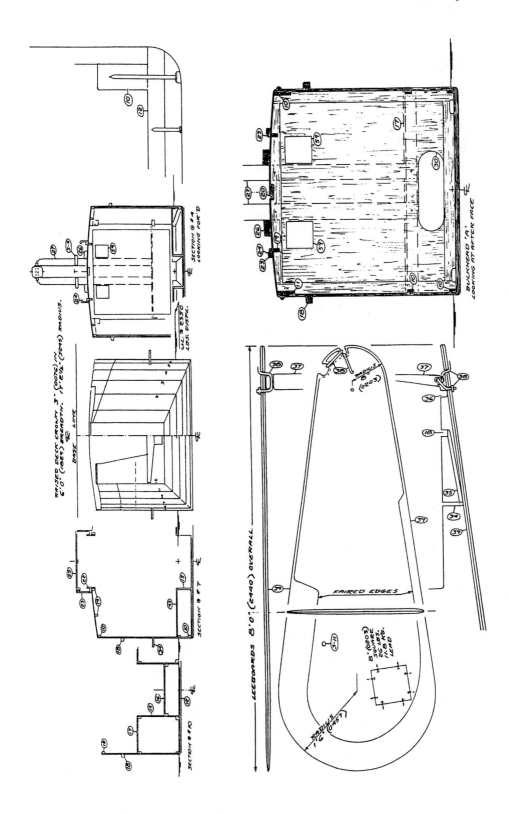

through stays reliably in spite of her slight momentum. The short waterline keeps her wetted surface small in smooth water, but the low overhangs use all her length heeled or among waves.

The vertical sides allow a narrower bow or a lower bottom forward without generating much turbulence under the chines. Martha Jane would sail and steer better in choppy water if her forward bottom rockered higher to match the curve of her sides, but she would be harder to build, slower in smooth water, less roomy, and noisier at anchor. Vertical sides suit leeboards better than flared sides, and reduce the weight of the deck on any given bottom breadth.

The leeboards are slung on rope pendants, to be cheaply installed and instantly removable. The inevitable play, especially broken-wing kiting, is irritating but worth putting up with for the simplicity and the flexibility under eccentric stresses.

Draft is 7 inches at full load without any fixed excrescences. The bottom is 1 inch thick under its sheathing, stiffly braced by the full-length keelsons. The inboard rudder is mounted in a pivoting panel of the bottom, in a free-flooding well to obviate any need to try to make it watertight. It remains steerable as it retracts. She is normally steered with the rudder when she's under power, the loosely pivoted motor automatically following the rudder movements. Under power she can be swiveled inside a circle of her own length, a relief if the bridge turns out on close approach to have less than 5 feet 9 inches clearance.

Water ballast totals 500 pounds, enough to give the high-sided hull a good range of stability. It is taken on and dumped by pulling two plugs, or it can be pumped out while afloat if necessary. The dry weight of the boat is in the order of 1,300 pounds—too much, in my opinion, but tolerable to many hardened trailer-sailors.

The rig is governed by the desire for quick lowering. The mainmast can be fully

Mark Lindgrum's Martha Jane

counterweighted to raise and lower at a touch, but the counterweight is hardly worthwhile with such a short mast, and its weight, high and forward, is undesirable.

These boats are exceptionally nice to maneuver in tight places, tacking and jibing with reliability and precision. Those blessed with mainsails built by sailmakers who know the art of the four-sided sail are close-winded and fast.

One or two Martha Janes have made offshore passages and kept the sea in gales. I wouldn't set out far to sea in one myself if I could help it. If I had to do it, I would be very careful, but not much frightened.

49 *Sea Bird '86*

23'0" × 7'9" × 2'6"

Dear Phil:

You have already updated L. Francis Herreshoff's Rozinante for us [oar auxiliary canoe yawl; *Sensible Cruising Designs*, International Marine, 1991]. Perhaps you'd like to update the old Sea Bird? In a trailerable, plywood version, the Sea Bird's shippy looks would really catch the eye and yet not tax the retirement budget too much.

I'd like the whole thing to trail behind a six-cylinder vehicle. We would plan to use a pickup with a cap for stores and onshore berths, cutting in and out of the Intracoastal Waterway and exploring the lakes and shores of the Northeast.

William Salter, Delhi, New York

Dear Mr. Salter:

What Thomas Fleming Day had in mind when he set Charles Mower to work on the plans of Sea Bird, and Lawrence Huntington to build her, was to show that a very modest boat could keep the sea routinely. Day was an offshore seaman and an advocate of "the strenuous life" in the Theodore Roosevelt mold. He was contemptuous of fair-weather yachtsmen and smooth-water boats. The racing rules of the time were producing some of the most unseaworthy boats that ever sailed, and Day was concerned for the health of the sport. Sea Bird was his illustration of what a sensible recreational boat should be. The year was 1901.

Day was a great spirit. He was always on the lookout for overlooked possibilities and was interested in anything that opened up boating to people who weren't rich and socially prominent. Sea Bird was designed to be cheap for small boatshops to build and

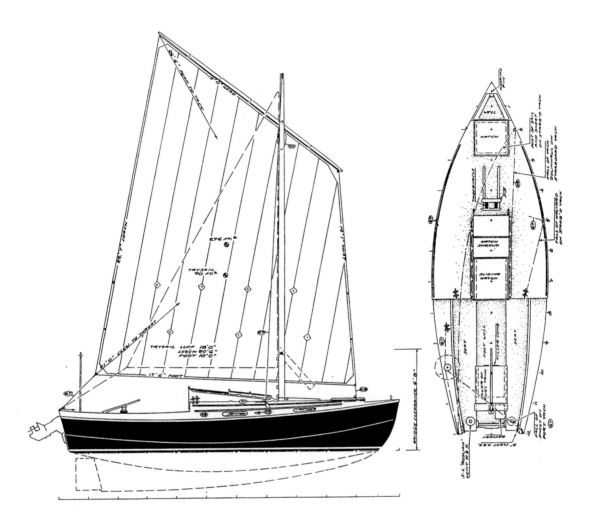

attractive to home builders. The hard-chine shape with straight frames was at that time, and for long after, supposed to be easy to build. That was a fallacy in pre-plywood times, but so widely held that it would have been a crusade in itself to combat it. It was a good construction for knock-down kits. The supplier did the lofting and beveling, making it fairly easy for a novice to get the shape accurately set up to plank. Quite a few Sea Birds were built that way, and a lot more were started but never finished, as was the way of kit boats then as now.

What Day did with Sea Bird was to take her out more boldly than was then usual. He sailed out around the Nantucket Lightship, and he offered a prize for an "outside race" from New York to Marblehead around Cape Cod, which was the beginning of modern ocean racing. A few years later, he navigated one of the first three yachts to race to Bermuda. It's ironic that Sea Bird is the ancestor of the IOR fleet. Day would have liked the way the IOR crowd go to sea but disliked the cost of the boats and the pervasive sea-lawyers. The OSTAR would have been more to his taste.

He demonstrated that Sea Bird could stay offshore for days and nights, heaving to

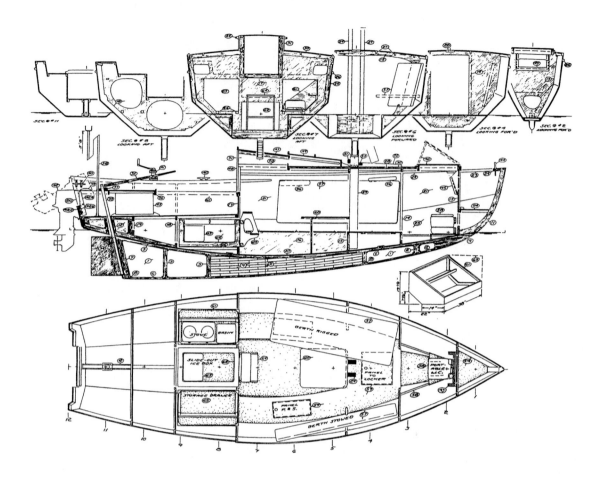

for a rest or if the weather turned dirty. Eventually, he sailed her across the Atlantic. He wanted it known that a cheap little boat could do more than slip timidly from one Long Island Sound harbor to another.

Having made his point and seen it absorbed, he turned to powerboats, and later to outboard motor boats, still with the object of showing that they could go to sea. He navigated two motorboats in races to Bermuda and took the powerboat *Detroit* across to Ireland and on to Russia. Later he took a tiny boat with one of the first Evinrude outboard motors from New York to Boston. All these exploits were desperately uncomfortable, but they weren't very dangerous (except for the carefree way they treated gasoline at the time), and they weren't expensive.

My proposed Sea Bird '86 is strictly in the Day spirit. She is a fairly cheap boat, suitable for an experienced home builder, fit to go to sea, and designed to use her motor with no inhibitions.

She's built of tack-and-tape plywood, prefabricated from diagrams of key panels to obviate lofting and jigging. She's biased toward the part-time builder who wants a boat, not a carpentry challenge, and who has to work in short stints. The shape would be good for an aluminum boat. Day would have approved of the no-maintenance quality of unpainted aluminum as soon as he could be convinced that it wouldn't evanesce

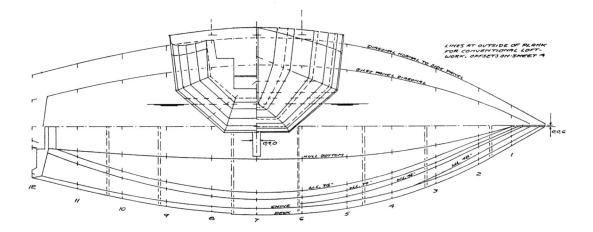

as the aluminum sides of the *America*'s Cup boat *Defender* did about the time Sea Bird was built. (*Defender*'s aluminum sides were riveted to a bronze bottom near the water-line. . . .)

The plywood boat is sheathed with fiberglass to speed up finishing and reduce the consequences of neglect. Day liked sailing better than polishing. His boats were plainly finished and not always squeaky clean.

The original Sea Bird was built as a centerboarder, with all her 1,000 pounds of ballast inside. I calculated her displacement from the published plans. Mower's designed waterline implies a displacement of 4,100 pounds. Her actual flotation shown in photos of her trials must be well upwards of 5,000 pounds. Since Mower was a good estimator of weights who did not make mistakes of that order, I surmise that he was thinking of much less ballast and gear than Day put into her.

Sea Bird was changed to a keelboat after a couple of years because the centerboard trunk spoiled the cabin. Day and Huntington had a difference of opinion about the shape of the keel, with the result that she eventually got a full keel much bigger than was necessary. The keel shown for Sea Bird '86 is like the one Day wanted, with the minimum depth that would ensure reliable handling in bad conditions. A short, deep fin would make her faster close-hauled with a skilled and alert helmsman; the shallow keel is stronger, calls for less concentration on the helm, is probably faster reaching and running, and hangs on better hove-to.

Sea Bird '86 is shorter, narrower, and shallower than the original. The difference in length is mostly due to cropping the stern overhang to take the outboard motor. The Evinrude demonstration mentioned is proof that Day would have approved of this cheap and simple power installation, which saves drag under sail and keeps all the fuel outside the boat.

I squeezed the breadth to bring her well inside highway trailer limits. The trailer boat, even those like this one that are not very practical to launch down a ramp, is a development that would have delighted Day.

The deck layout is as simple as I can make it. The raised deck saves labor in a one-off boat, adds interior space, and increases buoyancy and reserve stability—that is, sea-worthiness. It's not as good to work on in rough water as a deck with a cabin trunk, but deck work in this boat is meant to be done, for the most part, standing in the hatchways, because I wanted to eliminate a lot of expensive pulpits and stanchions.

The cabin is an updated imitation of L. Francis Herreshoff's H-28. Read his writings for its virtues, of which the first is that it's cheap to build, and the second that it can be kept really clean. Sea Bird '86 does have a portable toilet in place of Herreshoff's trademark cedar bucket, because in most places this side of Labrador there are too many people too close together to tolerate the implications of buckets. The current generation of portable toilets is wonderfully good; I use them in much more pretentious boats than this one. I've walled off the head for those who feel they need the privacy.

This cabin is designed to camp in for short cruises. It's possible to live comfortably for a long time in a cabin this size, but the stowage arrangements need long study and many hours of joinerwork, all of which is best done after the owner has grown familiar with the boat.

The dipping lug is my own campaign for an overlooked possibility. This sail is usually dismissed out of hand because it is so much trouble to tack it. Dipping lugs are powerful and close-winded sails that need no standing rigging, little running rigging, and only a short mast. The drawbacks for close maneuvering don't strike me as critical in an era in which all cruising boats do all their maneuvering with their engines. It doesn't make sense to give a full-powered boat a sail plan based on the assumption that the motor won't be used. Marina contracts commonly prohibit trying to make a berth under sail, and most cruisers don't set sail until they can lay their course.

The specified motor for Sea Bird '86 has power enough to drive her at hull speed against a chop. When she has to tack, she will steam dead to windward while the lugsail is being changed over for the new tack; likewise for beating through narrow passages. In a long-and-short-tack situation she would take the short tack under power, lowering the sail but not shifting it. She's a true motorsailer, with a higher performance under sail *and* power than that of comparable boats, especially boats of her cost. T. F. Day was not the man to lock into a line of thinking based on the fact that *racers* have to maneuver without their engines (which they start as soon as they cross a finish line).

The mast is stepped in a tabernacle with its heel above deck. It's so short that neither counterweight nor strut is needed to raise and lower it—handy if you lose the end of the halyard.

The trysail shown in broken lines is primarily for heaving to. Sheeted over to the weather quarter it will keep her steady and quiet, making a square drift with a big radar reflector displayed, while the crew rests. It can also be sheeted flat to steady her under power in a seaway. In either case, wind resistance is tiny compared with the tower of wire and struts vibrating aloft in most cruisers. In a hurricane, there's a chance that her mooring will hold her unless something with a tall standing rig drags into her.

Author's Note

I eventually had a good sail in a boat built to this design. She was tiddly at anchor on account of the narrow waterline, but carried her sail well in a good breeze. Nothing seemed to need alteration, though I would certainly rig her with a peak halyard now, like Bill McKibben's motorsailer (Chapter 61) and Ataraxia (Chapter 71). With that, there's much less hesitation to tack.

50 *Presto Cruiser*

27'0" × 6'10" × 1'3"

Dear Phil:

Magazine editors are really no different from readers; we dream of special boats, too. This one has been floating around my mind, in one form or another, for years. I have been patient, but position has its privileges, after all.

I'm a sucker for a handsome boat that sails well, and I can forgive a lot of sins against accommodations that are committed by a long, narrow, low-sided boat—one that recalls the past without being trapped by it.

I want a shoal-draft boat that I can beach, tides be damned, and that will dry out at a comfortable angle of heel. She should be light enough to transport atop and launch from a trailer when the mood strikes, but she will spend most of her idle time at a mooring.

I want a simple, free-standing rig that's easy for the solo sailor to handle underway and at the mooring. If two people can step and unstep the mast, so much the better. She should be a smart sailer, but I don't want her rig and form to demand my undivided attention. She should be handy in tight quarters and carry enough sail to be fun in the light airs of summer. Although I want to sail her into and out of as many places as I can, you should probably provide for an outboard auxiliary. Sculling is an alternative when the currents cooperate.

The boat and I will spend most of our time on the coast of New England and on large inland lakes. She'll have to deal with square waves and go to windward in a chop.

Below decks, all I really want is camping-style comfort, plus a little. A good-sized double berth, sprawling space, sitting headroom, and a cabin sole that's large enough to accommodate two children in sleeping bags will make a satisfactory sailing campsite for my family. When the children's bags are stowed, we'll have room on the sole for a couple of those nifty low-slung beach chairs. Good light and plenty of ventilation are important, too.

I'll need a flat for a camp stove, a place to secure a cooler, and stowage for galley utensils. I want to stow heavy items down low near the center of buoyancy. Hanging duffels will hold clothing, bedding, and other lightweight items. Although a bucket will be our sink, I do want stowage for a portable toilet.

A lot of this sounds like Black Skimmer, but since I read your comments on the bad effects of hard chines on sailing monohulls I have been attracted to Commodore Ralph Munroe's Presto boats. If Munroe's claims for his boats are accurate, a similar but small sharpie should be a wonderful little cruiser.

Dennis Caprio, Bennington, Vermont (then editor of *Small Boat Journal*)

Dear Dennis:

First about sharpies: A sharp-bowed boat with a flat bottom has to have more curve in her sides in plan view than she does in her bottom profile. If the stem cuts the water, the sides push the water out harder than the bottom pushes it down. This builds up more pressure against the sides than it does under the bottom. The water is pushed from the high-pressure area towards the low-pressure area; if it has to get around the sharp corner of a chine as it does so, it breaks into great eddies, producing high drag and wild steering. These eddies reduce the pressure under the bottom still more; the bow tends to drop, and you get worse eddies—a vicious cycle. This is why sharpies are poor sailers in a chop, especially when there's more sea than wind.

The wider a sharpie is for her length, the blunter her bow angle has to be. Blunter bows result in a greater difference between the sides and bottom, hence heavier turbulence. To minimize this effect, a big sharpie has to be long for her breadth. A well-designed sharpie carries her bottom high forward, to meet the water mostly with her bottom. But when she heels, the forward chine will dig in. A very small sharpie, that can be sailed upright by use of live ballast, can be wider for her length. Large or small, the high, sloping bottom is noisy and bumpy at anchor or anytime the boat isn't sharply heeled.

What Commodore Munroe did in Presto, in 1885, was, first, to round off the chine to eliminate the turbulence. That allowed him to fair the bow down to a comparatively deep forefoot that slices through a chop silently and lets the water flow smoothly under the boat as she passes.

Then he made Presto deeper amidships to get displacement for lots of ballast—4½ tons, he says, and he probably meant long tons, making the total over 10,000 pounds in a slim boat 35 feet 6 inches long on the waterline. A sharpie could be designed to carry that much ballast, but the bottom rocker would look freakish and the pounding would be exacerbated.

Outside ballast was rare in this country in 1885, so keelboats weren't carrying their ballast much lower than Presto's. She competed with them much better than she would have later on when outside castings and fin keels came in.

Presto's low freeboard was what was fashionable when she was built, but she had more freeboard for her *breadth* than most boats of her day. A boat that's low-sided for her breadth is the dangerous one. She gets her rail down at a small angle of heel. If she

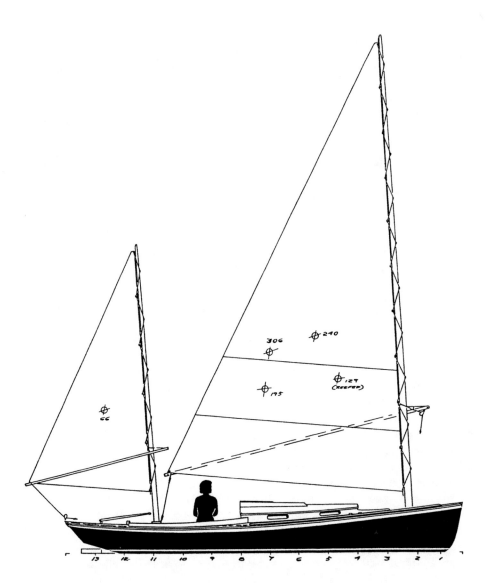

heels sharply, she will "cut under," as they said at the time—bury her deck deeply, put open ports and hatches under, and founder. She may trip and fall bottom-up. My proposed design is as low as I dare to make it, to please your eye. If you meant to take her offshore, I would urge, and might demand, higher sides, probably in the form of raised forward decks like those used in some of Munroe's later boats.

Low freeboard does have some real advantages, besides looking nice. It makes a boat smaller and lighter—that is, cheaper, though freeboard is the least expensive dimension to increase. Low freeboard lowers the weight of the deck and, more important in a small boat, the weight of people on the deck. Live ballast is much more effective in low-sided boats. In high-sided modern types, a man does more for stability by going below and lying in a weather-side bunk than he does by hanging an arm and a leg over the rail.

Low sides make boarding easier, either from a dinghy or out of the water. They make it easier to get a fish aboard, or to catch a bucketful of seawater, or to wash your boots. They make less wind resistance, though that is a petty matter compared with the windage of masts and rigging. They allow added sail area down low where it doesn't have much heeling effect. Sitting down close to the water enhances the crew's sensitivity to the speed of the boat. It's possible to be pleasantly hypnotized by the steady wash along the lee rail.

The upswept counter makes space for a good-sized rudder without adding draft. A rudder this size and depth is effective if it has big end plates. I guess we'll be seeing more and bigger end plates after the uproar over *Australia II*'s keel. I show the rudder hung on a skeg so it won't pick up weed and pot warp as a balanced rudder does. The skeg isn't big enough to keep her from turning quickly.

The raking transom is purely for looks. For all functional purposes it ought to be vertical or tumbled home as on the IOR boats. Reversed transoms often look well on racing craft, but they don't fit this boat's proportions. I've used the raking transom to make the outboard motor a little less of an excrescence, and I suggest painting the motor shroud to match the boat's color scheme. There's no obligation to carry a free advertisement for the motor manufacturer, and the motor is less likely to be stolen without it.

The deep belly and high ends will make deep waves when she's driven hard. She's not a boat that can take off and surf. At 7 knots the stern wave will be right up to the deck. For compensation she'll have momentum. I've learned to live with the way a light sharpie stops the instant her sails stop thrusting, but I miss the way fine-lined boats with heavy ballast shoot in stays and carry their way through flat spots. When I use the word "thoroughbred," that's part of what I mean.

I first thought of bent-frame carvel construction because that's the cheapest way to build a boat of complex shape in the Northeast. But I found that a surprising number of people liked her looks, and I began to think that it might pay to assume that there'd be more than one built. Cold-molded construction costs more than carvel, but it would stand dry storage better, have a little more space below, and be much lighter. The displacement and ballast marked on the drawing were for carvel construction and were supposed to include a generous allowance for crew weight, cruising gear, and soakage. With a cold-molded shell, say ⅝ inch thick to need no stringers, I'd guess, subject to more figuring, that she could carry 3,500 pounds of ballast without going deep of her designed lines in cruising trim. If so, she'll be much stiffer under sail than the Presto type usually is.

The ballast would be steel, preferably reinforcing bars, set in concrete and spread from side to side through the midbody of the boat. This combination is cheap and backs up the bottom planking so solidly that she should be able to run onto a hard beach in a slight surf with a good chance of taking no harm. Using a maximum of steel with just enough concrete to hold it together and encapsulate it, the top of the ballast should come no higher than the dashed line on the arrangement profile. Using lead would make a few inches more headroom below, but would cost more and not be so strong.

The proposed rig is a ketch by the usual definition, but it's a yawl in intention as the jigger is meant for balance, control, and steadying, not for serious driving power. The reefed centers marked show a major advantage of these proportions: You reef the mainsail, and the aggregate center stays in the same place. The mizzen, never reefed, is just big enough to hold her head to the wind while you get the main in, or to ride steadily to

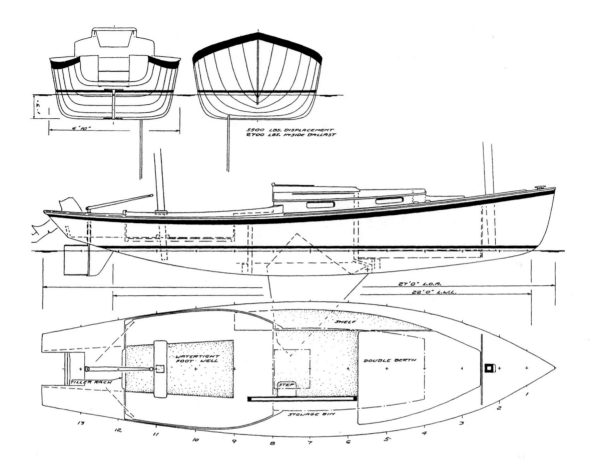

a drogue, but small enough to back with a hand on its boom to throw her head either way from irons. By setting up hard on the mizzen snotter, the sail can be flattened out to luff or feather without intolerable slatting. Its sheet can be started to correct weather helm.

Ken Bassett (the proposed builder) thinks she ought to have the sails tracked instead of laced. I wouldn't give him much argument. The lacings have to be tensioned by a long trial-and-error process, and they complicate the snotter attachment. The tracks are probably at least as good aerodynamically, certainly so if the masts can swivel in their partners. I showed the lacings because track and slides have become very expensive and lacing line has not. A point in favor of the lacing is that its tension can be varied to adjust the draft of the sail, a tedious and tricky business that can make a dramatic difference to the performance of the boat.

In your part of the world you can probably find a couple of trees that nobody wants, for the masts. Elsewhere, I'd favor building them up of thick staves. I'm unconvinced that aluminum is better than fir, spruce, or cedar for unstayed masts. Carbon-epoxy and other composites do look promising, but I take it their price is over your head for the present.

Commodore Munroe would have considered this boat much undercanvased. In his time, ghosting ability was important to get around without engines (though he lived to design some fine powerboats). Not only was ghosting ability desirable, it was possible. When the wind was light, the sea was usually smooth. The man who said that hell was paved with glassy ground swells obviously lived before motorboats kept the sea in a turmoil around every harbor, wind or no wind. The ingenious devices to add sail area to *Presto*, *Utilis*, and the others cost a lot more now than they did then, and they make an unholy clutter that does nothing for handiness when it blows harder. I would argue for the stark simplicity shown, with the small outboard mounted where it's ready for use at a moment's notice.

The cuddy may be just barely up to your specifications. It would be comfortable for a singlehander or a loving couple. I've lived for a month in a similar one with no hardship. The off-centerboard clears a flat sole 6 feet 6 inches long by 4 feet 3 inches wide, if the cooking shelf is made to hinge up and the portable toilet is put out in the cockpit footwell. Two youngsters could sleep on air mattresses—maybe three, if they're small and tired.

The deck is nice in decent weather. A hull like this is not very sensitive to placement of crew weight. The rig lends itself to putting up a tent or awning at anchor.

The off-centerboard behaves no differently from a centerline board, but it does have to be cased watertight right up to the deck. If the trunk opened inside the hull, as a centerline board often does, the off-centerboard could flood her in a port-tack knockdown. All Presto types need very big boards because they have no other effective lateral plane.

You're not to think that a boat like this will sail close-hauled with a bendy-masted sloop with a fin keel, unless it could lead the keelboat over a shoal. But, such boats sail most respectably with a relaxed crew.

51 *Grandpa's Pirate Ship*

22'0" × 8'11" × 2'3"

Dear Phil:

I've been wanting to build a "pirate ship" for my two young grandchildren to enjoy with me. It would be a floating playhouse, which would give me an excuse to take them sailing on weekends.

With this in mind, I fell in love with William Garden's Privateer. She's 30 feet on deck, which is almost reasonable, but she's 13 tons displacement and 13 feet beam. Although I've built two boats, this would be beyond my physical, not to mention financial, capabilities.

I looked at hundreds of other designs, to no avail. Then Mike O'Brien at WoodenBoat showed me the little triple-keeled sloop in your book *Different Boats*. He suggested that a boat of that basic size, with its sheer sweeping up towards the stern, might be a place to start.

Mike suggested further that I write to you for the impossible: a small boat with an after cabin. The after cabin need not be big enough for me. I would need just enough sitting headroom for two kids under 5 feet tall. Could there be a way to build such a cabin, complete with tiny stern windows, in such a small craft?

A boat like this would be so much fun, I just had to ask.

Warren Jennings, San Antonio, Texas

Dear Warren:

Quite a few years ago I took a notion to make plans for a model of *Hispanola* from Robert Louis Stevenson's *Treasure Island*. I reread the great book with minute atten-

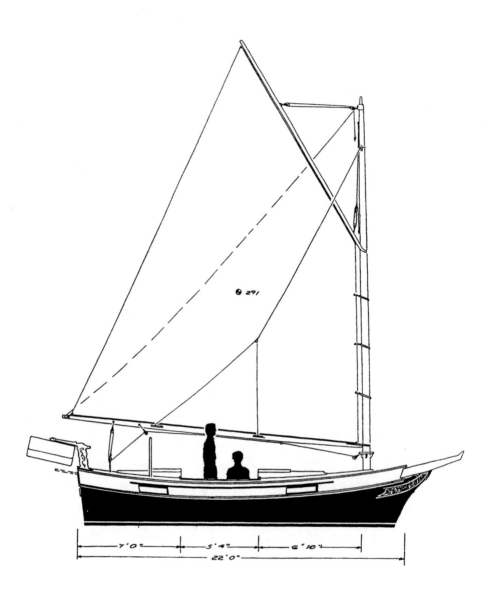

tion, concluding that the schooner was an American-built Baltimore Clipper on account of the way she lay over when she grounded out, and from Captain Smollet's remark that she would sail "a point nearer the wind than a man has a right to expect of his own married wife." But I found that Stevenson hadn't made the inside of his vessel match the outside. She's flush-decked when Israel Hands is chasing Jim Hawkins around on deck, but she has a great cabin, with stern windows, when there's action below decks. You can't have it both ways in a racy vessel even of her 200 tons (which would be about 90 feet long on deck at the time). So, I gave up the project. If I were directing a film of *Treasure Island*, I would do what Stevenson did: have a flush-decked schooner like

Pride of Baltimore for the sailing and deck scenes, and mock up the inside of a great cabin in a set ashore for the interior.

(Incidentally, Stevenson gives the date as "17__," but in fact only 1760 fits what he says. England is at war with France but not with Spain. Long John Silver claims to have lost his leg under "the immortal Hawke"—lying, but plausibly. Hawke became immortal at Quiberon Bay in 1759, though the leg was presumably supposed to have been lost in an earlier Hawke battle. Spain declared war on Great Britain in 1761. Q.E.D.)

It's possible to make the stern high enough for a great cabin and run the deck forward more or less at that level. But, if you want bulwarks (the action in *Treasure Island* calls for them), the boat has to be inordinately high-sided. If she's as small as the one you're projecting, she'll feel tiddly as the crew moves around on the high deck. To get security for the crew while keeping the stern cabin, you have to have a center cockpit.

Center cockpits are attractive in a good many ways: Crew weight is centered fore-and-aft; an inboard engine isn't jammed down into an inaccessible crevasse; it's usually convenient to lay off clear leads for the running rigging; and the view from the helm can be good. A center cockpit is in the way of heavy spray when the boat is close-hauled. The steering connections are complicated, and what would be the best part of the cabin in an aft-cockpit boat is preempted.

I suggest steering with a whipstaff—actually, a vertical lever hooked up to the rudder with quadrants and cables, since genuine whipstaffs were highly unsatisfactory. The mechanical connections are expensive and finicky to adjust, but once they are well done, the whipstaff should have a tiller-like feel with the bonus that the staff doesn't obstruct the cockpit as much as a wheel, and can be unshipped at anchor.

The cockpit is a likely width for bracing your feet on the edge of the opposite bench as the boat heels. This also keeps the footwell small. (It's always a shock to cube up cockpit volume and see what a weight of water it can hold momentarily.) A boat as buoyant as this one isn't likely to ship a green sea, and it's a safe assumption that in any conditions that could fill the cockpit, the water would be thrown high and wide at the next heave of the boat. Scuppers are for rainwater. The width of the benches and backs leaves a nice, flat deck outboard, so you can sit comfortably with feet on the benches for a better view or more exposure to a cooling breeze, or to help the boat stand up in a short, hard beat.

The forward "main" cabin is a minimum cuddy, but has just space for four people to sit down to eat when the cockpit tent isn't erected. The portable toilet would be moved to the after cabin for sailing, or the cockpit in sleeping hours. These things work extremely well, especially if they're supplemented by some hand urinals that can be dumped overside at once almost anywhere. The privacy phobia that most of us were brought up to is a great nuisance.

The after cabin probably looks better on paper than it really is. There isn't height enough for an adult to sit up straight, though there's slouching space toward the after end. I don't think 5-foot berths are a good idea. The foot and a half gained doesn't do a lot for the layout, and those 4-foot-tall youngsters will be looking down at you from 6 feet 6 inches before you know it.

The inboard rudder appropriate to the remote steering allows a stern window big enough to get out of, besides giving a fine view and ventilation. At appropriate times you can rig boarding nets outside. I doubt I'd bother with the fake diamond panes, but this stern could be elaborately decorated. I had in mind to combine the stern davits (for

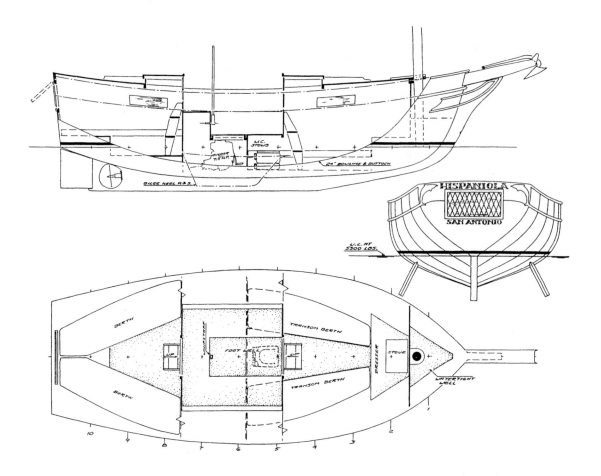

a 6-foot-6-inch punt) with some suggestion of the great battle lanterns of the ships of Queen Anne. I ran out of time and don't have the right kind of talent, but the possibilities are there. Anybody thinking of designing this kind of decoration should soak themselves in the paintings of Bjorn Landstrom in his book, *The Ship*, if they can't get to the Musée Maritime in Paris, as this kind of thing looks awful if it doesn't look wonderful.

The boat has to be wide and high-sided, and therefore heavy, for her length. I assumed that she'd be cold-molded, though she could be built carvel with plenty of steam in the upper forward planks and probably some cant frames in the bow. She would need a ballast keel of something like a ton. Her lines are far from clumsy. The easy sweep of the bow–buttock line and the fine waterlines indicated by the shape of the berths and flats, are those of an easily driven boat. The body plan, wide for its depth and bulk, suggests a stiff boat able to carry a big sail plan. I was tempted to put the ballast on a 4-foot-deep fin for windward speed—a pirate ship should be fast and weatherly— but I reflected on the nature of the coasts of the Gulf of Mexico and decided that the 27-inch draft shown would be more appropriate.

Bilge fins aren't a favorite of mine. Most boats that depend on them are slow, and they're apt to be weak. Those shown are tied into two deep bulkheads, and the amount of salient keel and forefoot allows them to be placed well aft where the deadrise is almost constant. Bilge keels that intersect varying deadrise, farther forward, cut across the natural lines of flow and generate massive turbulence around their roots. The alternative, apart from leeboards, is a centerboard designed long and narrow to fit under the sole and engine. She'd be faster with such a board if it had just the right sectional shape, but boards like that always get jammed sooner or later.

I've designed three square-riggers that were built, and not long ago got up preliminary work on a brigantine not much bigger than this (see Chapter 43). Small square-riggers that look at all traditional aren't practical, and the tone of your letter suggests that you'd rather have a real cruiser than a stage set. This boat is too short for the sail area she can carry, and that she needs to drive her, to be a good schooner or ketch. A ketch's mizzen would block the after companionway, and a schooner's mainmast would spoil the cockpit. A sloop's mast would spoil the forward cabin.

That leaves the cat rig, which is appropriate since the hull is a distant relative of a Cape Cod cat. The gaff sail suits a cat best because its center doesn't shift forward in reefing as much as that of a jibheader. (A short boom has the same effect, but means that the sail would be smaller since no boat can carry as much sail high as she can long. Tall, narrow rigs only pay when the sail area is artificially limited by some regulation.) The area shown is modest, but that's partly because the high hull and some respect for heads in the cockpit pushed the boom high. A 1900 cat would have set 60 or 80 square feet more sail on the same spars, and sailed faster for the difference. However, the bottom of a sail is the least effective part except in a deck-sweeper. The sail shown is powerful and, to my eye, not out of keeping with the style.

I thought of showing a squaresail, set flying in place of a spinnaker. It could be braced up very sharply since there are no shrouds in the way, and the yards could be stowed in crutches along the deck edge to form rails. I also though of a ringtail, a fore-and-aft studding sail (pronounced "stuns'l") set on light spars projecting beyond the ends of the boom and gaff. But one implication of your letter is a need to sail short-handed, and sails of that kind demand plenty of hands. When the youngsters grow up, you can keep them busy by adding the kites. It's to be hoped that they won't be grown before you get the boat.

52 *Singlehander Catamaran*

20'0" × 7'2"

Dear Editor:

Your "Cartoon" section is an excellent and interesting idea. I'm happy to be able to toss in my wish list. I'd like the boat to be:

Light. Light enough to be towed handily behind a car having a 1900-cubic-centimeter engine, and light enough for that car to be able to retrieve it from a reasonably steep launching ramp.

Fast. With only one person sailing it, this boat should be able to outsail most of the commonly seen trailerable cruisers and hold its own against most good daysailers its size. No gaff or sprit—it must be close-winded.

With overnight accommodations. Quite spartan accommodations; the user would bring aboard a single-burner stove, a bucket head, and other light gear. It probably would not be slept aboard more than two nights running, and usually by one person.

Without leeboards. And without any protrusions below the hull of more than about 10cm; more would interfere with trailer launching and retrieval. The centerboard trunk should not cut up the space in the cuddy any more than absolutely necessary, and I'd prefer no pendant in the water from the heel of the centerboard—too much drag.

That about sums it up, except for miscellany. Auxiliary propulsion is relatively unimportant; a boat that sails well can be sailed in most situations. It could have some provision for sculling, a minimum outboard motor, or both. I'd prefer that she not be double-ended unless at least four beams long—wide double-enders have too much helm when heeled. Also, it should be no Red Onion (that is, by William Atkin's definition from many years ago, so ugly it brings tears to your eyes).

Herschel Smith, Milford, Connecticut

Dear Herschel:

I don't think you had a catamaran in mind. Neither did I, until I sketched a single hull and found no way to get power to carry sail and no place to put a decent-sized center-board.

With no weight to be wasted on ballast, and the singlehanding requirement eliminating trapeze, sliding seat, and similar devices, we have to find a way to give her form stability that won't stop her as it comes into action as it does in a wide single-hull boat. I thought of a scow, but they're almost always homely and pound at anchor. In any case, the racing bilgeboard scows would have evolved into catamarans 80-odd years ago if the NAYRU hadn't prohibited tunnel-hull scows in a fit of stupidity, spectacular even by their standards, in 1899. (It is most frustrating to need to write a strong letter of testimony to a committee all of whose members have been dead for half a century!)

If you think of a catamaran as a special case of a scow, you're somewhat liberated in proportioning it. You can keep it narrower than usual, which is handy for the trailer. A boat like this would be faster in a breeze and not much slower in light airs if it were a foot or more wider. I kept her to 7 feet, thinking that the keels only 4 feet apart could go between the trailer wheels and so haul up lower and at a flatter angle. The all-up weight is a little less, and she will give more warning of being over-pressed in squally weather.

The hulls are 3 feet beam. It seems to me that almost all cruising multihulls would be better if they had more waterplane area. Exaggerated slenderness may pay if you're Dick Newick designing a boat for Phil Weld, though even there I'm suspicious that they're past the point of diminishing returns. Dick says not, and he should know if anybody does. But, if what you're after is all-around spirited behavior that doesn't demand fierce concentration, and if you don't want to have to hire a motorboat to follow you and right the boat when you capsize, there's a lot to be said for making the hulls wide and buoyant.

For one thing, it makes room for one good berth in one of the hulls. The centerboard and rudder go in the other hull very efficiently. If the asymmetrical looks bother you, she could have two smaller rudders, but she won't handle better, if as well, and the bare tail of the port hull would be a handy place to mount an outboard motor. I think she'll need the motor on account of the locations of many launching ramps. The one here in Gloucester, for instance, is between two bridges with strong tidal streams. A scull would work nicely between the hulls when the motor has been stolen.

The wide hulls and narrow overall breadth allow the connecting bridge to be light and simple. The wide hulls float the displacement high on top of the water, making them drier, less prone to bury when driven, and with less tendency to generate spreading waves. This last is why we get away with spacing the keels so close together. The keels are shown with plenty of rocker to make sure of smooth tacking, at some sacrifice of top speed.

Hulls like this are good-looking to my eye. They have real boat shapes with curves and hollows, instead of looking like two razor clam shells trying to hide under a bridge.

You didn't mention making this a cheap boat, so I've assumed the best construction for your purposes: WEST System cold-molded with two $\frac{1}{8}$-inch courses, bulkheads, and no stringers except the clamp and keel apron. The hulls are curvy enough to be stiff without more reinforcement. I guess they'll weigh about 250 pounds each; with trailer weight, around 800 pounds. The trunk cabin would be molded the same way. This high trunk would be ugly if it had windows, but it looks quite shipshape if it's all opaque like

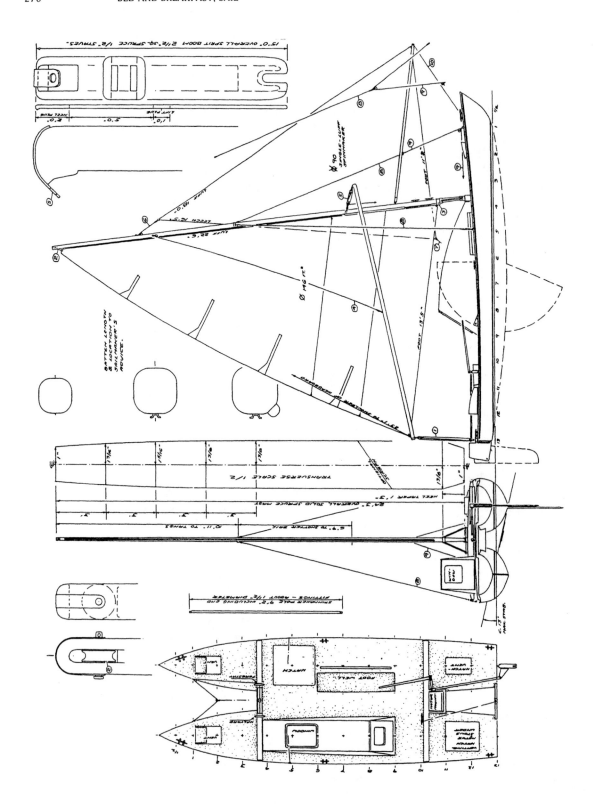

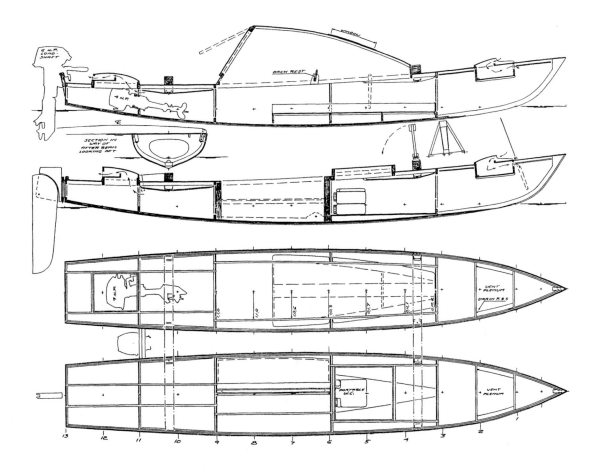

a spray hood. The door can have a window. With a backrest and a couple of candles, this cuddy doesn't look like a bad place for a singlehander to read himself to sleep. Two people could wait out a thunderstorm there, but unless they're quite intimate one would sleep on deck with an air mattress and a waterproof sleeping bag—not so bad, since the camping gear can be kept dry.

I agree with you about dragging centerboard pendants. Apart from slowing the boat down, I'd just as soon have a motor running as listen to the vibration. This centerboard doesn't need a pendant at all. It can be worked directly by grabbing a bar through the top corner. The triangular shape and large area make it insensitive to careless steering, and since the boat is a bit undercanvased for light airs it's just as well to have a shape that doesn't stall easily. I've shown it well forward to make the rudder carry a good deal of the lateral-plane load. She should come out about even on drag; rudder angle from weather helm will about eliminate hull drag from yaw angle. The main objective was to allow a deep reef without a lee helm that would kill her close-hauled sailing.

As for the rig, I always tend to suggest that one sheet and one halyard are best for singlehanded sailing. A sprit boom (it could be a wishbone, but I wouldn't bother with it myself) of this type has the virtue that the sail can be flattened on all points of sailing by setting up the snotter. That's almost as good as a reef and a lot faster to execute. To

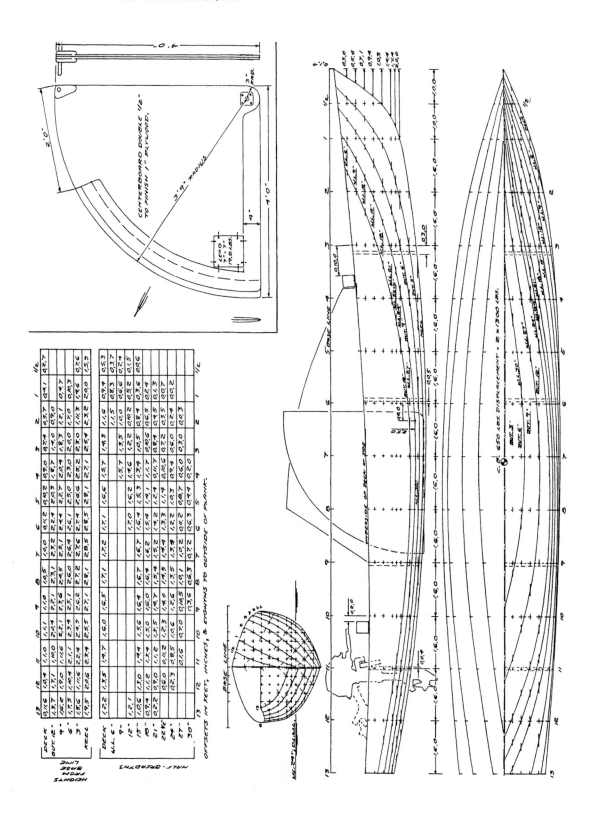

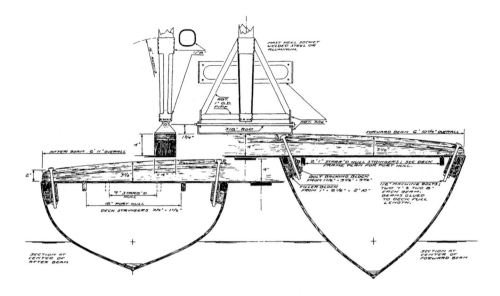

get the best use out of this procedure, the boom has to project some distance ahead of the mast, which doesn't marry well with a jib.

If you were to state a preference for as much as 3 or 4 feet more mast height and sail luff, I wouldn't give you much argument. The mast shown is 24 feet 6 inches overall. Its short length ought to save anxiety in squalls and rough water. Pivoted at the step, it should be easy to swing up and down if the twin forestays have neat releasing shackles. The staying can all be quite slack. I thought all that would be worth a good deal of drifting ability in a cruising boat. She's obviously not going to be a slug, even in light airs with the short rig, compared with the types you mentioned. But I put the point to you for guidance if we take the idea any further.

I looked up Red Onion, Atkin's work has been an inspiration to me all my life, but I have to agree that R. O. wasn't his best effort (though she isn't as homely as she looks on paper). This proposal ought to look like a thoroughbred, with graceful proportions and handsome wave and spray patterns.

[Aquila Chase, a Californian I've worked with before, commissioned working drawings of this concept meaning to build her himself, but an injury cancelled the project.]

53 *Berengaria*

32'0" × 8'2" × 1'7"

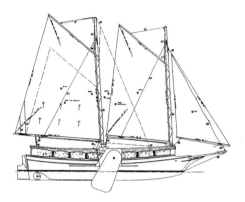

Berengaria was designed to be built on a mountainside up the headwaters of the Sacramento, used mostly for weekends on San Francisco Bay, but once a season trucked to Puget Sound, or the Sea of Cortez, or Lake Tahoe. A probably unrealistic dream of sailing to Hawaii was mentioned.

Two letters to her owner, Bruce Boyd, convey the spirit in which she was designed. The first, with a cartoon study, was my response to the wish list. The second, with a more formal drawing, is my reaction to his suggestions. He's an architect, better equipped than most people to translate a drawing into a mind's-eye image.

January 16, 1992

Dear Bruce,

This arrangement combining cabin and cockpit seems to me likely to be more and more accepted. The first boats I used it in, the 23½-foot Birdwatcher class [see Chapter 46], have been slow to catch on, partly because of the unfamiliarity of the concept but probably more because those boats were designed for oar auxiliary, which is still harder for most to take. The people who have built Birdwatchers like them very much.

The concept works better in this larger size, which is adapted to chair-height seats, and in which partners can be laid across for centerline masts at a height that can easily be ducked under. Nobody ever needs to be out on deck when she's underway. It's feasible to have some of the side windows open, but I would rather they did not because she depends on the high, buoyant sides of the raised shelter for stability in a knockdown; high freeboard is a substitute for deep draft in this sense. She is really a half-decked boat, but the long standing room is so narrow that she can lie on her beam ends without

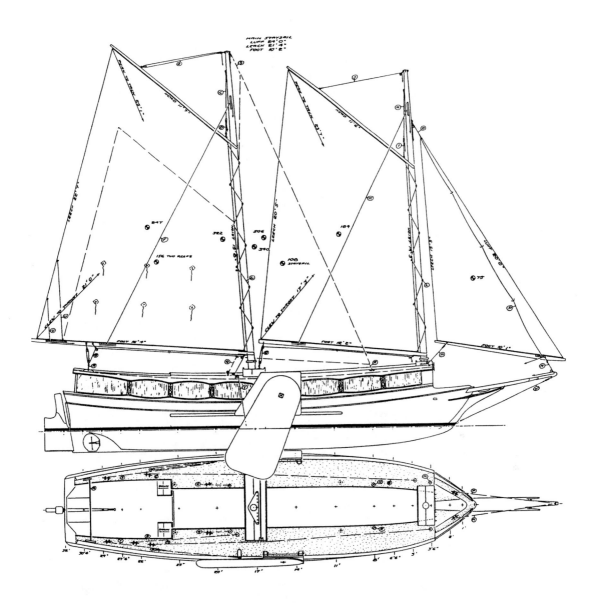

shipping water. The heavy ballast tanks would right her at once; they also give her the maneuvering momentum of a moderately heavy boat.

The small inboard diesel will be quite unobtrusive, and it weighs very little more than an equivalent outboard. It's less likely to pitch out, and cannot get washed in a bar crossing. It would be nice to have a feathering prop, but if she were to be mine I think I would have a two-bladed solid prop for low cost and reliability; the drag in the aperture won't be very important in a boat with this much displacement. The engine I have in mind is available with hand starting.

I have designed a fleet of schooners with rigs more or less like this one, and they sail well. An owner recently sent me a tape showing his 19½-foot sharpie schooner

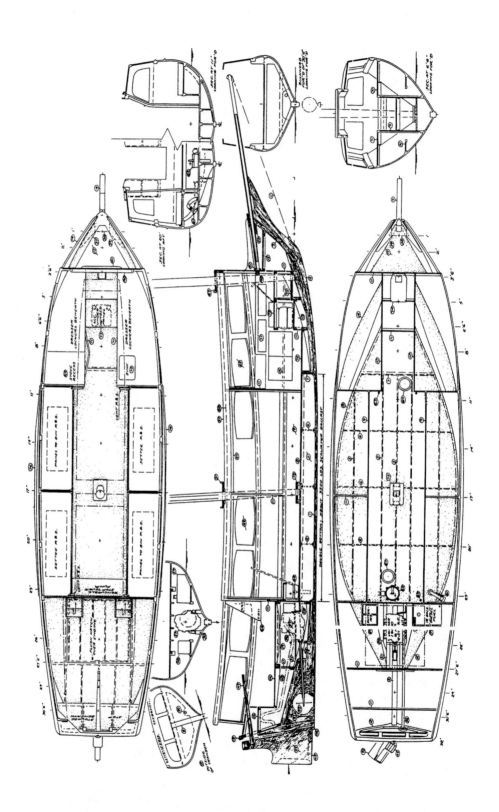

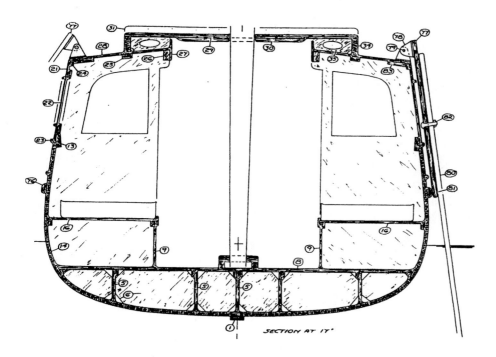

SECTION AT 17'

keeping pace with an L-16 close-hauled. The sloop was outpointing him, but not by much. It seemed obvious that the schooner would win if sheets were started. The mainmast in the proposal for you is only 29 feet long; it ought to be possible to put these masts up without any need for fixed tabernacles or counterweighting.

Using strip-Dynel-epoxy construction, I would hope to get the stripped weight for the trailer down to little more than 2 tons. A two-axle trailer should handle it, though my feeling is that using a hired flatbed rig is likely to be more economical than keeping a dedicated trailer sitting idle most of the time.

For offshore work, most of the standing room could be covered with solid panels, with hatches as needed. For ordinary cruising, assorted tents and insect screens, dodgers, and so on would be more flexible. Since she has full positive buoyancy, I don't think taking her to Hawaii with just the fabric covers would be very rash.

The general style was inspired by a galleass [a heavy, wide, high-sided development of a Renaissance war galley, used with great effect at the battle of Lepanto] model that is (or used to be) in the Arsenal museum at Venice, supplemented by, among others, a Swedish galley yacht design in Chapman's *Architectura Navalis Mercatoria*.

Phil Bolger

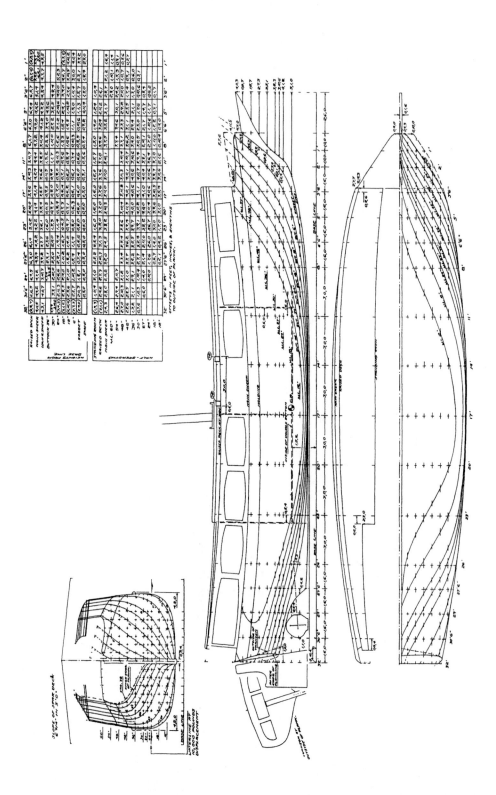

February 16, 1992

Dear Bruce,

Iona is good, though I always thought *Berengaria* was the best queen's name of all. I'm immensely relieved that you like the concept. I hesitated to let my enthusiasm have full scope for fear of conveying too much pressure.

I'll have to do some more figuring on the beam-ends flotation, but I think the wider standing room aft will work and be an improvement. It may have to be somewhat shorter to eliminate any hazard that she could flood by going down by the stern, as once happened to a smaller boat in which I cut that aspect too fine. If so, it will be too short to lie down in at full length, but she is not short of berth space for your purposes. The steps up to the awning deck will work better from this area and can be on both sides.

I'm all for the leeboards [the cartoon showed a centerboard]. I did not suggest them because I thought I might be straining your tolerance as it was. They are much in keeping with the style, though I may suggest a double pivot to allow the transverse pivot axis to go lower on the high sides. The boards won't travel so much fore-and-aft as they are lowered and raised. The fore-and-aft-axis pivot, which allows the boards to "broken-wing," would be at deck level.

I have several designs for small boats designed to be launched on end over high sides. My own boat has about 5 feet of freeboard where her boats are carried, so I've had some practice on this. Swimming just calls for some imaginative ladders, or it would be nice to arrange some real yacht boarding steps with a platform near water level. In any case, the rudder will have a big end plate and steps up the trailing edge.

If she were mine, the windows would be Lexan. It is soft and must be carefully cleaned, but inspires great confidence; e.g., I'm told (though I have not experimented) that a 9mm bullet hole will seal itself instantly, leaving a small mark where the bullet passed through. My Lexan windows lost most of their transparency in 13 years, but the makers claim the new ones will do better. Mine are ⅜ inch thick, but I think ¼-inch windows should do for your much lighter boat. I have no aesthetic objection to cutting them into smaller sections (diamond panes better?), but at least when they're new and clean the big clear area should be nice from inside. By all means, indulge any impulse to embellish and decorate; the 18th-century Chapman copies enclosed are a good guide to appropriate scale. In view of what happened to the *Vasa*, it's just as well to keep the weight of ornament under control! [*Vasa* was a Swedish sailing battleship that capsized and foundered due to top-heavy carvings.]

You have a point on the forefoot design. I was thinking of beaching, short turning circle, and reduced friction surface, but she would have a smoother action and a handsomer bow wave with more depth. I also like the rounded-out sides, which will give a little more sail-carrying power and suit the leeboards well. [The cartoon showed vertical sides, less breadth, and harder bilges.]

On the ballast, I question whether the added headroom would be an improvement, since the seat height would not then match up so well with the view. [He suggested using metal ballast, to fit lower in the hull than the bulky water ballast tanks.] She could be of much lighter displacement with fixed outside ballast, to the same draft but with a shallower body over a long salient keel. I indicated lots of ballast, since, being water, it can't sink her, and the momentum and deliberate motion would be pleasant. A minor amenity is that the comparatively deep bilges forward and abaft of the ballast tanks collect spillage and leakage. Water ballast is ineffective when the rest of the hull is flooded (that is, without buoyancy high up, say under the deck, she would float bottom-up if badly holed or otherwise filled). I would have the water.

These little Japanese diesels are astonishingly smooth and quiet. I think she would do upwards of 7 knots with the 8-h.p.; I'm sure you can cruise at 6 knots, 10 minutes to the mile. It does not weigh or cost much more than an equivalent outboard.

Cost varies so dramatically with how the stuff is bought, and what you count, that I don't like to make cost estimates. Around $20,000? Something like that, give or take 50 percent. . . .

The next step would be to work up a ¾-inch-to-1-foot study from which I can do more accurate calculations. This I would rather not do twice, so I hope you won't order it until you're reasonably sure the project will go forward along agreed lines.

Phil Bolger

Part Eight

Bed and Breakfast, Power

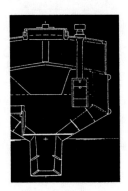

54 *Microtrawler*

14'6" × 7'11"

Nobody looks at a Microtrawler without smiling or laughing. She's a contribution to the public stock of good humor. She can take her place in a parade of toy tugs. The others will be plowing at 5 knots with impressive waves. Microtrawler is happy at that speed, but her waves aren't as photogenic—there aren't any to speak of, just a small feather at her bow and some minor, by 1990s standards, turbulence behind. She tracks and steers better than most, except for being blown away in a beam wind. If the water is choppy, her people don't get wet—only jarred a little.

After the parade, Microtrawler suddenly accelerates and skims away at 20-odd knots, leaving a long, narrow, flat, white trail. She rides on her central ski. Its up-curved forward end holds her bow up as its sharp waterlines slice through the crests. The vertical and horizontal curves are matched: Water encountered by the sides goes out around the sides; water encountered by the bottom goes under her. None has to go around the corner, the streamlining being as effective as that of a torpedo. She is stabilized, and the small amount of spray suppressed, by the wide, wide sponsons, which drum fiercely in the process. The half-scale model which proved the concept started to come unstuck due to vibration in her sponson bottoms after jumping some steep waves; longitudinal stiffeners cured the trouble within reason and were carried over into the bigger boat. The three web keelsons in each bilge of Hawkeye (see Chapter 17), a later and lighter design, are supposed to make her stand still more punishment, but I expect that a Microtrawler's crew will need to ease up before she does.

These shapes are not pleasant to ride at the wrong speed in the wrong length of head sea. Running down a sea they're very good, tracking straight and keeping their chins up, and they're steady in a beam sea. Though hard-riding in a head sea, they're dry, and they're not stopped if they're stuck together strongly enough.

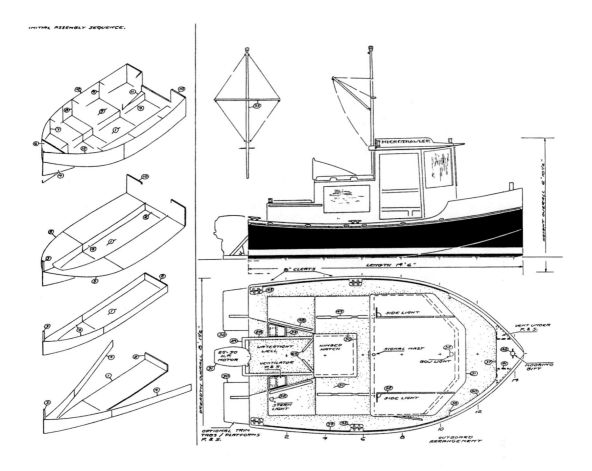

They don't bank on fast turns, but they don't skid, hence don't trip, at least at any speed that ought to be of interest to owners of such craft. I suppose that if a Microtrawler had power enough, she would take off and back-somersault. I won't be apologetic to anybody to whom this happens, since the boat will give fair warning that she's over-powered and overdriven to anyone in their right mind. There may be some risk of reckless euphoria from exposure to a boat that looks like Microtrawler, that performs as she does. . . .

The blunt-pointed upper bow is mostly cosmetic, though a case can be made that it is stiffer, lighter, and less in harm's way than the square-across bow like that of a garvey or jonboat that would be easier to assemble. The origin of the concept was an attempt to do something about the plowing, skidding, and air ingestion of a garvey by adding buoyancy under the garvey's toboggan bow.

Assembly is rightside-up, from the keel box up. When I built Hawkeye I thought it would be neat to assemble her bottom-up, using her flat deck as a building jig. This worked, but it didn't seem to save any trouble, and righting the 8-foot-wide hull without damaging the flimsy bulwarks was tricky.

(text continued on page 286)

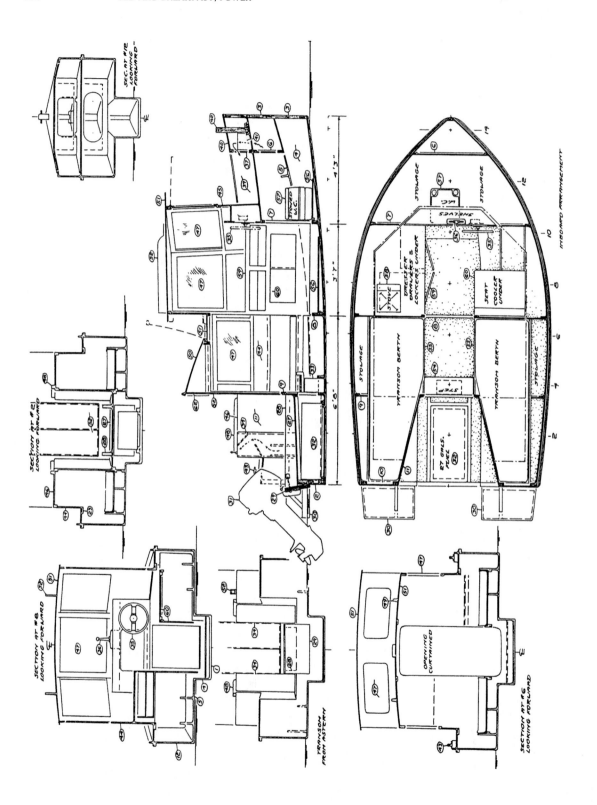

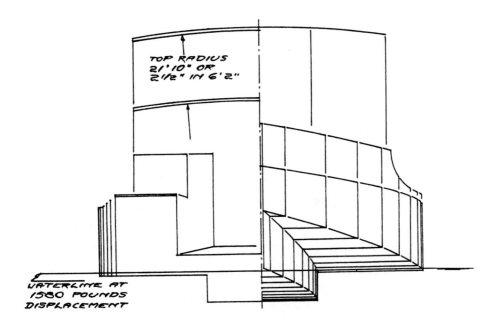

TOP RADIUS
21'10" OR
2 1/2" IN 6'2"

WATERLINE AT
1580 POUNDS
DISPLACEMENT

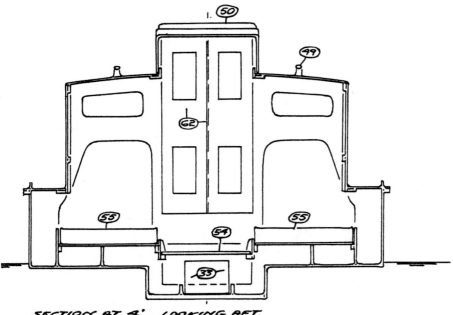

SECTION AT 4', LOOKING AFT

Microtrawler

Microtrawler is a small boat by any definition, and she's not very expensive for a high-speed cruiser with two full-size berths and a standing-headroom wheelhouse and galley. She weighs three-fifths of a short ton and may be the most expensive 14½-footer in existence. Compactness is desirable, but it's not equivalent to simplicity. But, if a Microtrawler replaced a 40-footer that was even more complicated and had to be taken more seriously, she might be cost-effective.

55 Miniature Steel Tug

15'11" × 7'9" × 3'0"

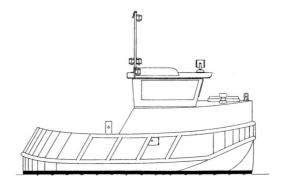

Dear *SBJ*:

The State of Washington has just imposed a new tax on all sail and power boats whose length exceeds 16 feet overall. There are many runabouts and planing boats under the limit, but few are suitable for heavy work. I'd like a maximum-displacement workboat just under 16 feet that is indestructible, economical to run, and has an easy motion. This boat would be a miniature tug that I could use for salvaging logs, setting moorings, taking small tows, and to beat the tax.

I was thinking of a deeply veed steel hull with plumb bow, sides, and stern (for maximum waterline) with one of these heavy 30-h.p. Chinese diesels for ballast. A speed of 5 knots or so would keep the motion easy in a seaway. A flush steel deck with bull rails would allow the boat to sit on a hook without collecting water. The pilothouse should be plywood, to lower the center of mass and to allow a compass to work. I'd like the pilothouse to be large enough for two friendly people to sit on stools when the weather cooperates. A small bulkhead heater to boil coffee would be handy. The pilothouse door would be in the after end of the house so that the side decks could be of reasonable width. Sounds like a tough but useful little workboat to me.

Bill Wald, Vashon, Washington

Dear Mr. Wald:

I'm all for dodging the revenuers, keeping in mind their habit of changing the rules in the middle of the game; I can see them thinking it clever to lower the limit to 15 feet

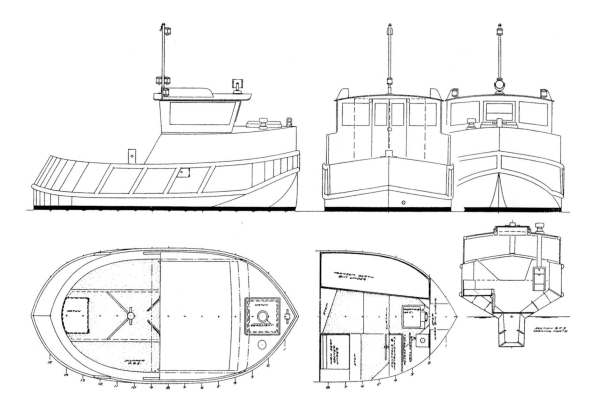

next year. In making a "neighbor gun" a few years ago, I cut down the barrel of an old shotgun to 20 inches instead of the legal 18 inches as a precaution against that attitude.

I started the boat with a box keel bulky enough to house the Chinese diesel with clearance enough to get an arm down past it on each side. The box is sloped and rockered enough at the forward end to keep the eddies from making her wild to steer. This keel has high drag at its after end because the water there has to turn a sharp corner before it's left behind. There's a lot of drag to any arrangement that will protect a 2-foot-diameter propeller, and this boat has so much drag from wave-making and surface friction that I doubt a little more from turbulence will make much difference.

The hull above the box keel has lots of reserve buoyancy, especially forward. Tugs are prone to burying themselves in their own waves, even to the danger point. This one won't. She'll be worth looking at at 6½ knots, with a frothing mustache up to the chine guard all around her bow, a frothing wake boiling back from the rub molding around her stern, and a long series of rolling swells following her. She'll look more at home with a barge on her towline, moving at 2 or 3 knots with a race behind her prop.

I'd expect her to be first-class at precision maneuvering, especially in a gale when a normal powerboat is blown out of control at low speeds. I picture this one in a yacht anchorage during a storm, picking up one boat after another as they start dragging their moorings. Making her fit for rough water is one reason I'm suggesting the raised deck forward. Its buoyancy would pick her up instantly if she were hove down on her side by a combination of a breaking wave and a skewed tow. It seems to me that the deck space

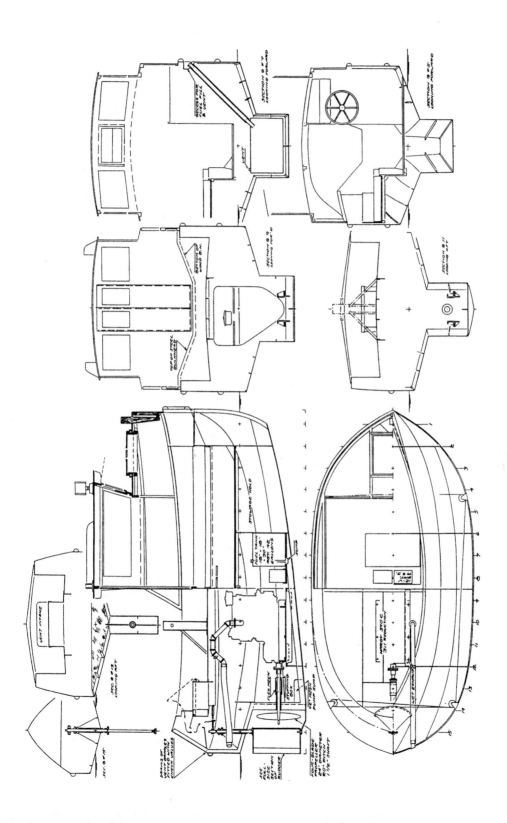

sacrificed isn't worth much. You can duck through the cabin to stick your head and shoulders out the forward hatch about as fast as you can walk around outside, without the risk of being crushed against the string piece of a wharf or a big boat's overhang.

The other reason for the raised deck is the room inside. Underway, standing in the wheelhouse of the type of tug you're thinking about is nice for a while; but at 5 or 6 knots it can get tiring before you get where you're going. That full-size berth is a great amenity. Four, even five, people could get in out of the wet to share your coffee. You could all sit down and be sociable after the tow has been delivered. A single man could make himself snug indefinitely, though in that case I would put a locker for oilskins in place of the high seat abaft the wheel, and make a few other adjustments. The portable toilet could go under the berth, but it would have to be at the after end where the flat sole is widest, which wouldn't be good when there are several people in the wheelhouse. There's room for a good-sized icebox under the sole, forward of the fuel tank.

The view ahead isn't as good with the raised deck as it could be without it, but the helmsman can see the water to within 20 feet of the bow right over the stem and much closer over the starboard bow. This shape won't squat at any speed. She'll settle down deeper in the water as she speeds up, but she'll settle all along, or possibly more forward than aft, so the view from the helm will improve rather than deteriorate.

In spite of the great flare of the bow, she'll be wet in a head sea, with streams of spray blown up off the crest of the bow wave. The forward-raking windshield, which I'm told is cultural in your parts, sheds spray best. I'm not fond of them as a rule, because in the usual case in which the windshield has to clear a companionway, a forward slope makes the whole house much bulkier than an aft-sloping windshield would. In this case the forward slope fits very well. A three-panel windshield with sides angled back for the lee panel to blow clear in a quartering wind would be an improvement in heavy spray, but there is not room for it, either inside or out. Perhaps we could knock just the corner off to make a narrow panel for a lee-side view ahead, but the straightforward flat slope looks better to me. The compass can mount up under the overhead, as far from the steel hull as possible; check to see what happens when you switch on the spotlight.

This boat will be corky and bouncy in a seaway, in both roll and pitch. I don't like the motion, but the only way I know to reduce it much is to cut down the reserve buoyancy and stability, which I like still less. A friend of mine was drowned a few years ago in one of these easy-motion half-tide rocks. He reckoned that she was invulnerable, like a submarine, but he lost power in among a mess of ledges in a winter northeaster. I surmise she took in a sea at her combustion air intake.

I show the exhaust out the stern instead of up in the air. The rounded stern will let the fumes go clear without any risk of their eddying into the wheelhouse. The Chinese diesel's exhaust is not hot or noisy compared with more modern designs. My Sabb engine, which was somewhat similar, had an unlagged exhaust, and you could put your hand on the dry section right next to the manifold with the engine up to cruising temperature. The hand would come away pretty fast, but leave no skin behind. The Chinese engine looks like a great bargain for any boat that can handle its weight and bulk. I assume that the low price comes out of the hides of the workmen in a country where the government owns the labor unions. Possibly the managers don't know what the engine costs to make, socialist bureaucrats being weak on economics by definition. I've seen only one of these engines installed, but it looked to me, and to some better judges, like an excellent job of engineering.

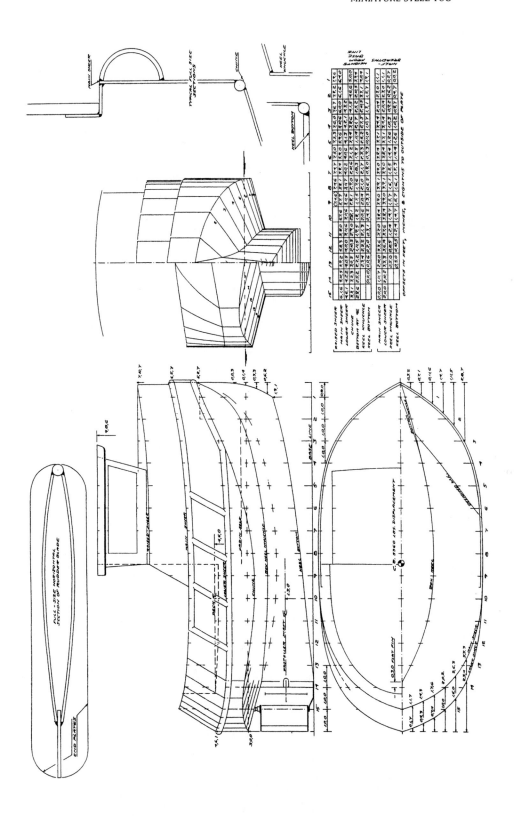

Construction would start with about ¼-inch plate for the flat bottom of the box keel; so much the worse for the rock you hit! On a level bottom she'd stand upright on this bottom pretty reliably, but she ought to be legged, as if she did fall over she'd go down over 45 degrees with a great bump.

The rest of the steel structure would be ⅛ inch and curvy enough to get along with very little framing. There would have to be an elaborate jig to form the plating, but once welded together she'd need only a few stringers in the after part of the upper hull bottom, and one each side of the forward end of the box keel, to prevent oilcanning.

I'd have the afterdeck and the bulwarks steel as well, because among other reasons, it might not be so easy to mount the towing bitt on the removable panel over the engine if wood were used. The raised deck and house would be plywood for the reasons you give. The whole thing could be built as a unit and bolted to a flange on the steel hull so it could be easily replaced if it got damaged or rotted out.

The rub moldings could be half-pipes, or the nice (but fearfully expensive) rubberoid extrusions. Condemned fire hose is very good if you don't care about looks, but I see this boat as somewhat yachty. She's going to be one of the most expensive 16-footers in history. The 5,000-pound-plus displacement is not reduced for cost purposes by being compressed into a very compact package.

56 *Plywood Diesel Cruiser*

23'6" × 7'5" × 2'2"

I've often remarked, half-seriously, that power cruiser design peaked in 1938 and has been going downhill ever since. It's not true, of course; the best of the current generation are miracles of capability, and some of them are good-looking. But the subtle elegance that seemed to come almost naturally in the mid-1930s has been lost.

I pick 1938 as the vintage year because I like the slightly softened lines that evolved out of the angular 1920s. These shapes, which took craftsmen to realize, would be much easier now in production boats. I wish some of the nostalgia caterers would try them rather than the older types they've concentrated on.

This small cruiser follows the older style because it's much quicker to build one-off. Warren Swan, who commissioned the design, is an experienced carpenter who wanted to build her in one winter.

I showed him an ultra-austere concept I'd published earlier, more of an exercise than a serious proposal. From that, we developed this comparatively livable craft, trading considerable labor and skill, and some trailer convenience, against more pleasant living quarters for extended cruising, better rough-water manners, and more shipshape looks. The 1920s style, besides being quicker to build, has better helm visibility than the late-'30s boats, which had to have flying bridges added for bare safety in crowded waters.

The boat will be based on the west shore of Michigan's Lake St. Clair. That used to be the greatest center of powerboat building in the world, with Chris-Craft at Algonac, Hacker at Mt. Clemens, and many more. Aside from being notorious for steep waves, the lake's exits are the Detroit and St. Clair Rivers, through which all the rains of Lake Superior run on their way to Niagara. St. Clair is said to have as much as an 8-m.p.h. stream on occasion. Warren reckoned that he needed 12 m.p.h., which is 10½ knots.

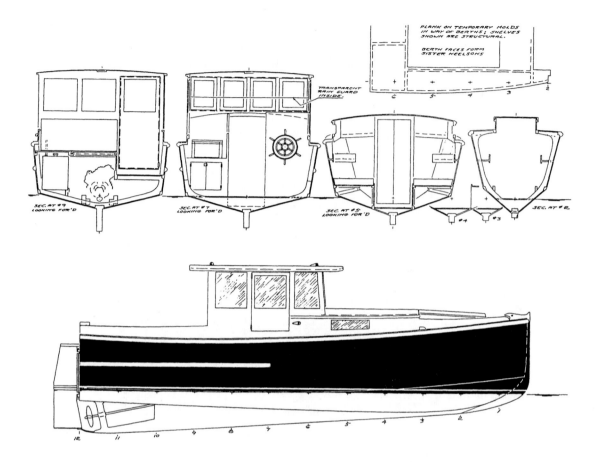

The dimensions had been set at 23 feet 6 inches long and 7 feet 5 inches breadth, for the obvious reasons and because it was a good size for Warren's shop. Ten-and-a-half knots is 2.2 times the square root of her waterline length in feet, meaning that she will generate a wave 60 feet long and "plane" by some definitions. Watching her run, most people will guess that she is doing 15 m.p.h. I think she can just make 12 at the top continuous speed of the 18-h.p. Yanmar, with a light load, a clean bottom, and not much wind. The speed would only be used for the St. Clair bottleneck and similar circumstances. Most of the time she will cruise at 8 m.p.h., 2,400 r.p.m. or 1,090 propeller r.p.m. Fuel consumption is 1.15 gallons per hour or 7 miles per gallon. She is much less efficient than a highway RV in level cruising, but she needs only a tenth of the reserve power and can be much lighter and simpler. I'd also feel more relaxed in the middle of Lake Huron than on a major highway. The lake freighters are even bigger than 18-wheelers, but it's possible to get farther out of their way.

The saving of weight and space by using the smallest possible engine cascades through the design, allowing the nice layout and economical construction. Ironically, in the creeks and canals that typify the St. Clair shore, she can go faster than the muscle boats because her light and shallow shape doesn't drag a heavy wake (and because she is not looked at so apprehensively). She will look and feel like elegant transportation in

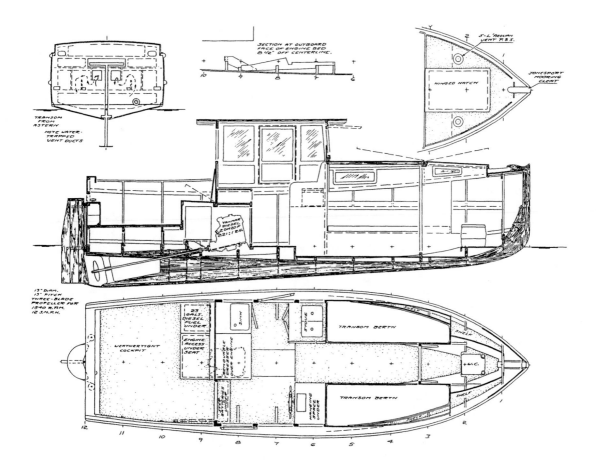

places where the heavy powerhouses are plowing clumsily. Once in the open lake, the modern boat will vanish over the horizon in a flash; they're not only fast, but able to cope with rough water in a fashion unknown even 40 years ago.

Plywood planking speeds construction and stands drying out on the trailer. The shape is freed by Warren's ability to loft and plumb without the Instant Boat shortcuts. The traditional setting up makes the consequences of design mistakes less scary since the builder can check against the loftwork instead of cutting blindly up to the moment of assembly. I'm always on edge with a new prefabricated design until the builder reports that the components fitted together reasonably well. Sometimes they don't on a prototype. (Sometimes they don't on the tenth or hundredth duplicate; builders as well as designers make mistakes!)

Avoiding dependence on precalculated panels allows some "torturing" of the plywood, forcing it out of its natural curves. With ½-inch plywood this can't go very far, but the sides forward are off the true expansions as they twist from the flaring side to the plumb stem. On the forefoot I cheated with an angle where the rabbet and chine come together, easing the curve of the keel edge of the sheet. The fairness of a stiff sheet of plywood is controlled by the curves of its edges. If the rabbet had a quick turn up onto

(text continued on page 298)

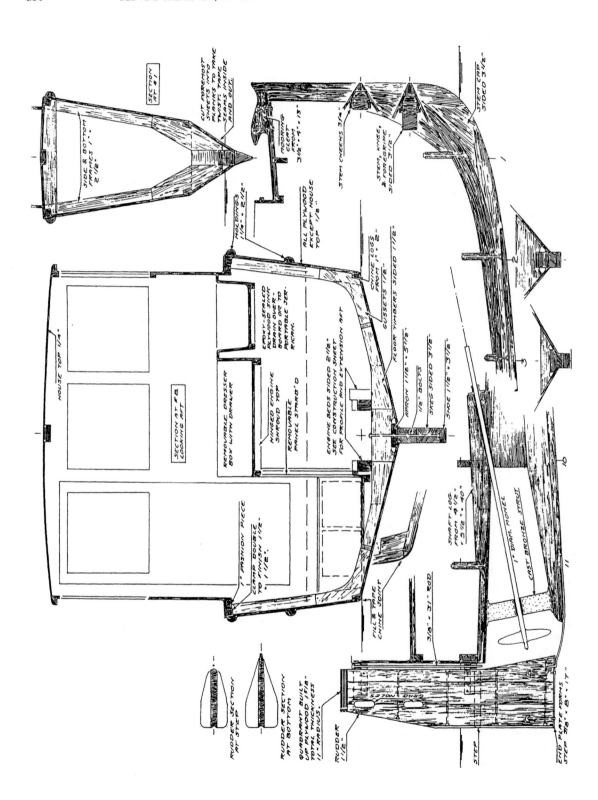

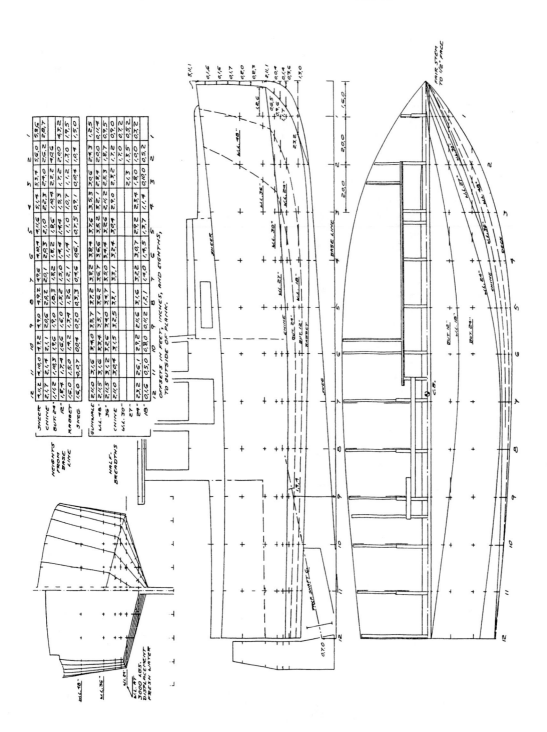

the stem, that short curve would be projected across the sheet, which would be hard to bend in, and when bent would show a bulging line that at the least would throw up spray and, at worst, cause unsteady steering.

I thought the resulting profile was ugly, so I profiled the cap outside the stem to produce the style of the period. The angle where the plywood meets the cap doesn't show much in the finished boat, and the sharp cutwater reduces the tendency of the spray to shoot upward. I don't think she will need spray strakes, especially since she will run with her bow well up. At full speed, the forefoot will be in the air back to frame No. 2. If it turns out that she does need spray strakes, they would start at the chine at the stem and run aft level with the waterline rather than following the chine, to deflect the spray with minimum force.

Given the curves of the chine and rabbet lines, the natural shape of the bottom sections is strongly convex. This would make the entrance lines too blunt, and the boat wet in a chop even with spray strakes. I show the frames straight and the foremost plywood panels sliced into narrow planks, the cuts taped back together when they're in place. The straight sections will make a cleaner bow wave in keeping with her period. In the days when boats normally looked like this one, a designer would have been humiliated if one of his boats splashed her bow wave ahead of her.

The forefoot is well rounded up to make running onto the trailer easy. It also allows her to turn more sharply. With her deep skeg cut away at the after end, shallow bow, and powerful rudder, this boat will maneuver at a standstill in a fashion now almost forgotten, an echo of the time when handling single-screw powerboats was a precise and rewarding art. She has a running draft of 26 inches including good prop protection, but this can be reduced suddenly by moving weight to the bow. She stands 8 feet 4 inches above the trailer rollers—not bad for a boat with 6 feet 5 inches headroom, but far above my ideal for a trailer boat. She is not meant to be trailered far or fast; the capability is to allow her to be berthed away from the crowded waterfront.

The first sketches showed her 6 feet 6 inches breadth; this was increased to 7 feet and again to 7 feet 5 inches without making her wider at the chine. The flaring side softens her looks and gives the gunwale a fairer sweep. I avoid flaring sides in small, light boats because they stagger when somebody steps out there, but in this case access forward is through the cabin, with anchor handling done standing in the big forehatch. Besides the obvious security, this saves some investment and clutter in grabrails.

The doors in the deckhouse allow leaning out for a better view, or to pick something out of the water; also for ventilation on hot days. If the helmsman needs to leave the wheel, it's much better to be able to walk straight forward or aft rather than out and around. A cushioned seat and backrest can be arranged across the after end of the deckhouse, easily wide enough for two people to sit together while the boat runs on autopilot in open water. When frequent maneuvering is expected, a standing helmsman is freer and can look around better than a sitting one, and fold-away helm seats are never very comfortable.

No anchor cathead is shown. This light and low boat's storm anchor will be a 25-pounder that can be recovered at arm's length, saving an ugly excrescence and some weight in a bad place.

The two nice transom berths are only possible by eliminating transverse framing in that area. She will be planked on temporary molds (removed when the plywood sheets are held at chine and rail), and stiffened by the shelves above the berths. The inboard faces of the berths, galley dresser, and washroom form stiff sister keelsons to help take up trailer stresses in the frameless area.

There's room for a refrigerator or portable cooler under the stove. The folding portable dining table may be used in either cabin or cockpit. The portable toilet has an integral holding tank. Water will be in jerricans stowed to trim the boat. A two-person punt can be carried across the stern. The cockpit will have a tent and awning. It's wide enough for an air mattress and double sleeping bag for another couple, but she is planned to be roomy for one couple for a month, rather than for a crowded weekend.

Part Nine

Vacation Homes

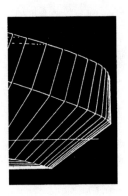

57 *Blueberry*

20'3" × 7'3" × 2'8"

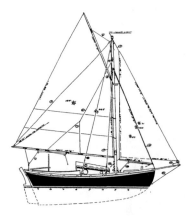

Blueberry was designed by her owner and builder, David Hume. I collaborated and had a lot to say about it, but I did my best not to tamper with the spirit of the concept, which contrives to be striking without being pretentious.

Part of her attraction is due to her high finish and general neatness. Her owner put seven years of spare time into building her, and it shows. There are no unfair lines, no rough spots, no makeshifts. In the fine arts, painting and sculpture, it's often taught that careful detailing takes the skill of a Wyeth to avoid a labored look, but *Blueberry* does not look labored to me. She's a busy design, but all the busyness is inherent in the concept. None of it is stuck-on decoration.

Hard-chined cruising boats go back to the turn of the century and before, many of them by amateur designers who found the "three-line" plans easy to make and the straight frames encouraging to set up. The first one designed for plywood planking was by Charles G. McGregor, who pioneered the use of the new material in the late 1930s.

Once it was understood that sheet material worked best when shaped to segments of cones and cylinders, the commonest way of projecting a plywood bottom was to fan out the lines representing the surface of a cone whose centerline was canted out from an apex below the hull and out ahead, on the opposite side of the boat from the panel being projected. This produces a raking midsection, deep and sharp forward, shallow and flat aft. This was a popular shape in any case—it's characteristic of the Friendship sloops, for instance—but in a plywood boat it usually produces a bow that is blunt as well as deep and can't go as fast as the long run to the stern implies. If you can make a boat's bow go fast, the stern will generally keep up, but there's no way for a fast stern to pass a slow bow.

Arguments about optimum shapes for sailing aside, a shallow stern exacerbates the

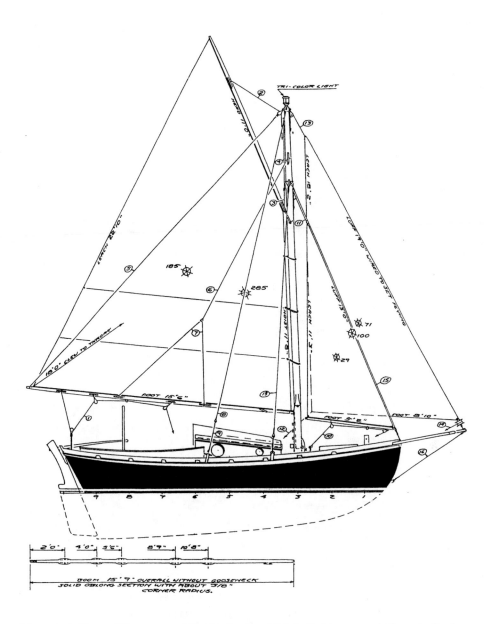

biggest problem of the very small cabin boat, which is that her crew is forced aft where the weight makes her drag her tail.

I put the projection apex on the near side above the waterline, the controlling lines fanning out across the chine toward the keel. With the projection apex near amidships, the two ends of the boat aren't so dissimilar, and the stern carries some depth where it will float the crew's weight without putting so much transom in the water. I've used variations of this shape in several other boats.

In this case I fudged the projection slightly; *Blueberry* is not a true developed shape, though she's close enough to it to get the plywood on without buckling the sheets.

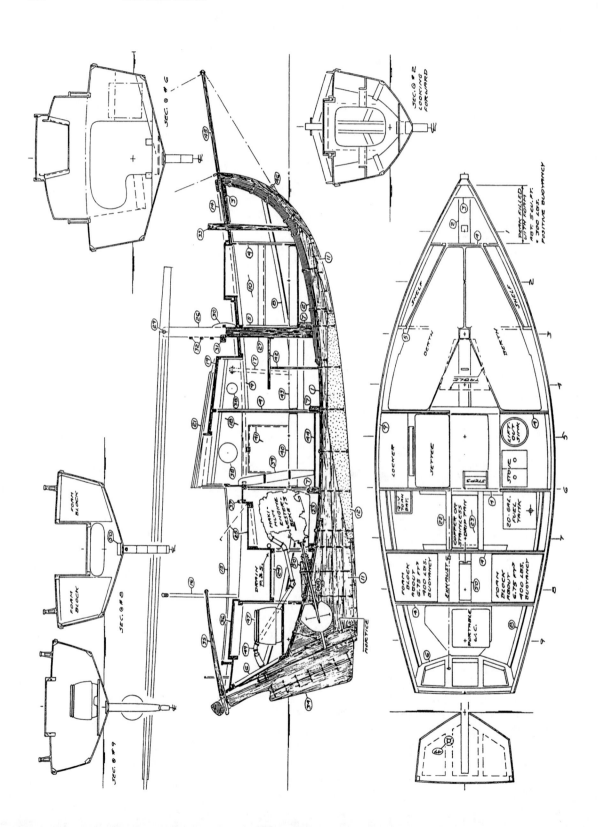

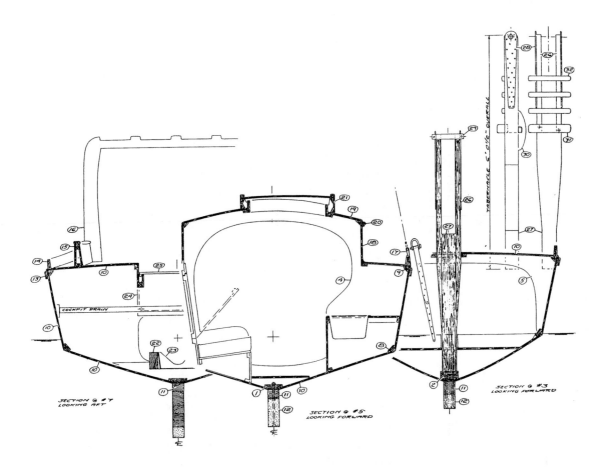

The deep body aft made room for the engine installation. The big 13-h.p. Westerbeke was drawn before the engine was chosen, to show the maximum that would fit. She actually got a 10½-h.p. Vetus diesel that drives her powerfully enough, especially since it's immune to pitching out. The prop is in a deadwood aperture to allow the use of a fixed-pitch propeller. My observation is that very small folding props are unreliable, I suppose because the blades are too light for the centrifugal force that extends them to overcome the friction that holds them closed. The hole in the deadwood no doubt has a lot of turbulence drag, but being well clear of the rudder it doesn't seem to affect the handling of the boat. There's supposed to be room in the aperture to get the prop off the shaft, and I've shown a hole through the sternpost so the shaft can be drawn from outside. It's rare to want to get a shaft out, and I suggested that this hole be drilled if and when it's needed.

The long keel with a lot of drag (that is, sloping down from bow to stern) doesn't place a ballast casting as low as it could be if the bottom of the keel ran forward level to a toe just forward of amidships, with a steep leading edge up to the hull from there. The sloping keel makes a slower-turning boat and probably needs more surface area to allow her to go where she looks close-hauled. Against that, the impact in a hard grounding is likely to be glancing, and the keel takes the ground so far aft that shifting weight forward may free the boat. This keel configuration is easier to get on and off a trailer. I used to think it tracked better in a following sea, but if so the difference is not great.

At one time I made builders take a lot of trouble rounding off the corners on such keels, on the theory that they should act like the leading edge of a highly swept wing. A couple of experiences suggested that I was giving away more in lateral-plane effectiveness than I was gaining in reduced drag, so now I show the edges square. (I doubt that a square leading edge would be an improvement in an extreme delta-wing aircraft like the Saab Draken, because the plane flies at very high angles of incidence compared with a good boat's yaw angle.)

I complained at an early stage of design that we were cheating on the cabin layout by making the berths impractically narrow at the foot. David retorted that one of the crew was much shorter than the other, so "our feet will overlap nicely. Anyone cruising on this size vessel is likely to be in a pretty affectionate relationship, surely, and close quarters for the feet would be at least supportable and perhaps pleasant." The easy chair carries out this reasoning, though my own picture of it in use is of the on-watch member sitting there, hove-to in a gale off soundings, exactly on the axis of pitch and roll, with feet braced against the galley dresser. A passing ship pauses, wondering if the tiny boat is in trouble, and the crewman shows head and shoulders, coffee cup in hand, sips calmly, lifts a hand in casual reassurance, and vanishes below again. During the design discussions there was mention, not very serious, of a cruise in the Davis Strait.

A lot of the livability of this cabin is due to placing the toilet in an outhouse. To use it, the tiller has to be unshipped, on the assumption that other arrangements will be made underway. Given fairly limber users, a boom tent, and plenty of lagging around the exhaust pipes to protect calves, it may be workable.

It would not have occurred to me to rig an 18-foot-waterline boat as a cutter, but it looks surprisingly unaffected both on the drawings and in action. The 29-square-foot staysail is probably worth more than its area suggests, as a "leading-edge slat" for the mainsail. It allows her to heave to in a stable attitude with a full or reefed mainsail set. This isn't done much now in this country, but it can be a useful maneuver. For this purpose, the staysail ought to have two sheets so it can be backed from the cockpit. But there are already a lot of lines in the rig, and it's only a couple of steps, with good handholds, to go forward and guy the sail out.

The cutter forestay supports the mast without depending on the security of the bowsprit. She's over 26 feet from the end of the bowsprit to the end of the main boom, setting 285 square feet of sail—a lot for her displacement. Thanks to its long base and the gaff mainsail, the rig is not high for its power. She's a stiff boat, with her shallow body and wide waterline, but even so, she couldn't carry this much sail if it had to be set inside a standing backstay. I'd be surprised if she doesn't often walk by boats of her size with conventional contemporary rigs.

The big masthead jib is both the strength and weakness of the rig. It's an immensely powerful sail, but to set it up tight for close-winded sailing in a fair breeze is more than it's fair to expect of the simple running backstays. The owner has talked of increasing the power of the backstays with purchases or Highfield levers. This would no doubt help, up to the point at which the bowsprit starts buckling in compression. In really strong wind, with the jib rolled up, the reefed mainsail and staysail will make a very stiff and generally weatherly rig. I'd guess that in open water, such as Long Island Sound, a wind in which she couldn't carry her whole mainsail would put up a sea that no boat this size can buck to advantage.

The running backstays aren't supposed to be necessary to the security of the mast,

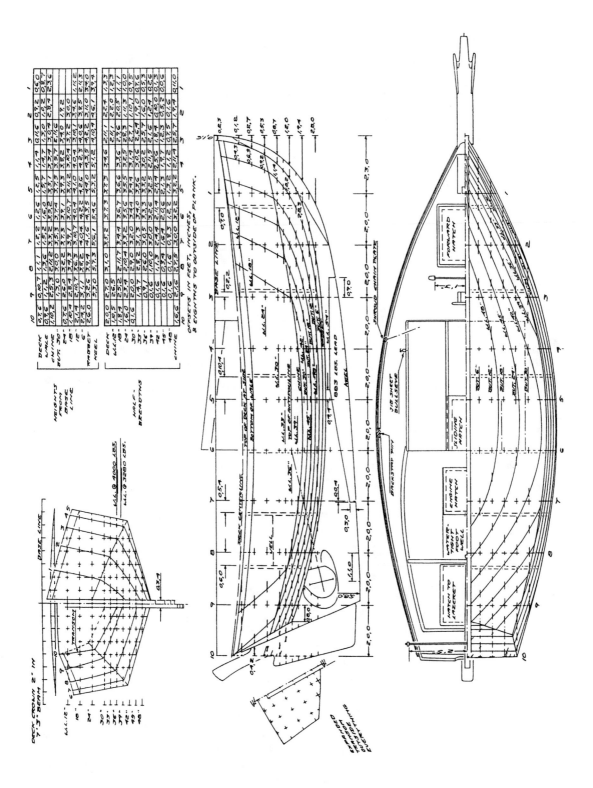

David Hume's Blueberry

except possibly before the wind in very heavy weather. Running or reaching in moderate weather, they can be tied off to the shrouds.

The tabernacle step braces the foot of the mast enough to allow the single shrouds without much drift aft. A deck-stepped mast would need better staying geometry than this, or else would depend more on setting up the running backstays on all occasions. Raising the pivot point so far above the deck leaves only 17½ feet of mast to swing down. The tabernacle is tapered below deck, taking up little more space than a through-deck mast and creating no drip. Tabernacles are expensive in both labor and materials, and with big masts they create tough problems of leverage for raising and lowering. In this miniature scale the design problem is trivial.

After droning on for so much space about why we did this instead of that to make *Blueberry* an efficient recreational vehicle, it's obvious that that is not why she is as she is. There was a time when taking this much trouble—much more than the function, if any, warrants—would have been called an offering or dedication. We don't have such good words for it now, or such an easy rationalization of the impulse, but there seems to be no diminution of the urge to create something admirable.

Author's Note

David Hume has written an engaging book about the designing, building, and cruising of *Blueberry* (406 Windward Drive, Wilmington NC, 28409). I was afraid that after seven years of enjoyable carpentry, he might find sailing the finished boat an anticlimax, but the transition went smoothly.

58 *Barge Houseboat*

25'6" × 7'10" × 10"

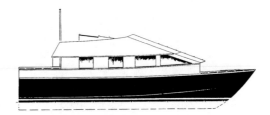

Dear Phil,

I live on a small island in San Francisco Bay, and I would like to move to a more mobile home: a barge-cum-houseboat. The barge would become mobile with the addition of a tug of some kind, and so would need no power of its own.

The barge would spend most of its time in one of the houseboat areas of the Bay. But summers, vacations, and just plain old wanderlust would find it under tow, meandering along the Sacramento River Delta, or up a river. The barge should also be easy enough to get underway so that a weekend or overnight trip would be practical.

Ideally, the barge could be seaworthy enough to be towed along the coast, given careful choice of weather. I've always wanted to travel the great American rivers, the Great Lakes, and the Intracoastal Waterway, and this barge-and-tug arrangement just might be the way to do it. The canals of Europe are long and inviting, too, so the barge and tug should make easily handled deck cargo.

Accommodations on the barge for two people and occasional guests should include a galley with two burners and, over, a sink, a cooler, and counter space; a permanent table that comfortably seats four and occasionally six; a head with shower; hanging lockers substantial enough for a set of business clothes for each of the two crewmembers; and bunks that take little effort to convert from whatever their daytime use might be.

There should be at least three comfortable places to sit. To provide a sense of privacy, one of the seats should look at something besides the other two.

Light, heat, and cooking energy can come primarily from diesel or kerosene. It would be nice to have 12-volt power as well, enough to power a portable microcomputer for 12 hours or so during a working vacation or a semi-permanent working holiday. Since it's always cold on the Bay, the barge needs a reliable source of heat.

The deck should have space enough for a couple of bicycles and a pulling boat or a couple of kayaks.

All these requirements will be difficult to meet in a small boat, I know, but I'd appreciate your trying. Think of it as a small barge. And please, if possible, keep it simple, as you did in your liveaboard lugger *Resolution*.

Philip Smith, Alameda, California

(This correspondence took place in December 1986. At the time, I had been living aboard *Resolution* for a year; as of summer 1993 I was still living in her with no immediate plans to change. She has to be quite big, 48 feet and 16 tons, because she's my office and workroom as well as my home.)

Dear Philip:

I have a weakness for scow houseboats, but they do have considerable drawbacks. They're noisy in rough water; they tow hard; they're apt to be badly maintained because the big, flat bottom is hard to get at; and they have trouble finding berths because they're unpopular with "real boat" people and more so with owners of waterfront real estate.

I played with a house that was to sit on multiple floats which could be taken out one by one for servicing, leaving the house floating on the remaining ones. This scheme had some possibilities for the muffling of slap as well. It did nothing for the towing or zoning problems.

The germ of a different approach lay in the amount of time I've spent trying to cope with the intrusion of engines, tanks, and controls in power cruisers. For years I've been pushing concepts based on small engines in unconventional locations. Lately, it occurred to me that if the power plant and controls were left out entirely, it would save even more space, to say nothing of expense. Your point about the tax and regulatory advantages of having no power is well taken.

It's surprising how little space is wasted in this design as compared with a rectangular scow. The drawings show something quite a bit smaller than I take you to have in mind, yet it has practically everything you put in your wish list. The bed is full queen size with headroom over it for sitting up straight. (I used to condemn double beds walled in like this because I thought they couldn't be made up, but I have found that with firm foam mattresses on plywood, the bedclothes can be tucked on the far side by kneeling on the mattress.) The bookshelves will hold a hundred pocket-size paperbacks and leave room for reading lamps.

The head and the adjacent shower are far from cramped. There's no room for holding tanks—portable toilets work better, anyway—but disposing of soapy shower water is a problem. I deal with it myself by using no soap aboard the boat and going ashore for a soapy shower when I need it. Without soap there's usually no objection to pumping gray water overboard, which can be done with a hand pump or a bucket and sponge out of the watertight stall.

The galley is complete enough, though it could stand more counter space. The dining table can seat six people if a couple of them are small. It forms two good berths for

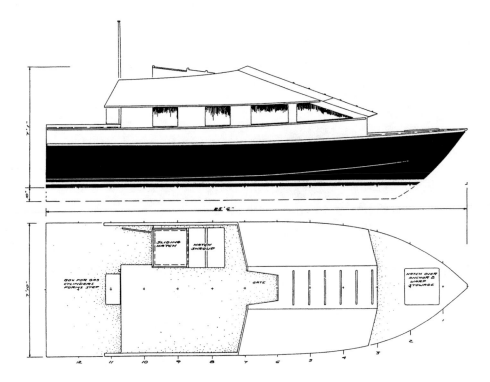

unrolling sleeping bags. Hardly anything is lost here to the pointed bow. The whole thing would be loosened up by making the boat longer, but it's interesting to see how small she can be in a pinch. This boat is well inside practical as well as legal trailer limits for an occasional trip. It could be launched and hauled on most ramps, and its dry weight could be kept under a ton by taking pains with the structure. I've drawn it to displace over 2½ tons to allow for generous supplies and personal possessions, and also to allow some ballasting to damp the motion at anchor.

The appearance of being a modest modern power cruiser is more than skin deep. I try not to design cruisers with bows as blunt as this, but others do and the boats aren't desperately bad. I picture this one hitching a ride along the coast behind a good-sized cruiser. A removable fin, or outboard rudder with a tiller, would make it behave in tow, and riding the cruiser's wake would cater to its deficiencies in head-sea encounter. It could be towed fast—15 or 20 knots easily. If the tug were a 300-h.p. 40-footer, and the towline were the right length to take advantage of the tug's following wave, the houseboat-barge would take almost nothing off the tug's speed. It'd just be a question of making friends with the right people along the way.

For inland waters, any outboard utility would get her along at good speed, either towing from ahead, or lashed up on one quarter for more precise control. It would be possible to design a dedicated push boat with a semi-rigid hitch to push from straight behind. Such a boat could be short, 8 feet or less, though a stubby scow pusher wouldn't be as useful a boat in its own right. An extreme pusher, 4 feet long and 6 feet wide, would be a buoyant and more or less flexible outboard bracket which could be taken away and stored after it had nudged the houseboat into a slip.

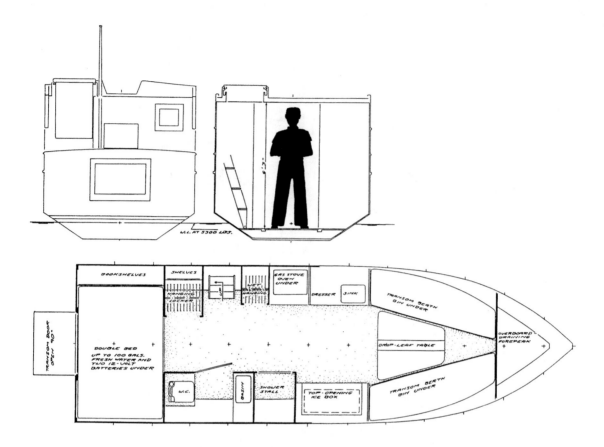

In waters with a fair range of tide, it's often possible to drive a bargain with a marina for a dry-out berth, one they can't sell to most people. That's what I do myself in summer. The drying out twice a day inhibits fouling—the copper-sheathed bottom of my boat went 14 years before it needed cleaning. In winter in a wet berth she would grow a short beard along the waterline, but the whiskers would drop off after a day or two in the dry-out berth. A wood, steel, aluminum, or fiberglass boat will need cleaning occasionally, but at much longer intervals than boats that stay afloat. A boat with a comparatively narrow bottom like this one is easier than a big scow to leg or cradle level on an uneven bottom. She is strong enough to stand uneven support such as drying out over a gully.

One reason the boat is more compact than most scows is that it devotes no space to verandas. If these are wanted, they can be in the form of separate, detachable floats along the sides and across the stern. I haven't dealt with boarding ladders in the drawing, but I see no special problems. The afterdeck, over the big bed, has room for chairs, and there's more space on top. With no engines, some ballast may be needed, starting with a thick bottom suitable for sitting down on clamshells, beer bottles, and marina mooring cables. The fresh water is indicated where it will help stability, but it may not always be there, as happened when the *Andrea Doria* (the Atlantic liner that was rammed off Nantucket, and capsized because her water ballast tanks had not been filled) was hit.

There are two general scenarios for the use of a boat like this. The more common one would have her tied up in a marina berth, plugged into shore current. She would be wired for alternating current and use regular 120-volt lights and appliances. Electric heaters can deal with a volume as small as this; their fans keep the air from layering. To use a wood-burning heater, or anthracite as I do, she'd have to be bigger to make capacity for the fuel. A two-hole Shipmate 212 like mine burns hard coal at a rate of 75 pounds a week in high summer and up to twice that in the dead of a New England winter. A wood-burner would call for a sizable hold or a wood scow alongside.

To lie off on a mooring, she would have 12-volt lights. The gas stove would still be appropriate. Space for batteries is noted on the drawing. For reading and fine work, an Aladdin mantle lamp gives brilliant light but is tricky to maintain and needs constant watching. I've used propane lamps and stoves. They're clean and effective but so dangerous on a boat that I decided the strain on the nerves wasn't worth it. If I were planning to lie off again, I would try a small AC generator in a deck box with its fuel also on deck. This would charge the 12-volt batteries and furnish bright lights when I needed them on an AC system.

Candles can provide reliable light, and heat, if you use enough of them. Four in a row on a secure bracket with a reflector make an adequate reading light. If the boat were to be used as a summer weekend camp, as a base for a sailing dinghy, or just to enjoy the scenery, that would be a cost-effective way to go, saving maintenance as well as first cost.

59 *Fast Sternwheeler*

25'6" × 7'8"

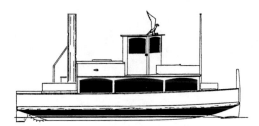

Dear Phil:

There are a growing number of people on the Ohio River with a consuming passion for paddlewheel riverboats. They gather about 10 times a year at festivals to "race" and form the focal point for outdoor concerts and so on. Some of the boats are old towboats over 80 feet long, some are steel-hulled yachts about 60 feet long, and some are trailerable day or cruising boats under 20 feet.

The boat I have in mind is a trailerable cruising boat for two that can be built Instant Boat fashion. She'll probably have to be a sternwheeler, as I can't imagine being able to get adequate fineness and stability in a sidewheeler in less than 50 feet. She should have the "Mississippi River" styling—that is, a raised pilothouse forward, an open stern wheel, some gingerbread, and either two smokestacks or none. To keep weight under control, I would expect to leave the interior wide open and use folding camp furniture. She'll spend her nights tied to the bank.

It would be nice to win races. Most of the competition will be heavy-displacement boats. We'd be among the hot boats at 13 knots. Seaworthiness doesn't seem to be much of an issue, but if you fall behind, you've either got to bust through the chop created by three or four tugboats running side by side or drop out. On the whole, though, the boat would spend most of her time meandering slowly along 400 or 500 miles of beautiful river over a season.

Wallace Venable, Morgantown, West Virginia

Dear Wallace:

I should say straightaway that the only paddlewheeler I ever designed was a pedal-boat—a sidewheeler with a 20-foot Instant double-ender hull. She went very well. Dynamite Payson, who built her, guessed she made 7 knots. I doubt myself that it was much more than 5, but at any rate it must have felt fast. It might be fun to take one of these to your paddlewheeler festivals. It would be easy to trailer and launch, and the only expensive component is the crankshaft driving the two wheels.

As for the proposed cruiser, I agree that the sternwheeler is the only way to go if it has to be trailerable. By juggling the headroom inside and making the pilothouse something like a truck cab with sitting headroom, the proportions of this little vessel work out quite attractively both for looks and for comfort. You can stand up in the kitchen and the washroom, and sit down next to windows of the right height and size elsewhere. She doesn't look like any existing riverboat, but I hope you'll agree that the atmosphere is there. She won't look out of place in the festival line-up, either underway or pushed up to shore with her boarding ramp down.

The cabin has more built in than you suggest. I've been through the portable-furniture idea myself. It's attractive until you try to stow things; then you find you have to have bins and chests and might as well use them to sit and lie on.

I couldn't resist showing the coal or wood range, with the magnificent chimney right there for the uptake. The chimney is so big and tall that the rain baffles hardly affect the flow, so it should give an unusually good draft in still air, compared with the various patent smoke heads. The other chimney takes the engine exhaust, and its size allows a huge dry silencer. At one time Maxim made dry silencers intended for stand-by power plants in hospitals where, so the catalog insisted, "*total* sound suppression is required." I remember that one of those, supposed to be suitable for a 100-h.p. diesel, was 11 feet long and 18 inches in diameter. Having "totally suppressed" the internal-combustion noises, you could play a tape of steam-engine sounds on a loudspeaker.

As to the speed, I'd be surprised if there were a paddlewheeler extant that can make 13 knots. That's fast! I have some reference plans of a 23-knot sidewheeler, *Commonwealth*, built in 1908 for the Fall River Line. I think she was the last and most elaborate coastwise paddlewheeler ever built. To make 23 knots she was 455 feet long and developed 12,000 h.p., besides using high-technology feathering paddlewheels which would be expensive if not impractical in a small boat.

However, I've often thought that it might be possible to build a fast paddlewheeler by using a fast-turning wheel with a small dip. Albert Hickman discussed this possibility in the 1900s but decided that the surface-piercing propeller had more promise. Uffa Fox patented an amphibious truck that was supposed to plane on buoyant, deeply flanged tires. I'm pretty sure this was never tried, and I doubt that it would work despite the way cars sometimes seem to plane on wet roads. I don't know of a precedent for the arrangement shown here, but I think there's enough chance that it would work to be worth trying. I've tentatively shown a wheel 36 inches in diameter by 6 feet wide; the diameter includes 2-inch paddle blades mounted on a 32-inch-diameter cylinder. Each paddle has a shade less area than the swept disk of an 18-inch-diameter propeller. They're mounted on a watertight cylinder to minimize the amount of water carried around the wheel instead of being driven astern. The wheel is supposed to turn 300 r.p.m., giving 22 statute miles per hour if the slip is 30 percent. I guess it will take about

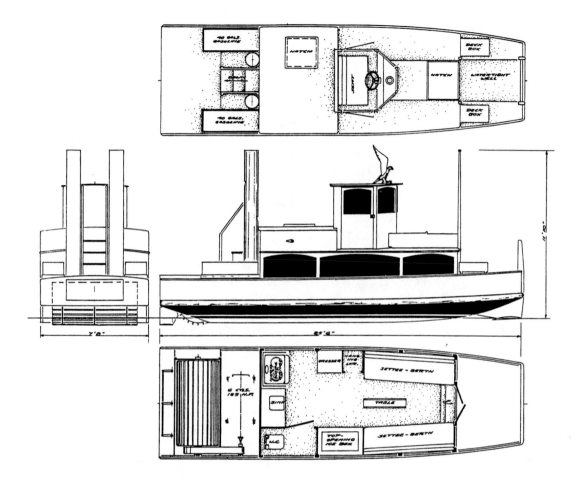

140 h.p. to swing the wheel that fast in a boat this big; preferably an in-line, athwartships-mounted engine, since the short fore-and-aft space for the engine would cramp a vee or opposed engine.

Somebody more knowledgeable than I am will have to decide whether an auto gearbox plus a toothed belt can be used for the reduction gearing, and to work out the installation in detail.

I've played with the idea of doing a cheap test of the principle by buying a junk motorcycle, preferably a fairly new one that's been bent at the front end, and hooking up its drive train to a stern wheel on a small jonboat. Some such "proof-of-concept vehicle" ought to be built before investing in the cruiser, as it's entirely possible that what would happen would be a cloud of fine spray, with rainbows, and not much progress. Or there may be some other unforeseen hitch. Years ago Eric Tasker and I got quite excited over a scheme for a sidewall trapped-air-bubble boat something like those that Bell-Halter built for the Department of Defense. It had hinged gates bow and stern to contain the trapped air, and the test hull flew spectacularly. The catch was that it would only go in a straight line. Even with a powerful bow thruster, it took a long time to get it pointed the right way to make a speed run. We finally concluded that surface-effect vehicles in general didn't offer enough advantages over free-flying helicopters to be worth pursuing. I still think that's probably true and that it also applies to foilboats and step hydroplanes. If you want to go really fast, it makes sense to get up well clear of uneven surfaces like land and water.

Twenty knots is not really fast in context, and at the least it's entertaining to imagine a boat like the one shown here backing off the riverbank and then accelerating to skim up the stream with a towering rooster tail like a prop-riding hydroplane.

The garvey or jonboat hull must be close to optimum for the speeds in question, especially since it will go fast without making any waves to speak of. I haven't calculated the displacement and she may float a little deeper than I've drawn her, but I doubt that she'll need more than 8 inches to run. Even a water-jet boat wouldn't be in the same class because of its underhull intake.

Most garveys and jonboats are too abruptly turned up at the bow to work well in waves. A bow with a gentle sweep like this one can get into trouble if it meets a wave with a steep face. The top of the bow may hit the crest before the buoyant breast can lift it, and the top of the wave comes back in your face as the boat shudders to a near stop. To deal with this I show another untried notion—a big foil fixed under the bow overhang, extending all the way across. This would be in the air when running in smooth water, but when you ran over the wakes of the tugboats the foil would cut into the waves and pick her up before the bow reached the crests.

This foil would be put to tremendous stress when it slammed down flat on the water, and would have to be very strongly built and braced. The supporting pylons are short and could be numerous. I'd expect to be able to make it stand, possibly after a destruction test or two. I once got as far as designing an 8-foot hull with a foil like this. Dynamite Payson would have built it if I'd given him any encouragement, but I backed away. [This letter was written in 1988. The box cutwater in Microtrawler (Hawkeye, Sneakeasy II, Shady Lady, Miniature Tug) is a much better solution; see Chapter 54.]

A problem with flat-bottomed boats with clean bottoms like this is that when you try to turn them sharply, they keep on going in the original direction, but sideways. Pretty soon they catch a chine and trip themselves with a great jolt. A high-sided boat like this one won't flip all the way over, but anybody who doesn't have a death grip on something quite strong will hit the water some distance from the boat.

Longitudinal skids along the bottom will stop the sidewise motion, and they don't have to be very deep to work. There should be at least two skids, placed well out to the sides; a single one on center can lose its grip. On a big powerboat I just finished designing, I've shown a pivoted, sailboat-type centerboard to hold her on turns. The builder and I are still arguing about whether it's worth the complications. She may end up with fixed skids.

I hope I've made it clear that nobody should go on with this design unless they're prepared to use it as a stationary houseboat or repower it with outboard motors if it should turn out that I've overlooked something about that "advanced" paddlewheel. A boat like this, with the stern pulled out enough to take a slower-turning wheel of conventional size, would be a safe bet. It won't make 13 knots.

60 *Breakdown Schooner*

46'11" × 7'8" × 1'6"

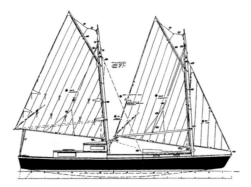

Bill and Beth McKibben thought they would like a faster and roomier boat than their 25½-foot Jessie Cooper sharpie (see Chapter 69). Bill suggested that we design it in several separable units which could be built independently and trailered to the water in two or three trips, to be launched separately and connected up while afloat. The process would be reversed when she went out of commission for any length of time, for economical storage. I had designed a boat on a similar principle a few years before, but she was an attempt to get all the components on one trailer and was bizarre beyond most people's tolerance, though she sailed quite well after some irrelevant details were straightened out. Bill's willingness to make several trips to the launching ramp improved the design considerably.

The bow and stern sections, containing the accommodations, are each less than 20 feet long and 8 feet wide, including the overlap of the central bottom section, which is also under 20 feet and which is flooded to ballast her. The central cockpit sides, seats, and sole are fitted in port and starboard units, with the centerboard dropping between them through a slot in the ballast tank. The height of these center-section sides gives a fair depth of girder for longitudinal strength of the whole assembly. She doesn't feel flimsy; the ½-inch plywood planking and deck, with 1-inch-thick bottom, is heavy for each of three 20-footers, and for any boat under 8-foot breadth, though it seems light for a 47-footer.

The schooner rig with big foresail and small main was chosen to limit the length and weight of spars, of which the 30-foot 8-inch mainmast is the longest. The mast locations of the schooner rig fitted the double-cabin layout. The mainmast is off-center to clear the aft-cabin door. The over/under mast partners make the masts comparatively

(text continued on page 321)

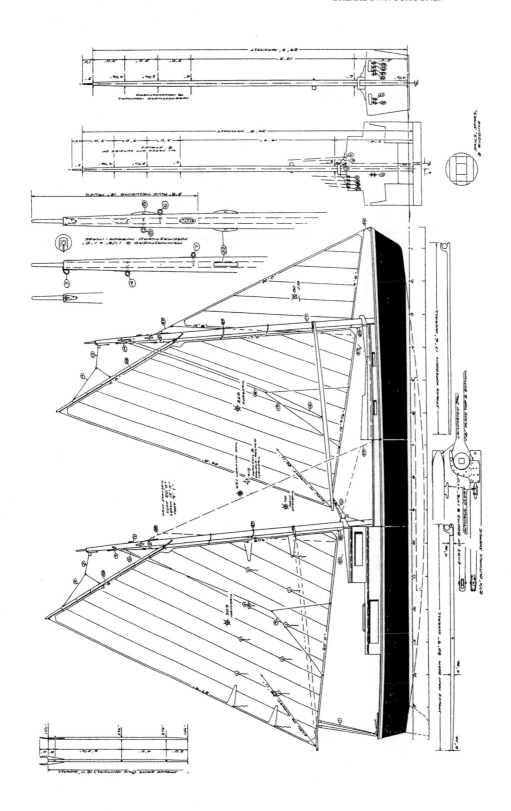

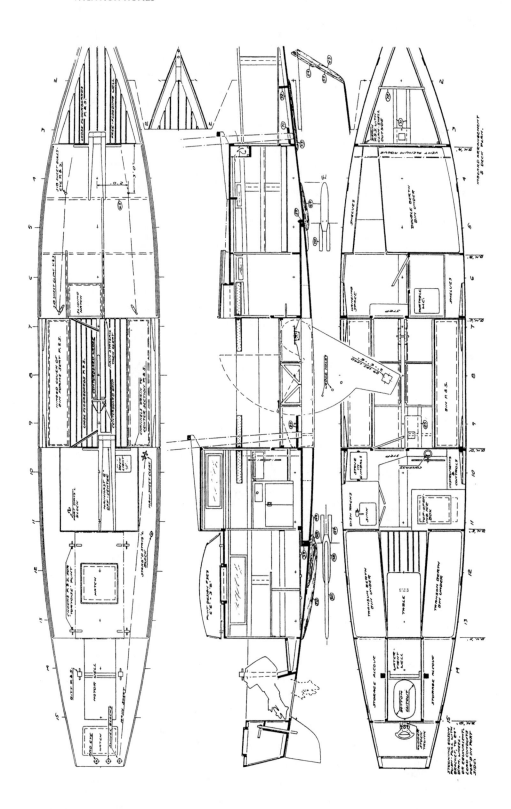

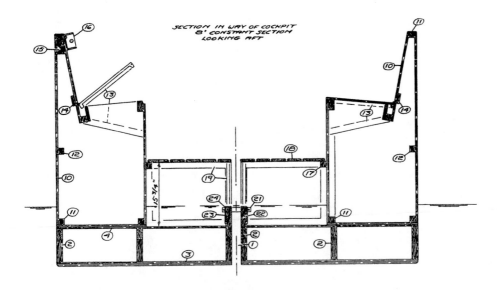

easy to unstep; the heel is run through the partner horizontally and the mast walked upright, instead of having to stand the mast on end and try to poke it down through the usual partners. With this size of masts, it's not something to do for every bridge, but it's good enough to be able to dispense with a crane. The arrangement is less bulky than a tabernacle pivot, cheaper to build, and more flexible in disposal of the lowered masts.

This vessel is very fast, under sail in a good breeze and under power. She normally heels enough under sail to meet a head sea without heavy pounding. With more than two short tons of water ballast and high sides relative to her breadth, her range of stability is reassuring, while she stands up well to the large but low sail plan. With stronger construction and the bow well decked in, she wouldn't need any restriction to protected

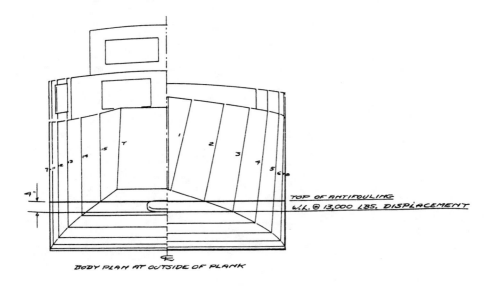

water, though that is her natural habitat. With an account of her behavior came a vignette of lying close in on a shelving beach as a mule deer doe brought two fawns down to the water close by, oblivious to watchers behind the main cabin windows.

Bill and Beth presently found maintenance of the long hull more trouble than they needed, and reverted to the 25½-footer and, later, a still smaller boat, an account of which is in the next chapter. The schooner was snapped up by a man who had been watching her. I heard that he moved aboard full-time.

61 *Fast Motorsailer*

22'7" × 8'0" × 9"

Bill and Beth McKibben built the fast motorsailer *Ada* (a 26-footer with 6 feet beam) and enjoyed her ability to run 50 miles in three hours and then enjoy a sail. From their Victoria base they ran her down to Seattle for a wooden boat show, whence a rumor reached me that Beth was delivering rude speeches to the passers-by on the deficiencies of her accommodations. Bill had lengthened the cabin over what my plans showed, but it was still a cramped cuddy. Presently Bill inquired if I could design a shorter boat with a longer, wider, higher cabin that would still sail and motor as fast as *Ada*.

By that time, I had tried Hawkeye (Chapter 17). I kept her box cutwater but ran the bilge panels down to meet the bottom of the box aft, to get more displacement while keeping the chine high. The cutwater end of the box emerged from the constant-deadrise bottom to carry displacement and running lines far forward. The result is not as simple as Hawkeye, but not complicated enough to slow Bill down. It throws out spray that would stay under the Hawkeye shape, but this boat is fast enough to run past the spray before it can blow inboard. It banks fast turns instead of tracking around upright, and is not quite as steady on course in a following sea. The main point is that this shape has more usable space, can carry housekeeping amenities, and is not as noisy. The protruding tip of the cutwater bottom slaps at anchor, but it is small and solid. It's the drumming of ripples trapped under Hawkeye's flat sponsons that wakes the sleepers.

The new boat uses the 35-h.p., four-stroke Honda motor and the dipping lugsail from *Ada*. Though 3 feet shorter on deck, she's practically the same length on the waterline and has finer entrance lines, with the upcurved bottom profile matching the plan-view curve of the cutwater sides. The blunt top of her bow is lifted clear of wave crests by the buoyancy of the cutwater. Enormous reserve buoyancy makes certain that she can't dive. A head sea stops her less than it does most 23-footers—not a strong state-

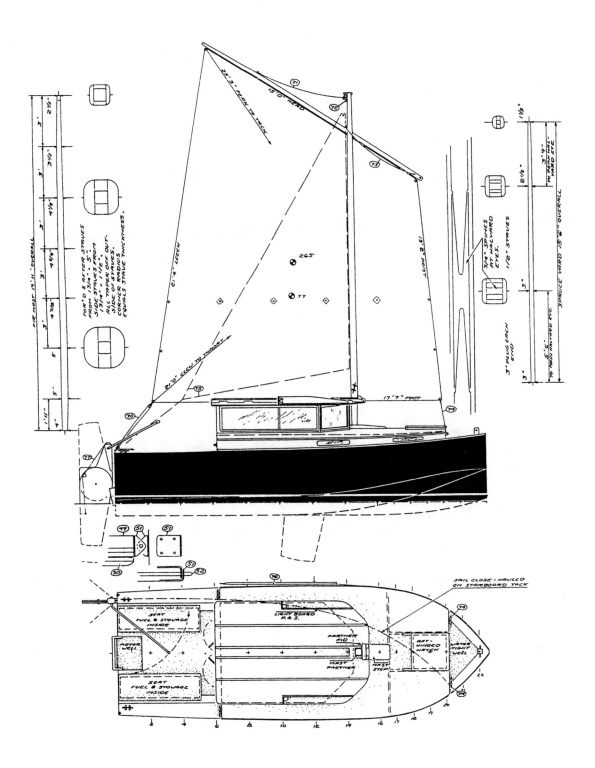

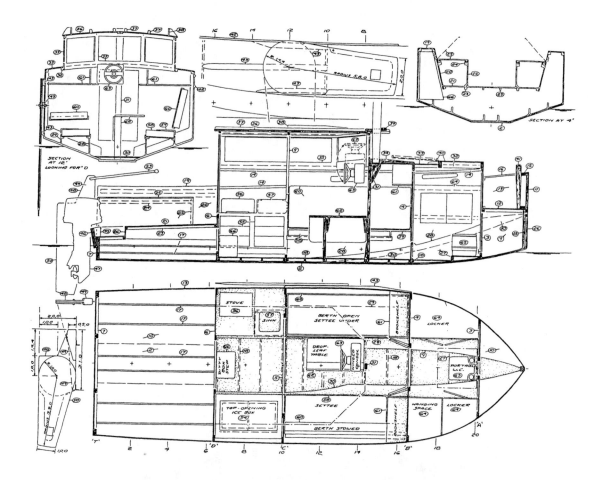

ment, but it stops her less than most 30-footers (still not a large claim . . .). With enough power she would touch down on every other crest like open-sea racers—if she and her occupants were built to take the punishment, which she is not, and they don't desire.

Close- or broad-reaching in a good breeze, she can sail by most sailing cruisers near her size, flaunting the tilted-up motor at them as she dwindles ahead. She's not close-winded by modern standards, and tacking the dipping lug takes either several minutes or a bigger crew than she accommodates cruising. The peak-halyard rig saves lowering the sail to the deck and manhandling it around the mast, but the tack has to be brought around and the sheet shifted to the new lee side as the yard hangs on the peak halyard with its heel just clear of the deck. It's possible to make a short board with the sail aback on the mast, and, with luck, get back through stays if the sheet is shifted. She's very slow on the "bad tack." Maneuvering is done under power except when daysailing with an active crew of three or four hands.

Before the wind, the dipping lug doesn't shine unless the long loose foot is poled out and the peak of the yard guyed aft. Taking that much trouble and adding a spinnaker, she would run well, surfing happily in strong wind.

The point of the dipping-lug rig is that it delivers great driving power over a wide range of courses, with a short mast and a minimum of spars and rigging. The sail has

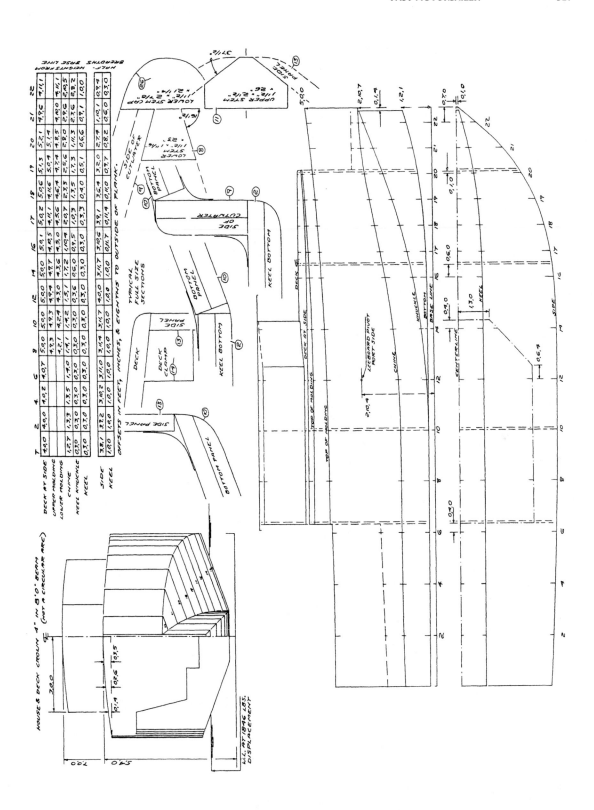

Bill McKibben tries out the first Fast Motorsailer

less heeling effect than most; with that and the righting effect of her high sides, she works and is self-righting without ballast. Performance under power is hardly degraded. The cost of the rig is not negligible, but it's cheap for its capability.

The cabin and cockpit are hard to fault except for the makeshift inside steering station, for which the most that can be said is that a helmsman can place her eyes close to the glass, and that it doesn't take a big bite out of the living quarters.

It's my belief that there has never before existed such a combination of sailing performance, power performance, usable space, lightness and compactness, and low cost.

62 *Samuel Clyde*

31'0" × 8'3" × 1'0"

Samuel Clyde was designed for day outings on the upstate New York lakes, and for canal cruising from that base. She was specified to be able enough to go out on the Great Lakes without trepidation.

She's similar in shape to my widely liked Diablo 15-foot outboard utility (a Payson plan), but in this large size it seemed prudent to erect her on a conventional ladder frame instead of prefabricating 33-foot panels.

The truck-cab bridge has a highway-type view for the canals, but rather than being cluttered with mirrors like a truck, the cab top has gull-wing hatches, the wheel and control console pivot up on the flexible hydraulic lines, and the seats drop out of the way. The helmsman can stand up, with the wheel horizontal at a comfortable height and his head clear above everything for an all-around view. Among other advantages in close quarters, bridge clearance can be sighted with confidence; she needs 6 feet 9 inches plus light staff, antennae, and so forth. It's also possible to get out and go forward or aft from the helm quickly, for shorthanded line handling in locks. Ventilation is very good.

The boat was wrapped closely around the specified accommodations. I meant to have only sitting headroom in the after cabin, but the owner called for the extended trunk over the passageway between the settees. I don't think I would have it if she were mine, but it does have advantages besides the upright walk-through. I had envisioned people sitting inside with a view through the seat-height windows. This is not changed, but now several people have backed seating on top, for short sightseeing trips, and the angle makes a secure resting place for boathooks, docklines, and fenders. The added windage in crosswinds is placed where it's as often convenient as troublesome. With no windows to attract the eye, it's unobtrusive. The main drawback is the blind spot in the view from the seated helm position.

(text continued on page 332)

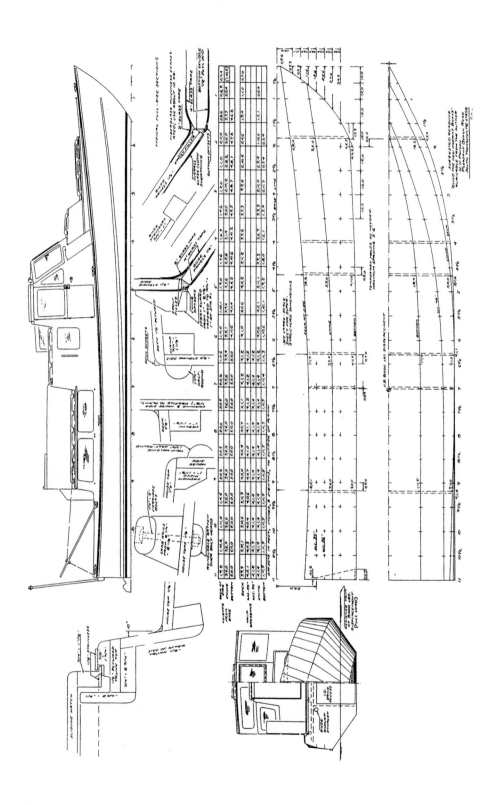

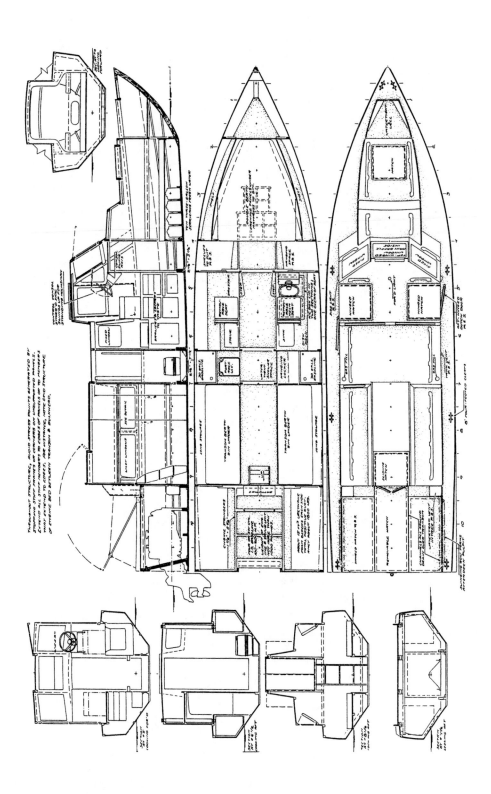

Samuel Clyde

The walk-through washroom with deep shower coamings to step over could be improved only by building and handling a much bigger boat.

The *Clyde*'s trial speed with the 160-h.p. MerCruiser-Chevrolet I/O drive was 23 m.p.h. I had expected her to be faster, and I think the fan of bow spray suggests that she trims too flat. I suggested to the owner, Joseph Spalding, that she would be happier with the drive swung back a couple of notches to let her bow lift more. He likes a level-running boat, and I haven't heard whether he tried it. If I were designing such a boat now, I would want to fit her with a box cutwater as in Microtrawler et al. (see Chapter 54). I'm sure she would be faster, and she might track better. The older shape is simpler and not as noisy.

Aside from the slightly disappointing speed, which did not matter much since she has 7 m.p.h. in hand above her designed cruising speed, the only complaint about the *Clyde* is that she blows away like a dry paper bag in beam winds. Not only is her hull very shallow (which is why she's as fast as she is), but its sectional shape drives sideways with exceptional ease. The cure would be a centerboard, but in very fast boats it's tricky (though possible) to prevent high water pressure from building up inside the trunk. The pressure can be relieved by a powerful spurt out of the hoist opening. A simple cure would be a big leeboard dropped through brackets on one side, but it would look ugly, and the crew would get tired of explaining to passers-by what it was for. They're thinking of having a recording made explaining the fold-over stern railing: "In locks and like that you may want it out of the way in a hurry."

63 *Red Zinger*

25'6" × 7'10" × 1'3"

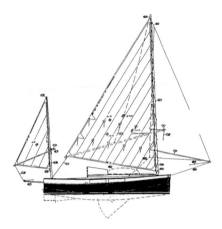

This was a custom design for Dr. Richard Zapf, who built her himself. If I had it to do over, I would make it easier for him by specifying 'glass-sheathed strip planking for the bilges instead of the panels cold-molded-on-stringers. These bilges can't be formed of sheet material; the sheets bulge off the stem from where they're held at the forefoot, no matter how they're tortured. I would use a thick pile of plywood instead of the splined planks for the bottom.

When *Red Zinger* was first tried, she sailed as though towing a bucket. I couldn't see what was the matter with her, until Mike O'Brien suggested that her mainsail was too flat. The results of recutting it were dramatic; she has since done well in handicap racing against more conventional boats. Sailmakers win and lose at least as many races as designers. . . .

In the following vignette, written for *WoodenBoat* magazine, the boat and the weather are real. The people are fictional.

The Guest

The plumb-stemmed cat-yawl is somewhere in the middle of Nantucket Sound—exact location arguable, because she's been in thick fog since leaving Edgartown. The three adults have retreated below, since they all wear glasses rendered useless by the clinging fog. The middle-teens boy is sailing the boat with one eye on the compass and an occasional glance at the Walker log astern. His father is not yet comfortable with leaving the boy in charge; he keeps breaking off the talk to stand up and peer ahead through the windshield, but all he can see is the forward end of the boat outlined against

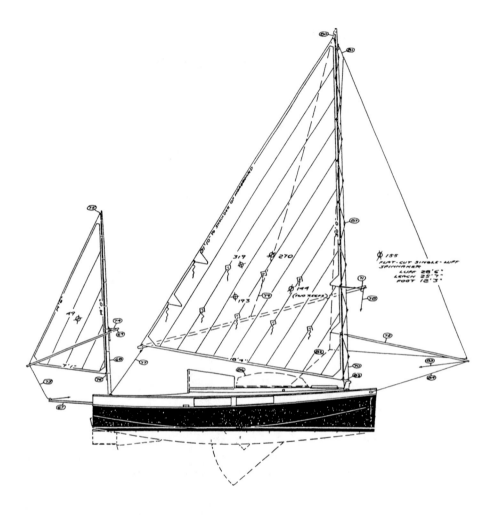

blank white. A radar reflector hangs from the mizzen flag halyard in response to a monster diesel engine heard but not seen some time ago.

The mother and The Guest are content with the eye-level view of the water racing past the big windows in the sides of the hull. The effect of speed is exaggerated beyond anything felt on deck, but the boat is in fact making good time with started sheets, riding the bow wave piled under her high and full forward chine. She is much faster than she looks to a casual eye.

The early-teens daughter has chocked herself off in the double berth, having said that she will take a nap in her watch below. She has a view out both sides, and has a copy of a magazine called *Pretentious Yachts* open on her lap, but her face is vacant under the headset of a cassette player. Her parents fear that she has it turned up too loud for the good of her ears, but they have noted that the epidemic of deafness predicted since hard rock came in has not materialized. The girl's brother will presently demand that she take over the helm, both of them having had enough experience to regard steering as a chore rather than as a treat. The lookout-helmsman is prohibited from using the cassette player.

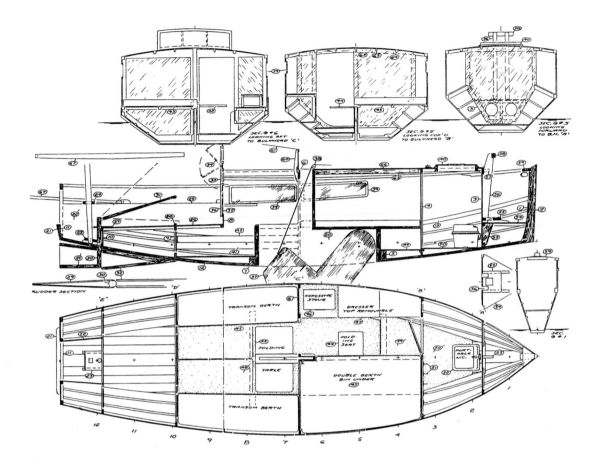

The adults are having what seems to them to be scintillating conversation. They're aware that this is one of the few occasions on which the boat is trimmed as the designer intended, with the live weight concentrated amidships. In better weather, a crowd like this usually insists on sitting in the cockpit, putting the light boat down by the stern. The big view windows, the cushioned settees, and the big deck opening with its windshield and translucent fabric cover, were all intended to encourage people to sit below while under sail. When the boat is pressed with sail, sitting below on the weather side helps her stability more than anything short of a trapeze. The more she heels, the greater the advantage of sitting low in the boat. Unfortunately, shade, shelter, and soft seats have all proved inadequate compensation for an uninterrupted view and the feel of the wind.

In any case, the boat hardly ever has this many people aboard, even for daysailing. The Guest, when he was invited, was promised a private stateroom: "We have a new boat." He can see his "private stateroom" if he looks astern, and it is indeed a new boat—an 11½-foot Cartopper dinghy (see Chapter 7), bouncing along in the wake.

It weighs only 75 pounds, including the tent tightly snapped over its gunwales. The flaring sides have so far kept it high on top of the waves; it has been seen at least a foot in the air several times. Planing on its 2-foot-wide flat bottom, it has no noticeable effect on the sailing of the mother ship. One of the points they've been discussing is the prac-

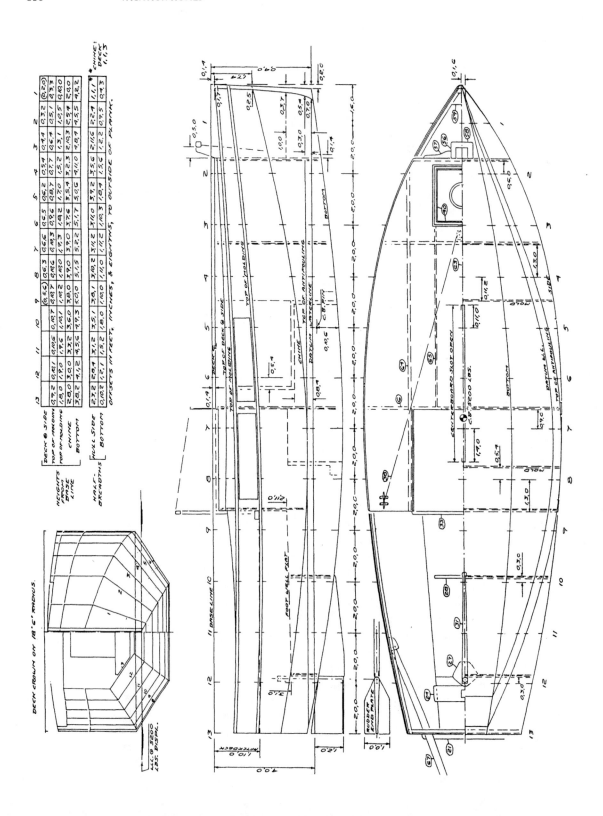

Richard Zapf's **Red Zinger**

ticability of towing a second one in tandem. If so, the suggestion is that the quarter berths in the cruiser could be dedicated to sitting, with their after ends used for stowage—of which there is not nearly enough for four people, let alone five. Unanimity about when to turn in would be unnecessary, and the occupants of the double berth would have more privacy at night. That berth is a trifle narrow for two people with no more than sleep in mind. The Guest suggested that since it's much wider at the foot than the usual boat double berth, a diagonal bundling board would allow sleeping head-to-foot in peace. This was not very well received.

They're ready to tolerate the fact that The Guest is a cigar smoker, having suggested that he feel free to light up, on deck, on the lee side, well aft. They have no understanding of how demeaning it is to a good cigar to smoke it while exposed to the wind, but The Guest forgave the dinghy-stateroom its several discomforts and inconveniences the first time he boarded her and lovingly heated the tip of a cigar, sheltered from the breeze and invisible to condescending looks. The ventilator built into the forward end of the tent could be adjusted to produce just enough draft to take the smoke out through the screen at the stern. The light of the battery lantern is adequate to admire the circulation of the smoke. It is not really good enough to read by, but he can quote Kipling on cigars from memory.

Leaning the filler block that carries the berth flat aft from the 'midships platform against the after end of the centerboard trunk, and bending the mattress up against it, made a tolerable recliner. The lantern hung from the forward bow of the tent. The portable rowing seat, and the bucket that shortens the waiting line for the use of the cruiser's washroom, lie at the sides of the centerboard trunk. His seabag "fits" on the foresheets.

The 'midships platform's original function was to make the crew sit where they trim the boat. The dinghy's short, rockered bottom makes it vulnerable to weight in the ends. Light weight and narrow waterline make it undesirable to try to get out under the sides of the tent. Boarding is over the stern, which has just enough buoyancy to allow it. A second painter has been made fast to the upper rudder gudgeon (the rudder is in the cruiser's after hold). With this, the dinghy can be hauled stern-to-stern with the cruiser. With the after tent bow swung forward, The Guest can shift one foot very carefully to the cruiser's motor board, using the foot of the never-furled mizzen to steady himself. A step cut through the transom at afterdeck level then allows climbing over into the cockpit.

The tiddly dinghy with its bow cocked high and back-to-front, and the man's precarious balance and footing, have possibilities for indignity, but inscribed over the cruiser's companionway is the generous motto, "Never grudge the neighbors a laugh."

64 *Bright Thread*

26'0" × 10'0" × 2'0"

Peter McCormick had been cruising in a big Cape Cod catboat for several years. Like the best of her kind, this cat was fast, weatherly, and handy, rewarding skill and experience with spirited performance. She was not a vehicle for tranquility. A bad decision, or bad luck, or distraction at the wrong time, had potentiality for embarrassment or worse. He decided to try for a boat that could be cruised in a more relaxed state of mind.

The Cape cat was also cramped below. The big centerboard split a wide cabin into two narrower cabins, neither very comfortable. Peter had once been a good draftsman; he boasts that Aage Nielsen offered him a job. But, he had been in business too long and was out of practice, not only in controlling pencil and pen but in the habits of thinking about shapes and proportions.

We agreed that most of the scary scenarios haunting the Cape cat could be exorcised by giving her a lot more freeboard and a ballast keel. If the freeboard were high enough, the keel need not be deep. With the boat floating flat on her side, the lever arm between a shallow ballast keel and the flotation of her high deck could be as long as that of a much deeper keel on a lower-sided boat, with the advantage that she would be floating higher in the water with less risk of flooding through open hatches.

The keel would add effective lateral plane, so the centerboard could be smaller and its intrusive trunk lower. The combination of the lower trunk with the higher cabin brought the trunk so far below eye level that it no longer dominated the cabin. With a suitable arrangement, the trunk could be turned to advantage, security against falling across the boat when she heeled suddenly. The long, salient keel made it possible to maneuver and to sail against the wind with the centerboard fully raised. The new boat would be at home in shallower water than the old one. The off-center folding propeller obviated cutting away any part of the keel, and the end plate on the rudder added power

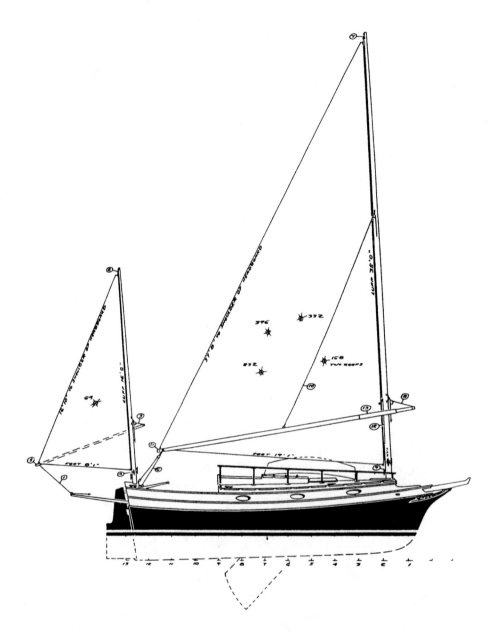

both to hold on against leeway and for control. (It's notorious that the sailing of fast cat-boats is degraded by cutting propeller apertures in their keels. Why it took so long for it to be noticed what an end plate could do for a shallow rudder is a mystery; there used to be enthusiastic racing among a fleet of big cats, and somebody could have swept a series by quietly making the improvement.)

The hull shape we settled on has a lot in common with the Cape cat. The bow has a deeper forefoot, accepting slower turning to reduce leeway with the board up, and to steady her on an anchor. The midbody is farther forward, as though a shorter catboat had been stretched out aft to a more pointed waterline and lighter quarters than is usual in

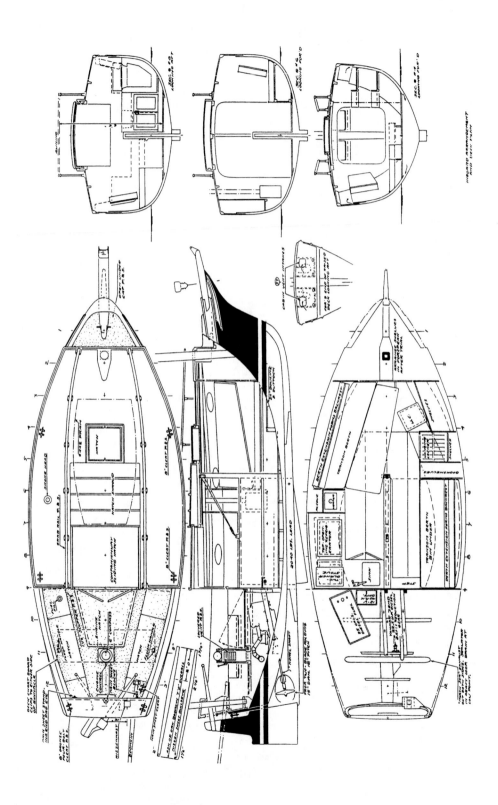

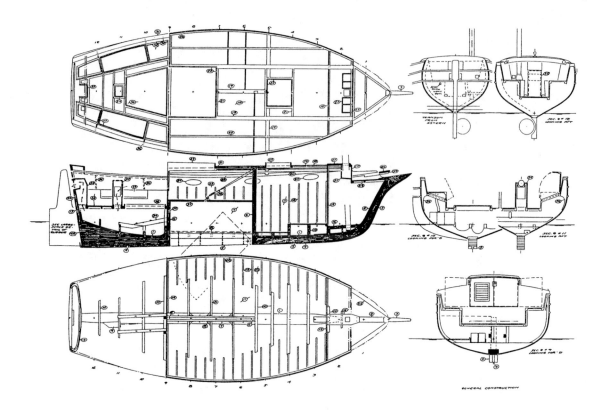

cats. For a given length this reduced her power to carry sail, but it also reduced the change of trim when she heels sharply. She can be driven through squalls carelessly, dry due to her high deck, and controllable due to her heeled balance. The long run, combined with the sharp entrance carried over from the cat, produces a fat midbody—not a shape that shines in a short head sea. I suggested that more length would pay, but Peter valued her compact proportions more. The trade-off is that a long, slender shape is good for progress, and a short, spherical shape good for survival (in a crowded port as well as a gale at sea).

A cat-yawl will always be slower than a comparable cat, because its mizzen has less area, and its area is less effective, than the area lost by cutting off the cat's long boom. (The cat-yawl is faster than a cat whose boom has been docked without adding a mizzen.) The jibheaded mainsail's center moves forward as it is reefed down, but the aggregate center with full mizzen hardly shifts. Reefing and anchoring are more comfortable with the steadying effect of the mizzen, which also has some damping effect on the bouncy roll of this cork-riding hull under power.

Paul Rogers cold-molded *Bright Thread* for Peter. Both of them are nit-picking perfectionists. Peter used to drive down to Maine on weekends and authorize tearing out some minute imperfection to be done over. She took a long time to build and may be the most expensive 26-footer ever built. She is the most perfectly finished and detailed boat ever built to plans of mine. I rafted with her in Lake Tashmoo when she was seven years old, and I thought Peter looked relaxed and contented.

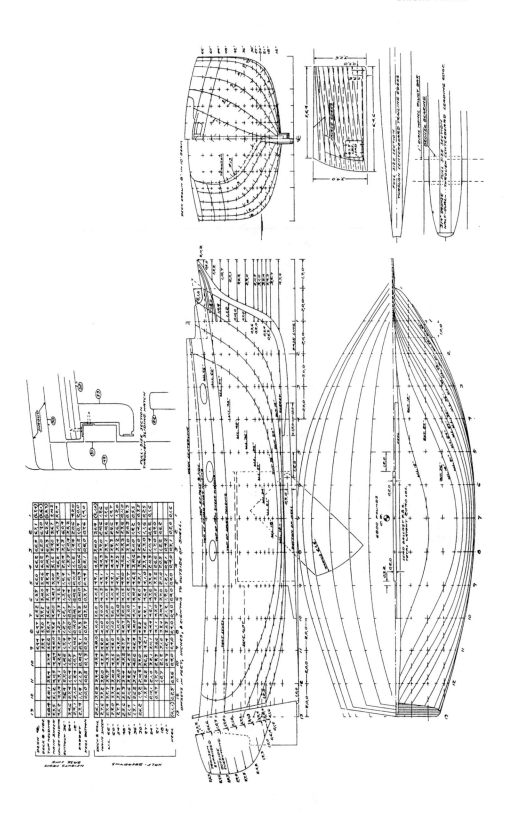

Peter McCormick and Bright Thread *(Norman Fortier photo)*

65 *Volunteer*

35'0" × 8'11" × 2'0"

Volunteer's design was directed to cruising in the Sea of Cortez (Gulf of California), with her 2-foot-draft flat bottom armored with ⅜-inch steel to go into out-of-the-way coves and lie on rough bottom. Her base is in southern California, where there's a shortage of berths. The poor utilization of small, privately owned cruisers is disturbing, as they lie in their berths for days and weeks. I have to remind myself that they're active in their owners' imaginations; a fictional pleasure is real.

The usual berth is expensive and sometimes a weather worry. The boats get foul and may be at an electrolytic hazard. Phil Truitt had practiced dry-sailing a conventional 27-foot, 10,000-pound auxiliary, ramp-hauling her with a 4 × 4 utility to a shore storage spot nearby, whenever she wasn't in use. He did not ordinarily drag her away from the vicinity of the ramp, which simplified the trailer and allowed the boat to be outside highway limits.

He wanted a boat with more room below and on deck, and faster-sailing, but not more than a short ton heavier on the ramp. We concluded that it could be done by using seawater for most of the ballast, to be pumped out before hauling her, and by eliminating the auxiliary engine and its tanks. The engine would be replaced by a yawlboat towed on a semi-rigid hitch and hauled out separately. It would be handy to guide her onto the hauling trailer, brought around to push amidships or forward to position her in a broadside wind. Phil built the yawlboat first, to try out hitches and handling with the 27-footer while the 35-footer was under construction. The boat was decked-in watertight overall, and we hoped to make the connections strong enough to stand heavy weather. The arrangement allowed the boat to pitch independently of the mother ship, keeping the propeller in the water as the ship's stern heaved up. The reasoning is doubtful, considering

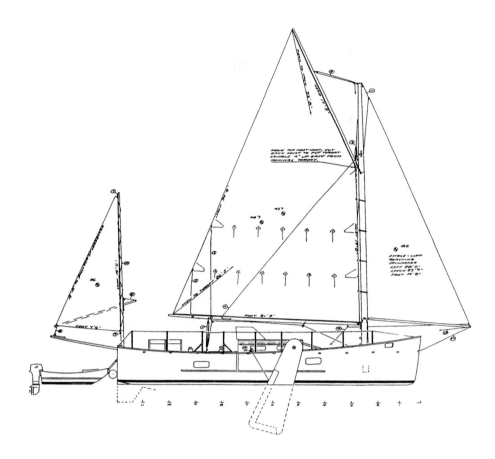

the possible stresses lying ahull in a gale, but the prospective cruising area is pacific and the connection is designed to fail safe, without damaging the mother ship.

A thick file of correspondence refined the concept—for instance, the following letter to Mr. Truitt, written April 7, 1988, to accompany the final preliminary drawing.

Dear Phil,

I guessed you'd rather have this fast than prettified. The water ballast is shown too far forward, but I didn't go on to the next redistribution since this one establishes that the volume is there, and then some.

Meeting the 11,000-pound limit now looks much more promising than I thought it would. If the shell is ⅝-inch strip with three courses of ⅛-inch sheathing (two diagonal and one more or less fore-and-aft), it ought to be stiff enough with very little framing beyond what will naturally arise out of the joinerwork and bulkheads; with some fairly deep-section stringers, I don't see why ½-inch isn't adequate for the deck. Given sparse outfitting, it looks to me as though the dry weight could come out well under 10,000 pounds plus the shoe.

As to the shoe, there doesn't seem to be any good reason to run it farther aft than shown here, and ⅜-inch, with 1½-inch plywood behind it, still is pretty solid. The resulting 1,200 pounds is enough to make sure than she won't capsize with water tanks

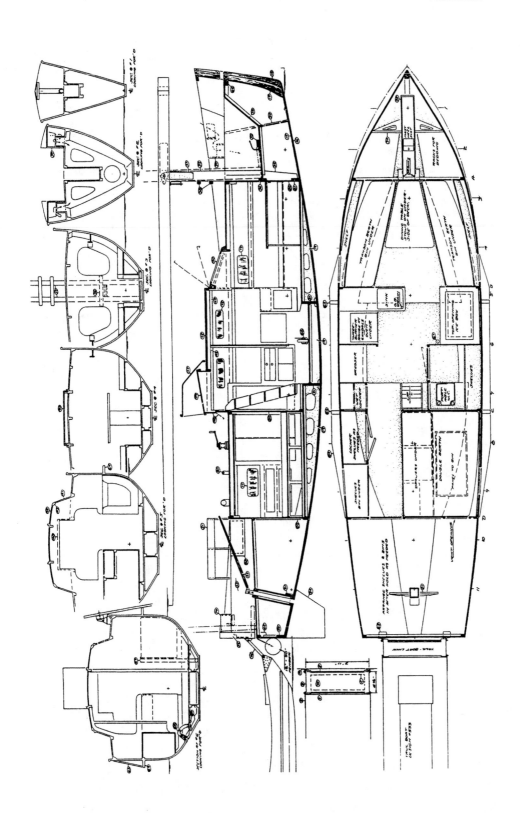

empty—though she will, of course, be very tiddly. I'd be tempted to make the shoe copper instead of steel. The coppered bottom of my liveaboard lugger *Resolution* has been a great blessing; in a dry-out berth eight months of the year and a deep-water berth for the ice months, it has not been cleaned or touched at all for nine years [see Chapter 58]. I haven't checked the price of copper lately, but I seem to recall hearing that it was still down. However, it's of course very soft compared with steel and would suffer in a hard grounding on a rough bottom, especially as, being denser, it would have to be thinner to keep the hauling weight down; $5/16$-inch comes out a bit light, but close.

To get the needed volume for water, I abolished the upper berths forward and raised the transoms and sole there as high as I could while keeping sitting headroom. I didn't like those spare berths much, anyway; as I noted, they reminded me too much of a troop ship. She's going to be crowded with six below, in any case—enough so for that number to be unusual, I think. I suggest that when you have six, you lay down a couple of air mattresses on the sole, which, thanks to its higher position, is now wide enough and flat enough for two (with a third one in the owners' stateroom, for that matter).

About the only other change worth mentioning is the sliding companionway hood, which I came up with on the job I just finished, an auxiliary to be home-ported on the northeast shore of Newfoundland. It seems to have several advantages, among others that a switch from a solid hatch to a screen cover for the opening is much simplified, while a look around is possible in rain or spray without exposing the opening.

I have not had any inspiration on swinging the mast (or rather, the one I had turned out to be geometrically unsound, to put it mildly). We can keep studying how to keep the top of the mast light, and plan to swing it by brute force with a powerful (ergo slow) windlass.

For the light-weather headsail, I'd be happy to draw another single-luff spinnaker, guyed out on a long pole. This is obviously a very powerful sail and will work much better than a centerline reacher before the wind and at least as well around to a close reach. The trouble is, I designed a fleet of boats that were supposed to have these, and have yet to see one set. I sailed hundreds of races 40 years ago in a class (left over from 1925) that had these. With a proper boom lift and other controlling lines led craftily, they're not that bad, but cruisers associate them with the damnable IOR balloon things and won't study them.

The transom gate works out beautifully: One step down to the deck of the yawlboat, with the mizzenmast to grab and the boomkin alongside your shoulder right back to the motor. This might actually work. . . .

The rudder should be very light on its tiller. It's meant to be a steel weldment but could be wood and bronze if you went for the coppered bottom.

The boomkin will be quite flexible, but maybe it would be smart to steeve it up a little more. If it got broken, the sail could be sheeted to the corners of the stern for the time being.

The leeboards will have an asymmetrical trailing-edge section that I think would make them inefficient on the weather side; it is supposed to be innocuous so the weather board doesn't have to be raised. I think she has enough lateral plane and that the board will only be all the way down when close-hauled in light airs. I'm more comfortable with boards that have some "broken wing" capability. It *may* be significant that the production Dovekies with two leeboards are demonstrably slower than the prototype with

(text continued on page 351)

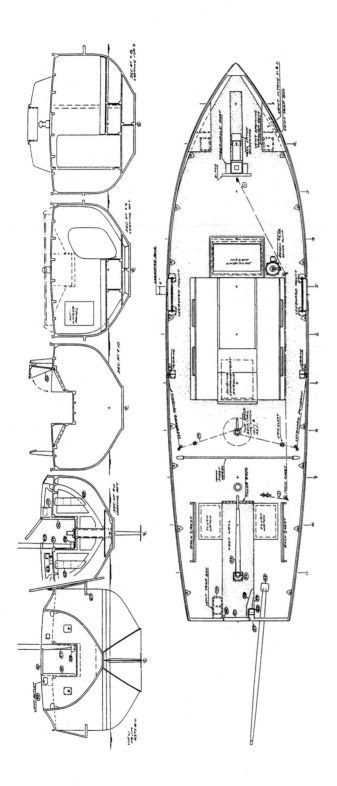

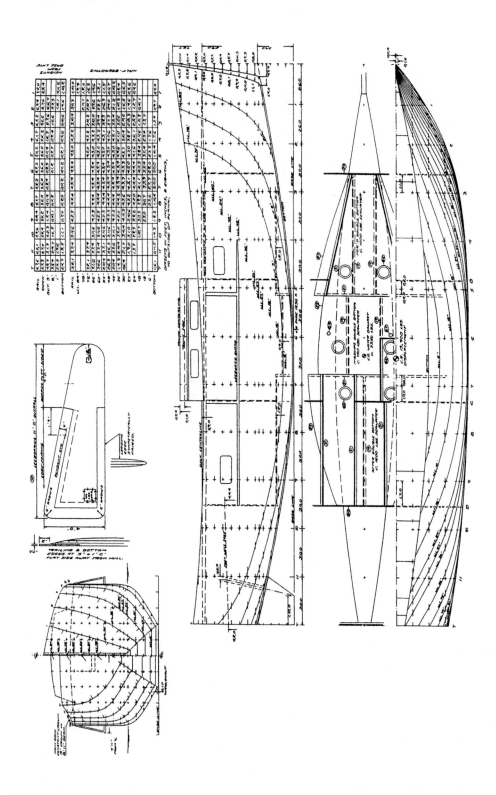

one; there are too many other differences to draw hard conclusions. Anyway, this is something that lends itself to experimentation later.

I think a single-luff spinnaker will do as much for her to windward as anything else you could set on the short mast, if you take enough trouble to guy it. Having no standing rigging takes some of the curse off the pole; e.g., you can let it go all the way around the bow to the lee side to take in.

A big, geared self-tailer is bound to come in handy, given enough snatch blocks. One of these, meant for a genoa, got me out of a big jam once in the Med, hooked onto a kedge anchor. With some cam cleats (I'm usually against these) it might handle the leeboards one at a time and save the wicked little foot-slicing trailer winches I was planning. A line led to the heel position of the mast has poor mechanical advantage at each end of the lift, though; I'll see if I can't do better.

Added freeboard here is 2 inches. It's not too easy to tell without a sail plan, but my impression is that it doesn't hurt. I suppose the settees could be arranged to drop down 6 or 8 inches, moving inboard as far as necessary to fit the flare of the sides, to get some vertical clearance for the pipe berths at night, but I would foresee some problems of discipline if you're talking about four youngsters arranged that way, even if the clearance were adequate. The temptations for those in the lower berths would be more than anybody that age ought to be expected to resist. I still think the extra pair would be better off on the sole!

Plumbing is up to you. I find I get along fine using jerricans and kettles, with no built-in water tanks and, especially, no piddling sink pumps. The only plumbing in *Resolution* is the seawater intake for the engine heat exchanger, and that almost sank her a year or so ago when the shore power grounded to the engine somehow and went out through the stiffening wires of the hose, which got hot enough to burn the rubber. We eventually realized that the flex coupling had insulated the prop shaft. The AC system has since been redone. . . .

I think you'll find that it's unnecessary to steer the motor; if left loose it will swing with the ship's rudder. But it would be good to have the gear and throttle control led up near the tiller. Incidentally, a tiller like this can be swung clear over to use it from the stern; the rudder can swing full circles, which is occasionally handy. Best place for batteries under the companionway ladder? Maybe the hold would be better; the weight there is no problem if anticipated. I'd be tempted to put the Honda there as well, though that will pose some problems of ventilation and isolation.

66 *Wyoming*

51'6" × 8'3"

This was a custom design for a Georgia man who eventually made the always-prudent decision that she was more boat than he ought to take on. (Wyoming, or Wyoh, is a "drawing board name," after the heroine of Robert Heinlein's story *The Moon Is a Harsh Mistress*.) He had the 150-h.p. outboard motor, wanted a boat that could run fast through the inland waterways without leaving chaos behind her, and thought of building her himself with semi-skilled help.

She's practically a two-for-one scaleup of Sneakeasy (Chapter 18), performance of which had been demonstrated. I guessed that the big old motor would drive her 26 statute miles per hour, and cruise her at 16 at what passes for good fuel economy among two-cycle motors of that size and era. The following wave would be 3 or 4 inches deep from trough to crest, since that would be the greatest depth of her hull at such speeds.

In a short sea, hulls like this are not especially heavy pounders because they bridge over several crests and don't develop much vertical motion. The 6-to-1 length-to-beam ratio allows the wedge of the bow to be very sharp. When it cuts through a wave crest, the pressure of water against the sides of the bow is comparatively small. The pressure under the forward bottom is still less, so water is forced downward across the chine and breaks into turbulence. The turbulent flow reduces the pressure underneath still more, allowing the bow to sink lower, increasing the pressure against the sides—a vicious cycle, accounting for the erratic behavior of sharp-bowed, flat-bottomed boats in rough water. The blunter the wedge of the bow, the worse the trouble. Hulls with bows as sharp as this one usually don't misbehave badly in waters narrow enough to have no swells. Increased rocker of the bottom profile forward, to make pressure underneath match the pressure against the sides, will cure the handling problems. The toboggan

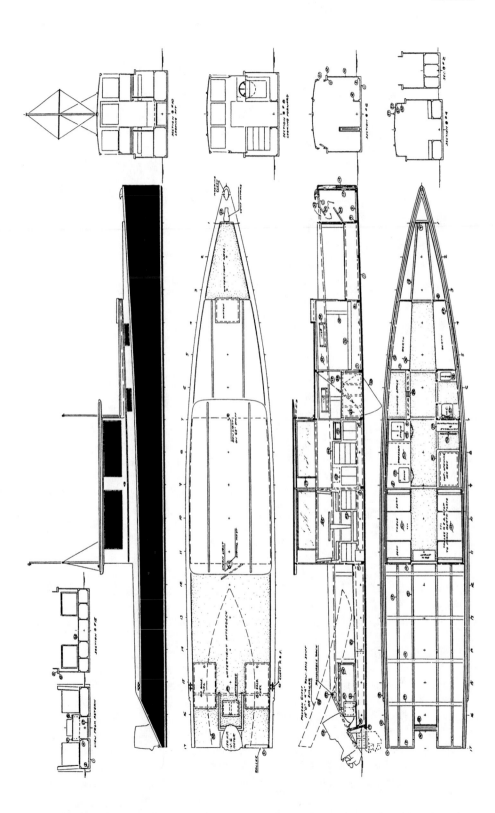

Wyoh's hull at half scale. The box shape is not obtrusive

bows of garveys behave well in that way, but they slap in a short sea and at anchor, and they don't drive as easily at low and moderate speeds.

The best excuse for a shape like that of Wyoh is the speed with which a boat of striking good looks can be assembled. Seventy-five sheets of ½-inch 4 × 8-foot plywood are cut out to diagrams and stuck together at the edges. Boats of this size have been built in a day, from unloading the 2-ton pile of plywood to launching (by a big gang, all of whom knew what to do). Wyoh is assembled rightside-up over her 1½-inch-thick bottom panel, saving a bad day when she has to be turned over. At some point she has to be jacked over on her side to be sheathed, but this can wait until the deck is on, for reassuring rigidity, and 90 degrees is not nearly as scary as 180.

Afloat, the box shape is not obtrusive. The knife edge of the long bow, and the slope of the stern, leave no impression of crudity from any angle. The effortless acceleration impresses people used to boats that have to fight their way up over their waves. The absence of bow spray and wake seems to exaggerate the speed as they skim past.

This last is a hazard of the type. Many boatmen are in the habit of choosing a motor according to the length of the boat instead of by breadth or weight. Wyoh could make 60 m.p.h. with quite modest power by present thinking. Running at that speed, jerking her into a sharp turn could roll her over with a neck-breaking snap. Even at 25 m.p.h. she could be treacherous, the more so because she banks smoothly up to the instant of tripping. She wouldn't capsize at that speed, but passengers could be thrown overboard. The centerboard is a preventive of this danger, as well as a help in windy maneuvering, but it might be housed at the wrong time. Centerboard trunks in fast hulls need venturi venting with deflectors at the forward end and rounding-back at the after end, or they build up pressure and spurt through the pendant opening.

Wyoh does need enough power to suit her speed to the length of the waves in an occasional open-water run. In waves of certain lengths, running slowly, she will run out from a crest and slam down hard on the next one. Speeding her up will bring her to the second crest before she has a chance to start dropping. I wouldn't recommend less than 40 h.p. for a top speed in the neighborhood of 16 m.p.h. A change of course, to meet waves at a different angle, can be as effective as a change of speed.

The view from the helm is not as bad as it looks, because the bow does not lift, nor the stern settle, at any speed. A hatch to allow the helmsman to stand up and look all around would be worth having. I wouldn't veto housetop controls, though I would comment about the effect on cost, maintenance, speed, handling in strong winds, and bridge clearance.

An alternative bottom, like that of the modified Sneakeasy, would cure the handling problems but would take longer to build, slap more, and need water several inches deeper. It would allow making her as much wider as one liked, out to Microtrawler proportions (i.e., 27 feet wide; see Chapter 54), for an entirely different, and much more expensive, boat.

All these warnings and reservations shouldn't obscure the rewards offered by boats like Wyoh: Treated with respect and sense, they have a unique elegance. The cheap and undemanding construction becomes irrelevant. Even the fact that they will bite if they're mishandled reminds me that I don't admire pets or people who tolerate bad manners.

Part Ten

Real
Cruisers

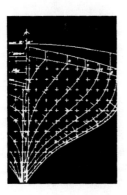

67 *Leeboard Catboat*

21'10" × 7'9" × 1'9"

This boat was designed for Hugh Miller, an Auckland, New Zealand, boatbuilder for his own use, usually singlehanded. The open stern was specified for rod-and-reel fishing, with the long boom topped up out of the way. She was going to be a 20-footer to fit in a particular shop, but I talked him into putting a temporary addition beyond the shop doors. I suggested that once the stern was allowed to stick out through the doors, the boat might as well be stretched to 25 or 30 feet, but he dug in his heels at 22.

The following fiction, which was written for *WoodenBoat* magazine, is loosely based on my own experience. My boat has to be much bigger than this one because she's my office and drafting room as well as my home, and because the books to which I'm addicted are heavy and bulky. She is moored as described, though not behind a service station. The small boats on my floats are *Spur II* (Chapter 11), a Shoebox Punt (like the Breakdown in Chapter 1, but one piece), and a nice kayak that Dynamite Payson built for me 20-odd years ago and which has always had more use than anything else I've owned. *Hawkeye* and *Spartina* (Chapters 17 and 22) are tied up as I write; we're about to launch a Microtrawler (Chapter 54). Others circulate through.

The Resident

The service station on the causeway across a salt marsh would not be allowed to be built nowadays. It is grandfathered and watched by agents of the EPA. Behind the station a creek twists off through the marsh toward a main channel of the estuary. It is now bare mud. A small cruising boat stands on the mud; she would be upright on her flat keel if the mud were level, but it isn't, and the boat is a little down by the head and canted to

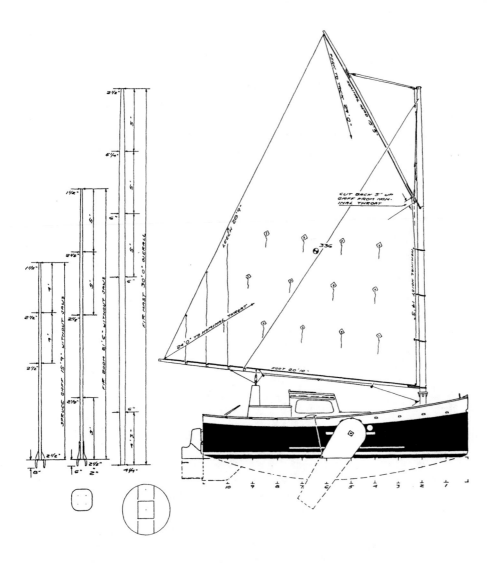

port. A string of floats extends over the marsh grass to high ground. A heavy electric cable runs from a meter in the station, down over the floats to the boat. The float complex is moored with anchors and is asserted to be temporary.

With the tide out, on a gray day in June, the boat looks forlorn, but if the owner were on board the cabin would look snug to him. The umbilical to shore power allows him bright lights and a clean electric stove. He has built a recess under the sink for an electric heater whose fan keeps the air from layering. The recess is high enough to be well above the bilge, and the AC wiring harness includes circuit breakers if anything is a little too sensitive. The 12-volt DC system is entirely separate, but a battery charger can be plugged into the AC outlets. The owner is defensive about his dependence on shore power but claims that he isn't trying to prove anything. Supposedly for cruising, he has 12-volt lights and an alcohol stove. In fact, he no longer cruises; he finds that there is no place he would rather be than here. A Laser dinghy lies on the outermost

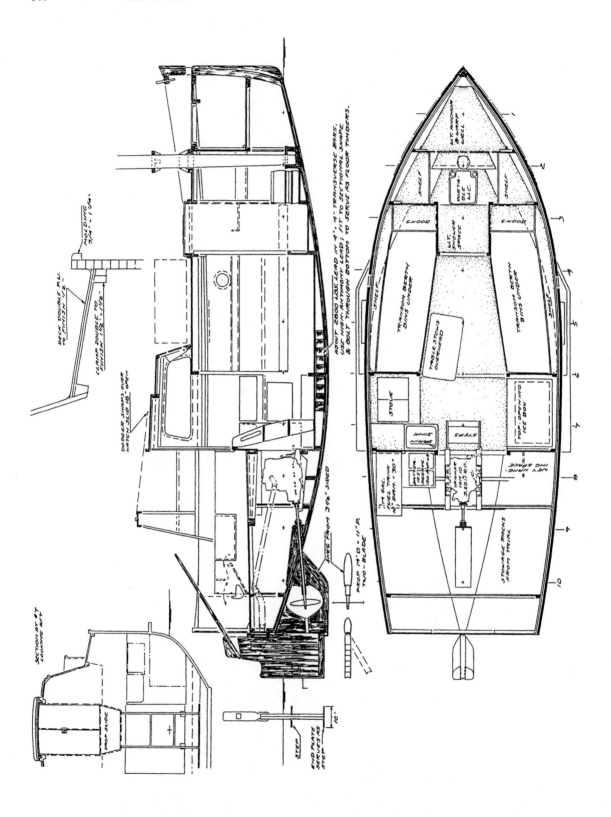

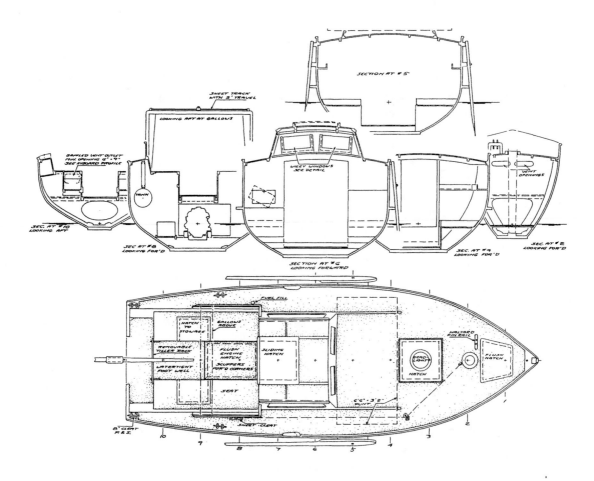

float—quick to launch and sail on impulse. Its winter equivalent is a wooden Whitehall pulling boat, now in covered storage.

He has lived aboard the boat for two years, since his wife invited him to move out of their house. At first he was in a marina, but his arrangement with the service station is better. It's cheaper because nobody else wants the dry-out berth, and he is closer to his car. It is quiet at night, and the view across the marsh is beautiful, if he turns his back on the old tires piled behind the service station. There are snowy egrets at half tide, and plovers and sandpipers and terns and ducks at various times and seasons; gulls in their evil beauty are always present.

The boat draws more water than the floats. When he first tied up, the floats dropped away with the tide until they hung all their weight on his breast lines. Eventually he worked out that the breast lines had to go under the boat's keel, made fast on the side away from the float, to go slack as the float went down on the mud. He expected to have a chafe problem where the keel sat down on the lines, but it does not happen. He uses very long spring lines.

In winter this berth is impractical because the ice builds up in jagged floes with the tides. At the end of November he moves to a deep-water berth vacated by a whale-watching boat that operates out of Key West in the ice months. She returns in April, but by then the dry-out berth is always clear.

Of course, the cabin was not designed for his present purposes. He bought the boat expecting his wife to go cruising with him. She seemed to like the full-headroom galley and commodious washroom. She wanted a door for the latter but got a curtain. This space is all fiberglass-sheathed, with a high sill to contain soapy water from sponge baths where it can be thoroughly mopped up. He now saves mopping by doing most of his washing at a health club. He uses no soap on board, unless you count packaged tow-elettes. Dishwashing is done with a pan of boiling water to rinse dishes scrubbed clean with damp paper towels.

When he moved aboard, he concluded that the second berth was expendable. He made a hanging space for shore clothes in one of the alcoves next to the washroom. These alcoves are the most reliably dry places on board. The bookshelf in the one on the other side now contains a big dictionary and about a dozen other books. He has a theory that good writers do their best work when they think they're potboiling. He has Robert Graves's *Homer's Daughter*, Jacques Deval's play *Tovarich*, de Camp's *Lest Darkness Fall*, Marjory Sharp's *Cluny Brown*, Harry Harrison's *Technicolor Time Machine*, Marion Zimmer Bradley's *The Shattered Chain*, and John Masefield's *The Bird of Dawning*, among others. There's usually a library book or two plus expendable paperbacks and magazines. The only "boat book" he has at present is Bruce Bingham's *Sailor's Sketchbook*, and he has made crude adaptions of some of its niceties.

Outdoor clothes are on the starboard side of the engineroom. The longer garments trail on the planking, and they're all awkward to reach. Other clothes are in the bins under the berths, which are top-opening and tend to be musty as well as inaccessible; the access panels should have been in the front faces, not under the mattresses. He plans to have a bureau built over the after end of the starboard berth. More of his possessions are in the hold under the cockpit with the life jackets. Some of this space is so hard to get at that he has forgotten what is there and is afraid to look on account of nightmares of rust, rot, and mildew. The empty part of the starboard berth is piled up with semi-transient items, all of which have to be moved to get at the bin beneath. He is lucky in having started with a heavy-displacement boat that easily floated half a ton of his possessions. She has nearly 3,000 pounds of inside ballast and is stiff enough to take some out if necessary, despite the big cat rig needed to drive her bulk. She is a good and weatherly sailer though she does bog down in her own waves when she's driven hard; she's at her best in light and moderate weather. Before The Resident took root, he used to sail her over to the South Shore, or down to Portsmouth via the Isles of Shoals, on weekends. In annual vacations he cruised to Narragansett Bay and down east as far as Boothbay Harbor. The boat handled any weather she met with in reassuring fashion. She has better manners in squalls than a classical catboat; the high freeboard and lifted quarters allow her to sail sharply heeled. She is quick in stays but also has good momentum.

The one usable berth is made up with sheets, since he decided that it was easier to get sheets washed than a sleeping bag dry-cleaned, and that the sheets were pleasanter to sleep on. The bed is made up by spreading the sheets and blankets in position on the mattress, then tipping it up on edge to smooth the bedding underneath on the off side; a very tight bed results. A durable bedspread covers the made-up bed for sitting and reclining in waking hours. A small television set is mounted on a swinging bracket in front of the bookshelves.

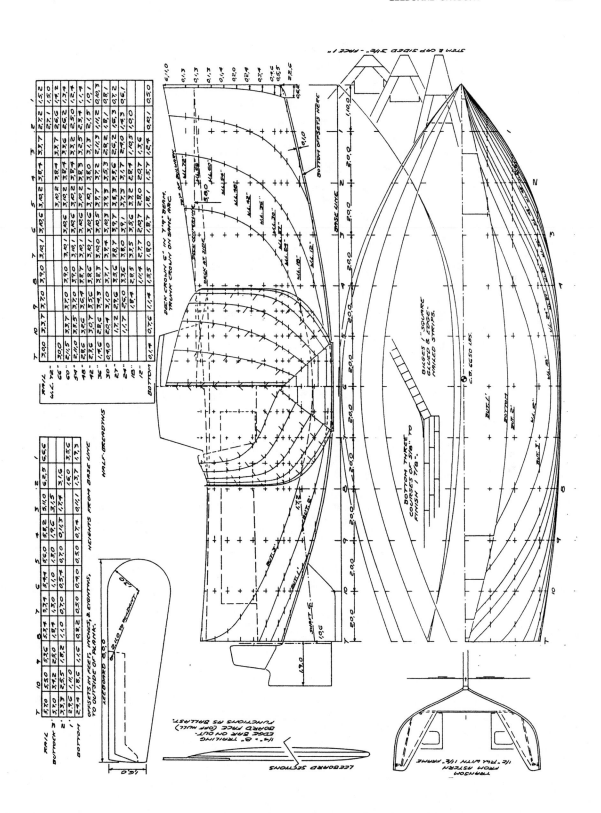

About every other week he has to carry the tank of the portable toilet up to the service station's flush toilet; oftener if he has company. He increases the intervals by pissing into 8-ounce instant-coffee jars. He empties the jars over the side, an army medic having once told him that urine was sterile and could be used as a disinfectant. He can recall when all marine toilets discharged straight overboard and a good many people thought buckets were better. The fish seemed to thrive, but he admits that if a hundred boats in a marina all flushed overboard at once, the effect could be depressing.

Thanks to the health club, he hasn't found the lack of running water a hardship. He has two 3-gallon jerricans of fresh water, but they last a long time because the melt water from his icebox supplies more than he uses. He boils it in case the ice company's machinery should be contaminated. (He bought supermarket ice until he found out where the supermarkets got it.) He has three plastic buckets, especially made to fit the bottom of his little icebox. Two of these hold a total of 30 pounds of chopped ice, which will last four or five days in warm weather. When it is almost gone he gathers the remaining ice into one bucket, salvages the melt water, and takes the two empties for a refill. Now and then he recalculates the cost of an electric refrigerator and puts off getting one, though he would like a freezer, in which he would keep ice cream.

He has a VHF radio but rejoices in the liberating discovery that life is possible without a telephone. He regrets the years he put up with its intrusions, and smiles a smug smile when nuisance calls are mentioned. The radio is seldom activated; once or twice he has used it to make collect calls to his lawyer.

The liberation extends to a new attitude about personal possessions. He walked away from a massive pile of *WoodenBoat* and *National Geographic* back issues; libraries keep them much better filed and indexed than his. A lot of tools, pictures, clothes, and toys that he took for granted that he treasured, he does not miss. If his company wants to transfer him, he will move like a hermit crab carrying its shell. He gets underway so seldom that it has crossed his mind that he might live comfortably in the boat in the middle of a sand desert.

He is plotting a bigger boat, however—or rather, a longer one—in which everything will be moved apart. The thing he wants won't be buried behind something else. He wants better access to the engine. Since he has to live with it at close quarters, he takes a few minutes daily to wipe it off, and as it is it takes a contortionist to get at the port side. He also wants a functional second berth, and lately an occasion came up that made him wish for a double berth. He thinks that all this could be arranged if the boat were stretched out 6 or 7 feet longer on the same midsection.

68 *Superbrick*

19'6" × 7'10" × 10"/ 3'6" (board down)

There have been shanty-boats time out of mind, some with sails for shifting berth. Outboard motors have been mounted on them since there have been outboard motors. Governments and owners of waterfront property have never liked them because they're hard to tax, intrude on expensively preserved views, and tend to be inhabited by primitive people who shoot the nice ducks instead of buying chicken killed out of sight in sanitary factories. Proper Boatmen look on shanty-boats with condescension as long as there aren't too many in the way.

The Proper Boatmen join the others in hostility when a shanty-boat shows pretensions to all-around sailing ability and even ventures into open water. It's reminiscent of the indignation of a medieval man-at-arms in expensive armor, faced by a peasant with a cheap bow and arrow. The reaction then and now is "no quarter."

Designing one of these is an exercise in malicious humor. Bad taste is not all it takes. The joke's edge is blunted if the thing doesn't work reasonably well. A double berth, two singles, an enclosed washroom, a stand-up kitchen, and appropriate closets and other storage—plus an effective sailing rig with lateral plane and rudder, ability to dismantle the rig without shore help, and an outboard motor placed to work clear of the sailing gear—can be fitted into a package less than 8 feet by 8 feet by 20 feet, by a planner without prejudices about symmetry or inhibitions about turbulent hydrodynamics.

The conclusion is an incivility to serious-minded people. The interior and deck joinerwork is almost as expensive as those of a genuine boat with a double berth, two singles, and the rest. The boat is expensive to berth because of its unpopularity. It's too wide, high, and heavy to be a good trailer boat, notwithstanding its paper legality. It's noisy and slow in choppy water, and prone to get out of control if it's driven hard in

(text continued on page 368)

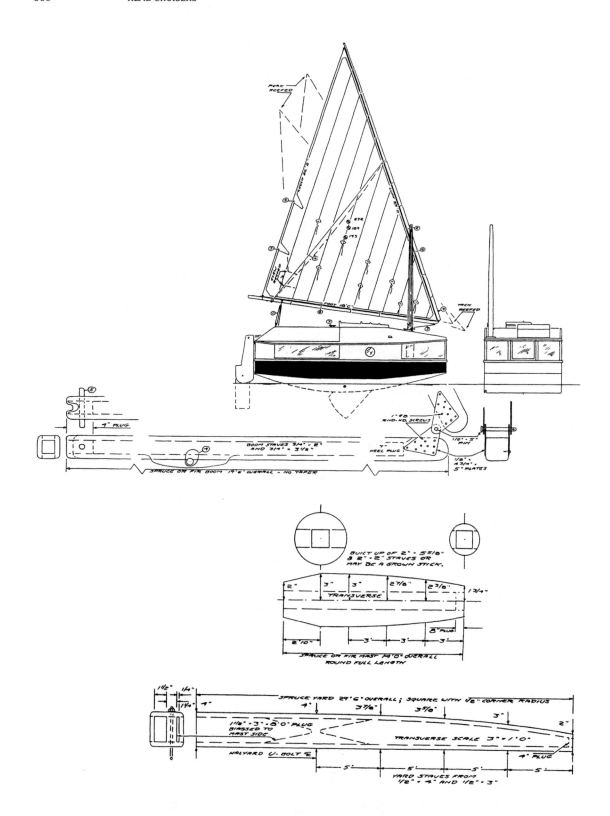

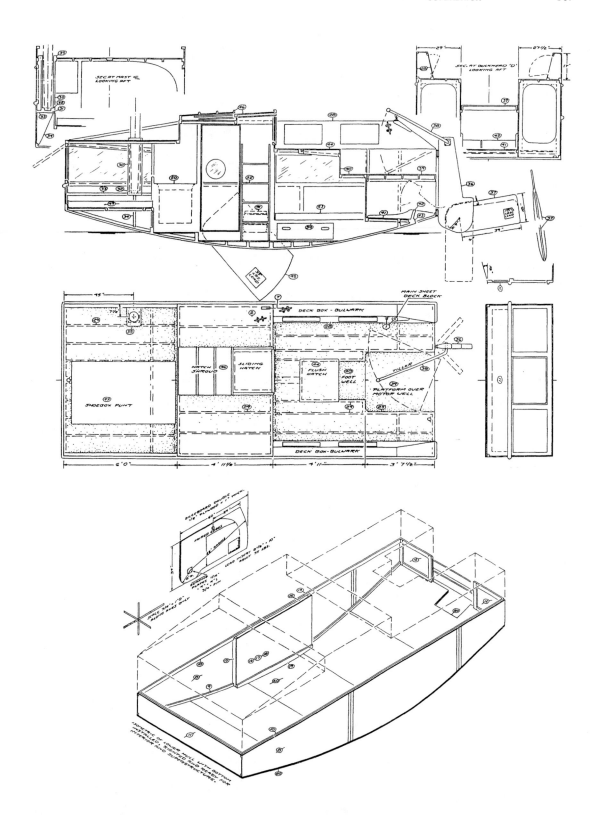

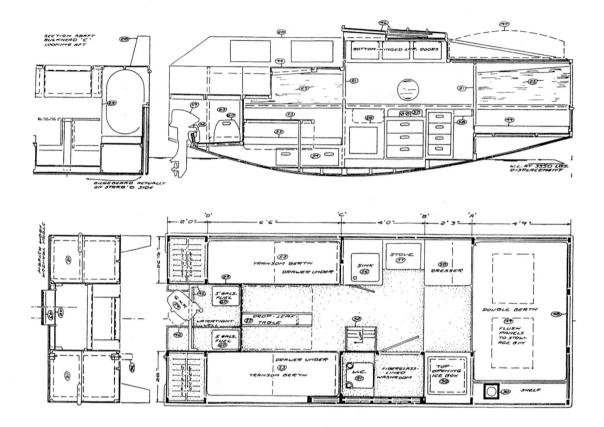

strong wind (if the square corner of the lee bow gets into solid water, it will keep dig-
ging in until the boat stops and broaches). Maximum speed, power or sail, is about 5
knots, with a rolling wake and a bone in the teeth.

It's self-righting, unsinkable, strong, and stiff, none of which entitles it to be called
seaworthy, if only because, in bad weather, at sea, it would jar and rattle its crew to
exhaustion.

Irresponsible. A gratuitous mockery of Right-Thinking Boatmen and other snobs.

69 *Advanced Sharpie 29*

29'6" × 7'10" × 1'1"

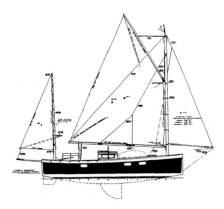

In 1980 I designed a short, high-sided, 25½-foot sharpie, later called Jessie Cooper, for a single man to live on board permanently. I had misgivings about the design, which was the antithesis of what I'd been brought up to think of as suitable sharpie proportions. The commissioned one never got built, but several others did, and they turned out to be surprisingly good sailers and easy boats to like.

Jessie Cooper was designed to have an old-fashioned cross-planked bottom, laid on the bottom-up lower panel of the plywood sides. The rest of the exaggerated freeboard was added as a raised deck after the lower hull had been turned rightside-up. After the first one or two boats, I was advising builders to use a thick plywood bottom that could be sheathed perfectly tight, the cost saving in the cross-planked bottom not justifying its irritations.

There were other weaknesses, not as easily corrected:

1. The deep daggerboard was good for sailing but very bad for shoal-water use; it collected weed, was heavy to lift, and jammed in an accidental grounding.

2. The heavy mast was stepped through the deck, needing a crane to lift it out.

3. The settees in the main cabin were too short to sleep on; she had a fine double berth, but no place to bed guests.

4. An outboard rudder shared the transom with an outboard motor, which looks, and is, a makeshift; the rudder is at risk of fouling the motor, and the motor is likely to pitch out of the water on one tack and get washed on the other. This last was exacerbated by the placement of her masts and daggerboard far off center, with the result that she had appreciably more stability on one tack than she did on the other.

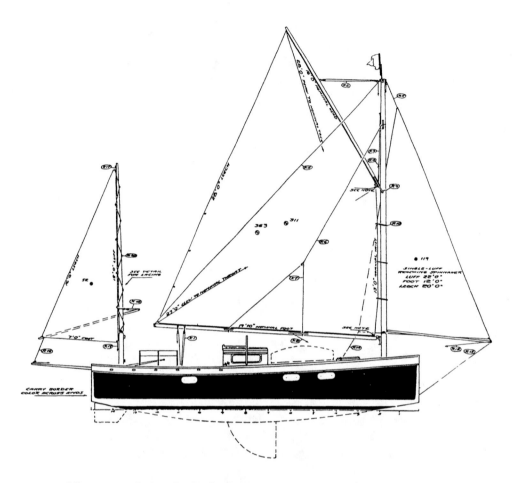

Nine years of sporadic ruminations, and some stimulation from would-be owners, led to what I boastingly named the Advanced Sharpie. (The design represented final emancipation from Howard Chapelle's tutelage and some justification of the great pains he took with my education. A lot of Ray Hunt's influence survived.) Those two, and Francis Herreshoff, shaped my style, which is ironic since they all despised each other. Hunt, who never knew that I existed, had the longest-lasting effect by the example he set of a technical open mind.

Advanced Sharpie 29 is 4 feet longer than Jessie on about the same midsection. The added length allowed sleeping-length settees and more stowage space. The rudder was brought inboard, clear of a shipshape centerline engine installation but in a free-flooding well to avoid the problems of rudder trunks. The mainmast was moved ahead of the cabin, to be centered in a tabernacle, with the bow opened out for the swing of the counterweighted heel of the mast.

The daggerboard was replaced by a pivoting bilgeboard in a similar but wider trunk. The geometry of the bilgeboard made it too shallow, so I duplicated it on the other side.

These boats are thoroughbred sailers with elegant maneuvering form. They can stay with most auxiliaries to windward, and outreach and outrun most, even without exploit-

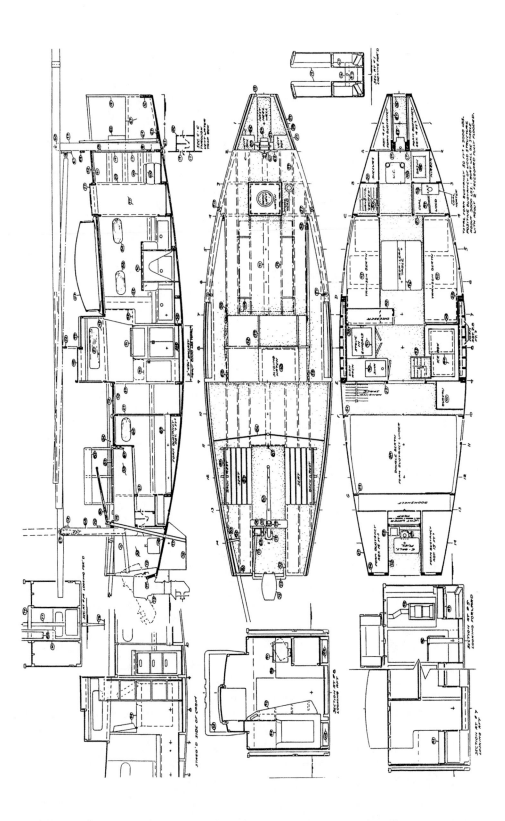

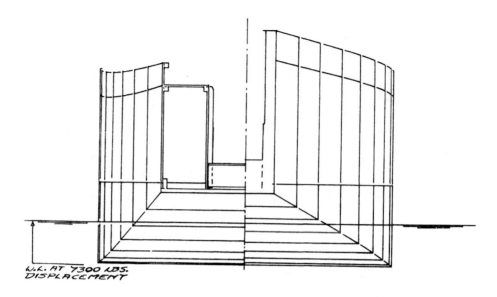

W.L. AT 7300 LBS.
DISPLACEMENT

ing shallow water and low bridges. They recover from knockdowns in reassuring fashion.

Enthusiasm usually begins with the cabin, prosaic as it looks. It doesn't photograph
well, some of its satisfactions being due to a lack of concessions to photography. Every
feature of it was directed by use scenarios.

When Bradford Story was building the cabin in which I'm writing, I had specified
how it was to be painted. He's not fond of painting, and one day he asked me what the
paint was for. I opened my mouth to answer, and no words came. No more painting was
ever done on my boat on any surface the sun's radiation can't attack. Decoration is several hundred battered books, and, temporarily tacked up, a local chart, a photo of the
haunting Lamborghini Countarch automobile, and a print of a Ross Shardlow painting
of the bark *Endeavour* in which each crewmember's individual personality appears.
This last has been up for some time, as it's hard to exhaust.

I have doubts about interior decoration as a profession. Susan Puleo, for instance,
is an artist of a high order. I applaud her attitude about design and I love to study her
work. But I would not want to live in a work of art day in and day out any more than I
want one of the Brandenburg Concertos continually playing. Some silence is needed.
The visual equivalent is spontaneity. In *The Common Sense of Yacht Design*, L. Francis
Herreshoff recounted his nightmare in the Edwardian version of an interior decorator's
dream: A "very sober voice" said, slowly, as he slept, "You will never again see frames,
nor deck beams, nor carlings. You will ne'er again see bolt heads, nor screw heads, nor
rivets; no, nor the clamp, nor the seams of the planking. No. never." L.F.H. was the
worst designer of cabins ever to make a mark designing boats, but he was a great
philosopher; the chapter on cabin arrangement is one of the best in the only great book
on boat design.

The Advanced Sharpies suffer from booming pounding at anchor. The square bow
throws out an intolerable amount of froth in choppy water. They're complicated and
expensive. I have the glimmerings of some ideas for improvements.

Advanced Sharpie 29s: Australia (top) and Chesapeake Bay (bottom)

70 *Loose Moose II*

11.5 meters (37.7 feet) × 2.4 meters (7.9 feet) ×
.33 meter (1.0 foot)

Bob and Sheila Wise built one of my Jessie Cooper sharpies on a French riverbank, as a stopgap measure until they could locate a real boat within their means. Like several other people, they found the boxy little boat unexpectedly competent. They lived in her for three years, until they had to conclude that if they didn't get a second working desk, one of them would have to go ashore.

Starting with the two desks, some more ambitious suggestions crept in, such as a proposed voyage from the Moselle in France to a West Indian island via the Rhone, the Mediterranean, and the Canary Islands. We didn't delude ourselves that a Bolger Box, even a long one, was the best possible vehicle for this enterprise; only that it was capable, that the modesty of the investment advanced the plan, and that the box *was* ideal for in-port living between passages. The shallow and compact boat could take choice berths not accessible to more conventional cruisers.

I don't have much respect for the architecture of Le Corbusier, but his "machine for living" concept is stimulating if you study, more than he ever did, how people can, should, and do live. If you try to disguise a machine like this, say by raking the ends or breaking the sheer, you produce a box with unconvincing concessions to style that only emphasize that you're ashamed of it.

I've been thinking that one of these boats might make a surface for mural paintings—say, an arctic seascape on the starboard side and a tropical beach to port. Or a fleet of vessels, or a crowd of people. The long, horizontal shape fits subjects hard to adapt to the usual proportions of a picture frame. The frame itself, the outline of the boat's profile, is suggestive. As a child I was fascinated by the carved and gilded Victorian frames on the paintings in my grandfather's parlor. It's a very healthy exercise to call up from memory the art objects that I enjoyed before I was taught by academic critics to despise them.

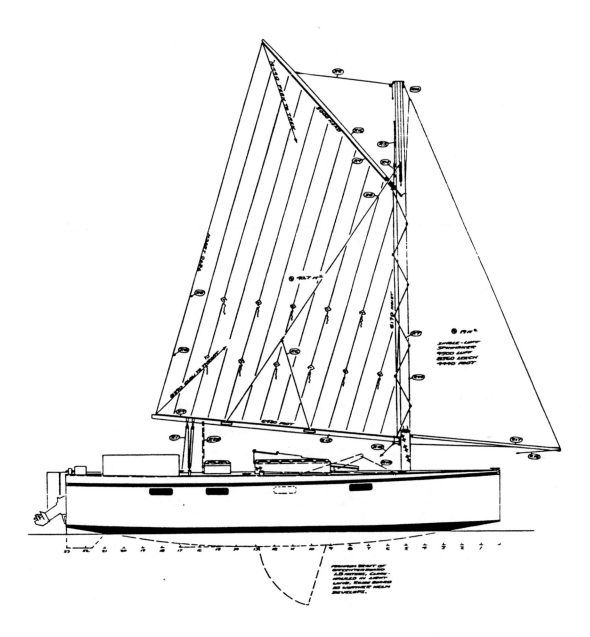

Whatever you think of that fancy, in this case we followed the implications of plywood panels to a logical conclusion and accepted the outcome. Bob assembled her in six months of near-full-time work, plus part-time work by Sheila. For her material and labor cost, Loose Moose is a fast, roomy, handy, and seaworthy boat, as shipshape as a supertanker.

The Wises wrote that Loose Moose accommodated ". . . a dedicated office with two desks (his and hers), a head with a bathtub (a small one), along with tons of room for books, film-video equipment, two computers, plus all the tools it took to build the boat,

(text continued on page 378)

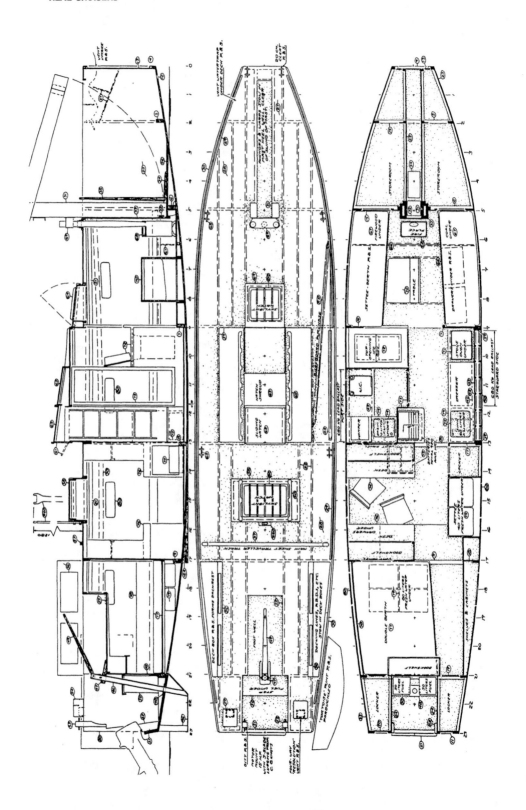

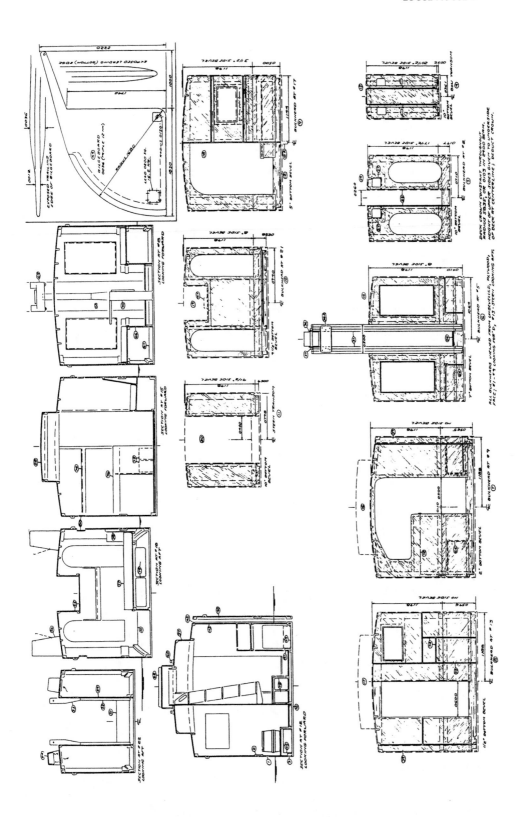

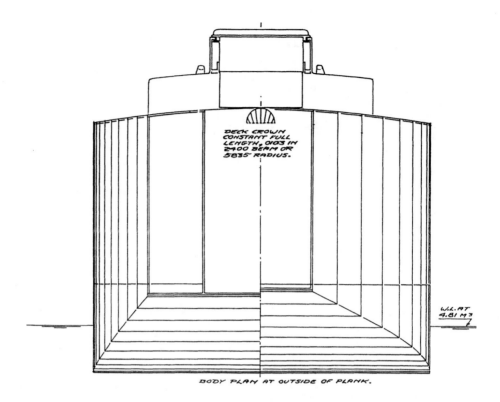

DECK CROWN
CONSTANT FULL
LENGTH, 0103 IN
2400 BEAM OR
5835 RADIUS.

W.L. AT
4.81 M³

BODY PLAN AT OUTSIDE OF PLANK.

and yet we are still on our lines!" I suppose the tub goes where the basin is shown on the plans. It's been upwards of a century since it was usual for a vessel to carry tools adequate to replace herself. The former capability didn't need access to manufactured plywood and epoxy, but it didn't produce boats as tight and light as this one.

The gaff cat rig met the requirements that the mast should be pivoted and counterweighted to be lowered at short notice, underway, and that the gear should work clear of a vane steerer. The absence of standing rigging allows the sail to be guyed out forward of the beam, with the big flat spinnaker on the other side; this combination has a course-keeping effect even without the vane gear, and it has less chafe hazard than most rigs.

It's possible that for running down the tradewinds she would benefit by a temporary extension to her bow, to mitigate the bow transom's tendency to bury, drag, and yaw in a steep sea. It wouldn't be much trouble to add, but it may be simpler to ease up driving her when she's unhappy. Ocean passages will be rare, and need not be fast.

On inland waters, she's capable of cruising at 8 knots, with great capability for shortcuts, no delay for bridges, and no propensity to wash the banks down behind her. The two punts parbuckled against her quarters are vulnerable, but they are Tortoises, the first idea of which was to be disposable. Think of them as crushable protection.

71 *Ataraxia*

11 meters (36.0 feet) × 3 meters (9.84 feet) ×
.7 meter (27.5 inches)

Ataraxia was built by Story Boatbuilding of Essex, Massachusetts, for David O'Neill of Hartford (he was living in Toronto while we were designing her). The following essay was written as a contribution to an as yet unpublished book about breakdown-proofing long-distance cruising boats.

Ataraxia was an illustration of what could be done at the design stage. In Greek, the name signifies "calmness untroubled by mental or emotional excitation."

Her proportions are as compact as possible without being snubbed, to make her undemanding in berthing and to minimize imposed stresses by waves and by taking the ground. Discontinuities were avoided in plan and profile, and as far as possible in section. Excrescences beyond the main envelope were kept to a minimum. The deck is a segment of a cylinder from bow to stern, with straight deck stringers replacing transverse beams. Among other advantages, this method of framing the deck furnishes overhead grabrails, and head contact is usually glancing.

The ends are upright to take all the available waterline length and to produce sharp forebody sections for smooth action in head seas. She is shallow-bodied and high-sided for initial and reserve stability with a minimum of ballast; has shallow draft for the obvious convenience; and is straight-keeled to avoid misunderstandings in docks and lifts.

Construction is carvel planking on steam-bent frames, a quick method of realizing a complex shape with reliable quality control. The many transverse frames accept a large number of closely spaced fastenings (silicon-bronze screws) to spread stresses widely. The frames carry a cedar sheathing inside; in the bays between the frames, air circulates continuously around the hull from the shaded side to the sunlit side at a rate of as much as one revolution per minute. The inner sheathing is always dry and radiates at the internal temperature. The wood structure in general has good insulating proper-

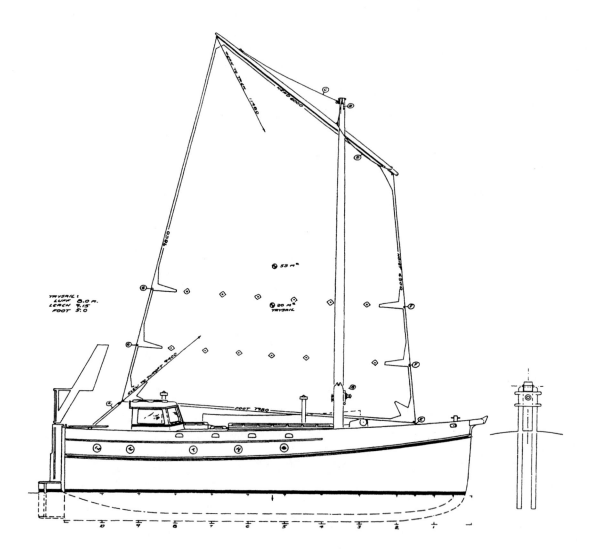

ties. No paint or finish coating of any kind is used inside the hull. The cedar sheathing is fastened with copper nails, which show a pleasant glint.

The cedar-planked bottom is tarred and sheathed outside with 16-ounce copper sheet secured with ring nails (perished copper can be torn from the heads of the nails, which are left in the wood). The copper has good antifouling and anti-shipworm properties and furnishes mechanical as well as chemical protection for the wood—from ice, for instance. It will last as long as 14 years if the boat is berthed most of the time, half

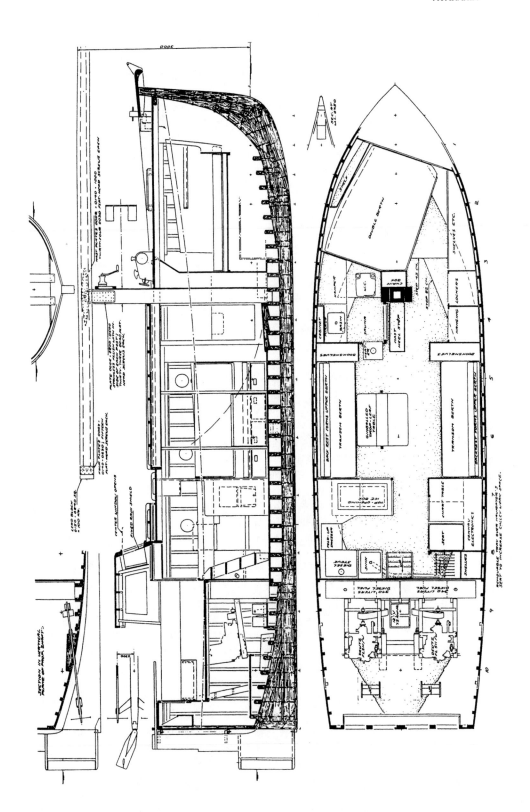

that if she is continually underway. The copper sheathing can be cleaned simply by drying it; fouling will drop off on the next tide. Electrical grounding is very effective. (However, the copper will react with lead to the latter's disadvantage; outside ballast should not be sheathed.)

The upper sides or raised deck, where there's no advantage in a complex shape, and where drying out and re-wetting create problems in traditional wood construction, is plywood, as is the deck, to be a stable base for a fiberglass-epoxy sheathing. External angles are rounded and internal angles coved to eliminate stress points and dirt traps. The whole outside of the boat is painted white for good sun reflection and ready touchup as and where needed.

Ataraxia has one mast, one sail, no standing rigging, minimum running rigging. Her critical components are an order of magnitude fewer than in a conventional contemporary rig. The few that she has are massive, such as the mast and tabernacle, or readily watched and replaced, as cordage and blocks.

It is assumed that she will do all maneuvering under power—although, with the peak halyard rig shown, dipping the lugsail is not much more laborious than tacking an overlapping jib. The peak halyard supports the yard and most of the sail clear of the deck while the tack of the sail is brought back around the mast. The process of tacking a dipping lug does not involve any parts sweeping across the deck, allowing tall smoke heads and other obstructions along the centerline.

The lugsail can be converted into a near-squaresail for downwind passages by bringing the tack to the deck edge abreast of the mast and poling out the clew. Chafe is slight, and the vessel can be brought to the wind quickly in a man-overboard situation. The small trysail is for steadying, as it can be sheeted flat, thereby needing no attention; she would be underpowered in strong wind without it. The sail area is only 53 square meters, but all of it is effective at all times, with no area wasted in acute angles, overlaps, or interference between multiple sails and spars.

The short mast is fully counterweighted to swing up and down at a touch for bridge clearance, but it will normally be carried erect to clear the deck. The deck slot for the heel is placed to drip clear of mattresses. The slot cover is utilized as a skylight and as a base for grabrails, besides being a useful toerail.

Two small engines allow each to be hand-started, saving concern about battery capacity. Belt drives locate the engines in a dry and accessible position; their light weight makes the high placement harmless. The propellers are low and close to the centerline; the lee-side one should always be free of air ingestion. The keel-mounted rudder is blown by the stream of either propeller; she can be held back by reversing either engine as the stern is swung by the other, allowing use of the more favorable rotation. The small propellers are solid three-blades, accepting the drag for propulsive efficiency and elimination of moving parts.

The diesels are air-cooled, eliminating sea connections. The open stern provides fast turnover of engineroom air and dissipates noise. Spray baffles and heavy-weather covers are provided. Nominal cruising range under power is 1,600 nautical miles at 6 knots, but she is supposed to use sail and power in conjunction to maintain a schedule in light-weather zones. The sail plan is powerful enough to dispense with other roll-damping devices.

The propellers can be reached by crouching on the bottom end plate of the rudder

(text continued on page 385)

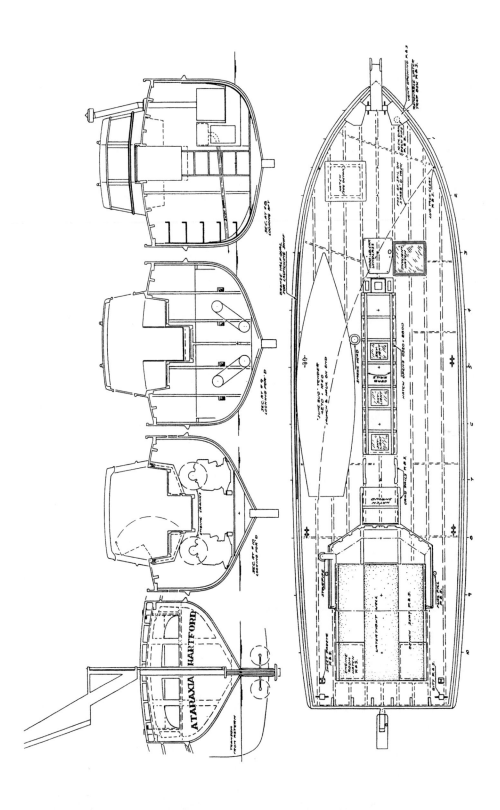

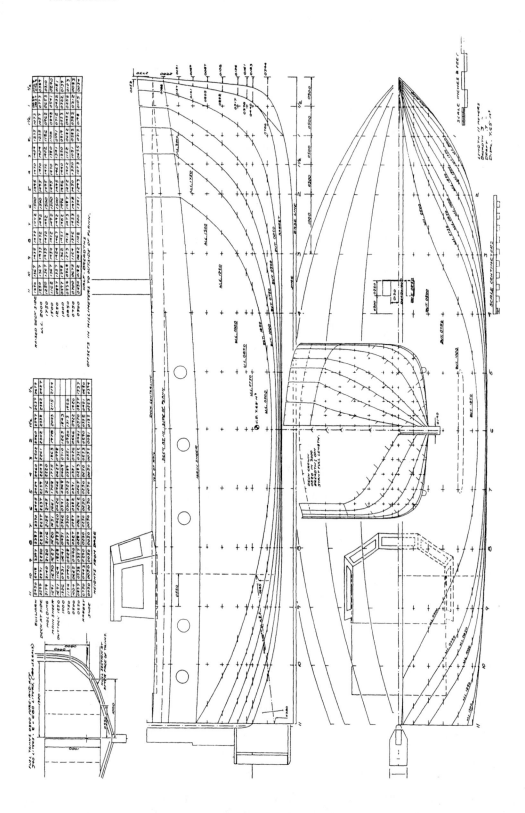

with head out of water. The rudder is instantly visible, well protected, and massively built and mounted. The vane steerer functions through a trailing-edge tab well out of harm's way, balanced for least power requirement, and actuated by a vane mounted on the rudder with the most straightforward linkage imaginable. She will also have tiller-mounted electronic Autohelm. When autopilot steering is inappropriate, the tiller will be used directly, with an extension for heavy-weather leverage. The doghouse is shelter for a solitary watchkeeper.

On deck, the bulwarks are high enough to take the whole sole of a foot. There are no outboard lifelines (the owner once lost a friend by a lifeline failure), but there are large and solid inboard grabs, and strong points for attachment of personal lifelines the full length. With this rig, it is necessary to go on deck to shorten sail, which at any rate eliminates jam-inducing turning blocks and lines stretched over the deck. The sail can be hoisted and lowered on any point of sailing including dead before the wind, and the low rig and exaggerated reserve buoyancy of the boat reduce the urgency of most sail handling.

Below decks, the unaffected layout reduces the distance it's possible to fall. She is well furnished with stanchions and grabs. The double berth forward is for in-port use; at sea the box berths will be used, adjustable for angle of heel and close to all the axes of rotation.

The sauna minimizes gray-water discharge. The portable toilet, with one or more spare base tanks, obviates all plumbing. Fresh water is carried in jerricans without piping or pumps.

All hatches are placed where drip is innocuous, except for the escape hatch forward, which has an oversize cover to be tilted for ventilation with rain protection in warm, calm weather. All stowage and mattresses are inside the inner sheathing of the hull.

The galley stove and water heater use diesel fuel from the main tanks, which are of 680 liters (180 U.S. gallons) capacity. Ventilation exhausts in the vicinity of the heat sources.

She will have current electronic navigation and piloting equipment, backed by sextant, Walker log, and lead. Kedge and bower anchors will be Bruce type, with a large Bolger anchor (a welded version of a three-piece Yachtsman anchor) carried in the bilge for crises. A saddle for her chain, with appropriate weights, will be carried to allow backing her anchors. With her mast down flat and her steady riding habits, she should have a good chance, anchored clear of the fleet in a gale.

72 *Offshore Leeboarder*

39'0" × 11'0" × 2'0"

Alert (ex-*Manatee*) is a 33-foot by 8-foot leeboarder designed for Jim Melcher for weekend cruising based on Pleasant Bay, Cape Cod. Loaded to double her designed displacement and floating 8 inches deep of her designed 18-inch draft with all the possessions of two people, she has been up and down both coasts of North America and through the Caribbean and Gulf of Mexico, and by sea, river, and canal around the Mediterranean, English Channel, North Sea, and Baltic. She also rode an old flatbed trailer rig from Tampa to Vancouver.

Romp, a similar boat but a centerboarder without auxiliary power, went through the eye of a Caribbean hurricane "without a moment's anxiety," according to her single-handed owner. In the oncoming quadrant of the storm she kept her bow up to the sea with her mizzen. When the wind came again after the passage of the eye, the mizzen blew away (definition of a hurricane "no sail will stand"); then she ran off at 8 knots with bare poles. Shallow-bodied hulls neither disturb the waves nor trip themselves; high freeboard buoys them over breaking crests. This experience suggested that the mizzen could be spared to clear a big steering vane.

Manatee and *Romp* are cramped for permanent living, and dispensing with wide-load highway permits hasn't seemed to justify the penalty on living space. When Alice and James Caldwell commissioned a new design for cruising the Great Lakes, and beyond into orbit, we planned the boat big enough to show generous elbowroom and weight-carrying capacity. Nothing in this cabin is stinted, for a couple indefinitely or four on a long vacation. The dedicated berths in the main cabin can be kept made up for guests, but their first function is for off-watch use in heavy weather, each of her two-person crew taking the lee-side berth in turn, exactly on the pitch axis.

This cabin looks roomy, but it's laid out for violent motion. The shallow, hard-

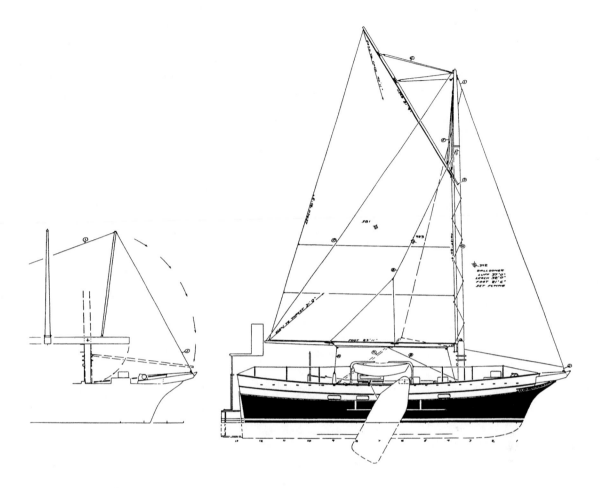

bilged hull has a slow and shallow roll and pitch as 40-footers go, but that is not always very slow or very shallow. The cabin is full of hip and shoulder bracing points, grabs and stanchions. The wide space in the galley relies on the overhead grabrails formed by the fore-and-aft deck beams (the deck is a segment of a cylinder inside the thick strip-built hull; the stringers all run perfectly straight, supported by bulkheads).

The fixed topside windows and the skylight are ⅜-inch Lexan, strong and shatter-proof though soft. The skylight can be removed to pass bulky objects below. It is placed to drip clear of cushions. The cockpit sole can be removed to open the engineroom.

Old-fashioned side davits carry two husky prams, swung out clear of the deck in good weather, or well inboard when necessary. The boats form part of the lifeline protection, leaving a wide gangway when they're in the water.

With such a shallow rudder, it's desirable to avoid cutting holes through the deadwood ahead of the rudder. These close-in, off-center propellers turn equally well either way because the rudder becomes a blown flap for the prop stream. Drag under sail demands a folding or feathering prop with moving parts that have been known to freeze up in their old age. Hulls with this much forefoot are slow-turning and blow away with

(text continued on page 390)

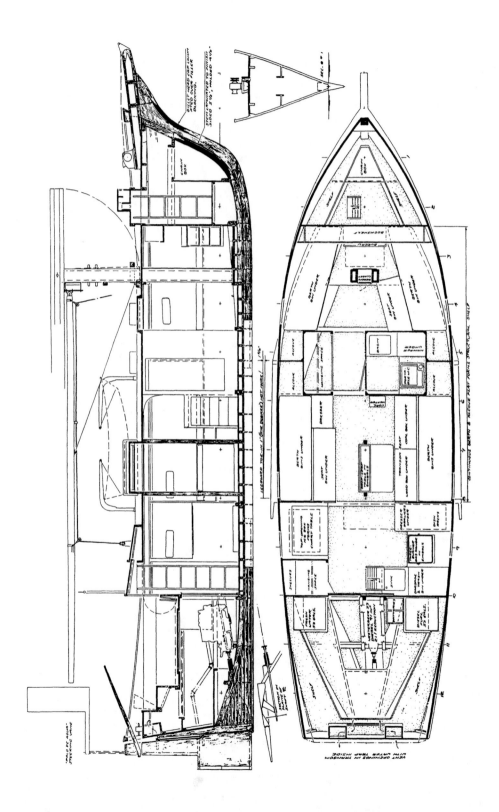

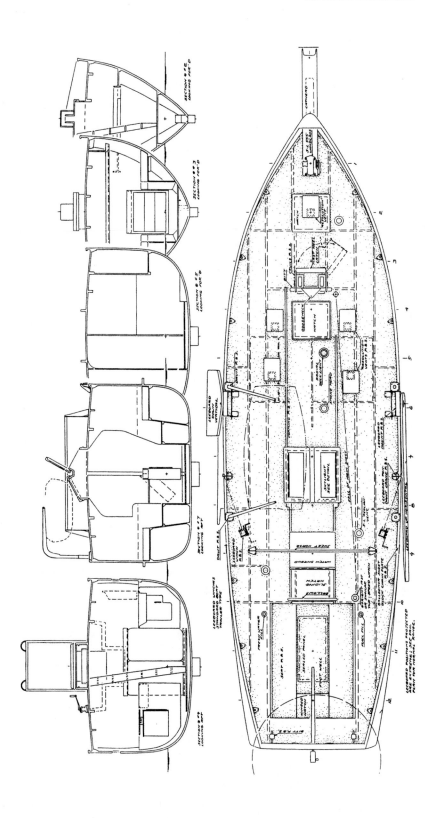

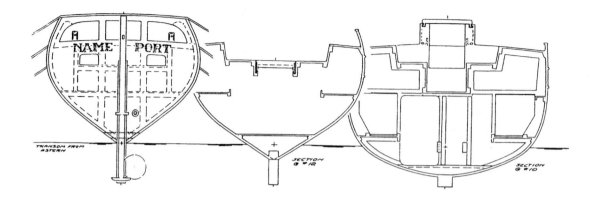

the wind in standstill maneuvering; use of one of the prams, with an outboard motor, as a docking tug is more practical than the complications of a bow thruster. Dropping a leeboard if there's water enough, or dragging an anchor if there isn't, helps. The forefoot can sometimes be butted against a shelving shore and the stern swung around it, either accidentally or deliberately.

The cat rig is not as fast or weatherly as a sloop but saves chafe and complications. The short, high boom, and mast well back from the bow, eliminate the tripping and diving habits associated with cats. The gaff head has minimum shift of helm balance when a strip is taken off the bottom in reefing. Gaff sails don't sag off at the top any more than jibheaded sails, though a sag is more likely to be noticed in a gaff-header. The cure in either case is an effective boom vang.

Sail area is small for the size of the boat, as it can be in an auxiliary, but it has more power than a comparison of areas might suggest because all of it is effective, with no backwinding or blanketing of one sail by another. Without standing rigging in the way, the sail can be raised and lowered broad-off from its topping lifts, and can be guyed forward of the beam with the ballooner out on the other side, to run down the tradewinds with some self-steering effect and minimal chafe.

HEIGHTS FROM BASE LINE

	13	12	11	10	9	8	7	6	5	4	3	2	1
RAIL	9.5.0	7.8.4	7.4.9	7.1.3	6.11.3	6.9.2	6.7.7	6.6.2	6.4.3	7.1.0	7.3.4	7.6.4	7.10.2
TOP OF DECK MOLDING	6.8.6	6.5.4	6.1.2	7.9.5	5.8.6	5.7.6	5.7.4	5.7.6	5.8.6	5.10.4	6.0.6	6.3.6	6.7.4
BOTTOM OF DECK MOLDING	5.8.0	5.7.0	5.1.0	4.10.0	4.9.5	4.9.0	4.8.7	4.9.2	4.10.1	4.11.5	5.1.6	5.4.7	5.7.2
BUTTOCK 4'	4.2.2	2.11.1	1.7.0	1.4.2	1.2.1	1.0.7	1.0.7	1.1.7	1.4.4	3.7.3			
3'	4.3.4	3.1.6	2.0.0	1.2.1	0.8.4	0.5.4	0.5.1	0.7.6	1.2.0	2.2.1	4.6.3		
2'	3.0.3	2.0.5	1.0.2	0.7.6	0.6.7	0.6.0	0.6.0	0.6.7	0.9.4	1.3.7	2.9.0	7.0.0	
1'	2.10.3	1.7.2	0.11.3	0.7.1	0.6.1	0.6.0	0.6.0	0.6.0	0.6.2	0.6.6	0.9.3	1.4.4	4.1.6
NOMINAL RABBET	2.4.2	1.3.4	0.7.5	0.6.0	0.6.0	0.6.0	0.6.0	0.6.0	0.6.0	0.6.0	0.5.3	0.4.2	
FALSE KEEL		0.0.0	0.0.0	0.0.0	0.0.0	0.0.0	0.0.0	0.0.0	0.0.0	0.0.0	0.0.1	0.2.0	1.0.4

OFFSETS IN FEET, INCHES, & EIGHTHS
TO OUTSIDE OF PLANK.

HALF-BREADTHS

	13	12	11	10	9	8	7	6	5	4	3	2	1
RAIL	3.3.4	4.0.4	4.8.0	5.1.1	5.4.1	5.5.5	5.6.1	5.6.0	5.5.1	5.2.2	4.8.0	3.8.4	2.2.5
W.L. 70"	3.7.2	4.1.4										3.8.3	2.1.5
84"	3.9.4	4.3.4	4.8.6	5.1.2						5.2.2	4.5.7	3.7.5	2.9.0
78"	3.10.6	4.4.6	4.9.4	5.1.4	5.4.1	5.5.5	5.6.1	5.6.0	5.5.1	5.2.1	4.5.3	3.6.6	1.10.2
72"	3.11.0	4.5.1	4.10.0	5.1.5	5.4.1	5.5.5	5.6.1	5.6.0	5.5.1	5.2.0	4.7.0	3.5.5	1.8.2
66"	3.10.0	4.4.7	4.10.2	5.1.6	5.4.1	5.5.5	5.6.1	5.6.0	5.5.1	5.1.7	4.6.1	3.4.0	1.6.2
60"	3.7.3	4.3.6	4.9.7	5.1.6	5.4.1	5.5.5	5.6.1	5.6.0	5.5.1	5.1.4	4.5.3	3.2.5	1.4.0
54"	3.2.5	4.1.6	4.9.2	5.1.4	5.4.1	5.5.5	5.6.1	5.6.0	5.5.0	5.1.0	4.4.0	3.0.0	1.1.6
48"	2.7.7	3.10.4	4.7.5	5.1.1	5.4.0	5.5.5	5.6.1	5.6.0	5.4.6	5.0.2	4.2.0	2.9.0	0.11.3
42"	1.11.4	3.5.4	4.3.1	5.0.2	5.3.6	5.5.5	5.6.1	5.6.0	5.4.4	4.11.1	3.11.2	2.5.6	0.9.0
36"	1.2.4	2.10.5	4.1.3	4.10.4	5.3.0	5.5.3	5.6.0	5.5.7	5.3.6	4.9.0	3.7.6	2.2.0	0.6.7
30"	0.9.2	2.1.6	3.7.6	4.7.7	5.2.1	5.5.0	5.5.6	5.5.4	5.2.1	4.6.0	3.3.4	1.10.0	0.4.6
27"		1.7.2	3.4.3	4.6.0	5.1.2	5.4.4	5.5.3	5.5.0	5.1.2	4.3.7	3.0.6	1.7.7	0.3.6
24"		1.4.3	3.0.0	4.3.2	5.0.0	5.3.5	5.4.5	5.3.2	5.0.0	4.1.7	2.9.7	1.5.5	
18"		0.6.7	2.1.3	3.7.4	4.8.0	5.1.1	5.2.5	5.1.2	4.7.3	3.6.6	2.3.1	1.1.2	
12"			1.0.7	2.6.7	3.11.4	4.7.6	4.10.0	4.7.0	3.9.6	2.7.4	1.6.6	0.7.6	
KEEL	0.7.6	0.2.6	0.3.0	0.4.4	0.6.5	0.8.4	0.9.0	0.8.3	0.6.7	0.5.0	0.3.3	0.2.6	0.2.6

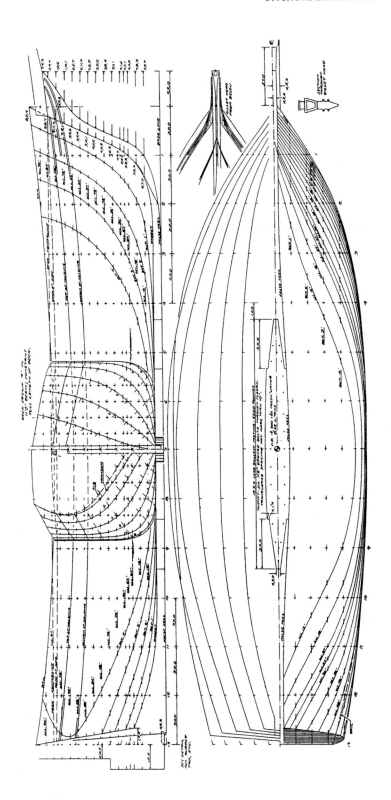

73 *Shady Lady*

39'0" × 14'0" × 3'9"

Mel Traber was, until he retired, a professional steelworker with a big, high, well-equipped shop, which his boat was designed to fit. A lot of the detailed design is his, but I have no problem with any of it and couldn't swear which of us suggested which feature. The cargo boom was his idea, its function being to swing his big Harley-Davidson motorcycle from the quarterdeck to a wharf. The box keel with square-cornered cutwater is mine—my favorite solution to the problem of getting some buoyancy out to the ends of a panel-construction boat without making her so blunt-ended that she pushes half the ocean ahead of her and drags the rest behind.

These keels drive easily because the profile rocker is similar to the plan-view taper. They push some of the water out to the sides and an equal amount downwards, with no tendency to eddy around the corner. That's on paper; in fact, there's some eddying there, certainly quite a lot when the boat pitches and rolls. I've designed a couple of boats in which this joint was formed from a segment of a big pipe. A good craftsman can do this smoothly with these gentle curves, but I'm not sure it's worth the complication of an extra weld line, especially since the comfort of the full-width, ½-inch-thick keel plate would be impractical. With that, braced by the stiff vertical beams of the keel sides, it's unimaginable that she could land on anything that could hurt her, short of high explosive, and even that might toss her away without holing her.

Grounded and left by the tide, she would stand upright if the bottom were level, an objection being that it would be hard to leg her level on a sloping bottom, and that if she fell over she would lie down more than 30 degrees.

She has a great reserve of buoyancy and stability, with high sides and strong deck-works, fit to roll over and over and finish the right way up and functioning. She's too

(text continued on page 395)

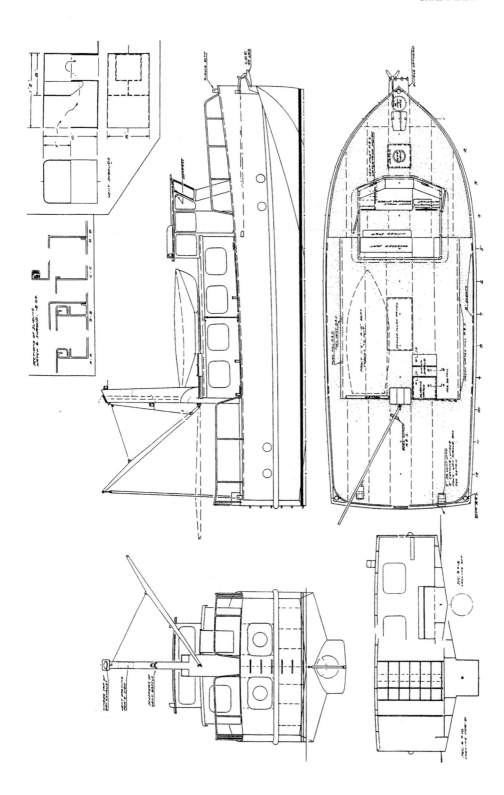

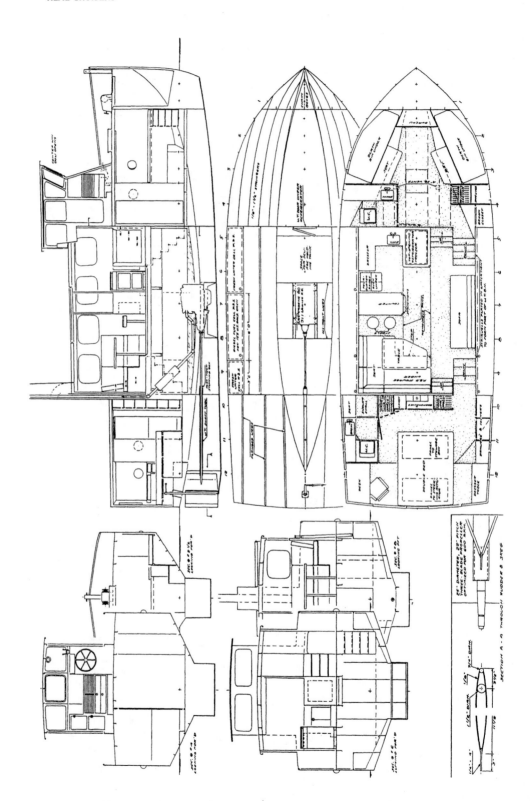

short to be an ideal ocean-crosser; her cruising speed for best range would be 6½ knots. Mel cruises her at 7½ knots, and she can probably come close to 9 wide open, with the 120-h.p., six-cylinder engine he substituted for the 80-h.p. four I showed on the plans. His reasoning was that the added cost was negligible at the scale of the total investment, and that you can't have too much power if you have sense enough not to use it until you need it.

For real ocean work she would need roll-damping paravanes; not that she's an exceptionally bad roller, but all powerboats roll enough to wear out their crews. However, Bermuda would be about the limit of her intended use, and three days of holding on tight is not too high a price to pay for saving the clutter of paravane gear. She's too stiff, and not fast enough, for hull-mounted anti-rolling fins to be effective.

The split-level cabin arrangement obviates steep ladders. Quick passage forward and aft is complemented by fairly wide waterways along the outside and a wheelhouse opening at deck level on each side, with chart table and navigating gear beside the helm. The view from the helm is as good as from some flying bridges.

I don't see anything missing that I would miss.

74 *Barn Owl*

15.2 meters (49.9 feet) × 3.8 meters (12.47 feet) × .90 meter
(2.95 feet)

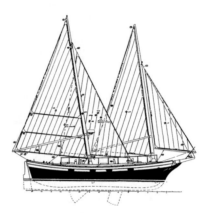

Simon and Juliet Bullimore's property is just east of Mistley on the Stour River on the north shore of the Thames estuary. Mistley used to be a port of the Thames barge traffic, carrying hay to the horses of London and returning with horse manure for the farms of Essex. Barges were built there, and they still come and go, loaded with euphoric vacationers instead of manure. *Barn Owl* has a Thames barge in her ancestry, along with Chesapeake pungies and Napoleonic gunboats, among other breeds of her shoal-draft heritage.

Paul Billings built her with spare-time help from Simon, in a former barn on the estate. Her berth is on a mudflat. The Stour is a beautiful estuary at high water, dwindling at low tide to a trickle running down out of green Constable country. Downstream is the giant port of Harwich-Felixstowe on the North Sea. A day's sail east are the islands of the Dutch and German coasts made fascinating by *The Riddle of the Sands* (the book; I was not impressed by the film except for the convincing reconstruction of the *Dulcibella*). Beyond again is the river and canal network of Europe, all interconnected from the Gulf of Finland to the Black Sea and the Mediterranean. Read Weston Martyr's *The £200 Millionaire* for a hypnotic account of the possibilities, which *Barn Owl*'s little sister *Alert* (ex-*Manatee*) explored at length. The malignant coasts fronting these lovely lands sent out Nelson and von Spee, Tromp and Shovel, Tasman and Cook.

Barn Owl is at home in those waters, but she is designed also to keep the sea in any weather, going anywhere, making modest demands of crew strength. As Captain Cook wrote of his bark *Endeavour*, "No sea can hurt her." The flat midsection with low, hard bilges rolls slowly, but her rabbet hogs down at each end to present sharp wedges to oncoming and overtaking waves. She is not stiff under sail, but her sides are so high that it's almost impossible to put her deck in the water. She can sail to windward in a meter

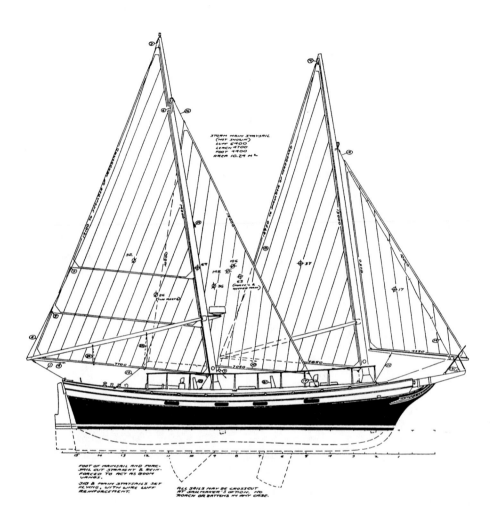

of water, but the two centerboards sharpen up her close-hauled sailing and stabilize her on course with any combination of sails. She has a high potential speed due to her shallow body and spread-out displacement, and her sail plan is large and tall, especially with the powerful main staysail set. The masts are thick-walled boxes stiff enough to set up the staysails in any weather in which her stability can stand them. The wishbone booms with twin goosenecks hold the shape of the sails without makeshift vangs or guys. The rig is designed to demand a minimum of force on any part of her running rigging. Dedicated winches obviate jam and chafe-prone purchases. Controlling lines lead to her secure cockpit-afterdeck, where the helmsman conns her from his seat on the high stern with the whole vessel under his eyes.

Below, she has a rich finish and lavish equipment, but it was steadily kept in mind, as this cabin was designed and built, that it should emerge from being stood on end, or rolled over, with its contents in place and its inhabitants uninjured. The intrusive cen-

(text continued on page 401)

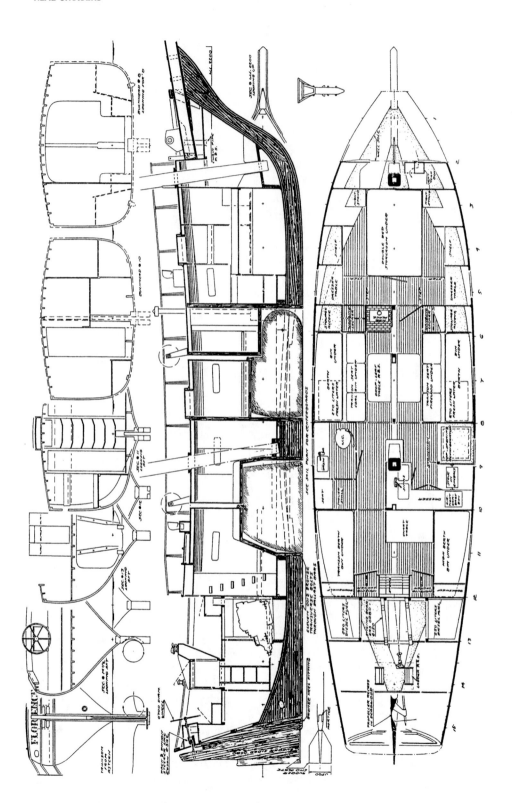

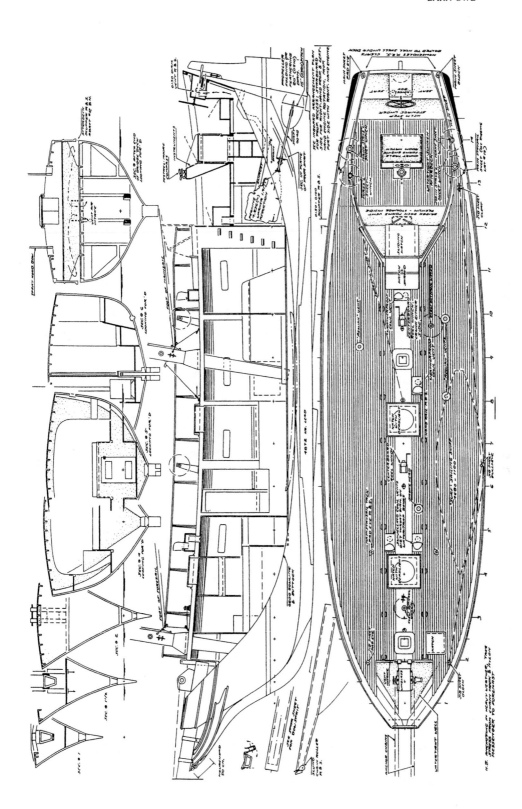

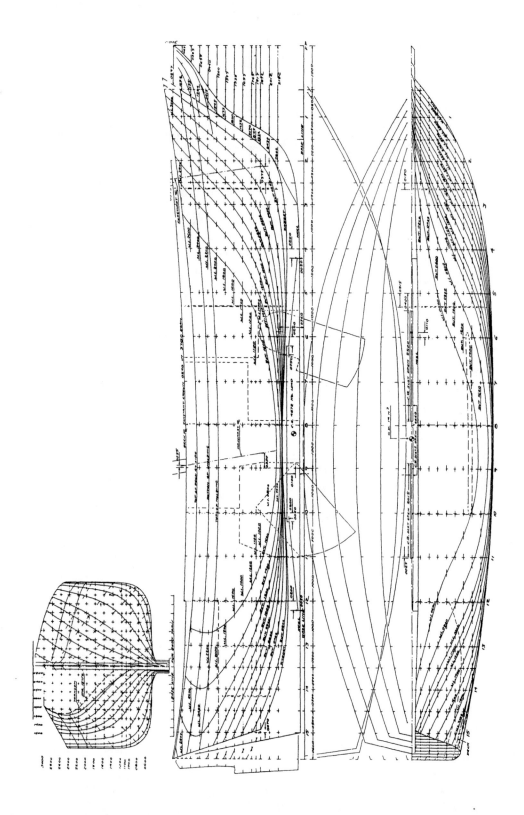

	15½	15	14½	14	13½	13	12	11	10	9	8	7	6	5	4	3	2½	2	1½	1	FP	
DECK	3000	2703	2830	2763	2703	2650	2566	2509	2473	2460	2468	2493	2940	2602	2692	2800	2868	2933	3012	3091	3200	
UPPER MOULDING	2707	2615	2543	2477	2420	2367	2285	2230	2193	2188	2181	2203	2246	2305	2388	2486	2540	2600	2664	2742	2836	
LOWER MOULDING	2246	2335	2290	2230	2180	2131	2059	2010	1978	1966	1972	1997	2039	2090	2163	2252	2302	2362	2430	2508	2650	
BUTTOCK 1600										1368	1049	0790	0640	0651	0740	0933	2322	2132				HEIGHTS FROM BASE LINE
1400				1823	1509	1049	0758	0608	0330	0360	0637	0769	1041	1560	2433	2851						
1200		2325	1995	1726	1423	1251	0899	0667	0593	0518	0520	0570	0684	0870	1253	2000	2450	2871				
1000	2239	1960	1720	1477	1280	1082	0780	0608	0522	0503	0710	0533	0620	0782	1071	1660	2091	2563	2989			
0800	2032	1768	1542	1318	1122	0940	0645	0565	0510	0500	0505	0516	0573	0686	0902	1367	1739	2230	2728			
0600	1853	1590	1368	1149	0968	0805	0617	0527	0499	0498	0503	0499	0527	0603	0753	1100	1421	1880	2418	2940		
0400	1687	1418	1183	0980	0813	0670	0528	0483	0485	0495	0500	0482	0482	0513	0611	0899	0738	1473	2030	2631		
0200	1500	1200	0966	0788	0636	0426	0422	0430	0475	0478	0490	0476	0440	0427	0481	0609	0738	1087	1568	2242	3072	
WL BUOY	1329	1029	0820	0646	0519	0437	0378	0400	0450	0470	0419	0467	0428	0400	0375	0499	0519	0692	1160	1919	2936	
KEEL	0100	0100	0600	0100	0100	0100	0100	0100	0100	0100	0100	0100	0100	0130	0148	0206	0336	0688	1500	2160		
DECK	0930	1049	1221	1330	1441	1537	1680	1783	1852	1880	1890	1880	1865	1814	1728	1553	1422	1248	1078	0722	0290	
WL 3000	0930																	1010	0648	0163		
2800	1050	1150	1235												1533	1382	1150	0852	0502			HALF-BREADTHS
2600	1100	1210	1292	1370	1458	1540							1819	1703	1468	1280	1028	0720	0382			
2400	1079	1215	1309	1400	1478	1558	1692	1786	1852	1880	1890	1880	1859	1800	1661	1384	1174	0902	0592	0273		
2200	0769	1157	1281	1383	1477	1560	1683	1788	1852	1880	1890	1880	1852	1778	1615	1298	1061	0785	0485	0181		
2000	0763	1030	1208	1340	1447	1547	1689	1797	1797	1880	1890	1890	1848	1752	1567	1200	0943	0673	0388	0104		
1800	0531	0838	1073	1249	1373	1508	1677	1788	1852	1880	1890	1880	1832	1728	1507	1088	0823	0559	0299			
1600	0299	0612	0862	1098	1273	1440	1654	1782	1849	1880	1890	1877	1817	1691	1421	0938	0709	0433	0211			
1400	0118	0382	0632	0890	1130	1330	1610	1769	1845	1880	1887	1868	1792	1630	1300	0823	0587	0353	0143			
1200		0200	0418	0699	0900	1143	1522	1729	1830	1872	1878	1843	1746	1531	1136	0677	0464	0274	0003			
1100		0126	0321	0720	0772	1088	1449	1639	1814	1859	1846	1827	1707	1436	1037	0600	0410	0353				
1000			0230	0572	0640	0982	1344	1645	1782	1844	1792	1651	1349	0922	0522	0358	0193					
0800				0229	0383	0592	1033	1458	1671	1760	1760	1660	1452	1050	0664	0361	0231	0111				
0600					0167	0289	0563	0970	1378	1534	1509	1312	0924	0598	0382	0194	0119					
KEEL		0075	0075	0075	0097	0113	0192	0150	0150	0150	0150	0150	0145	0113	0080	0075	0075	0075	0075	0075		
	15½	15	14½	14	13½	13	12	11	10	9	8	7	6	5	4	3	2½	2	1½	1	FP	

OFFSETS IN MILLIMETERS TO OUTSIDE OF PLANK.

Barn Owl *in the Stour River*

terboard trunks, not the structural problem they would have been in pre-epoxy times, are exploited to limit falls.

Barn Owl cost more to build than the estimate for Sir Joseph Banks in the next chapter, almost twice her length and five times her tonnage. Her running costs are smaller, her handling less demanding, and her social status higher.

75 *Sir Joseph Banks*

29.0 meters (95.1 feet) × 4.8 meters (15.75 feet) × 1.0 meter (3.3 feet)

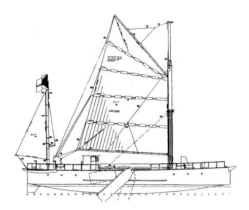

The Republic of Vanuatu is the chain of islands in the western Pacific Ocean, east of the Coral Sea, that Captain Cook called the New Hebrides. The people on the out-islands have always lived by subsistence agriculture. They don't have a maritime tradition; in Cook's time there was no communication between islands in sight of each other.

Now they would like some luxuries from abroad, but they don't make cash products to pay for kerosene or calculators. The exception is copra, dried coconut meat from which a vegetable oil is made. That they can sell for cash. Probably soon there will be more economical ways to make that oil, but it's to be hoped that by then there will be a service economy based on the work of people who can do business electronically, worldwide, but find these islands good places to live and work.

The present problem is to get the copra to market, and to distribute batteries and penicillin, economically. At present they do it in decrepit vessels condemned elsewhere. Such craft are cheap to buy but expensive to operate. If that's the best that can be arranged, the out-islands will be depopulated, or will cultivate cargo-cult subsidies from Canada and Australia.

Colin Pearson, a Canadian engineer who came to Port Vila in a cruising yacht and stayed to start a ship-repair business, thought he saw an unsubsidized possibility in the form of an auxiliary cargo vessel that would be cheap to run and maintain. Between us we worked out the design he named Sir Joseph Banks after the engaging naturalist, "a gentleman of large fortune," who sailed with Cook. The actual vessels would have names in Bislama, the principal local language.

The Banks is a giant sharpie, high-sided for her breadth for cargo volume and range of stability, designed to be welded together from prefabricated steel panels, rightside-up, on a Port Vila beach. The sharpie bow can run over dry land on beaches protected

from swells by coral reefs; there need be no investment in wharves or lighters. Close-hauled against the tradewind, she will heel enough to soften the action of the flat bottom, when a motorship with the beaching capability would be hammered. A small engine is adequate since the sails will be driving and steadying her whenever there's wind, while expensive light sails are replaced by engine boost. An expensive feathering propeller is unnecessary since the prop will always be driving her, but it will be lightly loaded much of the time, with very little fuel consumption. On paper she can maintain a 10-knot schedule; given the number of calls to be made, with short distances between, that's enough for good utilization.

Three men can sail the gaff cat rig, sheeted in the same fashion as a Chinese lug. Thames barges of larger capacity, without power, were sailed by three men at most, but the Banks' arrangement called for seven in the crew, partly for training. She's not supposed to carry passengers most of the time, but some informal ones may travel on deck. The hold can be converted to accommodate up to 80 people for special occasions, such as collecting youngsters for passage to a central school. This high-density layout, with four-high stacks of pipe cots in blocks of 16 with 45cm (17.7 inches) aisles, was standard in troopships, which I guess the designer's generation was the last to experience. It's not nearly as bad as it looks to live in for a few days, if the seasick-prone are in the lowest berths. . . .

The quick steering of the sharpie, with self-trimming sail and propeller boost, will enable her to thread the most intricate passages in the reefs. The steel leeboards reduce

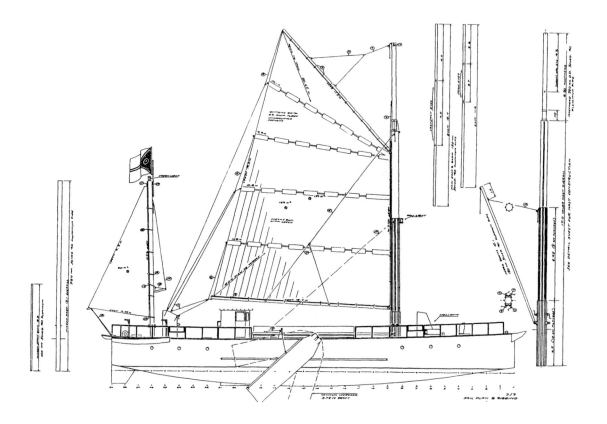

the draft when she luffs, to sail clear after touching bottom. The 20mm-thick (¾ inch) bottom plate, projecting a few centimeters beyond the thinner sides, will deal with a coral head in case of miscalculations.

Colin calculated that he could build this vessel, with all-local labor, for US$250,000 (1991) and that she could pay for operation and depreciation without subsidy. The potential returns were too small and dubious to interest unbiased investors, so the project had to go through various public and semi-charitable organizations. These found the design disturbing. There was a suggestion that officials doubted the seriousness of a scheme involving as small a sum as a quarter of a million dollars, and there was a rumor, no doubt apocryphal, that a million dollars was spent on fees to consultants passing on the soundness of the design. There certainly was pressure to replace the unfamiliar lee-boards with a centerboard, which I vetoed because, among many other obvious drawbacks, a centerboard trunk would require dangerously wide hatches for hold access. The range of stability was questioned, more reasonably since I had cut it very fine to keep as much paying capacity as possible. I had stipulated that the prototype be tested past 90 degrees with sail set, and more ballast added if necessary. The fatigue strength of the steel cantilever mast was not brought up, though it was my own major concern. I designed it with advice from Jim Michalak, an aerospace engineer to whom I appeal when I'm over my head, but it depends on some guesswork about the loading of the vessel and her behavior when rolling in calm and swell. The consequences of it buckling aren't lethal, though I hope it won't.

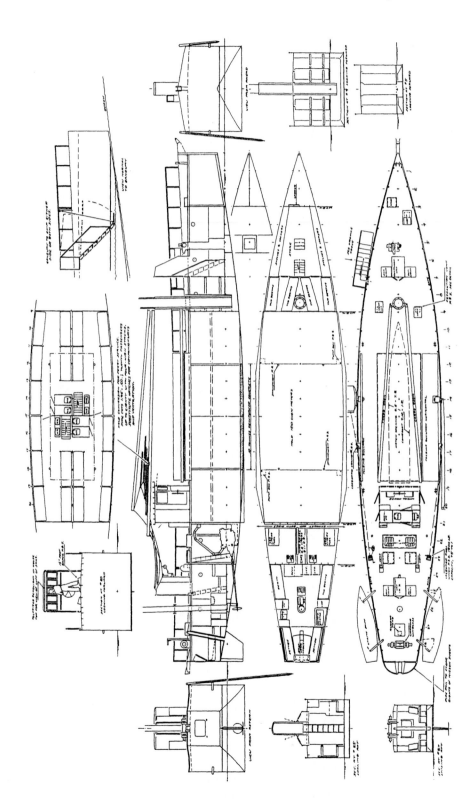

At this writing, the project continues to hang fire if it's not totally dead. I had an enchanting scenario of a fleet of these vessels, with crews competing for record times over the regular routes, and meeting occasionally for a regatta as the Thames barges used to do. In the future, when the economy can support more elaborate transports, these would carry tourist parties, as the Thames barges do, and race, with gambling as in horse racing. This last seems to me to offer a great business opportunity; I've suggested it seriously before, and written about it in my unserious fantasy novel, *Schorpioen*. Here the action is based on such a sport, *Schorpioen* being the name of one of a fleet of racers, all supposed to be a good deal bigger than the Banks, but with her principle of using sail and power in conjunction. For gambling purposes the power would be adjusted according to results to keep the racing close.

Sources

For Plans:

H. H. Payson & Co.
    Pleasant Beach Road
    South Thomaston, ME 04858
Common Sense Designs
    11765 Ebberts Court
    Beaverton, OR 97005
Phil Bolger & Friends, Inc.
    29 Ferry Street
    Gloucester, MA 01930

For the Novel *Schorpioen*:

Duff & Duff
    8 Harbor Road
    Mattapoisett, MA 02739

For Custom Boats:

Story Boatbuilding
    92 John Wise Avenue
    Essex, MA 01920

Periodicals:

Messing About In Boats
    29 Burley Street
    Wenham, MA 01984
WoodenBoat
    Naskeag Road
    Brooklin, ME 04616

Bibliography

The following information is as complete as possible; some books may be out of print.

Alden, John. *The American Steel Navy*. Annapolis, MD: Naval Institute Press. 1989.

Bingham, Bruce. *Sailor's Sketchbook*. Camden, ME: International Marine and Seven Seas Press. 1983.

Bolger, Philip C. *Different Boats*. Camden, ME: International Marine. 1980.

——. *100 Small Boat Rigs*. Camden, ME: International Marine. 1983.

Chapelle, Howard I. *American Fishing Schooners, 1825–1935*. New York: W.W. Norton & Co. 1973.

——. *American Sailing Craft*. New York: Bonanza Books. 1936.

——. *American Small Sailing Craft*. New York: W.W. Norton & Co. 1951.

——. *The Baltimore Clipper*. New York: Dover. 1988.

——. *Boatbuilding*. New York: W.W. Norton & Co. 1941.

——. *A History of the American Sailing Navy*. Avenal, NJ: Outlet Book Company. 1988.

——. *A History of American Sailing Ships*. Avenal, NJ: Outlet Book Co. 1988.

——. *Yacht Designing & Planning*. New York: W.W. Norton & Co. 1971.

af Chapman, Fredrik Henrik. *Architectura Navalis Mercatoria*. New York: Praeger Publishers. 1971.

Childers, Erskine. *The Riddle of the Sands*. Annapolis, MD: Naval Institute Press. 1991.

Clark, Roy. *Black-Sailed Traders*. London: Putnam & Co. 1961.

Herreshoff, L. F. *The Common Sense of Yacht Design*. Jamaica, New York: Caravan Maritime Books. 1974.

——. *The Compleat Cruiser*. White Plains, NY: Sheridan House. 1980.

——. *L. Francis Herreshoff Reader*.

——. *Sensible Cruising Designs*. Camden, ME: International Marine. 1991.

Hill, Thomas J. *Ultralight Boatbuilding*. Camden, ME: International Marine. 1987.

Howland, Waldo. *A Life in Boats*. Mystic, CT: Mystic Seaport. 1988.

Landstrom, Bjorn. *The Ship*. Garden City, NY: Doubleday & Co. 1961.

Moores, Ted, and Merilyn Mohr. *Canoecraft*. Charlotte, VT: Camden House. 1983.

Payson, Harold. *Boat Modeling the Easy Way*. Camden, ME: International Marine. 1992.

——. *Boat Modeling with Dynamite Payson*. Camden ME: International Marine. 1992.

——. *Build the New Instant Boats*. Camden, ME: International Marine.

——. *Go Build Your Own Boat*. South Thomaston, ME: Self-Published. 1987.

——. *Instant Boats*. Camden, ME: International Marine. 1979.

Villiers, Alan. *The Way of a Ship*. New York: MacMillan. 1981.

Worth, Claud. *Yacht Cruising*. New York: Yachting. 1934.

Index